Houle also discusses the roles of the major institutional providers of continuing education, including associations, professional schools, universities, employers, and others. He examines the ways in which the quality of service provided by a profession is influenced by continuing education, and he identifies guidelines for the future activities of both professionals and continuing education providers.

THE AUTHOR

CYRIL O. HOULE is senior program consultant at the W. K. Kellogg Foundation and professor emeritus of education at the University of Chicago.

Continuing
Learning
in the Professions

Cyril O. Houle

Continuing
Learning
in the Professions

Jossey-Bass Publishers
San Francisco • Washington • London • 1981

CONTINUING LEARNING IN THE PROFESSIONS
by Cyril O. Houle

Library of Congress Cataloging in Publication Data

Houle, Cyril Orvin, 1913–
    Continuing learning in the professions.

    Bibliography: p. 317
    Includes index.
    1. Professional education. 2. Continuing educa-
tion. I. Title.
LC1059.H68   378'.013   79-92462
ISBN 0-87589-449-6

Manufactured in the United States of America

JACKET DESIGN BY WILLI BAUM

FIRST EDITION
        First printing: April 1980
        Second printing: November 1980
        Third printing: February 1981

Code 8010

The Jossey-Bass
Series in Higher Education

Preface

A traveller who has just left the walls of an immense city climbs the neighboring hill; as he goes farther off he loses sight of the men whom he has so recently quitted; their dwellings are confused in a dense mass; he can no longer distinguish the public squares; and he can scarcely trace out the great thoroughfares; but his eye has less difficulty in following the boundaries of the city, and for the first time he sees the shape of the vast whole.

Alexis de Tocqueville

Today it is being said that the old concept of a profession is no longer suited to our times. The solitary, disciplined, highly educated, and deeply ethical practitioner dealing with clients one by one may always have been more of an ideal than an established reality, but this image is being replaced by that of a collective group enterprise that is shared by many people who represent layers of specialism and that is alleged to be flawed by a lack of concern for comprehensive and dedicated service, by a marked self-interest, and by incompetent performance. Something complex and strange is happening to the old idea of professionalism and some authorities argue that it must be replaced. By what, nobody can say.

It is not my intention in this book to map out a grand design for the future of the professions but rather to suggest how
some of the manifest needs of the present may be met by the
greatly extended and diversified use of continuing learning. Of
these needs, assurance of quality in meeting the intricate, changing, and interactive requirements of modern practice is at once
the most pressing and the most comprehensive. As Whitehead
(1926, p. 282) observed, "The fixed person for the fixed duties,
who in older societies was such a godsend, in the future will be
a public danger." As this truth has become more and more evident to the leaders of professions, a wide range of responses has
been forthcoming. The major ones will be identified later, and,
as will be noted, they are variously motivated by the desires to
reward excellence and to punish deficiency.

Each response to the need for assuring quality has had its
unique influence, but the general effect of all of them has been
to increase the provision of organized instructional activities.
This simple solution to complex problems will not be sufficient
to reestablish either the reality or the image of high-quality performance by the professions. In fact, many people are growing
irritated by what seems to them to be a mindless proliferation
of courses and conferences, each of which may be valuable but
which are not collectively undergirded by any unifying conception of how education can be used in a mature, complex, and
continuing way to achieve excellence of service throughout the
lifespan.

In the course of time it seems likely, therefore, that the
various kinds of control and incentive systems, which now operate separately and sometimes at cross purposes, will be brought
together into a concerted and highly developed effort to assure
quality. In achieving this end, education will be used in a great
variety of ways, being introduced at many places throughout
the lifelong work of professionals. Movement toward this future
synthesis is likely to be sporadic and evolutionary, though in
the future, as in the past, landmark statements by individuals or
groups will establish new levels of achievement and set the base-
lines for later development.

The purpose of this book is to advance the process by which greater conceptual coherence may be brought to the educational endeavors of practicing professionals in the United States. The key idea is that such individual and collective efforts can best accomplish their goals if they are closely related to the idea of dynamic professionalization that has grown up in the past quarter century, replacing earlier static conceptions that sorted occupations into ranked and rigid categories. Admirable reports and studies have already been made of various aspects of continuing professional education, and although the treatment of many topics may seem insufficiently detailed to some people, the book surveys a very large field of work. More important than depth of treatment is the achievement of a broad perspective and a greater awareness than presently exists of the interrelationships among themes that have almost always been considered separately until now.

The title of the book uses the word *learning* rather than the more customary term *education* chiefly because primary emphasis is upon the actions of individuals and groups who seek to fulfill their own potentialities. Learning is the process by which people gain knowledge, sensitiveness, or mastery of skills through experience or study. Secondary attention is devoted to the processes and procedures used by people who undertake to teach or to design formal systems of instruction. This relative emphasis should apply to all discussions of education (though it usually does not); it is essential when learners are professionals, people who, above all others, should have a sophisticated ability to guide their own careers. They will often wish to be formally instructed, but any such decision is a conscious choice that does not relieve a professional of ultimate responsibility for the conduct of his or her education.

The term *continuing education* also connotes—unfortunately and incorrectly though such usage may be—the idea of instruction, of varying degrees of formality, in which already-known facts or skills or defined awarenesses are transmitted from those who possess them to those who do not. A greatly heightened level of professional thought and behavior can never be accomplished by merely spreading present knowledge more widely. Therefore I have defined three modes of learning—inquiry, instruction, and performance—and have shown how they can be employed both separately and interactively.

This book is intended for anybody interested either in professions or in continuing education. Probably it will be of most concern to the diverse membership of each of three clusters of people. The first is made up of those who wish to advance a specific profession or cluster of professions, such as dentistry, nursing, or the health professions collectively. Among such people are association executives, editors, faculty members, persons on regulatory bodies, and, most especially, individuals who have full-time or part-time responsibility for educating practitioners. The second cluster is composed of all those who are interested in the general advancement of professionalization, including senior university administrators, officers of accrediting agencies, and behavioral scientists engaged in the study of occupations. The third cluster includes those people who have a concern for adult and continuing education, whether they be administrators, designers of programs, or research workers. For all such persons, continuing professional learning is but one field of application for theories, principles, and practices that are widely used; such people may find that the ideas expressed here can be helpful in a variety of situations.

My original explorations of continuing professional education were reported in various journals beginning in 1967. When it was suggested that this book be prepared, I thought that these earlier papers could be freshened up and linked together by a few bridging comments. It soon become clear that this course of action would be impossible. Matters were far more complex than had earlier seemed true, and the rush of events had already brought into being many accomplishments that could not have been forecast even a few years ago. Several passages from earlier papers reappear here, but all the rest of the book is new.

Help has been provided by so many organizations, groups, and individuals that it would be impossible to name them all. The Educational Testing Service made it possible for me to devote six months to the full-time investigation of the topic. William

Turnbull, president, and Robert Solomon, executive vice-president, gave this project its initial support, and Winton Manning, senior vice-president, served as a continuing liaison officer. Many professional societies—local, state, and national—have provided opportunities for me to learn from them. King Edward's Hospital Fund for London and its secretary, Geoffrey A. Phalp, have on three occasions provided me with a place to work and live. Many other institutions and individuals have allowed me to visit their programs and discuss their activities, and I have used many specialized and general libraries. Classes and seminars at the University of Chicago and elsewhere have provided vigorous discussions, which produced many of the ideas presented here. A long series of research associates, particularly Richard Yanikoski, helped with bibliographic sources and with lively personal interchanges. Dolores Ford and Leona Gilson greatly facilitated the tedious processes involved in preparing the manuscript. And, as always, my wife, Bettie E. Houle, provided intellectual support and stimulation as well as constant reinforcement throughout this, the longest and most complex single venture of my intellectual life. To all named and unnamed collaborators, I am grateful; to none of them belongs any blame for errors, oversights, and misjudgments.

This book is dedicated to all of my colleagues at the W. K. Kellogg Foundation, which I serve as senior program consultant. Work on this book was considered to be one of my responsibilities at the foundation. For three years, Russell G. Mawby, its president, and my other associates in Battle Creek have been constant sources of inspiration, instruction, and encouragement. I am deeply grateful to all of them.

Battle Creek, Michigan CYRIL O. HOULE
February 1980

Contents

The Author

CYRIL O. HOULE is senior program consultant at the W. K. Kellogg Foundation and professor emeritus of education at the University of Chicago. He was awarded both the bachelor's and master's degrees at the University of Florida in 1934 and the Ph.D. degree at the University of Chicago in 1940, all three in the field of education.

Houle served in various teaching and administrative positions at the University of Chicago from 1939 to 1979; his major academic interest was adult and continuing education. He was also a visiting faculty member at the University of California in Berkeley, the University of Washington, the University of Wisconsin in Milwaukee, Leeds University, and Oxford University. In various capacities, Houle has studied adult education in thirty-five foreign countries and has served as a member of national and international commissions and as consultant to governmental and private organizations in the United States and abroad. He is a member of the National Academy of Education and has been awarded honorary doctorates by Rutgers University, Florida State University, Syracuse University, New York University, De Paul University, and Roosevelt University.

xvii

He is the author of numerous books and other publications, including *The Effective Board* (1960), *The Inquiring Mind* (1961), *The Design of Education* (1972), and *The External Degree* (1973). Houle now lives and works in both Battle Creek and Chicago.

Continuing
Learning
in the Professions

Chapter 1

The Crisis
of the Professions

*Mr. Wolfe, I want to speak to you as one professional man
to another. You would be the first to agree that ours is
a dignified profession.*
> *Not explicitly. To assert dignity is to lose it.*

Rex Stout

The lives of some men and women are structurally shaped by the
fact that they are deeply versed in advanced and subtle bodies
of knowledge, which they apply with dedication in solving complex practical problems. They learn by study, apprenticeship,
and experience, both by expanding their comprehension of formal disciplines and by finding new ways to use them to achieve
specific ends, constantly moving forward and backward from
theory to practice so that each enriches the other. Such people
protect one another and are sometimes extended special protection by society far beyond that granted to other citizens. The
price of protection is vigilance against poor performance and
unethical behavior, and that vigilance is exercised by the privileged person, by others of similar specialization, and by society.
These people are called professionals.

This was the established conception which, by about
1960, had become a shining symbol throughout the world. The
honor arose not only from ancient antecedents but also from
gargantuan efforts in the nineteenth and twentieth centuries by
the leaders of numerous occupations to establish standards that
would entitle each one to be called a profession. People who
performed many kinds of specialized work desired the prestige

1

that accompanies that designation. This ambition led both the workers themselves and the general theorists of professionalism to suggest the criteria that would justify claims to inclusion within the favored circle of occupations.

This book is focussed on the ways in which professionals try, throughout their active lives of service, to refresh their own knowledge and ability and build a sense of collective responsibility to society. The first chapter suggests the nature and scope of this task; and, because such learning is ultimately based on the characteristics of the professionalizing process, Chapters Two and Three will deal with these in some detail.

The Established Pattern of Professional Education

The basic educational pattern of professional workers has long been established. At some time in youth—occasionally at birth—a choice of occupation is made by an individual or by the controllers of his or her destiny. This selection may carry forward an ancestral tradition, for example, of law, teaching, or military life; it may result from the conviction that the individual has been called for special service to God, to the state, or to humanity; it may be a means of economic or social advancement, possibly by the practice of dentistry, librarianship, or accounting; it may result from an awareness of personal interests or characteristics, which could most profitably be employed, for example, in engineering, nursing, or architecture; or it may arise from any of a hundred other causes, either purposefully pursued or resulting from chance.

At some time after the choice is made, formal education for the occupation begins. Specialized study is usually prefaced by years of basic training and often by general or liberal education, which establishes broad foundations of knowledge. Then comes a narrowing of focus. Occupational study may begin on a part-time basis, as when a college student is enrolled in a premedical or prelegal curriculum. At some point the original choice of an occupation by an individual is ratified by his or her acceptance into a course of study that calls for deep immersion in a specialized content and the acquisition of difficult skills and a complex value system. This formal process is reinforced by a differentiated life-style (perhaps in a hospital, a library, or a welfare agency), which separates the individual (psychologically if not always physically) from the general public and permeates his or her thought with a distinctive point of view. At the end of formal preparatory study and the reorientation of values, initial judgments are made about the competence of the individual, first by those who have guided the previous course of study and then, in most cases, by some larger authority—the organized profession, the state, or both.

A further process often ensues in which initial competence is deepened by the guided practice of recently learned skills. This enhancement of ability may be provided formally by an internship arrangement or informally by the supervision or acculturation provided by fellow workers. Fairly early in adulthood, however, the professional person becomes established in his or her practice. After that the need to keep up to date with new developments is considered necessary by both the members of the profession itself and by society in general, though decisions to learn are made chiefly by individual practitioners. If study does occur, it continues systematically or sporadically until retirement, senility, or death. The basic classic model of professional education can be economically sketched as in Figure 1. While "selection" and "certification" are usually clear-cut stages, the transition between "induction" and "continuing education" is often gradual.

The founders and leaders of most professions have long been aware of the need or possibility of postgraduate learning. Viner (1950, p. 2) noted that "the University of Avignon, in 1650, found itself faced by a candidate for the doctorate who had capacity but who had applied himself less closely to the pursuit of knowledge than to less exacting and more exciting activities. After some hesitation, it conferred the doctoral degree upon him with the notation *sub spe futuri studii*, which I am told can be translated as 'in the hope of future study.'" The hope expressed in this special case was eventually seen to be a general necessity even for the ablest students. Without this "future study" they could not use new techniques or be aware

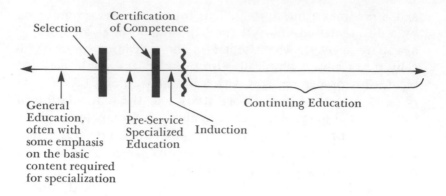

Figure 1. The Classic Model of Professional Education

of the growing knowledge bases of the professions themselves or of the disciplines in which they are rooted.

In the latter part of the nineteenth century, it became evident that maintaining and increasing adequate knowledge and competence could be achieved only by the use of systematic means. The processes originally developed for such purposes had neither a generic name nor a unifying conception. Journals published the results of research, the opinions of leaders, and the reports of commissions and committees. Societies held meetings and conventions. Publishers issued books and magazines. The manufacturers of supplies and equipment wrote brochures and trained salespeople to point out the advantages of their wares, thereby suggesting refinements or alterations of practice to their clients. Wherever the members of a profession congregated, shop talk conveyed content and points of view. In institutions of employment, systems of supervision were developed to provide both the incentives and the means for improved performance.

Supplementing these and other formal activities has been a frequently expressed but seldom systematized awareness of the educational importance of introspection on the situations encountered in practice. Sometimes this learning originates in uncertainty about how to handle a problem; for example, an engineer may seek the opinion of a specialist in coping with a technical difficulty. Sometimes study is needed because of competition; a lawyer may be spurred to examine references and seek legal precedents in order to be able to confront an opposing attorney who is examining the same kinds of sources. Sometimes the origin of this introspective learning lies in failure: an autopsy reveals physical findings the physician should have taken into account; a rejected bid reveals to an architect miscalculations in planning, costing, or other procedures. More generally and more positively, the professional develops an habitual detached viewpoint on his or her work and conceptions and from that perspective examines the uniqueness of each case dealt with, however routine it might originally appear to be.

The most conscientious professionals have usually believed that the formal and informal means of acquiring understanding and maintaining competence have not been used widely enough by their colleagues. Public opinion, always actively or latently opposed to any special interest group, has also served as a constant watchdog, pointing out the inadequacies of incompetent practice, ignorance, or a misguided or uninformed sense of ethics. Physicians, for example, have long been accused of cupidity. At the end of the first century, the emperor Domitian said that he had had "to curb by stringent measures the avarice of the physicians," whose practice, he felt, ought to be guided by "the financial ability of [their] patients, the success of the treatment, and [their] own dignity" (Bullough, 1966, pp. 25–26). Chaucer, in the prologue of *The Canterbury Tales*, said ironically: "God helps the doctor in ways manifold / He therefore has a special love of gold." And, at a meeting of the Fabian Society in 1927, one speaker said "Whenever you see a statement of public policy by the British Medical Association you always know that they are considering the private pockets of the doctors who are their members, and are never in the least degree interested in the public welfare" (Carr-Saunders and Wilson, 1933, p. 101). Similar lines of negative comments stretching back to antiquity could be cited for the progenitors of many modern professions.

This continuing buzz of criticism, which probably increases proportionately with the power and influence of the occupation concerned, has cast a shadow on the otherwise substantial rewards of the practice of established professions. That shadow has spread and darkened since 1960, as profession after profession—among them accounting, social work, teaching, law, and the armed services—has been viewed with increasing disillusionment. Deep concern is felt by some of the actual or titular leaders of most occupations. For example, in 1965, Derbyshire, president of the Federation of State Medical Boards of the United States, dealt directly with the topic. The only ideal solution to the problem of what the profession should do about incompetent physicians was, he said succinctly, "prevention . . . and here my story should end." But he went on to comment that many kinds of incompetence and disreputable practice exist, including ignorance, physical disability, a messianic complex, mental illness, unresolved emotional conflicts, alcoholism, senility, drug addiction, and negligence in diagnosis and remediation. (Derbyshire, 1965, pp. 119–120). The remedies he suggested are chiefly concerned with formal regulation and the application of professional sanctions, but the difficulties of using such methods were suggested in an interview with a senior physician, who commented to me, "We all know who the rascals and the sluggards are, but it is hard as hell to get rid of them." I have heard this kind of comment from members of all the professions studied in this book.

Since about 1965, the general public has also been more deeply and widely aroused over professional inadequacies than ever before. The specific charges against the professions will be summarized in Chapter Nine; here it is necessary only to note their existence. The isolated comments of the past have been replaced by widespread criticism or dedicated opposition. Federal, state, and local legislative bodies have taken action themselves or have empowered administrative bodies to establish regulations dealing with many aspects of professional practice. Countless court decisions bear on the competence of practitioners, and the rulings handed down by judges sometimes establish drastically different procedures and ethical principles from those which have previously prevailed. Professionally unorthodox ways of providing service to clienteles have been invented and are being widely adopted. Citizen action is sometimes forceful and direct. Mass meetings, picket lines, sit-ins, crowded and vociferous audiences at legislative and administrative meetings, and other ways of asserting public opinion have become commonplace, though each issue or incident always seems dramatically unique to the people affected by it.

As a result of countless pressures, militancy is also on the rise within the professions. The creation of unions or "positive action groups" is leading to confrontations, collective bargaining, strikes, and slow-downs in occupations whose members only a few years ago would have thought such activities to be far beneath their dignity. And organized groups of professionals, such as lawyers and physicians, are now attacking one another in courts, legislatures, and the mass media.

The Rise of Continuing Education

No single course of action can resolve the difficulties encountered in all these arenas of debate and conflict, but a pivotal need is for every professional to be able to carry out his or her duties according to the highest possible standards of character and competence. One essential way to meet this need is for every practicing professional to engage in lifelong study. Because earlier, less formal means of learning did not suffice, the concept of "continuing professional education" evolved, and the term itself came into general usage late in the 1960s. Initially it was restricted to only a few devices and techniques, the most common of which were the short course, lecture series, or conference, often housed in a residential setting. Gradually, however, the concept broadened to include all efforts to provide learning for active professionals. Most of these activities take place in familiar settings: lecture halls or amphitheaters; university conference centers; hotel ballrooms; or laboratories, clinics, or libraries. The materials and processes used may also be familiar—books, journals, lectures, films, slides, manuals, demonstrations, and discussions—but newer devices and techniques are becoming more common. Among them are telephone or radio networks; audiotapes and videotapes; closed-circuit, open-circuit, and cable television; programmed instructional materials; computers; satellite transmissions; simulations of practice; videodisks; and other inventions or processes that are still on the drawing board or are being field tested. New theories of learning and teaching are also being used as the bases for these programs. Among them are ingeniously devised systems of self-directed study, mentoring, mastery learning, modularization of instructional units, study leaves, techniques of intensive impact, and experiential learning.

As the amount of educational services has increased, following the general principle that "more is better," so has the skepticism of at least some highly qualified observers. It is easy enough, they point out, to measure the number of hours spent in any particular activity, the level of satisfaction of those who have completed it, and even the intellectual gain or accomplished skills that students may have achieved. But how much of the knowledge, ability, or sensitiveness that the activity was designed to convey has been fully absorbed into the understanding and practice of the learners? How rigorously and well do they continue to use that competence as part of their practice? How readily and frequently do they continue to build on what they know? When and by what means will they undertake new learning experiences?

In profession after profession, the answers to these questions have so far been discouraging; efforts at teaching and learning seem to have had all too little effect upon practice. A sense of despondency is sometimes expressed even by those who have devoted much of their careers to the process of lifelong learning. Miller (1967, pp. 320–321) has concluded that because of the failure of continuing medical education, "the exquisite elaborations of contemporary investigation are generally of major significance in the care of relatively few patients. . . . We seem most often to be working at the upper extremity of an S-shaped curve where an immense instructional investment is likely to result in a very small increment in the quality of patient care."

The failure of continued study to achieve an adequate adjustment of the requirements of practice has been well illustrated in a study of male high school physical education teachers in a northeastern state (Lindsay, Morrison, and Kelley, 1974).

The teaching profession has long stressed in-service education and has substantially rewarded those who take part in it by providing direct subsidy for study, by establishing differential pay scales based on education, and by using formal training as one means of promotion to higher ranks. In this study, an examination covering five essential fields of knowledge for male physical education teachers was administered by mail to the entire population (2,737 men) concerned. There was about a 50 percent response rate, and it is fair to assume that this half were generally more alert and knowledgeable than the nonrespondents. Yet the percentage of those who did not meet the criteria of adequate knowledge set by the experts in the five areas were 77, 77, 99, 89, and 94. The investigation points out that such deficiency of knowledge may help to explain the many observed consequences of inadequate practice, including the death of high school football players.

Rethinking Lifelong Professional Education

Long-accepted ways of "keeping up to date" and specialized programs of continuing education appear to be unsatisfactory in establishing and maintaining a desirably high level of professional practice; but what course of action would be successful? Ready answers to this question are constantly being provided but are often almost as quickly discarded. Methods or devices of teaching are put forward as panaceas; within a relatively short time, however, each one usually proves to have only limited application and either disappears or, at best, becomes one more resource among the many procedures available to the educator. Some suggestions call for more stringent systems of accrediting courses of study, of admitting people to professional practice, of vigorously enforcing codes of ethics, or of requiring repeated demonstrations of competence throughout a lifetime. But critics claim that this accountability is impossible to implement without traumatic conflict; and there is consensus that such measures would have the draconian effect of so severely limiting the number of practitioners that society's need for even imperfect service could not be met. Further, many present and future professionals capable of providing such service would be denied employment because they could not meet the impossibly high standards which exacting examiners might set.

No single solution appears likely to achieve the desired purification and enhancement of practice or to accomplish the heights of service that a more refined professionalism might bring. Certainly the mere addition of educational programs or systems of regulation, however enforced, will not suffice to bring about the changes needed. Instead the entire conception of professionalism must be rethought and its practices restructured. Every profession is a difficult art based on the application of complex bodies of knowledge. It is impossible completely to separate practice (and the external control of practice) from the ways in which it is learned. This premise establishes the background of the following chapters, though the focus of the book is on the ways in which continuing education may be used to raise the quality of service provided and aid the professionalizing process. Some implications of this point of view are presented here in order to indicate the magnitude of the changes that the future is likely to bring and to suggest the themes that subsequent chapters will develop.

The most profound revision of present conceptions may be in the very nature of the professionalizing process. Every occupation that lays claim to the distinction conferred by the term *profession* seeks constantly to improve itself in certain distinctive ways. These characteristics—such as increased competence in solving problems, a capacity to use more complex knowledge, and a more sensitive awareness of ethical problems— are related to the entire life career of the individual practitioner and to the stature of the occupation to which he or she belongs. Therefore a lifetime of learning is required to establish, maintain, or elevate the level of accomplishment suggested by each of these characteristics. This point will be amplified in Chapter Two, and in Chapter Three the specific characteristics will be described, and their function as goals for the total educational process will be indicated.

A new and far more complex design of education than that suggested in Figure 1 must come into being and, even though some of the stages may remain the same, changes must be made in them. Preservice curricula must be redesigned to do much more than is now the case to prepare students to be life-long learners. Many professional schools are reorganizing their courses of study so that their students will move more quickly than before into the world of work. The term *community-based education* is now common in law, theology, social work, and medicine (to name but four examples), the chief idea being to train the student not only within a specialized academic environment but also in settings similar to those which will later be encountered in practice. When this enlargement of instructional venue occurs, how will the practice of learning "in the field" be systematically used to encourage the process of subsequent life-long participation? Many university faculties are only now beginning to come to grips with this question.

Changes in the pre-service stages of learning have a powerful impact on the nature and variety of educational programs during the period of active service. In later years of life, a complex and subtly varied total offering of continuing learning opportunities must become available. This vast, intricate, and changing design cannot be achieved except by the application of greater resources, keener intelligence, and more creative approaches than are now customary, and the design will evolve more directly from the nature of earlier training than is now the case. This need has been recognized in many professions, particularly by leaders who have become disillusioned over specific teaching approaches. Blockstein (1967, p. 12), for example, asked his fellow pharmacists to join him "in scrutinizing the development and refinement of the many routes that can be taken" in continuing pharmaceutical education. And a distinguished panel of engineers dismissed earlier efforts in their own field as wholly inadequate and pointed out that continuing engineering studies must establish and maintain "an entirely new dimension of personal development throughout the engineer's career" and decide "what now needs to be done to assure the continual effectiveness of the profession" ("Final Report of the Goals Committee," 1968, p. 430).

The well-established flow of people through the formal training process will be significantly influenced by the growth of alternative lifelong patterns of preparation. For example, preparation for elementary or secondary school teaching is often followed, usually after years of experience, by preparation for school administration or some other specialized career. Experiments in similar "laddered" movements from one career line to another are now being tried in the health professions. The number of people who initiate professional careers in midlife or later is also rapidly rising, particularly as women enter the labor market after rearing their children or losing their husbands, as military or other careers lead to early retirements, and as individuals seek more challenging occupations than those in which they have been engaged. These and other phenomena will significantly change patterns of professional education. For example, skills learned by experience and training (perhaps as a community volunteer or an army officer) may reduce the nature and amount of what needs to be taught in formal pre-service and in-service preparation for another occupation.

In whatever part of the life-span it occurs, continuing education must facilitate the successful performance of practitioners in the diverse practice characteristic of professional work. In all curricula, pre-service and in-service, attention must be given to individual differences. In continuing education particularly, where the establishment of individual ways of work, of specialization of practice, and of various settings of employment all accentuate diversity, special efforts must be made to avoid a monotonous uniformity of training activities. The brilliant beginner, the seasoned specialist, and the dull plodder cannot all be expected to attend the same lecture series or routine workshop. A much greater individualization than at present must be provided so that a whole program does not rest on a single process, however established its traditions or intriguing its novelty may be.

Diversity of approach is required not only by human idiosyncrasies and diverse social settings but also by the fact that in most cases the forty to fifty years of active practice of a professional are not devoted to a single mode of work. Many kinds of changes occur in individual careers, including promotions, shifts in specialization, temporary assignments, retirements and returns to practice, and other modulations and mutations of a busy, usually prosperous, and frequently mobile life. Continuing education must be based not only on content-oriented goals of keeping up with new developments; it must also be designed to facilitate changes in life patterns or career lines. In many professions, for example, promotions to higher authority require the assumption of supervisory and administrative responsibility, the concepts and skills for which must be learned at the time when they are needed; indeed it is doubtful that they can be learned before then. In Chapter Four, an alternative to the classical model (Figure 1) is presented, taking account of some of the complexities of life and the ways in which they influence the practice of continuing education.

To achieve its greatest potential, continuing education must fulfill the promise of its name and be truly continuing—not casual, sporadic, or opportunistic. This fact means essentially that it must be self-directed. The automatic progression up the formal educational ladder that characterizes schooling in childhood and youth no longer exists in adulthood. Each professional must be the ultimate monitor of his or her own learning, controlling the stable or shifting design of its continuity. Even in the armed services, industrial and commercial corporations, and other large-scale institutions that maintain their own progression of training programs, much is left to the individual. In fact, the right to go to the next training program in an upward line of career development must often be earned by highly accomplished performance in active duty, and the desirability of the subsequent work assignment is determined by the evaluation of learning performance at the school. Chapter Five deals with the internalized zest for learning that must reinforce all forms of continuing education.

But reliance cannot be placed solely on self-direction. Many institutions offer continuing professional education; Chapter Six identifies the major organizations and associations concerned with such programs and suggests some principles that may help guide and differentiate their work. Chapter Seven describes the major ways in which organized educational programs are introduced into the professionalizing process.

Finally, Chapters Eight and Nine cover the ultimate role of the continuing educational process in the improvement of professional performance and in the maintenance of the quality of service provided to society. Both the collective existence of the professions and the ways of life of their individual members will be influenced in the future by scrutiny and control, the depth and complexity of which are scarcely yet realized. Formal and informal methods of professional and lay influence have long been used. Among them are accreditation, licensure or certification, legislative or other governmental controls and guidelines, judicial decisions, jury verdicts, policies of controlling boards, competition for clients, and appraisal of performance by colleagues, subordinates, supervisors, professional associations, clients or other users of services, and the mass media. The intervention of the general public and of specific clientele groups is becoming bolder than ever before—often with the overt and covert support of at least some members of the professions concerned. Lay citizens are being selected for boards, commissions, and policy committees that were formerly wholly professional in their composition. Periodic reassessment of competence is becoming commonplace. Bureaus representing clients in their dealings with professionals are being institutionalized in governments and corporations. Private associations of consumers and citizen action groups are springing up everywhere. The number and variety of cases taken to courts or other adjudicative bodies is increasing. Payment for professional services is coming to a much greater extent than before from government, insurance companies, or other organizations that demand both competence and cost effectiveness. All these measures encourage continuing education, because it helps safeguard and advance competence, because it advances the capacity of the professional to deal with the specifics of social policy formation, and because it gives tangible evidence of individual and collective efforts to meet the needs of clients and of society.

A Study of Similarities

This book stresses the fact that professions are markedly similar in their approach to continuing education programs. Every occupation has its own knowledge base and code of practice; its own lore, terminology, and point of view; its own mysteries and secret places; and a long-standing desire to repel invaders. Carr-Saunders and Wilson (1933, p. iii), in one of the early works on the professions, wrote the following somewhat mixed metaphor: "No man is a citizen of more than one country, and we have been mere hurried visitors to the homes of others." But even a few brief visits to the "homes" of other professions convince one that certain dominant conceptions guide all of them as they turn to the task of educating their members and that they tend to use essentially the same kinds of facilities, techniques, and thought processes.

At present this similarity of approach is not stressed in either theory or practice. Teaching and learning lie so near the heart of every profession that they seem to its leaders to have no other sources than the distinctive knowledge and tradition, the special history and belief, and the structures and forms of the profession itself. In developing the idea of continuing education, each occupation goes its way alone, winning its victories, making its mistakes, and maturing in its own conceptions. This implicit acceptance of uniqueness is reinforced by the fact that those who consider themselves to be professional educators of adults have not yet established a widespread recognition of their own expertise except in the health professions (and even there the acceptance is somewhat grudging). A bar association would not insist that its accounts be audited by a lawyer; nor would a welfare agency require its dental consultation service to be provided by a social worker; in fact, in carrying out such functions, the association would make sure that it had a qualified CPA and the agency that it had a dentist. Yet both association and agency would feel thoroughly competent to undertake their own educational programs and might even insist that nobody else could direct them.

Important consequences follow from the abandonment of the idea that the learning processes of each profession are wholly unique. In urging collaboration among professions, Enarson (1977, p. 114) observed that "the danger of contamination is slight, the possible dividends great." To look at efforts comparatively is to see that the needs, the general objectives, the specific goals, and the methods used all have a marked resemblance across professions. A study of similarities could result in an exchange of ideas, techniques, and solutions to problems that would greatly refresh and broaden practice in many professions. Staff members of associations, university professors, and other people with assignments to conduct continuing education for individual professions could collaborate on common topics and confront similar challenges, thereby advancing the work of all of them and avoiding that duplication of effort which results from the solemn belief that each occupation must find its separate road to a brighter future. In some cases, interprofessional educational efforts may provide new depths of insight. A special task force made up of a dentist, a pharmacist, a physician, a nurse, and a physical therapist concluded, after three months of intensive analysis, that collaborative study based on the care of the patient would be desirable and feasible for all the health professions, though such an approach "bore little resemblance to the conventional wisdom about continuing education" (University of Illinois, 1966, p. 31). Finally, specialists in the field of adult learning could be helped in their own professionalization.

While this book will stress similarities, it will also take account of basic differences. All professions resemble one another, but each has a unique expertise and point of view. Within professions, distinctive occupational groupings also exist. A difference in outlook separates an accountant employed by an industrial corporation from an accountant who comes from a governmental bureau to make an external audit of that corporation. Two clergymen may have the same kind of license to perform a marriage ceremony; but one of them may be certified by his denomination only if he has fulfilled a long and exacting course of preparation, while the other may need only to convince the elders of his church that he has been called to his mission by the voice of God.

In an effort (like that of Carr-Saunders and Wilson) to achieve some breadth of view of both similarity and diversity, I have studied, briefly or at length, seventeen professions or clusters of professions, to none of which do I belong. The occupational groups analyzed were accountants, architects, clergy, dentists, engineers, foresters, health care administrators, lawyers, librarians, military officers, nurses, pharmacists, physicians and surgeons, school administrators, school teachers, social workers, and veterinarians. Of these groups, the literature related to medicine is by far the richest and most profound, perhaps because of the eminence and antiquity of the occupation itself and perhaps because it has recently allowed itself to be thoroughly studied as an occupation not only by its own practitioners but also by sociologists, political scientists, economists, historians, anthropologists, philosophers, and representatives of other disciplines and professions. References to medicine will therefore be more frequent than to other professions simply because so much more data are available.

In addition to these seventeen, several other occupational groups that lack a formal sense of a closely associated identity (the presence of which is taken to be an essential element of professionalization) have been studied, though more briefly than the others mentioned. They include artists, business administrators, farm operators, general university administrators, home economists, musicians, public administrators, mass communications experts, and university faculty members. In addition, many authorities on the general nature of professionalization have been consulted. My process of visitation and exploration has taken me down many avenues; in some cases they led nowhere and in others I probably failed to notice side streets or even boulevards that would have been highly rewarding if I had been sensitive enough to follow them. The books and articles included in the References, however, offer a great variety of opportunities for readers who wish to embark on their own self-guided voyages.

To sum up, the comparative study of continuing professional learning appears to be a promising field of inquiry whose validity and utility are the subject of wide consensus. My aim here is to present a synthesis of the key ideas that guide the various professions in the continuing education of their members. The rewards of this study will be achieved only by dealing successfully with complexities of method and interpretation that are almost certain to be even more difficult than those that can now be recognized. Opinion and theory have been abundantly expressed by many people, and the structure and ideas of this book rest chiefly on them. Laborious objective inquiry on a comparative basis is also required, though it is now scanty and fragmentary. But, even granting such difficulties, any other alternative than comparative study seems impoverished and limited. To know but one profession is not to know that one, and to work wholly in terms of its specific dictates is to adopt a limited framework for thought and action.

Chapter 2

From Professionalism
to Professionalization

Professionals are not new to the world. But in the past, professionals have formed unprogressive castes. The point is that professionalism has now been mated with progress. The world is now faced with a self-evolving system, which it cannot stop. . . . If mankind can rise to the occasion, there lies in front a golden age of beneficent creativeness.

Alfred North Whitehead

Professions seem always to have existed and, in recorded times, to have been the subject of informed commentary. Only in the twentieth century, however, has a sustained effort been made to define them collectively, and only in recent years has it been understood that they can be conceived in a dynamic as well as a static fashion. This dynamism has powerfully reinforced the growth of lifelong education, particularly that which occurs during the years of active service. Therefore it is essential to sketch the evolution of this dynamic conception of "professionalization" as it has emerged from earlier and less practical definitions of professionalism and to examine how this shift in conception helps to define the nature and goals of continuing education.

The Rise of Professionalism

When it is said—as, indeed, it *is* said by every knowledgeable observer—that professionalism did not begin to take formal shape until the late nineteenth century and was not given its present form until the twentieth, the comment seems to belie much of what everyone knows of the past. The priesthood is recognized as a distinctive personalized role in every primitive society. Hammurabi, Solon, and other codifiers of the law appeared early in the record of civilization. Anthropologists have found evidence in skeletons and mummies of the use of complex medical and surgical skills; and every patient in a modern teaching hospital will empathize with Martial, who commented in the first century, "I was indisposed; and you straightaway came to see me, Symmachus, accompanied by a hundred of your pupils. A hundred hands, frozen by the northern blast, felt my pulse. I did not then have chills-and-fever, Symmachus, but now I have" (Epigrams, V, 8).

It has often been argued, most notably by Spencer (1900), that all professions evolved from the priesthood because originally only its members were allowed to acquire nonconventional knowledge, the possession of which has since been defined by many people as the touchstone of professionalism. But Thomas (1903, p. 256), while granting much of the truth of Spencer's assertion, thought it inadequate to explain the growth of the advanced occupations. "They need patronage," he asserted, "and when either the court or the church is developed, the patronage is at hand. . . . Some of the professions have received more encouragement than others from the church because their presence favored the needs and claims of the church. But their development must be regarded as a phase of the division of labor, dependent on economic conditions rather than on the presence in society of any particular set of individuals or any peculiar psychic attitude of this set."

Whatever the origin of a profession, its early practitioners remained essentially isolated or in touch with only a small company of their fellow practitioners. In ancient Greek and Roman days, the professional might well have been a slave, treating his master's illness, keeping his accounts, or instructing his children. In medieval times, with the rise of the guilds, collectivism began but without any overarching sense of a complete and universal system of practice and practitioners. The universities originated as efforts to provide better education for the learned occupations, sometimes concentrating on one of them and sometimes serving as centers for the study of several. The Council of Trent, which ended in 1563, condemned the Reformation and urged the education of a priesthood to combat its heresies. In 1605, Francis Bacon, in *The Advancement of Learning*, made a comment that was often to be repeated: "Amongst so many great foundations of colleges in Europe, I find [it] strange that they are all dedicated to professions, and none left free to Arts and Sciences at large" (vol. 2, Dedication).

But the educational system was too small, travel and communication too arduous, and the city-state too restricted as a governmental form to permit the growth of a strong, centralized, and widely spread organization for any of the professions. Moreover, the knowledge base on which some of the professions rested was too meager to inspire confidence on the part of the general public or to sanction any widely recognized certification as a prerequisite to practice. Nor did that knowledge increase rapidly or become broadly disseminated; indeed, new ideas were often regarded as heretically opposed to established doctrines, thus giving rise to factionalism rather than to a sense of common advance. The shortness of life and the slowness of change meant that whatever a professional knew or believed to be true would be sufficient to support his practice throughout his career.

The age of enlightenment in the eighteenth century and the industrial revolution of the nineteenth caused a break with the past for the professions as for many other aspects of life. Both theoretical and practical knowledge began to be built into complex systems. Simple skills taught by apprenticeship grew more refined; engineering, architecture, pharmacy, and nursing emerged as clear-cut separate occupations. The phenomenon of organized association became more highly developed than before, making possible interlocking networks of professional groups that could provide services for and exercise discipline over their members. Governments either took on the power of licensure or delegated it to other bodies. Some of these developments occurred naturally and spontaneously, but most came as the result of complex leadership patterns, some of them hard to identify. It has long been believed, for example, that Flexner's 1910 report to the Carnegie Foundation for the Advancement of Teaching revolutionized the teaching of medicine in North America, but a modern revisionist historian (Monahan, 1975) has argued that the book added little impetus to an already powerful movement toward change.

In both Great Britain and the United States, the emerging phenomenon of professionalism eventually became a topic for theoretical analysis. Beatrice and Sidney Webb—with perfunctory assistance from George Bernard Shaw—made a detailed study of the subject in 1917 as part of an analysis by the Fabian Society of the control of industry. In their work, a borrowed definition of the term *profession* was used, but its source was not identified and it was not applied with rigor as a basis for selection of the occupations to be studied. The next major British work was issued by Carr-Saunders and Wilson (1933). It referred to the Webbs' analysis as "admittedly slight and incomplete" but was itself arbitrary in its choice of occupations, observing, for example, that "the functions remaining to the Church are spiritual, and we are only concerned with the professions in their relation to the ordinary business of life. The Army is omitted, because the service which soldiers are trained to render is one which it is hoped they will never be called upon to perform" (Carr-Saunders and Wilson, 1933, pp. 2–3).

In the United States, the first classic work on professionalism was a paper published in 1915 by Flexner. To define professions, he set forth six criteria: they "involve essentially intellectual operations with large individual responsibility; they derive their raw material from science and learning; this material they work up to a practical and definite end; they possess an educationally communicable technique; they tend to self-organization; they are becoming increasingly altruistic in motivation" (Flexner, 1915, p. 904). These criteria have strongly guided the thought of many people, particularly because Flexner used his definition boldly. He answered the title of his paper— "Is Social Work a Profession?"—with a resounding negative. Social workers, he said, were mediators to other professions and had no distinctive purpose of their own; therefore they had no communicable content that was uniquely theirs. Further, he thought it possible that the altruism attached to the occupation was more strongly felt by the people who controlled it than by "the worker herself."

Almost sixty years and hundreds of definitions of professionalism later, another writer on the same subject, Rose (1974), gave a far different answer. After a survey of other definitions, he proposed his own, which, like Flexner's, contained six criteria: association with high-status knowledge; association with universities; association with high social class; association with activities that have high value to many people; association with beliefs in processes that have acquired a high degree of mystique; and association with power bases. On applying these standards, Rose thought himself warranted to entitle his essay "Issues in Professionalism: British Social Work Triumphant" (Rose, 1974).

Between the dates of publication of these two papers and subsequently, on both sides of the Atlantic, the study of professionalism has broadened in countless directions, its many facets being studied both theoretically and objectively. Despite the sophistication of much of this analysis, modern readers may well conclude that a comment made by Hughes (1962, p. 39) is still true: "When people say 'profession' nowadays, they often have in their heads a very fleeting model, the model of what the law and medicine are supposed to have been in the liberal nineteenth century—that is, . . . an esoteric art, practiced by a closed group of people, each by himself, each having relations to a number of separate clients, and each collecting his own fees." Hughes goes on to say that this model is no longer valid, even for physicians, but despite that fact, "if one were to do a content analysis of professional claims in this country he would find that when people say 'profession' they are talking about medicine and about this particular concept of medicine as they think it was at a certain time."

These three conceptions of professionalism suggest only limited goals for continuing educational activities. Rose's seems to advocate the study of how to achieve power, prestige, "high-status" knowledge, and an aura of mystery. The model that

Hughes suggests (and rejects) gives rise to various possibilities for action, but, if followed consciously or unconsciously, would lead most professionals ever farther away from the reality of the situations in which they find themselves. Flexner's criteria offer the broadest scope of the three but still suggest limited possibilities for learning. In his terms, an occupation either is or is not a profession. If it is, then its elements are known; continued learning must be chiefly an elaboration of the groundwork already laid by preparatory training. If an occupation is inherently not a profession, continuing education cannot make it one. Social work, for example, having in Flexner's view no possible ultimate goal or content of its own, could lead its practitioners toward many educational objectives, but all would be related to general bodies of knowledge already acquired by practitioners of the true professions.

Professionalism: A Static Concept

A comparative analysis of these and many similar definitions shows each of them to be chiefly an effort to reorder the importance of already stated criteria or to add new ones. Each analyst who addresses the subject seems to construct, either consciously or unconsciously, a two-way grid with the names of the authors of earlier treatises ranged along one axis and criteria of definition along the other. In the cells formed by the intersections of the grid, an "X" is then placed to indicate which authority chose which criterion. Sometimes the grid is actually presented; in other cases it is implied. Criteria have been intensively studied, singly and in combination, both generally and in the analysis of a single profession.

As early as 1938, DeLancy had concluded that whereas no authoritative definition of a profession had appeared or seemed likely to do so, it would only be necessary for any student of the subject to put together a list of criteria, each of which was basically arbitrary but which collectively made up a coherent pattern. This pragmatically chosen list could then be applied to the topic to be studied. This in fact became the practice used not merely by investigators but also by those who had to decide practical issues concerning education, licensure, specialty certification, and associational leadership.

These practical decisions became harder and harder to make because of the phenomenal rise in both the number and percentage of the work force engaged in what the United States Census calls "professional, technical, and kindred workers." Because of changes in definition from one census tabulation to another, data are not exactly comparable but are close enough to allow gross estimates to be made. In 1910, there were about 1,758,000 people in this occupational category and they made up only 4.7 percent of the work force. By 1976, there were 13,356,000 such people and they comprised 15.3 percent of the work force. Thus an increase of 660 percent occurred in the number of persons so employed in comparison with an increase of 135 percent in the total work force.

The growth in professional, technical, and kindred workers occurred not only because in 1976 more people were engaged in the occupations included in 1910 but also because the members of many other vocations (both old and new) asserted the right to be called professionals, hoping thereby to achieve greater status, power, money, and other psychic and material rewards. In 1965, Lynn exultantly proclaimed (p. ix), "Everywhere in American life, the professions are triumphant"; it seemed that many workers wanted to have a share in that triumph. Many people took it for granted that a constantly broadening network of existing and emerging vocations would claim membership in the company of the elite. However, Wilensky (1964) demonstrated that this result was unlikely as long as any "classical" definition of a profession was maintained. Despite the fact that thousands of distinctly identifiable occupations exist, he argued, protracted effort had led to the result that "no more than thirty or forty occupations are fully professionalized" and that the idea of a much more widespread growth "is a bit of sociological romance" (pp. 141, 156).

Many people would argue that Wilensky, even in his own terms, was overgenerous in his estimate that thirty or forty well-accepted and fully professionalized occupations exist. Events that have occurred since he and Lynn wrote have blurred rather than sharpened criteria and the distinctions they establish among occupations. As has already been noted in Chapter One, the members of no profession, however venerable or exalted, feel as triumphant today as they did in the middle 1960s. Moreover, even the assumption that qualifying criteria are essential has often been ignored. If definitions rest solely on unsupported claims, then any occupation can assert its right to enter the charmed circle of the professions, and indeed many have done so. For example, a group of graduates of a Federal New Careers program "decided to discard the stigma of being called 'para-professionals.'" They asserted, "We do not feel, as that title insinuates, that we are less than fully qualified. We decided to call ourselves 'New Professionals.' With this new title, we became even more highly functional in order to live up to our new name and its connotations" (Boyette, Blount, and Petaway, 1971, pp. 237–238).

If the professions are less triumphant than they were in the 1960s, the chief cause probably lies in growing concern about the extent to which the needs for a highly competent and subtle performance of essential services are being met for society as a whole, for some segments of it, or for some individuals. The rising level of criticism of the past quarter century suggests that the effort to give a restrictive and lofty definition of the term *profession* that places it at the top level of a rank-ordered work force has not been adequate to meet those needs. Still less progress is likely to result from the enunciation of self-serving standards that allow a vocation to define itself as a profession; even less good can come from the complete abandonment of all standards. If the concept of professionalism is to be preserved as an ideal that gives guidance and hope to reality, a basically different approach is necessary.

Professionalization: A Dynamic Conception

A new approach had already been enunciated by the mid 1960s, though it took some years for its application to become widespread. Essentially this change calls for a new use of the criteria long associated within the professions. Each criterion sets a standard that may be considered either in static or dynamic terms. In the past, the major search has been for absolutes that would identify those occupations that could properly be called professions. The more widespread modern trend is to ask what principles of action seem most significant to the members of a vocation as they seek to elevate and dignify its work so that it can become accepted by society as a profession. For clarity of communication, absolute criteria are here called *canons* and dynamic ones are called *characteristics*. For example, a canon might be, "A profession must have a clearly formulated code of ethics." A characteristic might be, "A professionalizing occupation should be concerned with the continuing refinement of the ethical standards that characterize its work." Characteristics, by their dynamic nature, can take the form of goals for a professionalizing occupation.

Thus the study of process replaces the identification of existing essentials. This approach carries with it the implication that all occupations seeking the ideals of professionalization are worthy of sympathetic study and that no clear-cut boundary separates the professions from other vocations. The former question applied in each case—"Does the occupation in its idealized form or in practice possess the criteria of a profession?"—is replaced by a number of questions, each of which is based on a characteristic and inquires "To what extent does the occupation possess this characteristic and how is it working toward its further refinement?" The latter approach was suggested for public administration, for example, by Schott (1976, p. 258), who concluded that the field should stop applying rigorous canons and "become more modest in its claims to professionalism. Such modesty may enhance the quality of its contribution to the practice of public affairs and avoid a frustration of its scholars, educators, and practitioners due to impractical or impossible aspirations."

This shift of conception toward professionalization grew out of the writings and discussions of Hughes (1958, 1962, 1973), was explored theoretically by Bucher and Strauss (1961), and served as the organizing principle for the influential book edited by Vollmer and Mills (1966), who take care (p. vii) to point out: "We wish to avoid discussion of whether or not any particular occupational group is 'really a profession,' or not. In accord with Hughes' experience, we feel that it is much more fruitful to ask 'how professionalized' or more specifically 'how professionalized in certain identifiable respects' a given occupation may be at some point in time." Thus the existence of a charmed circle of the professions becomes meaningless. Every occupation that is called a profession is, in reality, a semiprofession. The analysts of an occupation can assess its degree of professionalization in terms of the number and quality of performance of characteristics chosen as essential. An upwardly mobile occupation can try to influence not only the number of principles it seeks to apply but also appraise its excellence of performance on each one. It can therefore be validly compared not only with other occupations but also with itself at different periods of time or in various places. Thus its leaders or the independent analysts of its work can measure whether it is moving toward or away from professionalism, and researchers can determine the factors associated with such movement. For example, Males (1976) has described the decline of the profession of architecture in Sweden between the early 1950s and the mid 1970s and has suggested the causes for this loss of influence, drawing lessons for British architecture.

Is the dynamic concept of professionalization merely an abstraction, or can it be operationalized to serve as a guide for practice? The answer is still not certain, but at least one study suggests the latter conclusion. Hickson and Thomas (1969) ranked 43 British occupations on the extent to which they had achieved certain characteristics, basing the analysis on the formal associations which, in the United Kingdom, issue credentials admitting individuals to practice. An operational scale was developed wherever possible for each characteristic, thirteen of which were eventually identified as being of particular significance according to the statistical procedures used. Three medical specialty groups (obstetricians and gynecologists, physicians, and surgeons) had perfect scores. Three occupations scored zero.

In the natural development of the professionalizing process, does growth occur by an unchanging sequence of steps?

Or are the characteristics sought in a random order or one dependent upon local circumstances and the facilitations and barriers they impose? Wilensky (1964, pp. 145–146) argued strongly for growth by an unchanging sequence of steps, concluding: "In sum, there is a typical process by which the established professions have arrived: men begin doing the work full time and stake out a jurisdiction; the early masters of the technique or adherents of the movement become concerned about standards of training and practice and set up a training school, which, if not lodged in universities at the outset, makes academic connection within two or three decades; the teachers and activists then achieve success in promoting more effective organization, first local, then national—through either the transformation of an existing occupational association or the creation of a new one. Toward the end, legal protection of the monopoly of skill appears; at the end, a formal code of ethics is adopted." The study by Hickson and Thomas (1969, p. 49) tended to confirm the existence of this series of stages.

Should this sequence of "natural" steps be used as a guide by ambitious leaders of occupations? There is strong disagreement over this issue. Wilensky explained "deviations from the sequence" as being largely opportunistic. "Indeed," he said, "in a culture permeated by the idea of professionalism but little touched by its substance, many occupations will be tempted to try everything at once or anything opportunity and expediency dictate" (1964, p. 146). Those who disagree with this comment do so for one or more of three reasons. One is to suggest that taking advantage of opportunity or expediency is sometimes the surest path to progress, not just the surrender to temptation. Another possibility is that those people who deeply understand the dynamic nature of modern professionalization are not "permeated by the idea of professionalism" as a charmed circle of occupations, each of which has achieved its stature by taking one step at a time. Instead, the dynamic processes that guide their efforts lead them forward on many fronts at the same time, though they are not necessarily "tempted to try everything at once." Still a third possibility is that "natural" progression may itself have occurred as a result of the social trends and policies

of the particular era Wilensky studied, but these trends and policies will not necessarily continue. For example, in the first
seventy-five years of the twentieth century, as formal higher
education was rapidly expanding, preparatory training programs
of professions seemed to move inexorably toward the sponsorship of universities. The impetus of this movement may have
slowed down, stopped, or even been reversed. In some of the
most highly prestigious professions, such as medicine, new educational centers are being developed outside the framework of
the university or with only minimal connections to it.

The dynamic approach is used in this book because it permits an open rather than a closed system of thought. For example, if independent fee-based practice is identified as an invariable definitional criterion (as Hughes suggested it is often
considered to be), then the clergy and the military must forever
be excluded from consideration. (As earlier noted, Carr-Saunders
and Wilson omitted them upon even more specious grounds.) Yet
since ancient times, both have been called professions, both meet
most of the other important modern definitional tests, and, most
significantly for present purposes, both have developed patterns
of lifelong learning whose examples could profitably be imitated
or adapted by other occupations. Furthermore, the conception
of a profession as a fixed entity may cause its members to believe that their only need for learning is to maintain their individual careers and the collective status they already possess.
However, if many occupations (even the most exalted) are striving to become more professional than they are, then all of them
can be helped to identify and achieve goals that now lie beyond
their reach. No matter how the ideal of professionalism is described, it is never achieved universally. The needs of society
require that every professionalizing occupation become better
than it is, and at least part of the effort it must exert is the improvement of its patterns of lifelong learning. A dynamic concept of professionalization offers educators both the opportunity and the challenge to use active principles of learning to help
achieve the basic aims of the group with which they work. They
become not merely reinforcers of the status quo, as they so

often are now, but the colleagues of all who work to further the power and the responsibility of the vocation. They serve but are not subservient.

Three Modes of Learning

If lifelong education for professionalization is to be fully effective, it must be conceptualized and applied in a sophisticated fashion. Depending upon the circumstances, those who seek professionalizing goals for a vocation use one or more of three major and overlapping modes of learning.

The mode of *inquiry* is the process of creating some new synthesis, idea, technique, policy, or strategy of action. Sometimes this mode is employed in a structured fashion; discussion and encounter groups, seminars, clinics, and guided experiences can be used to help people achieve new ideas or new ways of thinking, though the outcomes of the process cannot be predicted in advance. More frequently in this mode, learning is a by-product (though sometimes an intended by-product) of efforts directed primarily at establishing policy, seeking consensus, working out compromises, and projecting plans. In the late 1970s, for example, the issue of whether fees and services should be advertised has been much discussed in several professions, including dentistry, law, accounting, and medicine. Members of each of these professions have been debating the subject and, as Darling and Bussom (1977) have shown, have come to surprisingly similar conclusions. At the time of writing this book, however, the issues are still being clarified and the outcome is uncertain.

The effectiveness of the inquiry mode is blighted by any tinge of didacticism, which destroys the spontaneity of the discovery process. Its degree of success is based on informed judgment after the occurrence of the experience and is measured according to the accomplishment of objectives that often are not evident until then, or, indeed, until they have been proved pragmatically to be successful. In some theories of education (most notably that of John Dewey) this mode is proposed as the basic method of learning, though the process of inquiry may sometimes include episodes of formal instruction or the establishment of recognized standards of good performance.

The mode of *instruction* is the process of disseminating established skills, knowledge, or sensitiveness. Those who use it assume that the teacher (a person, a book, or any other source) already knows or is designed to convey everything that the student will learn. Most people think of this mode as being the only form of education, chiefly because established institutions use it so extensively in working with children and young people, including those engaged in pre-service professional education. Skilled teachers sometimes use a simulated mode of inquiry even within the framework of the mode of instruction. For example, a professor of chemistry knows the composition of unidentified chemical compounds, but requires students to discover the identity of each component. The degree of success of the mode of instruction is measured by the achievement by the student of goals that are usually known to the teacher at the beginning of a learning episode—though they may be modified during its process. Evaluation of achievement may seek by various means to measure the students' sense of satisfaction or, alternatively, their knowledge, skill, or sensitiveness. In recent years many educators have been interested in finding ways in which learners demonstrate the ability to perform well in either artificially contrived or natural settings. "Competency-based instruction," as it is sometimes called, is easiest to use when it is concerned with skills; it becomes more difficult when it is concerned with knowledge or sensitiveness.

The mode of *performance* is the process of internalizing an idea or using a practice habitually, so that it becomes a fundamental part of the way in which a learner thinks about and undertakes his or her work. In pre-service professional education, the mode of performance is used chiefly in "practical" or clinical teaching, where it is inculcated by drill, by close supervision, by clinical presentations, and by long continued demonstration on the part of those who provide instruction. During the years of practice, the mode of performance may be fostered by formal use of the other modes of learning, but it may also be reinforced by rewards and punishment that require individuals and groups to maintain and improve their abilities and to avoid obsolescence. Evaluation of this mode is essentially in terms of the nature or caliber of actual performance as judged by peers, by supervisors, by external examiners, and occasionally by the courts. As Kubie (1970, p. 694) has pointed out, "The difference between learning about and becoming is basic." The use of this mode in the workplace is sometimes guided by what is called "change theory." Often it involves not only formal educational activities but also manipulation of various physical and social aspects of the environment.

The use of the three modes of continuing education may be illustrated by a single example. Changing social conditions or the invention of new processes often require a profession to establish a basically new theory or methodology of practice. The decision makers of the profession (sometimes stimulated or assisted by outside opinion) must use the mode of *inquiry*, sometimes in an elaborate and complex fashion, to identify the essential nature of the new method or theory and explore the ramifications of its application, thus educating themselves to both aspects. When a basic procedure has been established, it is disseminated by the mode of *instruction* to the other practitioners as well as to concerned external publics. The changed behaviors that should result are then encouraged by the mode of *performance* so that they become established in practice and are monitored by whatever means seem appropriate in the various workplaces in which professionals are employed. During this whole process, the advocates of alternative methods (including the traditional way of work) will usually actively advance their own views, but they too will shape and spread their views by using the same three modes.

In the next chapter, a number of characteristics of professionalization will be suggested, not as static or definitional criteria, but as dynamic, widely accepted potential goals for improving performance and hence as objectives for the lifelong education of professionals. As will be extensively illustrated in that chapter and later, the three modes of learning apply in many different ways to the achievement of these objectives.

Chapter 3

Goals of Lifelong Professional Education

Just as the whole world is a school for the whole of the human race, from the beginning of time to the very end, so the whole of his life is a school for every man, from the cradle to the grave.... Every age is destined for learning, nor is man given other goals in learning than in life itself.

John Amos Comenius

The dynamic concept of professionalization requires the broadening of the present goals of continuing education. Many leaders assume that the dominant (perhaps exclusive) objectives of such learning are the mastery of new theoretical and practical knowledge and skill relevant to a profession and the habitual use of this knowledge and skill to solve the problems that arise in practice. Because such goals are easy to understand, they have tended to become the all-absorbing interest of the providers of continuing education and of those who guard the gates of the professions.

But the professionalizing process is complex, and the lifelong learning to which it gives rise must have many goals in both pre-service preparation and in the active years of practice. Fourteen characteristics broadly associated with the professionalization process are here suggested as bases for such goals. Many more than fourteen could be identified, particularly if one included all the policies and principles that apply to only one or a few occupations and situations. The list proposed here has been distilled from many sources but chiefly from analyses of the general literature dealing with professions, views expressed in publications or directly to me by the leaders of various occupations, and my own observations. The characteristics could be stated operationally by way of scales indicating the level of achievement of an occupation on each one, but such quantification would require elaborate techniques of validation and the establishment of reliability, which may appropriately be undertaken only after the characteristics themselves have been accepted or modified by investigators who wish to use them in detailed inquiries.

The educational goals established by these characteristics must be sought in various ways throughout the lifespan of the professional. In Chapter Four, the various stages of lifelong professional education are analyzed in detail, but in this chapter only a general separation is made between the pre-service preparatory years—when the foundations of competence are established—and the later years of active practice—when increasing competence is constantly tested by performance. Because of the orientation of this book, primary attention is devoted to the latter.

The Conceptual Characteristic

The first and most dominant characteristic is that as many members as possible of a professionalizing vocation should be concerned with clarifying its defining function or functions. It is difficult but necessary to seek constantly to understand the structural tenets of a practitioner's work—those which give it focus and form. Nonexperts often have no trouble defining the central mission of a profession. To them it seems obvious, for example, that veterinarians provide health or custodial care for animals, architects design buildings, and hospital administrators administer hospitals. But anybody who thinks about the realities of the professions knows that such definitions are too simple to be useful in dealing with the priorities and ethical decisions encountered even in routine practice.

Many practitioners, particularly those who have long been engaged in well-established vocations, can get along fairly well much of the time without achieving any deep or subtle knowledge of their occupational missions. Studies show, however, that substantial numbers of these people are continually or periodically troubled about what they should be doing in contrast to their actual pursuits. Blizzard (1956), for example, once asked Protestant clergymen to rank six pastoral roles in terms of the satisfaction and enjoyment they brought to those who performed them. The resulting rank order was: pastor caring for a congregation, preacher, teacher, priest or liturgist, organizer of the church's work, and administrator of its activities. When Blizzard then asked his subjects to rank these roles in terms of the amount of time they required in actual practice, he found that the order was drastically changed: the clergymen were spending the major part of their time at tasks they thought least important, least enjoyable, and in which they felt least effective. Blizzard concluded that "no matter how different ministers' ideas of what is important in the ministry [may be], all wind up doing substantially the same thing" (pp. 509–510). The problem presented by Blizzard's study has never been solved for the ministry and is doubtless shared by at least some members of every profession. For example, a study of high school principals showed little relationship between the ways they spend their time and the ways they feel they should spend it. Of nine categories of responsibility, professional development ranked sixth in the list of what they felt they should do and last in the list of what they did (Byrne, Hines, and McCleary, 1978, p. 20).

Even more troublesome are those cases in which a professionalizing group has difficulty establishing its central mission because of circumstances beyond its control. Pharmacy is a good case in point; for many years it has struggled to identify the central focus of its efforts. McCormack (1955) argued that despite increasing requirements for pharmaceutical training, successful pharmacists find themselves to be essentially businessmen and that the ensuing role conflict gives rise to a dilemma few individuals can avoid. Denzin and Mettlin (1968, p. 378) returned to the same theme, defining the obstacle that "prevents pharmacy from stepping across the line of marginality" as its failure to gain effective control over the dispensing of drugs. Conversations with professors of pharmacy indicate that they center their teaching on the accomplishment of several different major missions. It is sometimes argued, for example, that the truly professional pharmacist must serve in a clinical capacity as a combined consultant to and educator of individuals and families (who are regarded as clients) concerning various forms of medication and must try to ensure that each medication is used properly and that no synergistic ill effects result. However, this conception has not yet been firmly established in field practice throughout the country.

Changing social conditions and the new values they create cause profound alteration in the conception of central missions. For example, the forester of 1909 controlled large tracts of lumber, with which he dealt in straightforward, utilitarian, underfinanced, and relatively primitive terms. By 1939, he had become a technical expert with a sophisticated view of land management and a need to make resource decisions that were still largely based on immediately utilitarian purposes. By 1969, however, social concern with the long-range ecology of the forest had brought to the fore, as Jones (1970, p. 31) has pointed out, "complexities from which the forest resource manager was formerly fairly well insulated." Among them were "policy issues relating to natural beauty, open spaces, wilderness preservation, property taxation, outdoor recreation, and land acquisition." Jones went on to argue that the forester "should be instrumental in the resolution of conflicts arising from controversies" based on such issues.

In most cases, alternative viewpoints about the central mission of a vocation exist simultaneously. Architecture is a good example. In 1970, the editors of *Architectural Record* asked a number of leaders of that profession to define its "principal activity" and were astonished at the variety of answers they received. One distinguished practitioner came out steadfastly for "the design and organization of individual buildings and groups of buildings. If a person is not involved in the above, he is not an architect." Another authority denounced that view as being "a narrow concept, and one that is historically false" and argued that architecture is centered in "organization, decision making, and judgment to create functional and enriching spatial relationships at any scale." The editors concluded that "the comfortable old realities are shattered when students begin seeing architecture as identical with life and with our society and when established practitioners think part of their professional responsibility is to be both a politician and a social activist" ("Education in the 1970's," 1970, pp. 128–131).

Perhaps the most characteristic change in the conception of a profession has been the broadening of concern to include both a range of content and a depth of treatment that go far beyond earlier ideas. For example, a survey of dentistry pointed out: "Twenty-five or thirty years ago, dental practice was limited to relieving pain and treating lesions of the teeth, the gums, and other tissues of the mouth. Today it is concerned with the comprehensive management of oral, facial, and speech defects and with the oral structures and tissues as they relate to the total health of the individual" (American Council on Education, 1961, p. 95). Engel (1977, p. 135) has gone even further to suggest that the basic model of all medical practice, including dentistry, is out of date; he has proposed "a biopsychosocial model . . . that provides a blueprint for research, a framework for teaching, and a design for action in the real world of health care." Change has also occurred less comprehensively to bring about refinements of practice that have created fields of specialization in the health professions, law, engineering, teaching, and other occupations that were formerly organized on generalized comprehensive bases.

These few examples suggest that a constantly changing sense of mission has come to be a widespread—perhaps universal—characteristic of professions, one which, if present trends continue, is likely to be permanent. The implications for lifelong learning are profound. Students are selected for a preservice professional curriculum in terms of what the faculty conceives the defining function of the vocation to be and are educated in terms of that conception. Even then, however, the training is not built on a consistent conception of mission, because faculty members often hold sharply differing opinions and sometimes use their classrooms and laboratories to do intellectual battle with one another. Students are also far from docile, and their views provide a structure for the knowledge they acquire, helping them to determine the degree of its relevance. Thus everyone who enters service in a profession already knows of the existence of divergent views of its central mission. The beginner may also quickly discover, however, that the theoretical and idealistic concerns expressed and displayed in the professional school may contrast sharply with the governing ideas encountered "in the real world."

But whether the young practitioner maintains a sense of central mission brought from professional school or adopts a new one growing out of an initial exposure to full-time service, he or she must expect to be constantly challenged by the assertion of new fundamental orientations and in all cases the three modes of education mentioned in Chapter Two may become operative. For example, a new intellectual abstraction of the vocation's central mission may be stated by an established leader or by some person whose unorthodoxy initially gives rise to indifference, anger, or ridicule. If the idea appears to have a sufficient promise or threat, it will be subjected to elaboration, refinement, and adjustment to the realities of practice through a process of discussion, argumentation, debate, and other activities customary to the mode of inquiry. The outcome may be reaffirmation of the old idea, acceptance of the new one, compromise, or the perception of deeper unities originally hidden by surface disagreements. Thus the new sense of mission develops out of a process of collective self-education among established or emergent leaders of the profession.

The second mode, instruction in the new or revised concept and its implications for practice, follows naturally from the first and may be a part of the reality testing that finally gives the new definition of central mission its authority among those who control the processes of instruction, accreditation, certification, and licensure within the profession. Acceptance is not fully effective until the new concept is implemented by performance—the adoption of the new mission as an internalized and habitually used concept.

The adoption of a new unifying concept is never easy, particularly if it requires a complete reorientation of practice.

Especially in ancient and well-established professions, the new idea may confront ways of thought that are now deeply ingrained, though they may once have been considered radical. A reading of history suggests that even as the dominance of a new central mission is established, the idea that will eventually overthrow it may be visible somewhere on the horizon.

The Performance Characteristics

The second, third, and fourth characteristics of professionalization are so intimately related that distinctions among them often overlap in both theory and practice. But each is essentially different from the other two, and that difference is often crucial to the professionalizing process.

Mastery of theoretical knowledge. The second characteristic of professionalization is that the practitioners of a vocation should seek mastery of at least the rudiments of the information and theory—originally derived for descriptive rather than practical ends—that comprise the knowledge base of the profession. Every profession is a system of applied content, skills, and principles based in part on theoretical areas of the arts and sciences. As Francis Bacon observed: "If any man think Philosophy and Universality to be idle studies, he does not consider that all Professions are from thence served and supported" (*The Advancement of Learning*, 1605). As new disciplines have emerged, basic fields of content have proliferated, but Bacon's point that theoretical fields contribute to the professions is still sound: teaching depends upon psychology, physiology, sociology, and philosophy; the health professions depend most fundamentally upon the biological sciences but are also influenced by psychology, sociology, economics, and statistics; and engineering depends upon mathematics, physics, and chemistry.

Each theoretical field has been developed on the basis of a search for truth rather than as a way of solving specific individual or social problems. For example, philosophy and economics have their own bodies of knowledge and methods of adding to them, and the topics concerned are inherent to the disciplines themselves. Philosophy has subfields such as epistemology, metaphysics, and logic; the principles of each are intended to be general truths, not guides to action in specific practical cases.

In the professions, theoretical knowledge may be approached by practitioners in either direct or indirect ways. Courses organized to convey basic bodies of subject matter are usually included in the years of preprofessional instruction, and a perennial debate exists between those who believe that the disciplines should be taught on their own terms as part of general education and those who hold that the content should be selected according to students' future professional specialization. In professional schools, the latter position almost always prevails. When ethics is taught in a law school, it is legal ethics, and when psychology is taught in a college of education, it is educational psychology. Because this practice is widespread, many people confuse basic disciplines with their fields of application and sometimes cannot even properly distinguish between the academic degrees to which they lead (for example, a Ph.D. degree in physiology and an M.D. or a master's degree in sociology and one in social work). The danger of ignoring this distinction has been roundly attacked in a paper by Truesdell (1976) entitled "The Scholar: A Species Threatened by Professions," which begins with the lament, "Progress cannot be reversed; what it has killed, we cannot restore to life. Professionalism, like pollution, is here to stay" (p. 631).

Crucial though these bodies of theoretical knowledge undoubtedly are, pre-service professional education seems less and less likely to be concerned with them than has been true in the past. Applied knowledge is expanding very rapidly at precisely the time that an urgent movement is under way in many professions to shorten the preparatory curriculum. For example, in some universities the M.D. may be achieved in only six or seven rather than eight years after completion of the secondary school. Basic theoretical knowledge, particularly that which lies near the periphery of an applied field or outside it altogether, is likely to be cut from the required course of study.

During a lifetime of practice, however, the professional is drawn constantly back to theoretical considerations and may come in time to perceive an interrelationship of all knowledge. The potential school administrator may take graduate courses in urban sociology and in basic theories of administration, but service as principal of a city school shows how much he or she still needs to learn about the complex processes of municipal operation and how to use supervision, delegation, and other executive procedures. The alert practicing professional constantly sees the relevance of knowledge whose significance was not fully understood when it was first studied. More than that, intellectual curiosity leads many people to want to understand advances and shifts of thought in the theoretical disciplines. Practitioners of the health professions, for example, may not find their work greatly influenced by recent research in genetics yet still be eager to learn more about it.

The effort to use the years of practice to acquire deeper understanding of theoretical knowledge is motivated by a constant interplay of both need and interest. Such learning may be sporadic or may result from a conscious plan in which the individual keeps in touch with the sciences most basic to his or her profession and makes occasional explorations into new terrains of related content. The forty to fifty years of a career pass all too quickly, but they do lend a scope and dimension to continued learning of theoretical disciplines that are denied in the cramped years of initial schooling. To the extent that practitioners take advantage of their opportunities to acquire basic knowledge, their professionalization is broadened.

Capacity to solve problems. A third characteristic of a professionalizing vocation is that its practitioners should seek to be able to use theoretical bodies of knowledge to deal competently with a category of specific problems that arise in the vital practical affairs of mankind. The responsibility of the professional is not to discover abstract truth but, as Tosteson put it (in Condliffe and Furnia, 1970, p. 48), to bring to bear, "on a specific individual problem the wisdom, the accumulated wisdom of mankind." The nurse, the librarian, or the public administrator (and every other professional) confronts one problem after another and is required, with the insight, skill, and knowledge available, to do the best he or she can to deal with each confronted situation. Upon each case is focused not only theoretical knowledge derived from many disciplines but also practical wisdom acquired by experience.

The ultimate test of the success of a professional is the ability to solve problems (or to decide that they cannot be solved), and those problems usually involve vital and deeply significant outcomes. Thus, the practitioner must be psychologically prepared to live in a world of uncertainty. Knowledge is growing at a far more rapid pace than is the capacity of the human mind to absorb it. As this expansion occurs, new frontiers requiring further study are discovered. The professional's essential task is not to apply a specific fact or principle to a particular case but to deal with it by the use of a synthesis of all relevant knowledge. As each problem presents itself in its own way (even though it may fit into a familiar general category), the professional must take account of the total pattern of circumstances presented and treat it in a unique fashion, with an awareness that the outcome is always in doubt. Freidson (1968a, p. 25) has written on this problem in a penetrating fashion, in one place referring to "the impurity of professional authority," and Fox (1957, p. 207) has explored the same phenomenon in a paper significantly called "Training for Uncertainty."

In pre-service education, the potential professional is usually introduced to the realities and immediacies of practice. The case method, fieldwork, moot court, externship, practice teaching, clinical experience, observation, and other procedures are used to illustrate the intricacies of problem solving. At present, profound shifts are occurring in the timing of this kind of preparation and the settings in which it occurs. In the health professions, for example, contact between students and patients often occurs earlier than before and is tending to take place in community settings, not exclusively in a university hospital.

By creatively dealing with problems, all practicing professionals have the greatest opportunity for continuing education. A major, never-ending task of every practitioner is to examine each situation encountered to see what can be learned from it. The professional wants to diagnose and heal the patient, win the case, bring a dissension-wracked institution back to harmonious operation, build a bridge in a difficult terrain, or deal successfully with any other problem presented. In complex and unusual cases, the need to learn is often starkly evident, and requires the practitioner to read, consult other professionals, make tests and probes, engage specialist advisers or advocates, and take advantage of other opportunities. Whether the result proves to be a success or failure, the practitioner learns from it— and his or her future practice should be enriched by that fact.

A difficult but essential task is to apply the same kind of intent inquiry needed in unusual cases to ordinary and familiar situations. At the start of a career, every professional must learn to perform many tedious routines and to use different kinds of information so that each can be utilized properly as required by the overall pattern unique to each problem. A beginning professional is thorough but slow in checking routines laboriously. As time goes on, greater speed is possible, and eventually the focus of the practitioner may be almost entirely on the pattern itself and not on its component parts. Such a broadening of perspective is desirable, but only when the practicing professional can also maintain a firm grasp of detail, constantly looking for the unique aspects of each case but never abandoning essential conceptions or routines.

The repetitiveness of practice, however, sometimes leads to staleness, boredom, dullness, acceptance of shortcuts, and routinization of thought. This deadly effect is suggested by a fictional description of a hospital chaplain: "He was just out of seminary and performed last rites without running the words together" (Newman 1966, p. 117). Many senior professionals, in one way or another, "run their words together." Some physicians, for example, do not keep adequate records on their patients, do not perform all the accepted medical routines, and do not examine the results of laboratory tests closely enough to detect abnormal findings or potential synergistic dangers. As Miller once noted (1961, p. 104), "There is a maxim in medicine that more mistakes are made because the physician didn't look than because he didn't know." To use the terms defined in Chapter Two, the instructional mode may once have succeeded with a professional, but his or her performance has since failed.

Boredom and routinized thought not only have ill effects on the satisfactory resolution of each problem as it is encountered but also hamper the continuing education of the professional if he or she fails to apply to customary and familiar situations the same kind of intense inquiry required in unusual cases. The difference between the two situations is one of degree as far as the benefits of learning are concerned. In every situation in which the professional works, complexities are present; otherwise trained talent would not be required. Experience may be a good teacher, but reflection about experience is a better one. A busy, possibly overworked person may resent the suggestion that he or she should bring a fresh and discerning eye to bear upon even the most routine situation (the treatment of dental caries, the drafting of a will, the making of a minor executive decision, or the designing of a culvert), but to the extent that there is failure to do so, learning dries up at its freshest and most fruitful source.

Use of practical knowledge. The fourth characteristic of professionalization is that practitioners should have available to them and actually use a substantial body of knowledge and technique that has grown out of the nature, history, scope, and processes of the vocation's practical application. In most instances, these scholarly resources result from the analysis of solutions to the problems with which practitioners have dealt or with the testing of hypotheses concerning the application of general principles to specific situations. The knowledge thus derived explains causes, describes results, indicates alternatives, presents techniques, identifies new approaches, challenges established routines and procedures, and in other ways suggests to the professional how to cope more effectively than before with the situations he or she confronts. It indicates with what degree of certainty the practitioner can diagnose, prescribe, design, teach, administer, or perform other skills. This professional literature supplements but does not replace the education acquired from an introspective analysis of continuing practice. From the literature, the practitioner learns the rules; from experience, the ways in which they should be applied.

The roots of this practical body of knowledge lie deep in the theoretical fields of inquiry, and therefore the two can never be wholly distinguished from one another. But the professionalizing process requires the building of a substantial body of supporting knowledge which practitioners can use in undertaking practical affairs. Goode (1961) has argued, for example, that librarianship does not have an adequate knowledge base of its own to entitle it to the status of a profession.

Each professional school relates its distinctive knowledge to its basic core disciplines in many ways. The instruction in a law school may be wholly professional in content, the basic disciplines being seen, if at all, solely in terms of their application to legal cases. In another educational program, perhaps on the same campus, the prestige of the basic theoretical fields may be so great that it overshadows the more purely professional discipline; for example a very skillful trainer of teachers may have lower status than his colleagues who teach educational psychology or educational sociology. In still another program, the interest of the faculty in the advancement of the knowledge base may lead to a virtual absence of concern with its practical applications. At a meeting of theologians, for example, one professor said with feeling: "If most of the faculty [do] not indicate their interest in the church and [if] their emulation of the profession does not come through in the classroom work, then it is awfully hard for some of us who are in the field of practical theology" (Craven, Todd, and Ziegler, 1969, p. 142). The reverse situation is noted by a dean of architecture: "Our profession should have room for a few who only think" ("Revolution in Architectural Education," 1967, p. 137). The division between theoretical and practical knowledge is often felt so keenly in professional schools that the resulting tension is felt by both faculty and students.

As was noted earlier, most of the subject matter of formally organized continuing education is focused on the exposition of the content, skill, and sensitiveness produced by growth and change in theoretical and practical knowledge. This subject matter is being enlarged so rapidly and upon so many fronts that it floods in upon practitioners in torrents that threaten to engulf them. But knowledge does not progress by simple addition. Sometimes a brilliant insight will give new unity or perspective to many ideas that had not previously appeared to be related. And, particularly in rapidly professionalizing fields, reversals of viewpoint occur. Marcel Proust once wrote, in his lightly ironic way, that "medicine being a compendium of the successive and contradictory mistakes of medical practitioners, when we summon the wisest of them to our aid, the chances are that we may be relying on a scientific truth the error of which will be recognised in a few years' time. So that to believe in medicine would be the height of folly, if not to believe in it were not greater folly still, for from this mass of errors there have emerged in the course of time many truths" (Proust, 1966, p. 409).

Self-enhancement. A fifth characteristic of professionalization is that the practitioners of a vocation should, throughout their years of pre-service learning and work, seek new personal dimensions of knowledge, skill, and sensitiveness by the arduous study of topics not directly related to their occupation. In the pre-service years, this criterion may be reinforced by the formal introduction into the curriculum of liberal or general studies, but later in life the interests and enthusiasms of the individual are paramount. Each practitioner must determine appropriate counterpoising fields of inquiry that can contribute to his or her process of self-guided development. But while the primary effort to achieve this criterion lies within the control of the individual, its effect is both personally and collectively important.

No sharp delineation can be made between learning related to worklife and that devoted to other such concerns as home, community, or the fulfillment of distinctive personal potential. The training of the senses to discriminate by the study of painting, music, or sport has important consequences for professional discernment or dexterity even as the study of linguistic composition aids the process of communication. Thus general or liberal education helps lay an indispensable basis for occupational excellence. The reverse is also true. Much of the instruction in every profession, drawing as it must upon basic disciplines, introduces learners to their distinctive realms of thought. Also in the learning that comes from experience, the alert practitioner gains insights into the vagaries of human character and behavior and acquires the habit of synthesizing a number of discrete elements into a whole. Thus professional and

general education are interrelated in personal self-enhancement
and professionals must be sure that in undertaking the first they
do not forget the second.

The acquisition of new dimensions of personality can un-
questionably have practical career values by providing a chance
for a practitioner to reach new clients or gain recognition by
moving in different social circles. More profoundly, and for all
professionals, the study of nonoccupational subjects can offer
relaxation. The more absorbing the interest, the greater the
profit in this respect. "The tired parts of the mind," Winston
Churchill observed, "can be rested and strengthened not merely
by rest, but by the use of the other parts. It is not enough merely to switch off the lights which play upon the main and ordinary field of interest; a new field of interest must be illumi-
nated." It is only "when new stars become the lords of the
ascendant, that relief, repose, refreshment are afforded" (Churchill, 1932, p. 297). Darwin pointed out that any specialist who
loses his or her broad interests comes to have a stunted mind
and can no longer work as creatively as before. Using himself as
an example, Darwin claimed that his devotion to science gradually dominated all his thought and action, driving out his earlier
enjoyment of literature, music, and the fine arts. Late in life, he
lamented his loss of taste for them. "My mind," he said, "seems
to have become a kind of machine for grinding general laws out
of large collections of facts, but why this should have caused
the atrophy of that part of the brain alone, on which the highest
tastes depend, I cannot conceive" (Darwin, [1887] 1958, pp.
138-139).

But the broadest value of this goal is not its utility, its
provision of relaxation, or its maintenance of breadth of viewpoint, but its significance as a corrective for the boredom and
routine often produced by professional practice. In too many
cases, work dominates life, and what an individual does becomes
a symbol for what he or she is. When one speaks of optometrists,
foresters, teachers, or priests, the intention is usually to refer to
the men and women who earn their living in these occupations.
But the part is often taken for the whole, and the individual is
submerged in what should be merely one of many roles. This

foreshortened view is destructive of the whole person when applied by others, but is even worse when applied by oneself. In either case, all of life comes to be viewed in the increasingly rigid framework of a single profession. Against this danger there is no sure safeguard, but the best preventive throughout life is to have other absorbing intellectual interests to serve as counterbalances to the profession. Even if the organized profession itself does not foster the development of such interests, more than a few practitioners will make the personal discovery that what they learn outside their profession gives them valuable new insights into the work they do. Then, later in life, when professional practice usually diminishes and finally ceases, the zest for experience will continue and an independent dignity and resourcefulness remain.

The Collective Identity Characteristics

Those who seek seriously to professionalize an occupation try in many ways to establish its collective identity by building systems and structures that foster and maintain conceptual and competency characteristics. Form is important in all such endeavors, but less so than the spirit with which those who seek professionalization try to suffuse it. For example, restricted membership associations, accreditation of instructional programs, licensure of practitioners, and similar devices and procedures are common to many crafts. The professionalizing occupations are distinctive from these other vocations because their leaders seek to encourage and regulate standards of practice based on a profound central mission and on advanced and esoteric bodies of knowledge.

The collective identity criteria differentiate to some extent the professionalizing occupations from other advanced fields of work. Artists, farm operators, commercial and industrial managers, and university presidents claim to possess conceptual and competency criteria but are seldom ardent seekers of a comprehensive and continuing collective identity. Some categories of skilled workers include specialized segments of people with a highly professionalizing attitude. One example is business administration, most of whose practitioners are not strongly concerned with professionalization but who include accountants, a sharply differentiated subgroup that is working hard toward professionalization in terms of the characteristics identified in this chapter.

It is true that the term *professionals* is often used to identify all workers who operate at an advanced performance level, who have had rigorous training, or who take pay for their work. It has become conventional, for example, to say that the whole university faculty has become professionalized. More specifically a "professional" historian may be defined as one who has been formally trained by a university in historiography, both in the broad content of the field and in the specific phenomena or major events that occurred during the period of time and in the place that he or she studies. The distinction between professional and amateur athletes, particularly those who engage in international competition, has become obscured in a fog of seemingly contradictory rulings. Although the use of these terms can be meaningful in a general conversational way, for the purposes of this book they are not helpful operationally in considering the professionalizing process and the education it requires both before and during practice. Therefore only those occupations whose members are deeply concerned with establishing their collective identities are considered "professions."

Ordinarily the criteria involved in the establishment of a collective identity are sought by one or more formal associations that accept major responsibility for advancing and protecting the interests of practitioners and maintaining their standards of performance. In the absence of associations, professionalization can be nothing more than a surging, inchoate movement in which progress or the lack of it is largely influenced by the pressure of outside forces. Futhermore an association usually fosters the growth of continuing education, both by providing it directly and by stimulating its provision by other agencies.

Carr-Saunders and Wilson (1933, pp. 298–302) vehemently urged the importance of organized and exclusive societies by observing that "a profession can only be said to exist when there are bonds between the practitioners, and these bonds can take but one shape—that of formal association." In the extended historical survey that follows this comment, evidence is provided by the authors that, in Britain at least, the creation of an association has served as the crucial point of self-awareness and social acceptance. Thus, the request in 1844 for a charter for the College of Veterinary Surgeons was based on the fact that such incorporation "would materially contribute to . . . the respectability" of the practitioners of that vocation; the resulting charter designated it as a profession. At about the same time the founders of the Pharmaceutical Society said that it "was designed as a means of raising the qualifications of pharmaceutical chemists and placing between them and unqualified persons a line of demarcation." Other writers have agreed with this general point; still others have taken it for granted. But not everyone agrees with the idea that professionalization requires a single dominant and controlling association or even that the nature of a professionalizing association can be defined. In the United States, at least, a single vocation may have many associations, at least some of which may be in open or hidden competition with one another. A comprehensive association is sometimes surrounded by many separate groups, each of which usually represents a special field of application, a geographic area, or both. Still further, it is sometimes impossible to establish to everyone's satisfaction the difference between a professional association and a craft guild, a labor union, or any of a number of other organizations that may include members of the same vocation in its membership.

Formal training. The sixth characteristic of professionalization is that formal procedures should be established to transmit the essential body of knowledge and technique of the vocation to all recognized practitioners before they enter service and throughout their careers. As already noted, Wilensky (1964) believes that this characteristic is the second to appear temporally in the rise of a profession. The first leaders of an occupation come to it from many sources, but immediately or eventually work at it full time, identify its mission, borrow and develop its content and techniques, and differentiate its role from those of other occupations. These pioneers then begin to think of the perpetuation of their work. As Goode points out (1957, p. 194), a new profession "does not produce the next generation biologically [but] does so socially through its control over the selection of professional trainees, and through its training processes it sends these recruits through an adult socialization process."

In the long history of professionalization, many systems of education have been used, including trial and error, self-instruction, apprenticeship, and formalized training. Professionalizing groups usually feel a sense of accomplishment when their work is accepted as a special department of instruction by a university or other established educational institution. It very often happens, however, that the pioneer practitioners want to be sure that the proper subjects are being taught in an appropriate fashion by a qualified group of instructors with high status in the sponsoring organization and with adequate resources to support the new program of study. Even at the beginning, the organized professionals assert their stake in the educative process. As the number of training programs increases, a process of periodic formal inspection, usually known as accreditation, is customarily created, falling under the control of a professional association or some other specialized body. Thus the guarantee of competence in a profession is often first established by the fact that a person is not allowed to enter its practice until he or she has satisfactorily completed a formally accepted instructional program. But while the idea of accreditation is common to virtually all professionalizing occupations, its scope, principles, and practices are unique to each one and are in a constant state of flux and change.

In the modern era the placement of specialized courses of study in universities or other higher education institutions—such as theological seminaries or technological institutes—has become such a dominant method as to be, in the opinion of many people, the hallmark of professionalism itself. The leaders of many occupational groups have campaigned vigorously, particularly in the twentieth century, to have their training programs accepted as integral parts of existing universities, as has been the case with nursing and social work, or to have such programs raised in status, as was true of teaching when normal schools evolved into postsecondary institutions. In recent years, however, some disenchantment with university-based professional education has appeared. The dean of the Harvard Medical School has argued that training of physicians should have both a university phase and a nonuniversity phase. The latter is conceptually necessary because, in his view, a teaching hospital is markedly dissimilar from any other part of a university and great tension "arises from the often artificial attempts [to describe] nonuniversity activities as being university ones" (Ebert, 1977, p. 171). Some observers claim to discern a countertrend toward the award of degrees by nonuniversity organizations (such as hospitals, industries, government bureaus, or associations), but no major thrust in that direction has yet appeared (and may never do so).

While universities and university-level institutions have become dominant in the pre-service education of a profession, they do not have a monopoly. For example, a large number of nurses are still trained in hospital schools of nursing and an increasing number are receiving their instruction at community colleges. Even within a long-established profession, several categories of programs may exist. In October 1979, for instance, 136 institutions belonged to the Association of American Law Schools. The American Bar Association approved all of these schools and an additional thirty-four institutions as well. About sixty additional schools had not been approved by either group.* As far as the clergy is concerned, almost every conceivable kind and level of educational preparation is accepted as a valid basis for practice, including the supernatural inculcation of knowledge by God. Serious problems of status have arisen because in many professions—such as journalism, architecture, or librarianship—some distinguished practitioners are products of nonuniversity-based schools, of institutions that rank low in prestige, of apprenticeship or other similar forms of training, or of self-guided learning. Thus the monolithic control over the professions which the pre-service schools are often accused of exerting is somewhat diluted by the differences of quality and point

*This information was supplied by Millard H. Ruud, Association of American Law Schools.

of view among them and by the fact that many outstanding practitioners have not been prepared by them.

The attention paid by professional school faculties to the pre-service curriculum has been so absorbing that they have taken relatively little notice of continuing education, though the amount and nature of that provision varies greatly not only from one profession to another but also among the schools that serve a profession. The situation is changing rapidly, however, and a major concern of the staff members of professional schools in the last quarter of the twentieth century is likely to be continuing education. This enlargement of scope will be encouraged by changes in the formal processes of accreditation, by the decline in the number of pre-service students, by the growth of relicensure requirements, and by the prestige achieved by practitioners who are constantly seeking to increase their professional competence. In particular, the agencies of accreditation are stressing more than before the need for professional schools to include continuing education as an integral part of their training responsibilities.

Universities and other sponsors of pre-service training have strong competitors in the provision of continuing professional education. Many people argue that other institutions—such as associations or employers—should have primary responsibility for such work. Other providers, such as salesmen of the products that professionals use, are said to have the chief influence on diffusing information and skills. Chapter Six will present an analysis of these and other major providers of continuing education.

Credentialing. The seventh characteristic of professionalization is that formal means should be used to test the capacity of individual practitioners to perform their duties at an acceptable level and, in some cases, to license those who are qualified to do so. Recognition of the need for formal credentialing systems was a key element in the evolution from individualized and unregulated practice to modern professionalism. The nature of an adequate system of certifying competence was concisely expressed by the Oxford University Commission of 1852 when it said that "to render a system of Examinations effectual, it is indispensable that there should be danger of rejection for inferior candidates, honourable distinctions and substantial rewards for the able and diligent, with Examiners of high character, acting under immediate responsibility to public opinion." The commission added that at that time at Oxford, all of these attributes were lacking (Oxford University Commission, 1852, p. 60).

In American practice, the major instrument for licensure is the state government, which usually fulfills this function with the guidance of a committee for each profession, which sets the examination policies and attests to the results of their application. (Traditionally each committee was composed exclusively of the members of the profession it licensed, but there is now a strong movement to include lay citizens on the ground that they represent the public interest.) In some cases, a de facto power over state licensure is exercised by accredited professional schools, because only their graduates are admitted to the licensure examinations. Sometimes licensure is established by meeting the requirements for membership in an association or qualifying for a registry it maintains. In other cases, graduation from an accredited curriculum may serve as de facto licensure. For example, among librarians, usually only those who work in elementary and secondary schools are required to be licensed, but the profession exerts a strong social pressure to have only people with appropriate library school training admitted to important positions. The American Library Association has mounted strong though unsuccessful attacks on two presidents of the United States because each of them nominated a non-library-school graduate to be Librarian of Congress. In other cases (the clergy is the most conspicuous example) licenses are issued by the state upon certification by recognized private authorities.

In many professionalizing occupations, the entire process of credentialing is dominated by a tightly woven network of relationships, partly formal and partly informal, established by clusters of leaders. The same names may appear in positions of prestige and control in associations, university instruction, accrediting boards (state, regional, and national), and licensing committees. As Egelston has pointed out in his study of several allied health professions (1973, pp. 221, 224), "Monopolies are developing. Professional associations control the education, certification, program accreditation, licensure and collective bargaining agencies for their professions. . . . The tight description of preparation and functions in a legal framework creates a closed guild arrangement antithetical to advancement of personnel and adverse to experimentation as the organization of services and knowledge and technology change." Thus for many vocations the professionalizing process has achieved control by a small group of practitioners over the right to practice, negating the general theory that narrow specialism exercised in crucial aspects of life should be governed by broad citizen responsibility. As a result, public distrust of the credentialing process is often expressed, sometimes in extreme forms. For example, Carr-Saunders and Wilson (1933, p. 104) describe what happened in Paris when "the authorities required all practicing doctors to deposit their qualifications. . . . On the last day to comply with the order a prominent practitioner, whom all thought to be unqualified, deposited excellent qualifications, which he implored might be kept dark, since his very lucrative practice depended upon the fact that his clients thought him to be without that contamination."

This discussion of credentialing has been concerned chiefly with initial licensure. Subsequent and more advanced credentialing has been largely under the control of private associations (sometimes called "colleges" or given other special designations), which may have elaborate requirements for further study, experience, and examination beyond that deemed essential for initial practice. Usually the resulting credentials are certificates of specialized competence, as in medical or dental practice, or of demonstration of proficiency, as in accounting or architecture. This additional licensure may be regarded as a reward for continuing education, because it comes after extended experience and study, but many of those who secure special credentials or designations do not regard them in this way but as the ultimate completion of formal study.

A different attitude is held concerning such other forms of credentialing as relicensure, the issuance of competency-based certificates, and the maintenance of membership in specialized societies. The issuance of a license or certificate or selection for membership in a highly qualified (and usually prestigious) group has customarily been for the lifetime of the individual concerned, being maintained only by the periodic payment of a fee. Strong movements are now under way, however, to require that professionals be obliged either to demonstrate continuing competence or to provide evidence that they have sought to maintain able performance. The use of credentialing for this purpose will be described in Chapter Nine.

Creation of a subculture. The eighth characteristic of professionalization is that the vocation should nurture for its members a subculture with distinctive attributes: lore, folkways, mores, traditions, role differentiations and relationships, variations in authority and power, personal prestige systems, language and special references not understood by the uninitiated, and clusterings of people with distinctive functions. The profession can become very much like a secret society and may even possess grueling initiatory experiences; the most often cited example is the course in gross anatomy in the first year of medical school. In every professionalizing occupation, the process of acculturation may begin in the home environment of a child if a member of the family practices the profession concerned. During the years of general education, it can be enhanced by elective courses, independent study, work, or volunteer experience. It is sharply intensified in the professional school. Later, when the individual enters active service, the effort first to become established and then to achieve suitable career advancement leads to an ever stronger commitment. At that point, Greenwood suggests (1962, p. 216), "the absorption in the work is not partial, but complete; it results in a total personal involvement. The work life invades the after-work life, and the sharp demarcation between the work hours and the leisure hours disappears. To the professional person his work becomes his life." The subculture expands to include most of the culture.

The most profound effect of the acculturation process upon continued learning is probably achieved informally. The hospital, the press club, the teachers' lunch room, the library staff lounge, and the lawyers' table at a social club, are places where professionals are frequently engaged with one another in shop talk. In any work situation, the juniors constantly observe the seniors and learn what to do or what not to do. At associations and conventions, conversations in the corridor, bar, and dining room are heavily devoted to the discussion of practical affairs. On such occasions, as Milton Stern once commented, "Gossip is elevated to the level of generalization." When two randomly placed seatmates on an airplane, bus, or train discover that they belong to the same profession, an immediate bond is felt which often leads to a conversation about work. Much of the informal interchange in all these situations is inconsequential small talk, but even that has the effect of strengthening the bonds of professionalization. In addition, the conversation can have intended or unintended educational consequences that result from efforts to seek or provide guidance; reports of unusual problems or unorthodox solutions; discussion of economic, political, or ethical issues; or debates among people with divergent views. The value of this informal reinforcement and interchange of knowledge is so great that many professional educators have developed special techniques to reach geographically or socially isolated practitioners who do not have constant association with their colleagues.

The process of acculturation is deeply meaningful for the nature and extent of formal continuing education. Most profoundly, the immersion of the individual into the life of the profession usually means that further study is guided chiefly by those who are themselves part of the special community or who have contributed to its development. This principle is not uniformly true, nor does it apply in the same fashion for all goals and all content. But the general tendency is sufficiently strong so that, as noted earlier, most professions move along separate paths even as they move toward similar goals. The effort to overcome this isolation and thereby provide broader and more effective continuing professional education is being carried out in three general ways. Some professional institutions are engaging trained or experienced educators to direct their programs. Other institutions are creating special cadres of their own profession who become expert in, among other subfields, continuing legal education or continuing nursing education. And these educators, both members and nonmembers of the profession, are finding their way toward each other in special projects, team efforts (most frequently in the health professions), or in subsections of associations whose broad focus is upon general adult education or university extension.

Legal reinforcement. The ninth characteristic of professionalization is that legal support or formal administrative rulings should protect the special rights and privileges of practitioners. All occupations are controlled by general laws—such as those having to do with child labor and minimum wages—and people who work in many nonprofessionalizing vocations, such as farm operators, labor leaders, and law enforcement officers, also receive special support of various kinds or are governed by legislation that applies only to them. But the members of a professionalizing occupation often believe that their mission has an unusually important significance to society. Therefore they seek special protections and privileges from legislative, judicial, and administrative bodies. Among these prerogatives are the exclusive right to practice their profession, the power to perform legally binding acts, the right to maintain inviolable confidentiality in their relationships with their clients, and access to financial support for their research and training activities. Sometimes professionalizing groups feel it necessary to try to restrain by law the actions of individuals or other groups. For example, psychiatrists may seek to limit the practice of therapeutic counselors, or physicians may try to have restraints placed upon the fee-setting policies of lawyers, hoping that such limitations will discourage malpractice suits.

Most professionalizing associations also try to influence public policy in the field of work in which they are engaged. In Washington, D.C., and the state capitals, some of the strongest lobbies are those representing the professions. This sphere of action severely tests a profession's altruism, for the expression of naked self-interest (or the allegation that it is the sole source of the policies advocated) leads to the rise of counterforces, to public disillusionment, to schisms within the profession, or to conflict with other occupations or consumer groups. But in a democracy a professionalizing vocation must usually devote much of its resources to advance those policies which it believes to be essential to its own existence or concerning which it feels it has special expertise. As Meyer (1959, pp. 319–320) pointed out, "Social work has long had a double focus: on social reform, on the one hand; and on facilitating adjustment of individuals to existing situations, on the other. . . . Mary Richmond, symbol of the case-by-case approach, is reported to have said to Florence Kelley, symbol of reform in the grand style: 'We work on the same program. I work on the retail end of it, but you work on the wholesale.' "

The effort to achieve new legal rights or favorable governmental policies and to retain the gains already won greatly influences the educational program of a profession. In the years of pre-service professional education, if not before, students become aware of their future privileges and responsibilities and often discover profound disagreements on matters of social policy among themselves, among their professors, and between the faculty and themselves. It is during the years of active practice, however, that the assertion or defense of legal rights and duties is most directly related to education, particularly that undertaken in the mode of inquiry. Ideally, policy should be developed on any given issue only after the careful study of alternatives based on the collection and interpretation of data. Even when decisions are ultimately made by association boards or other representative bodies who control a professionalizing occupation, an effort is often made to include as many people (and as many kinds of people) as possible in the deliberations, because involvement in decision making helps both to shape the ultimate policy and to provide an early sense of commitment to it which will be essential when the time for action arrives. Once policy has been decided, it must be interpreted to all the members of the profession. Persuasion may be required to win the support of dissidents. The education required may be one based on strategy as well as substance. In a democratic society, a large number of influential people, both inside and outside the ranks of the occupation, must be encouraged to support the adoption of major social policies, and members of the profession may need to be taught how to reach and persuade such people.

Public acceptance. The tenth characteristic of professionalization is that the general public should be encouraged to become aware of the lofty character of the work done by the
practitioners of the vocation. Becker (1956, p. 101) argues that
the term *profession* is best used as "what Durkheim called a *collective symbol*: one of the many labels current in the society by
which a work group may be designated, by itself and by others.
Any group is a profession, then, which is fortunate enough to
get itself accepted as such." In another paper, Becker (1962, p.
34) spelled out this approach to professionalization: "I have suggested that we view *profession* as an honorific symbol in use in
our society and analyze the characteristics of that symbol. . . .
In other words, we want to know what people have in mind
when they say an occupation is a profession, or that it is becoming more professional, or that it is not a profession."

Even when a strong case can be made for the high status
of a profession, increased public acceptance is difficult to
achieve. Veterinarians can present excellent arguments for the
scientific foundations of their work, for the economic benefits
it provides to society, and for the number of advances in human
health pioneered by specialists in veterinary medicine. The competition for places in the entering classes of accredited professional training programs in the field is sometimes even keener
than in medical schools. Yet researchers in veterinary medicine
believe that they receive far less support for their work than do
other health specialists and that the number of opportunities
to enter the profession is increasing only very slowly. Despite
determined effort, the situation seems not to have grown markedly better in recent years (Roark, 1977, p. 3).

The desire to achieve public awareness and acceptance of
a professionalizing occupation is different from the desire to
achieve a higher place in the ranking of all occupations, though
the two are related to one another. The data show that the
former is probably easier to accomplish than the latter. Hodge,
Siegel, and Rossi (1964) made a comparative analysis of studies
of occupational prestige (including some vocations not usually
noted for their aspirations to become professionalized) in the
United States from 1925 to 1963. They concluded that the
ranking had remained remarkably stable during that period. In

one of the studies cited, the same rating instrument was administered to large representative samples of the public in 1947 and again in 1963. The correlation of prestige scores was .99. Some systematic but small shifts occurred in both directions, but the general structure of esteem did not change; however, judging from the decrease of "don't know" responses between 1947 and 1963, awareness of the nature of occupations had increased markedly. Furthermore, in 1947 at least, all segments of the population had almost identical views concerning the prestige hierarchy of occupations (Reiss and others, 1961, pp. 189-190). It can be concluded that the various occupational groups (or their champions) are all so fully engaged in public relations efforts that while they have increased the awareness of the American public concerning the nature of their work, they have essentially cancelled one another's gains as far as the winning of greater relative prestige is concerned.

A detailed study of a single occupation, rehabilitation counseling, bears out this conclusion. Haug and Sussman (1968, p. 62), summarizing a complex study, concluded that "visibility of the occupation is generally low, increases somewhat in the public segment familiar with disablement, and is highest among those with possible workplace relationship. However, visibility has little real effect on prestige ratings. When the occupation is known it receives a slightly higher score, but so do other service occupations studied, leaving *relative* positions unchanged. Further, the segment likely to have the most thorough knowledge, the group working in public administration, actually rates the occupation lower than does any other segment."

In a well-known study published in the middle 1950s, Inkeles and Rossi (1956) compared the occupational prestige systems of six relatively industrialized nations: the United States, Great Britain, New Zealand, Japan, West Germany, and Russia. Despite the great geographic spread and the cultural variability of these nations, their occupational prestige systems were remarkably similar, particularly with regard to the professions, which apparently have inherent attributes that influence their rankings more significantly than do general social patterns and national beliefs.

The relative prestige of professions, either separately or collectively, may well have changed substantially since the 1950s and 1960s, but if conclusions reached in the studies just cited and others like them are still valid, an increase in prestige of a profession is not likely to be easily, quickly, or directly achieved. The arts of public persuasion are advanced and widely adopted. Professionalizing groups are well aware of the need to use them, though it may be true that some associations, training programs, and other seekers of acceptance may use only broad-brush mass approaches when they really need skillfully customized procedures to reach the opinion makers in society.

The effort to strengthen public acceptance does not appear to be a major goal of either basic or continuing professional education, though some useful efforts can be made to help practitioners know how to present themselves and their work more effectively to the general public, to policy makers, to associates, and to clients. But such efforts may boomerang if carried too far; the citizens of a sophisticated society are quick to detect and become cynical about obvious public relations efforts. Better general acceptance of a profession may best be sought as a by-product of continuing education that improves the performance of practitioners in carrying out the basic mission of their work.

Ethical practice. The eleventh characteristic of professionalization is that a tradition of ethical practice, sometimes reinforced by a formal code, should be established and then constantly refined in the light of changing circumstances. This tradition must ultimately become sufficiently strong so that it cannot safely be violated by practitioners or their employers and yet be sufficiently flexible so that it can accommodate a wide variety of cases. In achieving this characteristic, occupations encounter some of the thorniest problems of professionalization. One of the primary tasks of educational programs, both pre-service and continuing, is to provide settings in which ethical issues and their practical applications can be debated and discussed. When clear-cut principles emerge from either majority rule or compromise, they must be conveyed in a coherent fashion to all the members of the profession. Engineering and accounting, to cite but two examples, have recently been deeply engaged in efforts to clarify ethical standards.

Any such task always leads to contradictions and complexities. The essence of professionalism has often been declared to be altruism. For example, a widely quoted judicial opinion holds that the professional's "main purpose and desire is to be of service to those who seek his aid and to the community of which he is a necessary part" (*State ex rel. Steinver v. Yelle* [1933], 174 Wash. 402, 25 Pac. 2d 91). Yet the term *professional* has often been invidiously contrasted to *amateur*. In this comparison, the professional is seen as a money-grubbing opportunist, usually compelled by poverty or low social status to undertake his craft, while the amateur (the root of the word being drawn from the Latin verb "to love") engages in his work because he has a passion for it and for the service it enables him to provide. Part of the modern opposition to professionalism comes from those who say they would like to reinstate the supremacy of the amateur but, as Brustein (1969, p. 18) has pointed out, this argument is flawed because "today's amateur . . . seems to love not his subject but himself." Thus two terms, almost always used in contrast to one another, appear to shift their meanings in confusing ways.

The universal standards of ethical behavior—such as honesty, temperance, justice, and steadfastness—by which moralists usually hold that behavior should be guided sometimes assume strange and unusual masks or reversals when applied by professionals. A client may feel strongly the impact of a presumed injustice but find that the professional he consults displays no such feelings. As Braude (1975, p. 95) points out, "An occupation must look relatively at events and try to order them in such a way that future occurrences may be predicted. A technical language permits the practitioner to assume this detached, relative stance toward the layman. It is the realization that this relative, comparative approach has in fact been taken toward him that shocks the layman client. It is, to say the least, deflating to the ego to realize that one's own emergency is a routine affair to the practitioner."

Even more disturbing is the negation of customary morality by special professional rules. For example, the adversary system in law assumes that an impartial court will decide between contesting parties whose attorneys are required to represent their interests. The lawyer must not only declare his client innocent when he knows him to be guilty, but, as Schwartz (1972, p. 20) makes clear, the defense attorney "cross-examines to impeach opposition witnesses he knows to be telling the truth; he exploits evidence adduced by the other side which is in his client's favor, even though he personally believes or knows the evidence to be false or mistaken." He must not condone perjury or destroy relevant evidence, but it is hard for the layman to see these latter practices as different in anything but degree from legal actions that are not only accepted but expected.

The members of a truly professionalizing vocation must therefore learn to make subtle ethical distinctions that might never occur to a layman. In accounting, for example, Levine (1973, p. 92) suggests two practices that independent auditing firms should adopt. Can such a firm retain full independence of action, he asks, if it has a continuing fee relationship with a client? He suggests that there might well be mandatory rotation of assignments, designation by the Securities and Exchange Commission, or some other form of external allocation of clients. And is not the attestation of competent fiscal management usually so brief as to be misleading? "We certainly are not insurers of our clients' overall financial condition but, unfortunately, the conciseness of our opinion may make it appear so." The only way, Levine argues, that such ethical criteria can be identified is by a process of informed discussion within the profession—a process of learning by inquiry.

In the effort to develop codes of ethics, almost everybody begins with the Hippocratic oath, although as Sigerist (1941) pointed out, any physician who in modern times swears to the original version has no intention of abiding by it and is committing perjury by taking the oath. However the symbol of formal avowal is not a bad one. It may well be useful to try to identify, either in a code or by other means, the ethical rules of the profession so that they can be understood by those who practice it and so that major deficiencies in the present system can be put right. But the code should not be a tedious set of detailed and rigid rules but a broad summary of the moral be-

havior that is expected of every practitioner and that becomes
a guiding though constantly reinterpreted tradition, somewhat
like the American Bill of Rights. Because active practitioners
set the tone of the profession, this system of guiding ethics can
be created and disseminated only by the use of all three modes
of continuing education—inquiry, instruction, and performance.
Otherwise it is likely that the present attacks upon the professions will continue to mount, and advances made in other respects will be negated by the losses suffered in this one.

Penalties. The twelfth characteristic of professionalization is that penalties (including the ultimate—denial of the right
to practice) should be established and enforced for those practitioners who are incompetent or who fail to act in terms of
accepted ethical standards. The chief defense against malpractice lies in the sense of discipline that an individual imposes
upon himself or herself, and it is in the enhancement of an
awareness of personal capacities and limitations as well as in the
application of moral standards that lifelong professional education plays its major role in the advancement of this aspect of
professionalization. The second defense lies in the understanding of the mission and standards of a profession by its clients,
by the general citizenry, and by the authorities who control its
work, such as legislators, governmental administrators, and
board members of hospitals, schools, libraries, welfare organizations, and other private and public institutions. These various
publics should be reached by special programs designed to provide the understanding they need so that they can remain alert
to the standards of service they should expect from the members
of a profession. Contrary to many hostile comments, professions
are increasingly accepting the obligations to reach relevant publics. While these efforts are not themselves examples of continuing professional education, the attempt to clarify the essential
messages to be conveyed to target audiences deepens the understanding of practitioners.

In the past, the establishment and enforcement of penalties has been largely in the hands of association or government
boards, which have served as tribunals to judge charges of incompetence or unethical behavior. (There is a modest trend to-

ward including citizen representatives on such boards.) Such ultimate safeguards of individual rights are clearly necessary, even though the machinery of due process can be cumbersome and slow moving. The fear of being brought before such a tribunal may be more widely effective in deterring malpractice than the judgments that are actually rendered.

Recently, methods of establishing and enforcing penalties have been greatly increased to include court cases, selection into or exclusion from specialized or elite societies, peer review by colleagues, exclusion of the right to practice in a specific hospital or other work setting, and acceptance or rejection of the rights of individuals to receive compensation from the government or other sources. Such processes are stimuli to continuing education and will be examined in Chapters Four and Nine. Over two decades ago, Goode (1957, p. 198) pointed out that intraprofessional evaluations, then chiefly of an informal sort, created hostilities and anxieties. "The most successful practitioner," he added, "loaded with honors, worries about his failures and ineptness." Professionalization strengthens these evaluations and makes them more formal than before. If increased anxieties result, they are perhaps necessary penalties for the privileges that the practitioner seeks to achieve.

Relations to other vocations. A thirteenth characteristic is that the relationship of the work of the vocation's practitioners and that of the members of allied occupations should be clearly established and maintained in practice. As vocations move toward professionalization, a complex and usually ambivalent relationship grows up between them and each of the occupational groups with which they work, particularly those which are more highly professionalized than they are. This fact is nowhere more apparent than in the field of health care. Many listings of vocations in this field have been made, and the number of identifiable specialities is constantly growing and shifting in character and in form of classification. As long ago as 1969, Greenfield identified forty-six occupations that he felt could be classified within the general category of "health manpower," most of which are professionalizing vocations. Of these, five were listed as autonomous health professionals (such as physicians, dentists, and optometrists), thirty-two as allied health professionals (such as professional nurses, dental hygienists, and dietitians), six as allied health technicians (such as x-ray technicians and medical assistants), and three as allied health assistants (such as licensed practical nurses and nurse's aides) (Greenfield, 1969). Not everyone would accept Greenfield's list or his classification. Chiropractors, for example, are excluded, and nurses holding only associate degrees or diplomas are classified as technicians. No distinction is made among specialist groups (such as pediatricians or nurse anesthetists) as differentiated from the general occupation to which they belong, though that specialization is often more profound in the lives of the members of the groups concerned than any other factor in their work. A listing such as Greenfield's can never be definitive, because the number of professionalizing occupations is constantly growing; however, it does suggest how complex the patterns of interrelationship in the care of patients has become. Ironically, just as more and more attention is being concentrated on the treatment of the "whole" patient, the "whole" family, or the "whole" community, the health professions themselves are becoming more and more specialized and thus able competently to consider only a small fragment of that "wholeness."

Greenfield's analysis includes a distinction between central staff and support staff, the latter being particularly evident among those vocations grouped under the designations "technicians" and "assistants." It is also likely that the "autonomous" professionals may regard the "allied" professionals as being members of a support staff and that some of the latter agree with this belief while others emphatically disagree. The best-known example of perennial conflict in role clarification between occupations is that between physicians and nurses, though one of the most infuriating aspects of the situation to nurses is the fact that physicians are so often blandly unaware that nurses, because of their professionalizing status, regard themselves as having distinctive and collaborative roles to play. The problem is further accentuated because some nurses (often, to be sure, under the pressure of an overload of work) do not assert their own role individuality but consistently act as though they were supporters rather than allies of physicians.

The conflict is often reduced to the question of which kind of professional is permitted to do what, with each profession seeking the generalized right to use particular procedures or make distinctive kinds of judgments. The need for a well-established and consistent definition of role relationships (largely based on the right to use specific techniques) as the way to create more intelligent and practically rewarding collaboration among all groups in the health care field has been argued by Light (1969) in a long and closely reasoned paper. His approach seems typical of most people who grapple with the problems of relating professions to one another. Schlotfeldt (1965), in contrast, believes that such a procedure is not the best principle on which to establish interprofessional relationships, though it may be the only immediately available one in many situations. Instead she wonders whether eventually, on a case-by-case basis, the two groups "can, as true professionals, work together to determine which of them can best assume responsibility for a particular aspect of a patient's therapeutic regimen at any point in time. Here is the appropriate focus for discussion on realignment of functions, for the ultimate criterion of which decisions are made must be the welfare of the patient" (p. 773).

The relationship between professionals and the support staffs who assist them has become a topic for sustained attention in many work settings. Most such efforts have followed the policy suggested by Light. A concentration on job analysis and on role definition in terms of the kind of work performed are the two major approaches to the regularization of work relationships. For example, Asheim (1968) has proposed a master plan of manpower classification for five kinds of workers in libraries, two of them being categorized as professional, another as preprofessional, and two as technical or clerical. The definition of duties and the pre-service level of education required is indicated in each case.

A special problem of support staff relationships arises when representatives of clientele groups are trained for service as *paraprofessionals*, a term which, particularly when coupled with the word *indigenous*, often signifies people drawn from low-income, low-status, or ethnically determined segments of the population. These people have been shown to be effective

as bridges to new clienteles and as change agents to help introduce innovative practices. An enormous literature has now
grown up to indicate how these assistants may best extend the
service for which professionals have neither the time nor the
proper entrée. Loewenberg (1968) has advanced the thesis that
the chief deterrent to effective performance of duties by para-
professionals lies not in the nature of the concept itself or in the
personality traits of those who discharge this role but rather in
the definition and maintenance of careful structural relationships among different levels of workers.

It seems realistic to assume that these problems of role
distinction and collaboration among professionals and those
who work with them will never be finally solved, because social
and economic conditions are constantly changing. The very attributes of professionalization that give an occupation status
tend to accentuate its separate knowledge, cultural distinctive-
ness, and unique mission. But if ultimate success in achieving
harmonious relationships seems difficult, amelioration of present separation is well within reach. Here again pre-service and
continuing education may help. Experiments are now under
way to interweave the preparatory training of various groups of
health professionals and to help the members of each group
understand its relationship to the others. Later in life, in work
settings within employing institutions as well as in training
opportunities provided collaboratively for several professions,
efforts can be made toward a team approach. Thus both a ra-
tionalistic structuring, which marks out and conveys roles and
responsibilities, and a human relations endeavor, which provides
mutually shared acculturation, could help to provide better collaboration among the different kinds of professionals who must
work together.

Relations to users of service. The fourteenth and final
characteristic is that the formal relationships between practitioners of the vocation and people who use their services should
be clearly defined. Ordinarily the discussion of this criterion is
cast in the framework of a relationship of professionals to
"clients," but no other part of the literature of professionalization bears out more clearly than this one the narrowness of view-

point of which Hughes (1962) spoke when he referred to the continuing dominance of the nineteenth-century conception of the role of the physician or the lawyer. As Bidwell (1970, p. 93) has pointed out, "The classic professional-client relationship is voluntary, dyadic, and centered on the exchange of service and fees." Yet this traditional view of the professional-client relationship has no meaning when it is related to the work of the clergyman, the naval officer, or the public school teacher; even in medicine, particularly in pediatric or psychiatric practice, the identity of the true client may be uncertain. Efforts to lay down general rules on the basis of practitioner-client relationships have limited or no application and seem to be less and less significant as time goes on. The maintenance of confidentiality, for example, used to be an almost sacred principle in many professional-client relationships. Now record-keeping systems in hospitals, clinics, and elsewhere make it not only necessary but advisable to record in the patient's case history diagnostic test results and medical comments, which then become available to the eligible categories of health care personnel.

The continued use of the word *client* may be a disservice to understanding because of the difference between its past and its present associations. It still remains true, however, that in every profession some people are supposed to benefit from what the practitioner does. The beneficiary may be a single person, some defined group of people, or the general public. In each professionalizing occupation it is apparently necessary to establish the rules that govern the appropriate relationship with the person or persons served. In journalism, for example, strong efforts are being made to protect the right of the practitioners not to reveal the sources of their information on the ground that if they do so, they will imperil their future ability to serve readers, even though the result may be that innocent people are punished or criminals allowed to go free. The mandate of the clergyman is to give solace but also to warn, and this fact is true whether he is dealing with individual parishioners or with his whole congregation. The appropriate relationships between practitioners and beneficiaries of services are never easy to establish, particularly because other important obligations must also be considered. For example, professionals such as administrators of schools, hospitals, or social welfare agencies, who work generally for the public but directly under the control of a lay board, have responsibilities to the public, to the board, to the individuals served, and to the profession itself. It may not be easy to strike a balance among the loyalties owed to all these general and specific entities.

Only the simpler forms of relationship can be learned in the pre-service years, because the niceties of human interaction are often obscured by the need to acquire initial work competence. The young student is apt to see matters in a very simplistic fashion. When a senior physician, making rounds with house staff and students, enters the hospital room of the city's mayor, he or she may perceive three constituencies at once: the patient as a person needing medical attention; the patient as an occupant of an important role who can make decisions that influence the quality of health care in the city; and the accompanying present and future colleagues who wish to learn. The young staff members may not perceive the intricacy of the situation and may evaluate the senior physician on the basis of service to only one of the three constituencies. It is the physician's task to help associates understand his or her behavior as fully as possible.

The understanding of complex relationships between practitioners and users of service can usually be acquired only during the practice of a profession. Much learning is acquired through introspection and through an awareness of what activities are favored or resisted in the immediate subculture in which the practitioner works. Another source of changed practice is the degree of stress placed upon the profession by the community, particularly by consumer groups and power centers, which can control freedom of operation. But the relationship of the work of practitioners to the users of their services can also be made the subject of more formal kinds of education in any of the three educational modes. The development of various "bills of rights" and "guidelines to practice" illustrates such efforts, as does the attempt to secure agreement on the opening up of previously confidential areas, such as the announcement of the fees charged for various services.

In most professions, a practitioner who gains outstanding competence and status is often called upon to accept supervisory or administrative responsibility. When that happens, the individual concerned must learn how to discharge new duties and, in particular, how to relate to new associates. Thus, as a career line advances, a continuous formal or informal learning process must occur, one which will be described in the next chapter. This changing relationship and the educational activities it requires can sometimes be anticipated. Often, however, no exact prediction can be made even of the next move in a career, much less those which will occur subsequently. Therefore, education must often take place on the job after the change has been made. For example, a particularly troublesome difficulty results when a professional becomes the executive head of an agency and must work under the direct control of a lay board. These boards are required by law or custom to exercise generalized authority as the designee of the community, thus guiding and strengthening the service provided and, by their breadth of resources and knowledge, tempering the narrow and angular view of the specialist professionals. It is probable that the only people who can grasp the difficulties of such a situation are those who have themselves experienced it.

The Combination of Characteristics

While each of the foregoing characteristics is involved in the professionalizing process, none is uniquely related to it. For example, the thirteenth criterion, the effort to differentiate the work of a vocation from that of allied occupations, is common to most crafts and, in particular, has been a strong preoccupation of the members of the building trades. It has been argued by some authorities that professionals should be more concerned than workers in other vocations with treating the task of differentiation in a positive spirit so that it can become the basis for cooperation, but it would be hard to maintain this point of view in any examination of actual practice. It seems preferable to suggest that all vocations working to strengthen a characteristic (even if some of them are uninterested in professionalization) can find a community of interest in this goal and can learn from one another how to accomplish it.

None of the characteristics can ever be completely and finally achieved, and the race for professional accomplishment therefore has no finish line. But as an occupational group raises the level of its performance of various characteristics, its right to call itself a profession increases, as does its right to expect society to view it as one. Ordinarily the members of a professionalizing vocation recognize that they must strive toward many goals, and therefore they try to achieve some or all of the characteristics suggested here as well as others that may be unique to their particular work. The sense of assurance of professional status by the members of a vocation as well as acceptance of that status by the general public or by an authoritative external body depends on the balancing out of the level of achievement of several traits or qualities. Failure to reach some objectives may be compensated for by strengths in the achievement of others. Ultimately self-assurance cannot be justified, nor can social approval be assured, without substantial strides toward accomplishment of a number of the characteristics.

The Ultimate Aim of Continuing Education

No easy or automatic method of continuing education can be found to ensure the establishment and maintenance of ethical, intellectual, and social standards in a professionalizing occupation amid the stresses and temptations of practice. As Sancho Panza remarked, "each of us is as God made him, ay, and often worse" (Cervantes, *Don Quixote*, pt. 2, chap. 5). Each vocation wishing to professionalize itself must try to elevate its dignity and maintain its integrity by the use of precept and practice, by the positive force of education and the negative force of self-regulation, by open and free discussion, and by a full opportunity to scrutinize the principles that govern practice. The pre-service educational programs of many professions have often achieved a high level of intellectual strength and ethical force. Past success at this early stage may give hope for future success at later stages.

The ultimate aim of every advanced, subtle, and mature form of continuing education is to convey a complex attitude made up of a readiness to use the best ideas and techniques of the moment but also to expect that they will be modified or replaced. The new machine will soon be antiquated, the new drug will be outmoded, the new principle will yield to a more profound one, and the revolutionary approach will become first familiar and then old fashioned. Everyone must expect constant change and with it new goals to be achieved and new understanding and skill to be mastered. The major lesson of continuing education is to expect that the unexpected will continue to occur.

Chapter 4

Lifespan Learning of the Professional

The great lawyer has always been a great teacher and his best pupil is himself.

Charles Evans Hughes

To be aware of the value of continuing learning is not the same as to be a continuing learner. Many a professional can report almost verbatim and with an air of conviction whatever he or she has been taught about "keeping up to date" but show few signs, by either participation in educational activities or by performance at work, of putting that knowledge into practice. In contrast, countless professionals engage in intense and prolonged learning without ever paying special attention to the fact that they are doing so. This latter situation is particularly true when education is a by-product of experience or of the use of the mode of inquiry.

In this chapter I suggest how, in the customary patterns of early development and mature activity, the practitioner gains both an awareness of the values of continuing education and the habit of participating in it. Traditional ways of teaching and work have been established without very much attention being paid to these values and habits; therefore, suggestions will be made about how they can be introduced or fostered.

The central framework of this necessarily discursive account is the occupational lifespan of the individual professional. As was indicated in Chapter One, a succession of roughly similar events in the careers of most members of an occupation influences continuing education or readiness for it. This normative pattern of learning occurs not only during the years of practice but also during the earlier years of childhood and youth. The term *continuing education*, whether it designates the improvement of professional competence or any other goal, implies some form of learning that advances from a previously established level of accomplishment to extend and amplify knowledge, sensitiveness, or skill. But the nature of a superstructure is determined by its foundation; thus the amount and kind of study undertaken at forty, sixty, or any other mature age is likely to be determined, at least in part, by what has happened earlier in life.

The effort to discern general patterns in the customary flow of life does not mean that they are either arbitrary or universal. Every member of a profession (even a person who follows a traditional sequence of study and practice) has a distinctive style of lifelong learning influenced by an individual background, a unique combination of character traits, and the special circumstances of his or her immediate environment, including stimuli provided by people and institutions who seek to advance continued education. As personality and circumstances change, so does this pattern of learning.

An increasing number of people do not follow the normal sequence used as a central theme in this chapter. The variety of new approaches to professional competence is so great that it cannot be charted or categorized, but at least three recent trends have significantly changed the customary course of events. First, many people are entering professions later than at the traditional time; therefore their education may occur in previously unorthodox sequences. Second, many people, through choice or necessity, are shifting to second professions, and are therefore following atypical pre-service and in-service training patterns. Third, the avid desire to learn may sometimes make its initial appearance somewhat later in life than traditionalists have assumed. Therefore, everything in this chapter should be tempered by an awareness of these and other exceptions to customary sequences of learning.

The Years of Early Youth

When does the eager and sustained desire to learn, which will eventually lead to continuing professional education, first appear in the individual? Some people say that the trait is associated with intelligence, physical vitality, or other innate characteristics and is thus hereditary. Other authorities stress the formative years of early childhood, when the values of home and neighborhood, the availability of cultural resources, and the behavior of admired or disliked adults or other companions establish lasting patterns of choice and rejection. A third group points to the later years of youth: Young people often follow the same careers as their parents, because of admiration, because no better choice appears available, or because of such tangible reasons as the possibility of inheriting a family pharmacy or architectural practice. Other young people reject family traditions and choose a pattern of life (sometimes including a career) by emulating some model, by chance, or by the need to fulfill a sense of personal mission. In any of these cases, the habits of later associates also have either a positive or a negative effect on the learning desires of the individual.

Little is known about the effect of schooling upon the enhancement of the desire to learn. Those who accept the values of a sound formal education are sure that schools and colleges equip children and youth with the abilities needed to learn, broaden their range of interests, and encourage them to explore the vast realms of knowledge. Opponents of the schools accuse them of deadening natural curiosity and stifling rather than creating interests. Both points of view are valid for some children and in some situations, but they are also extreme. For the vast majority of young people, schooling has some positive and some negative impact, but the range of effects has not been definitively studied.

As will be shown in Chapter Five, many studies have measured the extent and nature of learning undertaken by adults, both in their leisure time and while at work. This research shows that the length of formal education in youth is positively associated with the extent of participation in education (both professional and nonprofessional) during the years of maturity, but little is known about the relationship between the extent of such participation and the quality (however measured) or nature of early schooling. Even the positive association between the extent of early schooling and adult participation in learning does not prove a causal relationship, because both are related to many other economic, social, and personal aspects of life. Furthermore, because the members of a profession all tend to have about the same number of years of basic education, the quantity of early schooling as a predictor of differentiated participation of in-service learning tends to be minimized. Even when the extent, nature, and quality of preparatory formal study vary greatly from one person to another—as with teaching or in medical specialty groups—all three factors may be only indices of other factors, such as the amount and kind of family resources, and not themselves causes of further learning.

It has often been argued that "getting hold of the students early" will help to acculturate them to a profession and encourage them subsequently to pursue its study ardently. The most common way of doing so is to concentrate students' learning so that it centers ever more heavily on professional instruction. It was shown in 1978 that "faculty members in nine fields where the first professional degree is the baccalaureate are less favorably disposed toward the liberal arts today than were their counterparts in 1958" (Vander Meer and Lyons, 1979, p. 201). However, any proposed narrowing of secondary school or collegiate courses of study arouses the opposition of those who champion liberal or general education, either for its own humanistic values or as a necessary basis for a broadly trained and continuously inquiring practitioner of a profession. But the chief deterrent to highly increased specialization in pre-professional-school years is the fact that most young people change their career plans, sometimes several times, or do not decide until late in youth what occupation they wish to undertake.

American colleges and universities are relatively liberal in their willingness to permit students to change their academic objectives, including those related to their occupations. A massive shift in undergraduate majors occurs among students. The most complete data available are for the early 1960s. While the nature and direction of these changes may have altered significantly since then, the magnitude of the shift has probably remained about the same. In any case, the people who were graduated from college in 1965 would, if they went into professions, be the relatively young but well-established practitioners of the late 1970s. Astin and Panos, in their study of a very large sample of students who entered college in 1961 and who indicated their career choices both then and four years later, reported that "about three fourths of the students changed their long-term career plans after entering college. The percentage of those who changed, however, varied greatly from field to field, ranging from less than 50 percent in a few fields to more than 95 percent in others" (Astin and Panos, 1969, p. 132).

Those graduate professional schools and departments into which admission is eagerly sought can, to be sure, choose only students who have earned a large number of credits in profession-related courses. Even now, however, many professional schools do not have a sufficient number of applicants to allow them this freedom, even if they wish to exercise it. The ability of admissions officers to exercise selective choice will decline significantly if the number of young preprofessional baccalaureate students drops drastically during the 1980s and 1990s, as it seems certain to do. The desire of college faculties and administrators to preserve their institutions and programs may cause them to be more responsive to student demands and less compliant to professional requirements than has been true in the past.

It can be argued that either constancy or variability of career choices during the years of pre-service professional training may be related to the extent of participation in continuing education in later life. An equally good theoretical case can be made either for steadfastness of purpose, which permits the building of a powerful cumulative effect, or for breadth of knowledge, which stimulates and challenges the free play of an inquiring mind. No substantial research has yet been undertaken to discover which theory is the more valid or, indeed, what other factors associated with continuing professional education might be discernible at the time the student makes a major commitment to the profession by entering its formal training program.

Admission to the Professional School

Many criteria are used as the bases for selection into a professional school. Among the most common are grade-point averages in earlier schooling, general and special aptitude as measured by tests, and personal interviews held by representatives of the school. The aim of the selection process is to discover which of the applicants will prove to be the most intelligent, stable, well prepared, and deeply committed students. It is assumed that, later on, these people will be the most accomplished practitioners.

Among the people selected, however, there does not seem to be a strong positive correlation between the methods used and actual performance in the professional school. A study by Gough (1978) of 1,135 medical school graduates examined the influence of four measures of admission: Medical College Admission Test (MCAT) Science subtest scores, premedical grades in science courses, preference for scientific subjects, and an equally weighted composite of these three measures. All four proved to be moderately related to academic performance in the first two years of medical school, a fact which is not surprising because study during that period resembles earlier kinds of formal education. In the latter two years, however, when students are more directly related to the practice of medicine than was earlier the case, the four measures were almost completely unrelated either to grades or to faculty ratings of clinical or general competence. Seventy premedical students were also given day-long personality assessments. While the results are too complex to summarize here, it can be noted that the students with "above average scores on the four measures revealed them to be narrower in interests, less adaptable, less articulate, and less comfortable in interpersonal relationships than their lower scoring peers" (Gough, 1978, p. 291). A new version of the MCAT was introduced in 1977 in an effort to make it a more broadly predictive instrument than before.

While Gough's investigation deals only with medicine, discussions with leaders of other professions indicate that many of them feel that the admissions tests for their own schools are seriously deficient in predicting which students will most satisfac-

torily achieve the criteria of success established not only by the
faculty but also by the demands of practice. Fields (1978, p. 1)
has described major efforts, under significant national sponsorship, to improve the admissions process "by trying more systematically to identify personal qualities and traits that can be
linked with competence in various professional careers."

If continuing education is crucial to the profession and
therefore to the people who are preparing to enter it, some attention should presumably be given in the admissions process to
the selection of individuals who have already given evidence that
they have a thirst for knowledge and that they are likely to retain that thirst throughout their careers. Professional schools
now say that they seek intelligent, stable, well-prepared, and
deeply committed potential entrants. An estimate as to the possession of an inquiring mind can probably be made about as
well as an estimate of any of these other desired characteristics.
Upon the validity of this estimate all further efforts at continuing education crucially depend. While the persistent desire to
learn can be created during the later years of adulthood, it is
probably present in most young people by the time they are
ready to enter professional school. If so, how is its presence
demonstrated?

Despite a ten-year search, I have never found any admissions committee that had considered the possibility of estimat-
ing the continuing education potential of its applicants. Studies
to lay the groundwork for doing so would not be hard to design.
For example, an analysis could be made of the differences between two matched groups of practicing professionals, one of
which engages extensively in continuing education and the other
of which does not. What apparently related characteristics or
habits that were already evident at the time of entry into professional school distinguish the first group of practitioners from
the second? One difference might be a record of independent
and self-initiated study. Another might be extensive participation in youth groups, clubs, public libraries, museums, and literary and cultural societies. The zest to learn can lead a child or
youth far beyond classroom instruction at a fairly early age.
Perhaps such an appetite is likely to persist when compulsory

and other directed schooling ends. Creative research could test that hypothesis as well as others.

Basic Professional Education

Once admitted, the students in a professional school enter a special subculture, which blends both formal instruction and the customs and behavior patterns established by the social and physical milieu. Traditionally most of the studies of the pre-service program have concentrated on the first of these two elements, identifying the subject matter to be learned, the sequence in which it is to be presented, and the methods of instruction to be used. As sociologists and social psychologists have turned their attention to the study of professional schools, they have tended to examine the customs and behavior patterns of the faculty and students. For example, Kay (1975, p. 35) has said of schools of architecture: "It is a manic life-style; see the gaudy plumage on this strange bird of campus. Architecture students look more—well—vivid. Even their deans wear polka-dot bow ties, desert boots, and beards. . . . [The architecture students] were the first to first-name their teachers, the first to see work-study programs as valid, the first to move out of the linear, straight-line route of education." Every other profession develops its own style and patterns of behavior, and the basic learning acquired by its students reflects that fact.

In every professionalizing occupation, strong doubts have been expressed about the nature of the basic preparatory curriculum. As long ago as 1956, Peterson and others published a detailed study of the competence of practice of ninety-four physicians in North Carolina, using measures that are generally accepted as valid. This study revealed that rank in medical school, prestige of medical school, and quality of internship were not related to the adequacy of performance of physicians over thirty-five years of age (Peterson and others, 1956). It has been widely accepted, on the basis of other studies and of anecdotal evidence, that a similar lack of correlation exists in other professions.

It seems likely that at least part of the discrepancy between basic education and later demonstration of competence is a result of the amount and quality of continuing education undertaken by practitioners. Consequently it is probable that one way in which a basic professional program might enhance later competence would be by ensuring the fact that, during the years spent in the school's subculture, the students' personal commitment to lifelong leraning is firmly established both by curricular changes and by efforts to alter the customs and behavior patterns of the students.

This change process involves acceptance of the fact that much of the traditional curriculum must be rethought and that some of it must be left to be learned in later years. The great advance of knowledge in most fields of study means that the learner must enter a sequence of activities far too brief to include all that he or she will later need to know. The professional school must separate essential from nonessential knowledge so that its students can master basic knowledge or gain crucial beginning skills and insights but not get lost in the vastness of accumulated content. In law schools, for example, as Freund (1967, p. 44) has pointed out, "There is an intensified effort to explore fields of law by sinking shafts rather than covering the ground." Another policy that can help a beleaguered faculty avoid an overcrowded course of study is to exclude any subject from the pre-service curriculum that can be learned better later. Teachers' colleges used to crowd into a four-year undergraduate curriculum all the courses (including those in supervision and administration) that a student might possibly need during a fifty-year career. Today young men and women are educated to be teachers, often in five- or six-year programs. If they subsequently wish to become supervisors or administrators they return to the university to secure the specialized education they then require, a body of learning for which experience has provided a depth of meaning not possible for them to have understood earlier. The same trend is occurring in engineering, and many law schools provide relatively little direct preparation for "lawyering skills," expecting that they will be learned later, usually by on-the-job training and tutelage.

The necessity to keep on learning throughout life seems so obvious to the leaders of most professions that they believe that its self-evidence will cause it to be internalized within the value system and pattern of actions of every practitioner. But an examination of the practices of professional schools often shows that this idea is nowhere communicated systematically and thoroughly. For example, a highly respected report issued on behalf of one category of professional schools announced that one of their primary goals should be to help their students establish the habit of continuing self-education. Despite this fact, the volume that identifies these goals and describes the training that should be offered to achieve most of them does not suggest the ways in which this habit is to be acquired.

If the custom of continuing to learn is not established in the years of pre-service instruction, the failure to practice it will have increasingly serious consequences: Pre-service students do not have time in school to "cover the ground," and later they will not know how to do so. Also, most beginning professionals have been taught dated theories, facts that are no longer true, and skills that will soon be discarded as obsolete. Even though faculty members remain marvelously up to date and have not themselves been caught in the eddies of a cultural lag, knowledge increases so rapidly that what a student learns early in the pre-service curriculum may be out of date or wrong by the time of graduation. He or she may suspect that, to the very last class, error is being taught; so may the faculty; but neither is sure exactly where the errors lie. In 1969, Zelikoff reported a study of engineering curricula at five-year intervals beginning in 1935, noting courses that had been dropped and others that had been added. Assuming that the existing curriculum represents the best available current application of knowledge, Zelikoff found that only about 5 percent of the content in electrical engineering taught to the class of 1935 could still be accepted as valid. The rate of erosion grew steeper in later years because of the more rapid growth of knowledge. About 45 percent of the content taught to the class of 1960 had become obsolete by 1969 (Zelikoff, 1969).

In the light of these facts, how can the professional school convey the habit of continuing self-education and thus help save its students from later obsolescence? Some answers to that question are evident and can be briefly stated. Excellence of teaching can create or further stimulate interest in a subject. As much as possible, instruction can be cast in the mode of actual or simulated inquiry in which the student (sometimes with the faculty, sometimes in collaboration with other students, and sometimes alone) seeks the answers to questions. Facts are thus taught within the context of a constant and continuous exploration of the unknown. In many courses and many ways, faculty members can give direct instruction in the practical values of continuing education. The need for perennial renewal can be included at any place in the curriculum where it seems appropriate. The complexity of the learning goals identified in Chapter Three can be taught to the student so that he or she knows that it is necessary to do far more than to keep up with new content and techniques. The continuing educational activities conducted by a school for its own staff and for in-service practitioners can be carried out in such a way as to be brought meaningfully and strongly to the attention of those who are still acquiring their basic education. These students can be introduced to the techniques and resources of continuing education, particularly those which have specific reference to the profession being learned. The method of constructing a personal learning plan can be taught, and supervised practice in doing so can be provided. Students can also be taught about the evaluative and quality control systems to which they will become subject during practice, including peer review, relicensure, and self-administered examinations.

Formal means of instruction such as these will do no more than lay a foundation for later learning. Furthermore they are not very attractive to students whose dominating concern is with the immediate need to master the skills and content required of them by their instructors. Becker and others (1961, p. 61), in their study of medical students in one school, show how deeply obsessed the students are with the major tasks of each part of their curriculum: When they "pause to take up a mental stance outside the present knife-edge of their experience and think of medicine, the medical profession, and their goals within it . . . they use a wide-angle lens [and] their thought refers to many years which they lump together in time. . . . Their long-range perspective may be emotionally intense, but it is necessarily vague." Even this indistinct conception does not usually include continuing education, though one freshman quoted in the study commented that he thought of medicine as a staircase he will have to climb all his life. This awareness of the need for lifelong learning, however, is not revealed in most of the numerous and lengthy quoted comments in the study. Twenty years later, in a study of the students in another medical school, it was found that most of them, when pressed on the point, expressed "definite patterns of attitudes toward continuing medical education," which had emerged early in their doctoral programs. The investigators felt that some of these patterns were discouraging and believed that they indicated a need for action on the part of the faculty (Krowka and Peck, 1979).

Much thought has been given by educators in the professions to the ways of changing the informal socialization process during the course of basic professional education so that it can reinforce the formal processes of instruction. One hypothesis in the rich and complex literature on this subject was made by Simpson (1967, p. 47) with reference to student nurses: "Socialization into a profession takes place in three analytically distinct phases, each involving some learning of the cultural content of the role and some self-identification with it. During the first phase, the person shifts his attention from the broad, societally derived goals which led him to choose the profession to the goal of proficiency in specific work tasks. During the second, certain significant others in the work milieu become his main reference group. Third, he internalizes the values of the occupational group and adopts the behaviors it prescribes. These three phases may overlap, but in general they constitute a sequence."

This concept suggests how a professional school faculty can introduce the idea of continuing education into the socialization process as well as into the curriculum. The behavior and viewpoint of a beginning professional is often based on the work habits and beliefs of one or more of the instructors in the professional school. If any person who serves as role model is visibly and continuously engaged in learning, an example is set and may be followed. But, as Phipps (1977) has demonstrated for baccalaureate nursing programs, the students' perception of the interest of the whole faculty in continuing education is more influential than their perception of the interest of even their most preferred instructor.

Some years ago, Miller (1956) described how twelve faculty members at the University of Buffalo School of Medicine reexamined their fundamental conception of teaching. The students of these faculty members must have profited from an awareness of what their instructors were undertaking. This endeavor of professional schools constantly to upgrade their work has now become fairly common, and some institutions maintain committees, specialists, or outside consultants to help design their curricula and teaching methods. Miller forecast this development when he concluded by saying: "Is it all worthwhile? My biased opinion is often balanced by those who call this talk of educational principles nonsense, who remind me that the work of the teacher is to cram into the student as many facts as possible in the time allotted. . . . And they may be right. But while they man their bastions against attack, we, the enemy, will be having a rousing adventure in pedagogy" (Miller, 1956, p. 1450).

This "adventure" benefits the students not only because of the improved instruction they are likely to receive as a result of their professors' increased competence but also because they have visible evidence that their mentors consider learning to be important and furnish examples of how it should occur. The influence of clinical or practical instructors may be particularly great as role models, because they lead busy problem-solving lives similar to that which the student feels will be his or her own. To witness a faculty member under heavy pressure demonstrate that he or she feels the need to broaden knowledge or to begin the study of new fields of inquiry gives the student a particularly potent example of the importance of continuing education.

One effort to stress continuing education in the pre-service socialization process flows from the recent emphasis in many professions on a community orientation. While the main purpose of this approach is to improve the service provided by the profession to a broad-based constituency, an increased awareness by pre-service students of the need for continuing professional education is often an intended or unintended consequence. This fact was made clear by an unidentified participant at a symposium on theological education (Craven, Todd, and Ziegler, 1969, p. 138).

> What's wrong with theological education is that it works on a model that conceives of the student as still in preparation. He's putting on his armor, and then at a certain point, varying according to his profession, the door is flung open and he rides forth into the world. . . . Instead of this, there ought to be a way in which the man starts to "live" right from the very beginning. In this way education is conceived always as continuing education, and never preparatory education, particularly in the professional school after he's gotten his college degree. From then on, he wants to be somebody, he wants to be in the decision-making process, he wants to be in the community. . . . Instead of [being] in a cocoon for three years, getting ready for this great breaking-out process, when he enters theological school he's immediately put into a situation where he is somebody, related to some concrete situation; and his education from this point on is a continuing process, except that here it will be a little more structured and intensive. . . . One of the ways in which we can see this really working is by abolishing theological school residential campuses, and instead, having students live in apartment houses in cities. By setting up the students in community situations as actual participants, they can then come to the campuses to take such courses and reading as can be related to the situation where they live.

A community orientation is now advocated by some faculty leaders in virtually every kind of professional school. National attention has been given to community-related innovations in, among other fields, architecture, engineering, law, and social work. Funkenstein (1971) has suggested that the community approach has brought university teaching of medicine well into its fourth era. The four are: the general-practice era, 1910–1940; the specialty-practice era, 1940–1959; the scientific era, 1959–1968; and the community era, which began in 1968. The data with which Funkenstein supports this analysis are drawn from interest patterns and other characteristics of students in the Harvard Medical School and therefore immediately reflect only the student-value characteristics of the socialization process in one high-prestige school. The community era appears, in a sense, to be a return to the values of the general-practice era. A student of the class of 1972 had a pattern of interest closer to that of a 1938 physician than did the members of the classes in the intervening years.

In some professions, the entire faculty may be providing leadership in the move toward the community approach but, because the tenure of professors is long and their sudden conversion to new value systems rare, it is safe to say that in most cases the new emphasis, even for most of those who share it, is an overlay, or in some cases only a slight modification, of accustomed ways of work. A specialist or research-oriented professor seldom becomes a champion of the community approach overnight. To the extent that the new approach is accepted, it may lead to habits and practices of pre-service socialization that put the student into close contact with problems of actual practice, thereby causing deeper awareness than before of the continuously perplexing difficulties that will need to be confronted later in life.

Whatever the processes of formal education and socialization may be, much of every professional's attitude toward future learning and the ability to undertake it has been established by the time of entry into service. Each beginning practitioner starts forth on his or her life work with a high level of knowledge, skills, and perceptions. But—here as elsewhere—anybody who has been taught only what to learn has been prepared for the present, which will soon be the past; anybody who has been taught how to learn has also been prepared for the future. The individual must ultimately accept responsibility for knowing and serving, for facing the daily tasks of applying specialized knowledge to particular cases, and for guiding and shaping a career. Otherwise external forces may push him or her to and fro without resulting from any personal decision or leading to any increase in the power to deal with subsequent problems.

This section should not be concluded without explicit recognition of the fact that professional schools vary greatly in the motivation of their students and in their attitudes toward the occupations for which such schools offer preparatory study. It is customary to assume that all students have broadly similar aspirations, but this is not the case. In many programs, the students have mixed, ambiguous, and uncertain purposes and display highly varied abilities and seriousness of intent. Bowers (1974) has shown that in one school of journalism, which he believes to be typical, only 55 percent of the students expect to have newspaper jobs at graduation and only 30 percent expect to be working for newspapers five years later. Many people may enter law school because they plan to practice law, but many others do so because they believe a legal education is the best preparation for a career in business or politics, because they have been told that the study of law is the culmination of a liberal education, because they have not as yet "found themselves," or because they have nothing better to do. In every professional school, some students enroll but never finish the sequence of instruction because they choose to leave or are required to do so. Despite this diversity, the patterns of every professional school's instruction usually rest single-mindedly on the assumption that students will enter the occupation for which the school prepares them. Even people who have no intention of following such a career must learn by the pedagogical rules established by that assumption.

It is not clear what implications the homogeneity or heterogeneity of student intentions have for the inculcation of the desire to learn. The topic appears to be one that could lead to fruitful study. Meanwhile any consideration of the linkages between basic and continuing professional education must take into account the fact that no invariable correspondence exists between the two career stages. Many people prepare to practice but do not actually do so, just as many people who do practice have prepared themselves by other means than attendance at professional schools. All studies that rest on contrary assumptions are open to question.

Assessing Readiness for Practice

In many professions, the securing of a credential to practice becomes the next step in the professional's career after the completion of formal schooling, although sometimes such a credential can be awarded in other ways. Licenses are issued by an agency of government, usually the state, and certificates are issued by a nongovernmental organization or association. In either case the individual must meet certain predetermined qualifications. In many cases, students study intensively, either alone or with the aid of colleagues, tutors, or cram schools, to prepare themselves for the examinations that must usually be passed by anyone who seeks a credential. Usually they are based almost entirely on the grasp of subject matter and the ability to apply it, though some assessment of personality characteristics and value systems is occasionally made. The writers of the tests generally do not seek to measure the extent to which the beginning practitioner is aware of the necessity of continuing study or the means to undertake it, a strange omission in today's world. As has already been noted, the issuance of a license or certificate usually guarantees the right to practice for a lifetime, though periodic and often perfunctory renewal processes, such as the payment of a fee, may be required. In recent years, however, relicensure has been taken more and more seriously as a stimulus to continuing education; its use for such purposes will be described in Chapter Nine.

Induction into Practice

The transfer from the controlled instruction of the school to the actual practice of the profession is a time of great significance for continuing education (particularly self-instruction), because it is then that each individual must face directly and responsibly the challenges which must be met in a world centered on performance. Those who enter practice have knowledge, techniques, and attitudes; now they must learn the art of blending the elements of their competence required to deal with each new situation they confront.

The development of systems of careful induction into practice is characteristic of many professions today. Lortie (1975, pp. 59, 70) has developed the concept of "mediated entry" in which "typically the neophyte takes small steps from simple to more demanding tasks and from small to greater responsibility under the supervision of persons who have attained recognized position within the occupation." He asserts that arrangements for such mediation are primitive so far as school teaching is concerned and that practice teaching is only a "mini-apprenticeship." Induction to service in such cases is usually through trial and error, more or less interpreted by introspection, though new practitioners who work in collective or institutional settings may be guided by supervisors or mentors and sometimes by an organized process of training, rotation of assignments, and special tutorial assistance.

At the other extreme is the celebrated case of medicine, where mediated entry has been crystalized into formal residency systems and clerkships, the purposes of which are both the provision of care to the patient and the acquisition of advanced practical knowledge by the doctor. The people undergoing such training in medicine and other occupations perennially complain that they are made to carry out too many routines and are not given enough opportunity to deal with unusual and therefore interesting cases. These comments indicate that the practitioners have not yet learned the valuable lesson that much of the work of a profession is routine and requires vigilance on the part of the practitioner to discern any elements of the unusual that may appear.

Many patterns of mediated entry have been worked out in the several professions. Some, as in social work, are incorporated within the program of basic training. Others, as in accounting, occur in a formalized system of advanced apprenticeship during the early years of practice. Throughout the 1960s and

1970s, clinical education has also been a major concern of the law schools, with many distinctions being made between "law" and "lawyering" and an infinite variety of practices being espoused.

The problem of induction into service in the professions is becoming more complex because specialized practice rather than general service is becoming more and more common. In medicine, the extended development of hospital residencies and the admission requirements for certified specialty groups may require years of both service and instruction; the results are tested by an examination, the satisfactory completion of which confers both a designation of distinctive competence and the ability to demand increased compensation. A study of physicians who were graduated in three sample years in the 1960s shows that by 1976, 81 percent had either been certified by specialty boards or were in the process of seeking certification, and that it is not until an average of twelve years after graduation from medical school that certification will be achieved (Levit and Holden, 1978). In these cases, the M.D. degree is actually awarded nearer the beginning point of the total period of pre-service education than the end. In school teaching and librarianship, specialization is strongly emphasized, but the nature and extent of preparation for either is less prolonged than in medicine. In other professions, special competence is created and maintained by practical experience and independent study rather than by formal instruction. In a general law firm, for example, one partner may become adept at handling certain types of cases and before long will be either directly representing the firm in all such matters or counseling the other partners as they need special expertise.

It is impossible to draw a sharp dividing line in many of these cases between initial and continuing learning; the first merges gradually into the second. The intent of the practitioner must always be considered. One person may decide to be a pediatrician even before leaving high school and may then move systematically through twelve to fifteen years of training to achieve full certification of specialized competence. Though the practical experience provided in such a program is vital, it is chosen

in terms of its potential educative impact and must therefore
be considered part of initial training. Another person may not
decide on a specialization until a general background of competence is established or even until after some time has been spent
in practice. For example, a nurse may work in general service
for several years before deciding to specialize in psychiatric
nursing. Also it often happens that people who are fully qualified and have practiced in one specialization decide to qualify
for another one. As these various examples suggest, the whole
period of induction into established and permanent practice
cannot be reduced to any straightforward and uniform pattern.

The situation is made even more complex because in a few
of the emergent professions, specialized training may come before rather than after general training. In the health professions,
for example, one may acquire special qualifications as a physician, a nurse, or a hospital administrator before securing a degree in public health. Students receiving advanced degrees in
adult education may already be credentialed specialists in librarianship, agriculture, home economics, school teaching, or any of
a number of other professions or scholarly fields.

Because of these variable situations, which may occur on
several occasions within a single lifetime, only the orientation of
the individual indicates whether a given episode of learning
should be characterized as basic or as continuing education. As
long as a person feels that he or she is in a preparatory phase
carried forward from the years of earlier schooling, is essentially
under the guidance or control of mentors, and is preparing for
a culminating credential or established privilege, the education
undertaken should probably be classified as pre-service. To be
sure, the years spent in such pursuits are rich in opportunities
for the creation of a zest for independent learning, as individuals
acquire new interests, as the occupational acculturation process
has greater impact, and as learners grow closer and closer to
their teachers until a true colleague relationship emerges. In
contrast, an individual who has prepared for a career, practiced
it, and then decides to resume study brings to his or her learning an independence of perspective quite different from that of
a person who has always been under tutelage. Such a person has

(ideally at least) internalized the values of continuing education, knows the goals to be sought, possesses a sense of self-sufficiency, and respects any formal instructor in terms of demonstrated competence rather than generalized authority. Most experienced teachers of both pre-service and in-service students can readily recognize the differences between them.

Learning During the Years of Practice

The individual who leaves the professional school, is licensed to practice, and has completed whatever form of induction training may be necessary begins the active practice of a career. From that point onward, continuing education starts in earnest. During the course of a lifetime, learning in one or more of the three basic modes is usually directed in some fashion toward all of the fourteen goals suggested in Chapter Three, though the relative importance of each one for each individual varies with many factors, such as the work setting, the maturity and responsibility of the person concerned, the particular deficiencies felt, the richness of opportunities provided, and the length of time spent in the career. Special assignments may also require distinctive learning needs: A practitioner may be appointed to a committee assigned the task of establishing ethical standards for an association or to a group of representatives from several professions to establish an interrelational pattern among them. Either assignment may require extensive educational commitments, including obligations to study, discuss, agree, and eventually to persuade. While these are special cases, they illustrate the collective responsibilities which, at some point in a career, an individual often undertakes, adding them to a continuing requirement to keep up to date on the evolving mission and the growing and changing subject matter of the profession so as to be able to maintain and advance personal ability and occupational stature.

The pattern of learning of an individual at any time during the years of practice is always unique, as are the shifts in pattern over time. However, at least four aspects of service have an important generalized influence on the nature and extent of every practitioner's continuing education. They are: the basic settings in which professionals work; the changes in career line that often occur with increasing age; the quality of the formal and informal worklife; and the age of the individual. Each of these must be analyzed separately, though in practice all four have intricately interwoven influences.

The Basic Settings of Professional Practice

A practicing professional is employed at any given time in any one of a number of different settings, of which five are most common. These settings are elemental. They can be combined and interwoven in ways that will become evident in subsequent pages, but usually an individual realizes the dominant setting in which he or she is employed.

In the *entrepreneurial* setting, the practitioner (either alone or in partnership with colleagues) organizes, operates, and assumes the risk for work done, offering direct service to clients as they require it. This form of practice was once uncritically assumed to be the essential work setting of the professions, and much modern discussion (for example that dealing with relationships to clients) consciously or unconsciously reflects this view. It was never a valid assumption, however, as the cases of the ministry and the armed services suggest. Today entrepreneurial practice can even be viewed as outmoded. Dentistry is, in fact, called a "cottage industry" by some of its practitioners because it has not developed the collective and interactive supports of some of the other health professions.

In the *collective* setting, the practitioner works with a group of colleagues who share in goal setting, organization, and operational procedures. For example, a library or a social service agency is a setting in which interactive staffs of professionals offer a mutually facilitative service. The homogeneity of the professionals involved varies greatly. In an elementary school, only four or five occupations may be represented; teachers will make up the majority of the persons employed, with perhaps only one nurse, one librarian, one social worker, and one dietician. In a hospital, thirty or forty kinds of trained specialists may combine their efforts. Each collective unit may be wholly independent or part of a larger institution, such as a city-wide school or library system. Even when these organizations have many branches, each professional person finds a primary focus of service in the collective action of the immediate group with which he or she is associated.

In the *hierarchical* setting, the practitioner is employed by an institution whose basic mission is identified with that of the profession. For example, a school administrator customarily works in a formal educational system for children. The expertise of people who work in hierarchies may not lie so much in their provision of direct service to the people served as in their capacity to operate an ordered structure of authority and to initiate or enforce the policies that best foster and maintain it. In some cases, most notably the armed services, there is only one employer in a country. If the practitioner leaves the employment of the sole possible user of his most highly developed talents, he leaves the profession (though he may enter a related one, as when a colonel becomes a police chief or the head of security for an industrial corporation). In other examples of the hierarchical pattern, such as school or health care administration, alternative employers exist and the individual often gains advancement by moving from one to another.

In the *adjunct* setting, practitioners use their expertise in the service of an institution whose basic mission is different from that of their profession. An industrial corporation may hire an attorney, an accountant, an architect, and members of various health professions. Each such person has a distinctive status that is not possessed, for example, by the directors of purchasing, sales, production, or personnel, although members of this latter group may have higher special status, salary, and prospects for advancement within the corporation than any of the adjunct practitioners. The latter may, in some cases, be content to agree with decisions or to endorse actions that violate specialized expert judgment, but if he or she does refuse to agree, that action has a special influence different from that exerted by purely personal authority and that grows from an established social responsibility and sometimes from law. If

a professional leaves the adjunct pattern to become, for example, executive vice-president of the company, he or she loses
the special social protection which was earlier possessed. In
some organizations, such as the armed services, adjunct professionals are so numerous that they make up special corps, such
as those established for medicine, nursing, or the chaplaincy. In
these cases, an adjunct setting takes on its own distinctive structural form even as it becomes part of a larger setting, thus leading to a new complexity of relationships. A new hierarchy has
been created within another very different kind of hierarchy.

In the *facilitative* setting, the practitioner, though usually
fully qualified as a professional, is no longer actively engaged in
the work of the occupation itself but aids and advances its progress. Such a person may be employed by a professional school,
a voluntary association, a government bureau, a publishing
house, a foundation, or a special research laboratory.

A professionalizing vocation never has all its practitioners
working in a single setting. Every occupation has many alternative forms of employment, and this fact is particularly true
when the number of practitioners is large. On January 1, 1976,
for example, 30,427 pharmacists were owners of community
pharmacies, 56,444 were employees in community pharmacies,
15,588 worked in hospital pharmacies, 4,273 worked for manu-
facturing companies, 8,760 worked in teaching, government,
and other facilitative positions, and 10,739 were not in practice.*

A professionalizing occupation does, however, tend to
orient itself to the setting in which most of its members are engaged, and variance from that pattern may cause uneasiness.
The attorney employed on a full-time basis by a corporation
(often called a "kept lawyer"), may feel removed from the
entrepreneurial mainstream of legal practice. Many nurses, even
those on private duty, like to have the sense of collective effort
that the hospital, the school, or the clinic provides. Public administrators who go into (or, as they often say, "retire to") university teaching may grow nostalgic for the former command

*This information was provided by Fred T. Mahaffey, National
Association of Boards of Pharmacy.

post. Sometimes a multiple shift of patterns imposes a series of difficulties of adjustment, for example when an accountant leaves entrepreneurial practice to serve a government bureau as a facilitator and then becomes an administrator by climbing the hierarchical ladder of the bureau.

Whenever a large number of practitioners moves from a traditionally characteristic pattern of service to a new one, a strain may be put on the profession itself. For example, many physicians have changed from an entrepreneurial to a collective practice, and some have shifted to work in hierarchical settings. These alterations in the pattern of service have led many people to call for a new definition of the role of doctors and of their relationships with allied health professionals. An even more striking case has occurred with the Roman Catholic clergy, where the objection of many priests to the traditional rule of the hierarchy and their desire to shift to a collective pattern of decision making and service have caused a number of personal and social crises throughout the world.

Even in esssentially nonhierarchic professions, such as engineering and pharmacy, the movement from one position to another tends to be upward in a chain of command. In this case, the new knowledge and skills that must be learned are usually those of management. In some such cases, a new professional-izing vocation may come into being, as has happened with school administration. While preexisting service in another pro-fession (teaching) is almost always required, the school admini-strator is expected to undertake a distinctive program of training based on the expectation that he or she is moving permanently from a collective to a hierarchical setting. The new profession has its own set of titles, which tends to set it apart from the earlier occupation. The head of a school is a *principal*, of a local school system a *superintendent*, and of a state school system a *commissioner*; derivative terms are devised for their assistants, associates, and deputies. These people almost never refer to themselves as "teachers."

In some cases, the shift in career emphasis may not lead to a new professional status, even though it may sometimes lead to an ambiguous sense of mission. Pharmacy tends to encounter identity problems of this latter sort, and many of the problems of engineering may be caused by the same division. In other professions, however, the commitment to a function or, at least, to the tradition of a function has given the practitioners a sense of basic unity. Nursing is a good example of this phenomenon: every position in the field—from the most recently awarded R.N. to the highest nursing official in a government, a university, or elsewhere—always has the word *nurse* or *nursing* in its title. Indeed, the same term is used for the members of two non-professionalizing vocations, practical nurses and nurses' aides. The sense of identification is not unique to nursing, though it is perhaps most deliberately fostered there. It is also held by architects, accountants, librarians, social workers, and others. Perhaps the differences among the professions suggested by these semantic distinctions of title are not as great as they might at first appear, but in dealing with each occupation, the provider of continuing education is well advised to keep the occupation's sense of common identity in mind.

The influence of the work setting on continuing education and the stimuli that lead to it will be explored at some length later in this book. For present purposes, it is useful only to highlight them. In entrepreneurial and adjunct practice, contact with other people possessing the same kind of competence tends to be more casual and intermittent than is true in collective or hierarchical settings. In the latter, fraternal, evaluative, supervisory, and stimulative measures can reinforce learning, and the concentration of employees makes economically feasible the provision of a richer variety of learning resources than would usually be the case elsewhere. In hierarchical settings, the structure of overall authority makes it possible to establish procedures and policies in which great attention can be given to fostering competence, creativeness, and leadership. In comprehensiveness and completeness of design, for example, no system of lifelong learning can match that provided to the members of the officer corps of the armed services.

Changes in the Career Line

Many people spend their entire professional lives in the same kind of setting as that in which they began their work, the

only changes in their lives being advancement in seniority and
sometimes in status. The dentist serves succeeding generations
of clients; the lawyer becomes a partner and then a senior partner but remains within the same firm or one very like it; and the
teacher, the librarian, and the social worker carry on essentially
the same duties as those with which they started their work.
Many other professionals, however, have shifts in their career
lines, often of numerous and varied sorts. Some of these changes
are from one situation to another, for example when a journalist
works for one newspaper and then for its competitor. Some are
movements upward in a hierarchy, for example when a second
lieutenant becomes a first lieutenant or a pastor becomes a bishop. Some are movements from generalist to specialist or the reverse, for example when an architect specializes in mass-produced
homes or a pediatric nurse becomes a general nurse. Some are
movements from one level of performance to another, for example when a suburban superintendent of schools becomes an
urban superintendent—or vice versa. Some are movements from
one function to another, as when a lawyer (who is supposed to
be an advocate) becomes a judge (who is supposed to guide the
application of law in particular cases). Some are movements
from one setting to another, as when an independent certifying
accountant becomes the employee of a corporation or a social
worker ceases active service in the field and joins the staff of
a professional association or a government bureau. Some are
movements from one specialization to another, as when a path-
ologist becomes a psychiatrist or a public librarian becomes
a university librarian. The examples are limitless in the volatile
life of professional service, which offers great scope for mobility.

Many accounts have been given of the impact of such
movements upon the individual. *The Rabbi*, a novel by Noah
Gordon (1965), describes the shifting patterns of confrontation
faced by a sensitive professional religious leader as he served five
congregations. A witty account, *How to Become a Bishop Without Really Trying* by Smith (1966, p. 130), suggests the following timetable: age 26, first miserable pastorate; age 28, second
miserable pastorate; age 30 or 31, county-seat parish or Grade
B city church; age 35–38, first major-league pastorate or new

suburban church with tremendous potential for growth; age 43–
50, second major-league pastorate or important board job or
presidency of church-related college; age 50–55, become bishop.
Career mobility studies have been undertaken in many professions. For example, an analysis of 1,220 accounting graduates
of Ohio State University showed that they had already had an
average of 1.6 changes, most of them not from one firm to another but from one area of accounting to another (Kollaritsch,
1968). The complex career mobility of the allied health professions is described by Perry (1969), who points out that the
ladder (implying upward or downward movement) or the lattice
(implying upward, downward, or lateral movement) must be
replaced by the jungle gym, (implying movement in all three
directions within a vocation and also entry into a different
though allied occupation).

Whenever any shift in the career line occurs, it provides
an incentive for formal or informal continuing education to
which the individual must respond. It has been ironically suggested—in the so-called Peter principle (Peter and Hull, 1969)—
that every worker rises to the level of his or her incompetence.
Perhaps a truer statement of the principle might be: Professionals rise to the level at which they no longer learn how to deal
with the problems they confront.

The need to adjust to change is particularly acute when
a professional moves from one kind of work setting to another
or leaves active practice to become a facilitator. For example, in
any move away from entrepreneurship—when a dentist leaves
private-duty service to work in a clinic or an independent accountant is employed by a business firm—some formal or informal induction training may be provided by the employing
institution. If not, the person concerned must learn independently how to mesh his or her work with that of colleagues or
people at other levels of the hierarchy. The person who moves
from a collective or hierarchical practice into an entrepreneurial
one—such as a hospital pharmacist or a government lawyer who
establishes an independent practice—often has a hard time learning how to work effectively, because customary forms of collaboration, reinforcement, and recruitment of clients are no longer

available. Particularly difficult problems of adjustment occur when a professional leaves an occupation based on a hierarchical monopoly, as has already been noted in the cases of Catholic clergy or the armed services. A different but allied kind of education is essential when an active professional becomes a facilitator and, rather than serving clients directly, must learn to stimulate and support the efforts of those who do.

A strong incentive for continuing education is also required when an individual who has not recently engaged in practice returns to the work of his or her profession. It is necessary to find some way to learn the new theories, knowledge, and practices introduced since the time when previous service ended as well as to become oriented to the new conceptual and collective identity characteristics of the profession. Such a person has inherent encouragements to learning: the desire to perform adequately in a new, strange, and sometimes threatening situation; the formal or informal requirements that may have been established as a condition prerequisite to readmission to practice; the awareness by the practitioner, in the early days of resumed service, that colleagues, supervisors, and clients are looking carefully at his or her performance; and a concomitant sense of comradeship flowing from the special help given by new associates at work, particularly if some of them are willing to serve as guides or mentors. If these encouragements and challenges are not already present, they can be introduced, though it is harder to do so in entrepreneurial than in other work settings.

In all the changes of the career line—both those that are related to entering a new work pattern and those that are not—the movement from one post to another sometimes occurs so informally that no provision is made for learning the new role. The individual must stumble along as adequately as possible, learning on the job by trial and error, relying on associates, observing, remembering previous actions by other people in the same situation, seeking advice, reading, taking courses, hiring consultants, and using other available processes. When a satisfactory adjustment to the new position has been made, maintenance of high performance standards once again becomes the guiding principle of continuing education.

To a rapidly increasing extent, however, continuing education is being offered by various providers to meet the needs of professionals who make changes in their career lines. In the armed services, special schools prepare officers for their new assignments. The graduate may also have an overlapping period of service with the person he or she is to replace before actually assuming command. This pattern is described by Jessup (1971) in terms of its application by the British Royal Air Force. Many organizations offer special training programs for people who assume new responsibilities. For example, New York University has long maintained an annual seminar for judges appointed to state appellate courts. Employing organizations, acting either alone or in concert with universities or other authorities, may carry out systematic programs of staff development. Kortendick (1967) has described one such program designed for librarians. In other situations, the pattern of learning is informal but still well understood. A new assistant director of a welfare agency may be appointed a year before the director retires in order to "learn the ropes" before assuming the senior post; or the principal of a school may take courses in planning, budgeting, or personnel management to learn duties carried out in the central office of the system to which he or she hopes to move. When such changes are made, it is often understood by persons in authority that a period of learning on the job is necessary before a fully competent performance of all duties can be expected.

The prevalence of changes in the worklife suggests that Figure 1 in Chapter One must be revised. Its static picture of the nature of professional education during the worklife must be replaced by a more flexible conception. Figure 2 is a simple and general version of how professionalizing occupations must design their total educational programs to take account of the career changes suggested in the preceding pages of this section. Each profession will develop its own distinctive pattern, but it will usually be a variation of Figure 2. It should be noted that the basic design of Figure 1 is still present in Figure 2, because many professionals remain in the same position throughout their lives. For them, continuing education is solely the main-

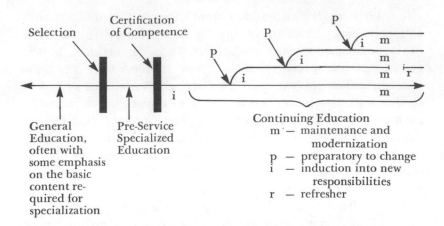

Figure 2. An emerging model of professional education

tenance and modernization of their basic professional abilities. Maintenance and modernization are also necessary in each of the other roles a professional is called upon to play. But this form of education is different from preparatory, induction, and refresher training, the distinctive goals of which require in each case that efforts to achieve them be especially tailored to their distinctive purposes.

Education as a Consequence of the Worklife

The chief lessons learned by a professional during the years of active service are the intentional or unintentional products of the work itself. The stimuli to learning inherent in the practice of a vocation are presented to an individual as an opportunity (such as increased income), a threat (such as a crisis of self-identification), or, most frequently, as a challenge combining both opportunity and threat (such as the need to discover the best solution to an unusually difficult and perplexing problem). These stimuli arise as part of the individual life of a professional as he or she takes part in collective informal activities. Some of the most important stimuli will be considered separately here, though all are interwoven in the life of the practitioner.

Problem-oriented information search. When the professional enters service, the problems presented by particular cases

become the absorbing center of attention. The confrontation of
these problems is the most significant stimulus for continuing
education throughout the whole course of an active career.
Margulies and Raia (1967) asked 290 scientists and engineers,
"What was the most fruitful learning experience you have had
over the past year or two?" and found that the most frequent
response, given by 42 percent of the respondents, was "on-the-
job problem solving."

A problem confronted by a professional may require
searching out and examining all available facts, studying distinctive aspects of the particular situation, seeking basic information from books or other sources, consulting with collaborators
and colleagues, or securing formal advice from experts. As has
been noted earlier, it often happens that the professional is
working competitively. Other practitioners are also centering
their efforts on the same problem in order to win a conflict or
to secure a different settlement of an issue. For example, architects and engineers hope to triumph in competitive bidding for
a contract, lawyers want to secure favorable judicial decisions,
and surgeons recognize that their clients are likely to seek another opinion about the need for an operation. Even when direct
competition is not present, relative success is often judged by
colleagues or supervisors in terms of the welfare of a client, the
meeting of a social need, the improvement of the environment,
or other evidence of the solution of a problem.

In the early years of practice, problem solving is a particularly effective stimulus to learning, because the responsibility
to handle each situation is continuously novel for the person
concerned, however familiar it may be for the profession as
a whole. As time goes on, however, and the solution to most
problems becomes routine, some of the sense of challenge is
lost and with it some of the stimulus to learn. Burkett and
Knafl (1974) have emphasized the almost endless combination
of variables that can be encountered in a fairly restricted area
of medical practice, and this same complexity is present in other
professions. However, it is possible for a practitioner to develop
standard solutions to problems and apply them almost without
considering the fact that unique elements are present in every
case. It is also true that the routine inspections required by

many professions (such as a forester examining his assigned terrain or a dentist giving a twice-a-year check-up) require vigilance and care so that they do not become automatic but continue to provide the freshness of experience that leads to inquiry and eventually to personal enhancement. The growth of routinized treatment becomes the precondition of failure to learn about new conceptions, techniques, processes, or treatments. Monotony becomes the enemy of learning.

"The old ways suffice; why not use them?" This question is most difficult for proponents of continuing professional education, applying, as it does, not merely to problem-oriented information search but to all other forms of learning. The maintenance of a freshness of viewpoint depends ultimately upon internalizing a way of work that must be individualized and self-imposed. Sir William Osler (1906) tried to record in his notebook the unique aspects of every case he saw, however routine the diagnosis and treatment, often keeping a large retinue of attending physicians waiting while he did so. The professional who adopts Osler's point of view is required not only to engage in practice but simultaneously to be an independent observer of what he or she is doing, not merely dealing with a problem but handling it in such a way that it enlarges the scope of his or her abilities. If this value has not been achieved by the time of entry into service, if it is not stimulated by the nature of practice (as it is, for example, with trial lawyers), if it is not learned directly by some of the organized means to be later described, or if it is not efficiently monitored by colleagues and supervisors, the individual practitioner will be cut off from the most rewarding and immediate form of learning the profession provides.

Crises of self-identification and stress. During the course of the worklife, all professionals probably have periods of frustration in which they doubt themselves, their goals, and the values of their work. Such frustration can sometimes bring on a catastrophic crisis, leading even to suicide. Individuals who manage to remain in practice may find it impossible to do anything but carry out routines mechanically. Their energy is not sufficient to overcome the inertia of the system. Counselors and psychological therapists are familiar with this phenomenon in its various manifestations and degrees and have many strategies to deal with it, among which education is often one ingredient.

Few studies have been made comparing the practice of professions, so nobody can say with certainty whether crises of self-identification occur more frequently within one occupation than within another. It would seem likely, however, that if any profession were to be particularly prone to psychological trauma, it would be the ministry, where from the beginning to the end of a career the individual must be sustained by a sense of vocation in its original meaning: a direct calling by God to lead a religious life and to guide others to do so. Brown (1970), basing his analysis on a long career of counseling ministers, has identified seven kinds of crises to which his clients are subject: (1) the crisis of integrity, in which the minister no longer believes in the creeds of his church; (2) the crisis of power, in which the minister feels that neither he nor his church has significant community influence; (3) the crisis of capacity, in which the minister feels personally inadequate to deal with the situation in which he finds himself, either because of his own ineffectiveness or because he is caught in a social situation with which he cannot cope; (4) the crisis of failure, often felt by older ministers, in which the individual sees himself on a downward path that will lead to a sad termination of his career; (5) the crisis of destination, in which the minister does not know how to plan and advance his career; (6) the crisis of role, in which the minister cannot resolve satisfactorily his indecision about whether to be primarily spiritual leader, executive, shepherd of a flock, ritualist, or the player of some other part in the drama of religion; and (7) the crisis of meaning which, in a sense, pervades all the others because it suggests that the profession has no place in the modern world. While these crises arise essentially out of work-life, they also influence and are influenced by all other aspects of the minister's social and personal life.

One has only to read this list of crises to realize that a similar categorization could be made for any profession and that it would probably include at least some of those felt by ministers. The stresses just mentioned are somewhat timeless; but others are produced by perceptions of new threats from colleagues or society. Longitudinal studies of physicians show, for example, that in the late 1970s they felt four major kinds of stress that had not previously been reported: a fear of malpractice suits, a fear of accepting the full consequences of responsibility for patient care, a fear of physical violence, and a fear of peer review (Mawardi, 1979). Such crises and stresses, however stark they may seem to those who experience them, can in one sense be viewed as positive because they make manifest the fact that the individual continues to care deeply about his or her work and has been neither routinized by its performance nor obsessed by its rewards.

Many crises cannot be met by remaining in the profession, a fact that helps account for frequent mid-life changes in vocations. Nor are such changes necessarily bad; they may indicate that an individual has rectified an earlier error in choice of career or has outgrown the capacity to be of service in the occupation. But the great majority of the people who face crises probably remain in their professions, perhaps living in a continuing state of frustration and accepting the feeling of monotony or crisis as an occupational way of life. Alternatively, they use the crisis as a stimulus for a positive program of action, often facilitated by outside assistance. The professional seeks out a formal counselor, finds a mentor, friend, or family member to serve as an informal guide or therapist, or works out a plan of reading, conferencing, or study of his own. Many people, as a result, move from one work setting in the profession to another.

The sense of crisis can become the stimulus for formal instruction. Some people seek release by learning new skills that will improve their competence, studying content to deepen their ideas or understanding, and investigating new fields of knowledge to give them breadth and perspective. In many educational activities, the latent curriculum may turn out to be more important than the formal one. For example, a lecturer may describe some technical advance, such as genetic engineering, only to find that the ensuing questions and discussions deal not with its procedures but with the ethics of its application. The session can become a semitherapeutic one dealing with the crises of values felt by individuals in the audience more than with the acquisition of content or the perfection of process that was presumably the focus of the meeting.

The informal collective life of the professional. In the normal course of life, most practitioners have a more or less continuing informal contact with other members of their professions. As noted in Chapter Three, this relationship occurs in many ways: being associated with them in a common work setting as colleagues, consultants, and collaborators; eating in the dining room at the local bar association or at the "doctor's table" in a social club; socializing on an interfamily basis; and jointly undertaking hobbies, recreation, travel, and social or political causes. Some people, by either design or necessity, do not share these patterns of association because they are wholly concerned with their own entrepreneurial practice or for other reasons. Many of them are geographically remote, are concerned only with a distinctive clientele, are inclined toward solitude or independence, or are unpopular and, for personal or professional reasons, isolate themselves or are excluded from social contacts. Individualists are often either innovators, who are impatient with what they believe to be the low level of common practice, or laggards, who find it uncomfortable or impossible to associate with their fellow professionals.

At this point, however, it seems appropriate to concentrate upon the normal rather than the exceptional situation. The influence of informal professional association as it operates with the customary expectations imposed by the general professionalization process can lead to greatly improved learning benefits, which are worth mentioning before considering unusual circumstances and special cases.

Social status. In an early and widely cited study, Hall (1948) analyzed the social structure of physicians in an American city. He identified an informal "inner fraternity" that dominated the practice of the profession, controlled access to the most prestigious hospitals and clinics, and had a membership well aware of its collective role as the guardians of standards and policies. This group was self-selected on the basis of age, family background, reputation of medical school attended, and other similar factors and tended to be made up of Anglo-Saxon males, though "recruits" with other backgrounds were introduced if they handled their careers prudently and if they acquired the proper sponsorship. Commenting on Hall's study, Braude (1975, p. 81) observed that all that the "essentially disfranchised physicians could do was to segregate themselves in their own sociological colleague groups—the Italian group serving Italian patients, blacks treating blacks, and the like." According to Solomon (1961), the importance of acceptance into "inner fraternities," whether general or specialized by sociological colleague groups, is very much on the minds of medical students and residents who use their personal contacts and influence with professors and colleagues to establish advantageous places for themselves in their later practice.

All professions have systems of informal social status similar to that of medicine, although the growth of specialized fields of practice as well as such social trends as movement of people away from big cities and from one region of the country to another have made prestige patterns far more complex and fluid than they used to be. These systems help establish the values of the professionals who belong to them. If continuing education is looked upon favorably, it will occur naturally and will be likely to succeed when it is fostered as a formal activity. The informal system of learning gains its influence because of the operation of familiar procedures and activities, a few of which will be mentioned here.

Colleagueship. In the study by Margulies and Raia (1967), the second most fruitful learning experience of the engineers and scientists studied (mentioned by 20 percent of the sample) was interaction with colleagues. This stimulus comes up again and again in the literature of continuing professional education. People who have been acculturated by a common process usually enjoy the quickness and intimacy of discussion that results from a shared background.

Professions are notable for the nurturance they provide to their members, beginning with the mentor-novice relationship that characterizes at least part of basic education and proceeding through a lifetime of colleagueship and supervision. During the discussions of any cluster of professionals, new ideas and techniques are spread. This process is particularly effective when it occurs in the easy familiarity of work settings in which people see one another day by day. Coleman, Katz, and Menzel (1966) have shown that the most significant factor causing physicians to prescribe a new drug is the "density" of their formal and informal associations with other physicians. Presumably this colleagueship increases the influence of doctors who believe in the drug's effectiveness. The effect of familiar association operates throughout the world of professionalism and is shared by all but solitary practitioners and supreme heads of hierarchies.

Many strategies exist to make colleagueship more educative: the encouragement of shared off-duty experiences; the designing of meetings and conferences so that they include opportunity for unstructured discussion sessions; the creation of journal clubs, discussion groups, special interest associations, retreats, and colloquia; and the reservation of special tables for interest groups at mealtimes. The ways of using these practices for the advancement of knowledge are usually fairly obvious in any given situation once the need for doing so has been realized.

Consultation. In dealing with particular cases, professionals often help one another on an informal basis, giving assistance when it is requested or needed—and sometimes when it is not. In many professions—such as law, accounting, dentistry, teaching, and medicine—some practitioners have clearly defined areas of specialization and are called in formally for consultation by colleagues when their expertise is required. In other situations, a team approach is used, with members of several professions working together to facilitate one another's effort. In all these cases, the dominant goal is the provision of a service or the resolution of a problem, but the side effect is a deeper understanding by each professional concerned of how colleagues go about their work and a growth of knowledge which, while particularized to the case being dealt with, may provide broader perspectives for future use. In a few professions, the processes of consultation may sometimes be so devised as to be deliberately educative, for example, when a social work case is presented and analyzed before a group of students, staff members, or trustees.

Both colleagueship and consultation can have negative as well as positive influences on continued learning. A group of colleagues may share a cynical view of any practice or principle that is not in accord with an accepted dogma, may scorn new knowledge or even the effort to secure it, or may deride colleagues who take part in learning activities. It is hard to change a negative social climate into a positive one, although strong, persistent, and charismatic leadership can sometimes bring about such a reversal. The threat of punitive action by some authority outside the profession may also be helpful; unity is fostered by the appearance of a common enemy. In the effort to avoid governmental regulation or rampantly negative consumer attacks on conservative or self-serving vested interest groups, leaders in many professions frequently urge their colleagues to police themselves. It is not clear, however, whether such pleas have yet had more than occasional and moderate success.

As for consultation, the advice and support given may be ill informed or out of date. The authority from whom help is sought may prove to be a laggard in his own field of specialization, and the persons involved in a team approach may drag one another down by inefficiency or antagonism rather than reinforce each other by informed and positive support. Any practitioner who hopes to learn by collaborative efforts must therefore be sure that he or she is consulting a competent authority or that fellow team members are able and willing to carry on effective collaboration. As a matter of fact, team practice often requires special training for those who take part in it.

Establishment of role models. The importance of role models in pre-service education has already been mentioned. Lord Jackson of Burnley (1971, p. 7) has suggested that this stimulus is also necessary for effective lifelong education in the professions. All technological scientists and engineers, he observed, should have "a sense of responsibility to maintain and enhance their own competence [and] also that of their associates, especially their more junior colleagues. Each of us can remember men who at various stages of our careers have stimulated, if not inspired, us by their encouragement and example.

And yet it is disappointing to observe how many men are apparently unable or unwilling to appreciate [that] the difficulties and frustrations their junior colleagues are experiencing are much the same as they themselves had complained about at an earlier date, and to recognize that they have a responsibility toward their junior colleagues and subordinates." The absence of positive and strong personal leadership is detrimental to growth during the course of a career. Lord Jackson quotes Sir Arthur Fleming: "A poor environment can rapidly convert a first class man into a mediocre one—if he stays"; to this, Jackson adds, "The nature of an environment is largely determined by the senior men in it."

Any strategies involving the use of this stimulus must be handled with care, particularly because any senior professional who fancies the role of mentor is likely to overplay it and achieve the opposite effects from those intended. In the pre-service years, the teacher or work supervisor is supposed to set an example to the people being taught, but this expectation is often thought not to be appropriate in a work situation in which people are presumed to be colleagues. Nevertheless, individuals are often chosen for positions, particularly in hierarchical or collective settings, because it is believed that they have personality traits that are lacking in the present mix of staff members. Among these qualities can be a personal enthusiasm for continuing education and the desire to foster it. Although such a staff member may not necessarily become widely viewed as a role model, his or her influence on colleagues who do serve that function may help to advance their forward-looking sense of the need to achieve the aims that only education can provide.

Institutional climate. Closely allied to other stimuli to continuing education is the existence of an institutional climate that formally encourages and provides education for the professionals engaged in it. Such a climate is possible wherever two or more professionals collaborate in any work setting. An educative climate can be fostered in many ways, of which three mutually reinforcing approaches are particularly significant.

The first approach is to design within the setting as many educative features as resources will permit and usage justify.

These might include, among many other features, a well-stocked
and well-staffed library, colloquia in which members of the professional corps make presentations on their specialties of practice, lectures by outside authorities, demonstrations of new theoretical or methodological approaches, released time and tuition
payments for study, and reimbursement for conference or convention attendance. In many institutions, staff members are
assigned, part time or full time, to foster and administer such
activities, and, in hospitals and other health care centers, a new
professionalizing occupation, the directorship of education, is
becoming established.

　　　The second method of fostering an educational climate is
the systematic use of the already mentioned team approach, in
which various specialists, often from different professions, work
together on selected cases that offer an opportunity for interactive instruction. This approach is, in a sense, an elaboration of
the problem-oriented information search and the consultation
process, but it has the added advantage of providing new applied
insights for each member of the team as he or she becomes aware
of the knowledge and expertise of the other members. Within
the professions of teaching, nursing, and social work, the team
approach has been strongly advocated by many leaders, and
Mauksch (1966) has shown how an entire hospital can be organized to provide it.

　　　The third approach includes the first two but goes far beyond them. It is the creation of an atmosphere of all-encompassing mutual growth and stimulation. The basic work of the
unit must still provide the paramount goals, but their accomplishment is accompanied at every point by a desire to probe,
to learn, to exchange ideas, and to open vistas. The shared intellectual excitement of such an environment, once experienced, is
never forgotten. Margaret Mead (1964) has described workplaces
that create an air of shared growth as centers offering the potential of a continuous social evolution. It is hard to say how a per-
vading sense of intellectual growth of this sort can be developed;
presumably some of the ingredients are the values and beliefs of
the leaders, the introduction of as many devices of fruitful communication as possible, and the insistence that the quality of

work performed by the professionals must constantly be improved. A sense of an increasingly powerful capacity to deal with the tasks at hand is crucial to the continued well-being of a functioning center and keeps it from the inbreeding and introspection sometimes found in well-endowed but complacent centers.

The use of the decision-making process. In every situation in which two or more professionals are engaged—whether it be in an entrepreneurial, collective, hierarchical, adjunct, or facilitative setting—decisions must be made about the work itself and the circumstances under which it is to be undertaken. For example, two architects practicing in partnership may work together on a building's design, may assign it wholly to one or to the other, or may give primary responsibility to one partner with review reserved to the other. Also the two must make many decisions about the general conditions of their work, such as where their office will be located, how clients are to be secured, what auxiliary personnel are needed, and how and when earnings are to be allocated. In entrepreneurial settings that involve more than two professionals or in collective or hierarchical settings, the increase in the number of people involved and in the intricacy of their interrelationships cause decision-making problems to grow ever more complex and often to become staggering in their scope.

In general, professionals believe that the right to make or help make decisions about the principles and practices of their work is inherent in the very nature of their professionalism. People in solitary practice or who try to be autonomous in collective or hierarchical settings are asserting their right to control what they do and how they do it. In other cases, job descriptions are carefully prepared and coordinated with one another so that each person knows the nature and scope of the responsibility to be exercised in a position. In hierarchical professions, there is an old proposition, "authority should go down the line"; "ideas should go up the line" is also ancient though perhaps much less frequently practiced. In every organized setting, collective decision making occurs in meetings of partners, in staff meetings, and in committee work.

The opening up of the decision-making process to include as many people as possible is a way of using the mode of inquiry to expose professionals and their collaborators to problems and thereby inform them of aspects of work with which they have had little or no previous experience. This result is likely to be enhanced when problems require the collection of data, the solicitation of authoritative viewpoints, or the use of other ways to enlarge understanding of fundamental issues or crucial points of decision. In a school, for example, teachers are regularly involved in faculty meetings in which time is devoted to revising the curriculum, to discussing policies of grading, discipline or other similar matters, and to considering special problems presented by students, parents, or other persons affiliated with the school. Such collaboration is undertaken primarily because of the belief that it will produce wiser decisions than otherwise and that they will be effectively carried out because of the involvement at the policy-making stage of the people influenced by them. Another important intended value, however, is the enlargement of understanding of the individuals concerned and the belief that their participation will help them make wiser decisions in the future than in the past.

The broadening of the decision-making process presents special problems for the administrator who must accept ultimate responsibility for the action which the other persons involved do not share. The managing or senior partner of an entrepreneurial firm, the director of a collective group of professionals, or the administrator of a hierarchical structure cannot avoid this responsibility and therefore must have an authority not shared by coworkers, even though they have helped make the relevant policies. Furthermore any such person must usually make decisions that deeply influence the lives of his or her work associates—hiring, promoting, setting compensation and fringe benefits, determining working conditions, and perhaps terminating employment—and the duty and power to carry out such actions always limits the full sharing of the decision-making process.

Another problem that may result from an inept broadening of involvement in decision making may be that the mere processes of participation assume too great an importance. The wisdom or the correctness of what is decided becomes less significant in the eyes of the professionals concerned than the procedures that are followed or the extent and nature of involvement of the persons concerned. The danger of this form of dogma is especially great in the case of collective work settings, but it can also occur in the other two basic patterns. However idealistic the practice of full involvement in decision-making may initially seem, it must be introduced and maintained with tact and skill in the realistic settings in which professionals work. Just where the lines of authority and participation should be drawn is hard to identify, either theoretically or in practical cases.

Avoidance and exclusion. An awareness of the possibility of avoidance and exclusion has a general salutary effect upon all members of a profession, many of whom are stirred to maintain or strengthen their performance by a realization of the consequences of a possible decline in practice or a boycott. The dramatic fate of some incompetent or unethical professionals is to lose their licenses and therefore their right to practice. Less conspicuous but far more common ways in which such practitioners are punished is through avoidance by colleagues and exclusion from needed resources. If a professional loses the confidence of colleagues, they are likely to withdraw from association with him or her, deny access to facilities needed for practice, or fail to refer clients. The suspect practitioner is thus gradually or speedily cut off from the right to work. The entrepreneur finds that habitual clients disappear and new ones never come; the person who works in a collective setting cannot find or keep a job; and the member of a hierarchy is demoted, told not to expect further promotions, "put on the shelf" in an inconsequential position, scheduled for early retirement, dismissed, or "kicked upstairs." In these circumstances, many professionals become resigned to their fates and live as best they can, but others are challenged to do anything necessary to rehabilitate themselves.

It is commonly believed that people who work in collective and hierarchical settings usually receive more direct and continuous warnings of poor performance than those in entrepreneurial settings and are therefore encouraged to remedy their ways by education and other means. The argument for this position is that the daily interaction of professionals keeps all of them on their toes. This viewpoint is often challenged, however, by those who assert that the people who work in hospitals, schools, welfare agencies, military services and other similar collective and hierarchical settings offer shelter and protection to incompetent and unethical practitioners, being encouraged to do so by the kindliness of colleagues, the protection of the institution's resources, and the need to maintain accreditation or a favorable public image. Blanket indictments of various kinds of work settings are probably less meaningful, however, than the ways by which each situation is operated. Well-informed and active citizen boards and effective practices of peer review and supervision can greatly strengthen the sense of continuing responsibility that every professional should feel.

The Influence of Age on Learning Patterns

In addition to the factors already mentioned, increasing age undoubtedly affects the practitioners of a professionalizing vocation. Sir William Osler, the great exemplar of the general-practice medical era, had clear ideas about the principles that should guide the physician and showed how they should be applied in the early, the middle, and the late years of practice, which as far as Osler was concerned should end at the age of sixty (a view to which he adhered steadfastly in precept though not in practice). His schematic view was not recorded systematically in any one place but was profoundly and consistently held and can be readily fitted together by those who read the full body of his writings. He felt strongly that at each age of life, the physician should be an active student, and on this point his practice was in full accord with his precept.

Aside from Osler's expression of his beliefs and a few other similar dicta, however, most attempts to indicate the direct influence of age and experience on the practitioner of a profession and upon his or her need for education have been heavy-handed attempts at humor or exaggerated comparisons between "the old guard" and "the young Turks." While the systematic study of the general life-span has been burgeoning, specialized applications of general theory to professions and particularly to the lifelong learning of their practitioners have not yet emerged into a significant body of literature. A few serious treatments exist; Farmer and Williams (1971), for example, have mapped out a typical career strategy, which indicates the kinds of personal and educational needs that occur during career changes at various stages of life. In George Eliot's great novel *Middlemarch*, she vividly describes how the ardent sense of mission of a brilliant young professional (in this case a physician) is dulled by the demands made upon him to achieve a successful career. Many analyses veer away from a full treatment of the subject. For example, Hall's paper, "The Stages of a Medical Career," (1948) actually deals with the process of adjustment to the established specialists who constitute the inner core of the medical profession. There have also been many studies of educational needs and interests, extent of participation in learning, and reactions to continuing education in various professions, some of which have considered age differentials, but this material treats the topics in such diverse ways that it cannot be readily summarized.

The Continuity of Continuing Education

In a major analysis of theological education, Niebuhr, Williams, and Gustafson (1957, p. 209) commented that "the greatest defect in theological education today is that it is too much an affair of piecemeal transmission of knowledge and skills, and that, in consequence, it offers too little challenge to the student to develop his own resources and to become an independent, lifelong inquirer, growing constantly while he is engaged in the work of the ministry." Without always making the same connection between pre-service and continuing education, a number of representatives of other professions—such as Gaver (1971) for librarianship—have recognized the importance of sequential experience in which one module of learning, however independently valuable it may be, gains force and direction from the cumulative impact of its integration with other modules. At present, however, the recognition of such relationships is the exception, not the rule. The most startling and ironic characteristic of continuing education, except in a few of the hierarchical professions, is its discontinuity in the experience of the individual practitioner.

A lifelong continuity, even one that offers many options, cannot be charted in advance as a basic curriculum can. Nobody would expect or want a lifelong curriculum with course following monotonously upon course. The patterns of individual life and personal desire are far too varied and lengthy for any such master plan to be useful. But anecdotal examples drawn from individual lives convey a sense that in many careers, a glimpse is being caught of what lifelong continuing education might mean. Gutzman (1969), a librarian, has coined the phrase "career-long sabbatical," to indicate a frame of mind which he feels is difficult but necessary to maintain. In an engagingly witty essay, Posnak (1970, p. 61) has described how, emerging into the world of work with a baccalaureate in English literature, he managed to find a job in accounting, learned its fundamentals on the job and, by part-time study, secured his CPA and became convinced that he was "on the verge of obsolescence at the age of 27. So began the effort to keep abreast of the profession and the world it serves, which I have since realized is a lifelong commitment of no mean consequence." Perhaps the four years that ensued before Posnak published his essay is too short a time for him to have tested his commitment, but the reader senses that he was off to a good start.

Gustafson (1970), a coauthor of the book in which Niebuhr's comment appeared, argued thirteen years later that a significantly different situation had, by then, been brought about in the churches and in society so that the need for lifelong professional education had become "a burning necessity." Gustafson believes that this fact is also true of other professions: "It would be unrealistic to expect moments of high excitement week by week in any profession; certainly potentially outstanding legal talent is exhausted in writing wills and closing real estate transactions, potential judicial talent in judging routine traffic cases, potential medical talent in ordinary obstetrical practice and routine surgery, potential architectural talent in designing schools and telephone equipment buildings at the lowest possible construction costs, potential teaching talent in trying to discipline adolescents who are uninterested in the subject matter" (Gustafson, 1970, p. 15). But if practice dulls the keenness of knowledge, skill, and commitment, education can resharpen it. Gustafson goes on to say that "the ministry, like other professions, desperately needs the objectivity of a continuing education that evokes not only new motivation to do old things, but also the vision to alter the practice of one's profession, the courage to seek to transform the institutional purposes and structures in which one is embedded, and the simple inspirations of finding fresh points of view" (pp. 21–22).

Chapter 5

The Zest
for Learning

The most important thing about education is appetite. Education does not begin with the university and it certainly ought not to end there.

Winston Churchill

Professionals vary greatly in the extent to which they feel and act upon the zest for learning that Gustafson described at the close of Chapter Four. Active practitioners include those whose constant effort to learn leads them to an ever more refined conception and execution of their responsibilities as well as those who seem content to grind through their days practicing routine skills and using long-familiar knowledge. The extent of the desire of an individual to learn ultimately controls the amount and kind of education he or she undertakes. If learning is eagerly sought, its burdens are light and its rewards great. If it is dreaded, regarded as an onerous chore, or viewed with indifference, any external stimulus (whether encouragement or threat) can do no more than assure a grudging and minimal participation.

It is not hard to determine by observation and interview the extent of the zest for learning of individual professionals, the knowledge they seek to gain, their motivations for study, and the actual and imagined barriers to their increased participation. In fact, when members of a professionalizing vocation are in close touch with one another, they tend to have a fairly good idea about the extent to which each one is seeking the goals suggested in Chapter Three. More general assessments of the extent and nature of the zest for learning of all the members of a profession or, indeed, of all professionals are still not available, but good beginnings have been made on such inquiries. It is with the methods and results of such studies that this chapter will deal.

The scope of the discussion of continuing education must now be broadened beyond the conceptions presented in Chapters Three and Four, where attention was paid almost entirely to the ways in which the preparation for a profession and its practice can educate its members. However, for most people, "continuing education" means some organized effort to teach or to learn. In later chapters these purposefully structured programs will be described in some detail. Here it will be assumed that their general nature is already known to the reader either from personal experience or from the brief accounts given in Chapters One and Two. The studies of the zest for learning that are reported in this chapter are based on the educative enrichment of practice, on organized instructional efforts, or on both.

Some Specific Studies

Even a quick survey of journals and bibliographic indexes will reveal hundreds of investigations of how much time groups of professionals spend in continuing education, what they learn, how deeply they value the experience, what desires for further learning they express, and other related factors. A brief summary of the findings of several investigations suggests their scope and diversity. These studies also set forth the basis of the hypotheses and conceptions to be described later.

Castle and Storey (1968), by analyzing the self-reports provided by 426 physicians and surgeons in Utah in 1966, found that the typical doctor worked 53 hours a week. Of this time, 32 hours a month were spent on continuing education (16.4 in reading, 6.3 in contact with colleagues, 3.5 in group discussion, 1.5 in rounds or clinics, and 4.3 in other forms of learning). In addition, 55 hours per year were spent on meetings and courses. Surgeons spent substantially more time in such pursuits than did either general practitioners or internists. The chief obstacles to continuing education cited by all doctors were:

Response	Percentage
Away from family too much	38
Too many patients	37
Not what's needed	27
Can't fit it into my schedule	27
Too many meetings	23
Can't leave patients	21
Expense	18
Nothing available	14
Postgraduate courses are a waste of time	13
Hard to learn after a certain age	4

The authors note that dissatisfaction with the poor quality or irrelevance of previous or current continuing education is not listed by the respondents as an obstacle.

An interesting parallel study was reported in 1970 by Brody and Stokes, who arranged for students, in the summer before their entry into medical school, to observe the professional activities of twenty California doctors engaged in either general practice or internal medicine. The average observed workweek was 35.1 hours, though the physicians reported to the observers that about an additional hour each day was spent on profession-related activities. Of the average total of 450 minutes observed each day, 14 were spent on continuing education, though the physicians reported that an additional unobserved 30 minutes per day were also devoted to this activity. In the coding chart of the observers, reading medical journals and attending lectures and seminars sponsored by hospitals and voluntary organizations counted as professional education. Brody and Stokes believe averages are deceptive, because the pattern of physician behavior that emerged ranged widely between two extremes. At one end of the spectrum was the isolated general practitioner in solo office practice who treated many patients for brief periods each day. This physician spent little time in either continuing education or patient referral. At the other end of the spectrum was the internist in group practice who spent much more time in consultation and referral of patients to other physicians, despite the fact that he saw fewer patients in his combined office and hospital practice. He participated much more regularly in all kinds of continuing education, even during July and August when organized continuing education was at a seasonal 'low' (Brody and Stokes, 1970, p. 748).

These differences among individuals can also be found in the desires for continuing education of specialty subgroups and of physicians working in different locations. A 1967 questionnaire study of 2,600 California physicians ("Physician Opinions. . . ," 1969) revealed many patterns. Physicians in rural areas seemed to be more satisfied with available learning resources than were those in urban areas. In terms of the desired content of instruction, substantial differences occurred among localities. For example, in Stockton, 23 percent of the physicians would have liked to know more about cancer and cancer chemotherapy, whereas only 4.3 percent in Ventura-Oxnard desired such knowledge. Similar differences were found in every other field of content. The preferred methods of learning varied somewhat among specialty groups, though two- or three-day symposia and reading led the list for all groups. However, ear, nose, and throat specialists liked three- to six-month traineeships almost as much as they did short symposia, orthopedists had a broader tolerance for various methods than did most other specialist groups, and anesthesiologists particularly liked tape-recorded digests of research. Thus, at the time of this study, successful continuing medical education in California would have needed to be highly flexible in terms of preferred content, modes of instruction, and specialty groups to be reached.

In a detailed national study of 1,509 cardiologists (Adams, 1974), it was found that annually 79 percent attend at least one cardiovascular course and 68 percent attend at least one national cardiovascular meeting. About 10 percent do neither. Despite this substantial involvement, the members of the group said that they desired a great deal of additional classroom and laboratory training.

Benthall-Nietzel (1974–75) made the familiar distinction between legal education and lawyering skills, the first having to do chiefly with the basic principles of law and the second with their application in specific situations. Included in the latter

category would be understanding human behavior, quick thinking on one's feet, persuasive expression of ideas under pressure,
and negotiating. In a questionnaire investigation of 416 Kentucky attorneys, it was found that most respondents believed
that many of these skills could be taught in law schools but that
if they were not, they would have to be learned by experience
or by some organized means of continuing education. Most of
the respondents had engaged in some form of continuing education. Nearly 85 percent had read books, 68 percent had attended
formal continuing legal education programs, 28 percent had
taken part in trial advocacy institutes, and 26 percent had enrolled in specialized training under law firm sponsorship, attended tax conferences, or secured advanced academic degrees,
among other activities. At first glance these figures seem impressive, but it should be noted that the respondents spanned the
full age range for practicing lawyers, 5 percent of whom had
had more than forty years of experience. In the perspective of
a professional lifetime, the amount of activity seems slight.

   An important section of the literature dealing with continuing education in specific professions is concerned with the
causes for participation; three studies from the field of nursing
illustrate various approaches to that topic. One investigation
(Price, 1967) was based on the belief that the desire to learn
arises from the intensity with which a practitioner feels a sense
of personal inadequacy in difficult situations. A questionnaire
sent to 1,000 nurses asked for a self-report on the needs they
had experienced and also for anecdotes to illustrate situations
in which such needs were paramount. The following categories
of needs were expressed by at least 10 percent of the nurses:
direct care of a specific patient, 56.6 percent; attitudes and
interpersonal relations, 43.7 percent; management/leadership,
33.6 percent; use of equipment or procedures, 18.9 percent;
communications, 13.1 percent; personnel functions, 12.5 percent; and medications, 11.4 percent. For these nurses, the need
to solve specific patient care problems was important as was the
necessity of practical and theoretical knowledge and the capacity to relate to fellow professionals and clients. Many of the
goals of professionalization suggested in Chapter Three were

evident in these accounts. The anecdotes illuminate the realities behind the general list of problems. A single episode suggests both the stress and the varied nature of the problems that many professionals confront (Price, 1967, pp. 40–41):

> One evening I was working as charge nurse on pediatrics and was also leader on a team whose patients included three critical children. Of two children who had IVs running, one went to surgery for correction of a bowel obstruction during the evening. The other baby had had surgery to correct several birth defects, but was not expected to live through the night. The entire evening was hectic because I felt I should be everywhere at once. I was unable to delegate much of the work because of my lack of experience. Besides, much of the work required an RN. When one baby returned from surgery, the doctor needed assistance setting up suction, and the equipment available did not work. As we were working on this an LPN informed me that she was unable to hear the heartbeat of the dying baby. The baby's father was standing there crying, and I was unable to offer any consolation. The doctor was impatient because his patient needed the suction, and I was frustrated because I could not handle the situation.

A second effort to discover the causes of educational participation (Berg, 1973) drew inferences by comparing the personal traits of those who participate with those who do not. Berg studied 102 staff nurses in general nonprofit hospitals in New York City. The 45 nurses who had participated in an off-duty course, conference, workshop, or institute during the preceding year were designated as Participants; the 57 who had not done so were designated as Nonparticipants. Berg found a few factors that differentiated these two groups: The Participants were less likely to be married, less likely to concentrate on surgical practice, and more likely to be encouraged to study by friends and relatives than were the Nonparticipants. But the chief differentiating factor associated with current participation was that the habit of learning had become deeply ingrained in the Participants. They had long been engaged in education and they were accustomed to reading, to using libraries and museums, and to belonging to associations.

A third approach to finding the cause of participation was an effort to link it to the value system of the individuals concerned. Bevis (1975) studied 106 nurses who had had only one year of experience after being admitted to practice. Using complex measures of participation, she scored each subject in terms of the degree of activity during that year. She then used another instrument to determine the extent to which each nurse valued the nursing profession ("the professional component"), the particular hospital ("the bureaucratic component"), and care of the patient ("the service component"). She found that those nurses who had the highest loyalty to the service component were the ones most likely to participate in continuing education, but that the other two components could act as reinforcements. If conflict between the bureaucratic and the service components existed, however, it had a negative effect on participation in continuing education. Thus it appears that the oldest and perhaps the deepest motive for becoming a nurse (care of patients) is more strongly associated with the desire to learn than are the other two components.

The studies summarized here and the many others that resemble them provide valuable insights into the realities of specialized sectors of continuing professional education. It is not yet possible to assemble this large body of knowledge into any coherent or comprehensive synthesis. Most investigations are descriptive, not analytical; few of them test hypotheses or permit comparisons. The scope of each study is restricted to one profession or a cluster of professions, and the data collected are local in place, specific in time, and restricted in range. Moreover, the identified goals of continuing education are usually limited to the acquisition of knowledge or skill in subject matter related to the profession. The studies have seldom considered the far broader range of goals required if education by all three modes is to have its proper effect on the whole process of professionalization. Also, because broadly descriptive studies of continuing professional learning are rare, anybody who wishes to know more about the nature and extent of participation in learning activities must often use data secured from other populations, bearing in mind that members of a profession are distinguished from other people by length of formal education, acculturation, and income, and that these differences are likely to be significant.

Content, Motivation, and Barriers to Learning

The most comprehensive recent national study of participation in continuing education was conducted in 1972 under the auspices of the Educational Testing Service. A brief report of the findings has been published (Carp, Peterson, and Roelfs, 1974) and a fuller treatment by the same authors is also available in manuscript. ETS has been kind enough to make special tabulations available to me so that the responses of the professionals involved could be analyzed and their behavior compared with that of the total sample studied. The following account is drawn from these published and unpublished data.

The investigation was based on a sample of the approximately 104 million persons between the ages of eighteen and sixty who were living in private households in the continental United States and who were not full-time students in the middle of 1972, when the data were collected. The people in this sample completed a lengthy interview schedule in which they were first asked, "Is there anything in particular that you'd like to know more about, or would like to learn how to do better?" Of the respondents, the 77 percent who answered "yes" (here called the Would-Be Learners) were asked a number of probing questions. All of the respondents were then asked, "Within the past twelve months, have you received (or are you receiving) instruction in any of the following subjects or skills? Please include evening classes, extension courses, correspondence courses, on-the-job training, private lessons, independent study, TV courses or anything else like that." This question was followed by a list of subject matter areas of concentration. The 31 percent who checked one or more of these areas (here called the Learners) were then asked a number of questions concerning their participation.

All respondents were classified in various ways, one of which was occupation; therefore it is possible to provide data on those who were identified by the investigators as being either professional workers or administrators in large businesses, the two groups forming one cluster. For the sake of convenience, this group will here be called "professionals." None of the tabulations of data dealt with learning that was undertaken only because of employment; therefore this study deals not with continuing professional education so much as it does with the continuing education of people who happen to be professionals. This distinction is an important one, although many kinds of educational activities are undertaken for professional advancement which do not appear on the surface to be directly related to it.

The authors of the study note that the closely related characteristics of education and occupation substantially differentiate Learners from Would-Be Learners as well as from people in the general population. Adults in America who engage in learning activities tend to be people who are already relatively well educated: nearly twice as many of the Learners (42 percent) have had some postsecondary education as have all respondents (24 percent); and while 33 percent of the total sample had never been graduated from secondary school, only 17 percent of the Learners had not. Similarly, with respect to occupation, Learners are underrepresented among the unskilled occupations and particularly well represented among professionals.

Table 1 indicates the various areas of content studied by the Learners and most eagerly desired by the Would-Be Learners. Because of important differences in the methodology of questioning and treatment of answers, the responses from these two groups are not directly comparable, but it is interesting in each case to see the comparisons between professionals and all respondents. Among the Learners, the professionals were significantly more involved in vocational and general education and significantly less involved in hobbies/recreation than was true of the total group of respondents. Aside from these three categories, the differences between the two groups of Learners is not great, though it may be noted that the total group of respondents participated to a somewhat greater extent in home and family learning and in religious activities than did the profes-

Table 1. Percentage of professionals and of all respondents
among Learners and Would-Be Learners who studied courses classified
in various areas of content

| | Learners[a] | | Would-Be Learners[b] | |
	Professionals	All Respondents	Professionals	All Respondents
Vocational	45	35	32	43
General	33	25	16	13
Hobbies/recreation	33	42	22	13
Home and family	9	13	9	12
Personal development	10	11	12	7
Public affairs	7	6	6	5
Agriculture	2	3	2	3
Religion	11	14	1	3
Other; no reponse	5	7	1	2

[a] All courses studied were included.
[b] Only the area that the Would-Be Learner was most likely to choose was included.

sionals. Among the Would-Be Learners, the professionals are more eager to learn about hobbies/recreation and personal development and less eager to learn about vocational advancement and home and family improvement than are the total group of respondents.

Table 2 provides a comparison of the reasons for learning or wanting to learn given by professionals and by the total group of respondents. It must again be noted that methodological differences in data collection prevent exact comparisons between Learners and Would-Be Learners. Some of the striking parallels between the two sets of figures may be accidental or may indicate that the same result would occur no matter what method was used. Both Learners and Would-Be Learners were asked to check all the reasons that applied to their actual or desired participation in education, so that totals for the columns exceed 100 percent in every case.

Among Learners, the professionals were less interested in getting a new job and more interested in advancing on their present job than were the total group of respondents, a finding that seems consistent with the fact that professionals are more established in their careers than are people in other vocations. There are many other differences between the professionals and

Table 2. Percentage of professionals and of all respondents citing various reasons for learning or wanting to learn

	Learners[a]		Would-Be Learners[b]	
	Professionals	All Respondents	Professionals	All Respondents
Become better informed, personal enjoyment, enrichment	61	55	64	56
Curiosity, learn for the sake of learning	33	32	43	35
Help get a new job	10	18	13	25
Help to advance in present job	35	25	13	17
Work toward certification or licensing	16	14	14	27
Work toward a degree	14	9	16	21
Better understand community problems	4	9	12	17
Become a more effective citizen	6	11	21	26
Work toward solution of community problems	5	9	11	16
Better able to serve my church	6	10	8	12
Improve my spiritual well-being	9	13	15	19
Meet new people	12	18	15	19
Feel a sense of belonging	4	9	11	20
Get away from the routine of daily living	11	19	18	19
Get away from personal problems	2	7	6	11
Meet requirements for getting into an educational program	3	4	5	13

Meet the requirements of my employer, profession, or someone in authority	32	27	11	24
Be a better parent, husband, or wife	12	19	17	30
Become a happier person	20	26	28	37
Learn more about my own background and culture	2	8	13	14
Other or no response	4	5	21	18
Total	301	347	375	476

[a] Only the activity in which the most time had been spent was included.
[b] Only the "very important" reasons were included.

all respondents in the Learner group; none seem to be strikingly significant, but the general pattern, judging by the totals, is of a somewhat narrower range of interests among the professionals than among the total group of respondents. It is not possible to interpret this finding with the data available. Some people might argue that professionalism is inherently narrowing, despite the fact that those who belong to this group have had much more education and possess greater economic and social resources than do other occupational groups in the population. Others might argue that the relative narrowness of range reflects the scarcity of available time for learning among the members of the professional group or of the advanced kinds of learning opportunities they would find profitable.

Among the Would-Be Learners, the pattern of motivations is roughly similar to that of the Learners, the chief differences being that the professionals show relatively less interest than do all respondents in seeking a new job, in working on certification and licensing, in meeting external requirements, or in being better family members. Other variations may or may not be significant. The much greater breadth of interest of all respondents than of professionals should be noted here as well. In interpreting this difference, it may be worth noting that while the Learners have given tangible evidence of their desire to learn by actually participating, the Would-Be Learners, far larger in number than the other group, may only be expressing a superficial desire. This may account for the relatively large percentages in Table 2. It is tempting to accept a positive motive even though the subject does not really intend to act on it. The relatively narrow range of the professionals may suggest either more realistic expectations or more focused interests than is true of all respondents.

A topic of interest is why content and motivation were treated separately in the analyses of the ETS data, given the frequent assumption that the goals of adult learners can be determined by knowing the subject matter of the activity in which they are engaged. In the literature of education, there is much discussion of liberal versus vocational studies and of personal benefit desires versus those for social gain, the source of the evidence cited usually being enrollments in courses that are inferred to have these benefits as their desired outcomes. In the past quarter century, however, there has been growing doubt of the validity of this inference. The assumption that the motives of learners can be determined by the nature of the content they study was tested by McGrath (1938) in a large-scale investigation in 1936 and found to be true to only a limited extent, a conclusion that has been confirmed in subsequent inquiries. A broad comparison of content and motives has never been made for continuing professional education. In the ETS study, however, it was possible to make cross-comparisons for all respondents in the Would-Be Learners category. As Tables 1 and 2 have shown, both content and motive are distributed among professionals in a pattern somewhat congruent with that of all respondents; therefore it seems likely that cross-comparisons for the latter group would bear substantial similarity to similar comparisons for the former group, at least in terms of general principles of interrelationship.

In Table 3, the subject matter category most keenly desired by the Would-Be Learners is analyzed in terms of all the reasons considered very important by those who chose it. The most significant fact about this table is the wide spread of motives. In every content field except agriculture, every motive proved to be important to some of the people who chose it as their major learning priority. Some of these choices appear to be directly related to content. For example, those persons eager to learn a vocational subject say that they want to do so in order to get a new job or advance in a present one, to meet the requirements of a program or an employer, or to secure a certificate, license, or degree. Upon reflection, other motives are readily understandable. Vocational study can be expected to bring economic advancement, thus enabling the individual to be a better parent, escape routine and personal problems, and perhaps to serve the church, be a better citizen, and, in general, become happier. Meeting new people also has obvious advantages in some occupations. With some motives, however—such as understanding the community, establishing a background of culture, and achieving spiritual well-being—the linkage to voca-

Table 3. Motives for desiring to take courses, by types of subject matter desired (expressed in percentages)

Reason Considered Very Important	First Choice Learning Interest in Field							
	Vocational	Hobbies/ Recreation	Religion	General Education	Home/ Family	Personal Development	Public Affairs	Agriculture
New job	37.8	13.4	9.9	21.5	12.2	14.8	11.1	32.0
Job advancement	25.6	7.5	5.2	15.7	8.0	12.8	10.4	15.0
Information, enjoyment	51.6	70.2	66.7	64.8	49.5	54.1	64.4	47.0
Meet new people	17.2	26.6	22.7	16.5	16.1	14.4	26.6	17.1
Requirements for educational program	16.9	7.8	8.0	24.0	8.9	5.5	6.5	0.0
Better parent	26.9	23.9	60.3	26.0	53.3	28.0	32.9	3.9
Escape routine	15.4	39.3	9.4	18.0	15.9	14.9	13.7	31.0
Certificate, license	41.9	20.2	6.7	19.7	11.3	18.0	14.6	12.2
Understand community	15.0	10.6	30.0	15.2	14.0	17.9	59.9	12.2
Serve church	10.1	12.2	68.4	14.4	12.9	4.3	11.3	4.6
Requirements of employer	38.8	9.0	13.1	17.3	8.4	12.2	20.3	23.6
Effective citizen	26.0	15.0	41.5	28.0	21.6	25.0	59.0	21.7
Degree	31.3	9.7	4.1	17.8	11.3	18.0	10.3	14.4
Background of culture	10.2	18.6	24.8	19.2	13.2	14.8	18.0	5.6
Sense of belonging	19.9	16.7	28.5	23.5	17.9	8.5	31.0	13.5
Curiosity	30.0	45.2	7.1	40.1	40.0	33.0	44.3	36.5
Become happier	34.6	38.6	46.3	35.1	43.3	30.4	41.5	54.9
Solve problems	14.2	11.9	31.9	18.1	14.4	14.0	40.0	25.5

Escape personal problems	9.8	18.5	17.0	6.9	12.6	9.5	9.3	17.3
Spiritual well-being	14.3	23.9	80.2	21.4	22.1	13.2	12.1	22.7
Other reason	3.4	8.8	5.6	2.5	3.0	2.9	1.2	00.0
No important reason	13.9	13.7	3.2	12.5	17.9	23.4	11.3	9.0

Source: Special tabulation made for the author by the Educational Testing Service.
Note: The columns should be read down because the independent variable is content and the dependent variable is motive.

Table 4. Types of subject matter desired by persons with very important reasons for wanting to learn (expressed in percentages)

Reason Considered Very Important	Vocation	Hobbies/Recreation	Religion	General Education	Home/Family	Personal Development	Public Affairs	Agriculture	Other	No First Choice
				First Choice Learning Interest in Field						
New job	63.9	7.1	1.2	10.6	5.8	4.0	2.0	3.6	0.9	1.0
Job advancement	64.8	5.9	0.9	11.5	5.7	5.1	2.8	2.5	0.8	0.4
Information, enjoyment	39.3	16.7	3.5	14.4	10.5	6.5	5.2	2.4	1.2	0.3
Meet new people	40.0	19.3	3.6	11.2	10.4	5.3	6.5	2.6	0.8	0.4
Required for educational programs	54.0	7.8	1.8	22.4	7.8	2.8	2.2	0.0	0.0	1.3
Better parent	38.6	10.7	6.0	10.8	21.4	6.3	5.0	0.4	0.5	0.4
Escape routine	34.3	27.4	1.5	11.6	9.9	5.1	3.2	4.6	1.4	0.9
Certificate, license	65.7	9.9	0.7	9.0	5.0	4.5	2.4	1.3	1.0	0.7
Understand community	38.2	8.4	5.3	11.3	9.9	7.2	16.1	2.0	0.0	1.7
Serve church	35.2	13.2	16.9	14.7	12.5	2.3	4.1	1.1	0.0	0.5
Requirement of employer	69.2	5.0	1.6	9.0	4.2	3.5	3.8	2.8	0.4	0.5
Effective citizen	43.0	7.7	4.7	13.5	10.0	6.5	10.3	2.4	1.0	0.9
Degree	64.4	6.2	0.6	10.7	6.5	5.9	2.2	2.0	0.7	0.8
Background of culture	32.0	18.2	5.4	17.6	11.6	7.3	6.0	1.2	0.3	0.5
Sense of belonging	43.7	11.4	4.3	15.1	11.0	3.0	7.2	2.0	1.6	0.9
Curiosity	36.8	17.3	0.6	14.9	13.7	6.4	5.7	2.9	1.0	1.0
Become happier	39.9	13.9	3.7	11.8	13.9	5.5	5.0	4.2	1.2	0.9
Solve problems	37.3	9.7	5.8	13.8	10.5	5.8	11.0	4.5	1.1	0.6

Escape personal problem	37.3	21.8	4.5	7.6	13.4	5.7	3.7	4.4	1.2	0.6
Spiritual well-being	31.8	16.6	12.3	13.9	13.7	4.6	3.0	3.4	0.5	0.3
Other reason	39.4	31.8	4.5	8.6	3.2	5.3	1.4	0.8	6.0	0.0
No important reason	41.4	12.7	0.6	10.8	15.0	11.0	3.5	1.8	1.4	1.8

Source: Special tabulation made for the author by the Educational Testing Service.

Note: The rows should be read horizontally because the independent variable is motive and the dependent variable is content.

tional content is hard to establish. Here the respondent is apparently fulfilling other needs for learning than those which the content suggests. It is possible, for example, that some individuals choose vocational content because they believe it to be acceptable to family and friends, but such a connection is only conjectural. In each of the other types of subject matter, some motives are immediately obvious, others can be found by inquiry to have linkages, and still others remain hard to explain.

Table 4 reverses the direction of the analysis and shows what type of subject matter was the first choice of those who had a very important reason for studying it. As was shown in Table 1, vocational subject matter was chosen by 43 percent of all Would-Be Learners; therefore, it is natural that this field would dominate the ratings. No matter what reason is considered very important, from one third to two thirds of those who so identified it chose some vocational activity as their first-choice learning interest in the field. Once again, as in Table 3, some of the relationships are immediately clear, some can be interpreted rather easily, and some appear to be inexplicable. It is hard to see, for example, why those for whom spiritual well-being is very important should give vocational training as their first-choice learning interest.

The data presented in Tables 1 through 4 suggest that the pattern of learning activity undertaken by professionals (as by other adults) is probably far more complex than is sometimes thought by people who limit education to the straightforward teaching of content drawn from a knowledge base in order to achieve a single purpose. The list of fourteen characteristics identified in Chapter Three has not been tested in any comprehensive study to see whether it would conform to the educational goals that actively motivate professionals to learn. Any effort to force the list of reasons used in the ETS study (which, it must be remembered, was concerned with all adult learners—not merely professionals) into the list of goals of continuing professional education in Chapter Three would be tortured and ultimately frustrating. Nonetheless it is interesting to note that some items on the latter list—such as the effort to understand basic and applied knowledge, to escape boredom and routine, to seek formal credentials, to establish individuality as a person, to cultivate new intellectual interests, to work effectively as a citizen advocate, to discover the nature of ethical practice, and to collaborate effectively with other people—can be roughly paralleled in the lists of content and of reasons given for educational participation in the four tables just presented.

In the ETS study, Would-Be Learners were asked to indicate on a suggested list all of the reasons that kept them from studying what they very much wanted to learn. A tabulation of the responses for professionals and for all respondents is presented in Table 5. Here the differences between the two groups are striking and wholly consistent with the way of life of professionals, who are more highly paid, more mobile, more confident of their abilities, and better established in the community than are the people in the total sample. In contrast to the latter group, professionals care less about cost, feel more heavily pressed for time, have fewer problems of child care, transportation, or red tape, and are more confident of their ability to learn. However, they have less time available, have difficulty in finding courses (particularly those scheduled at times that suit their convenience), have heavier job responsibilities, and are more tired of formal instruction.

The term *Would-Be Learners*, while technically correct, does imply that all such persons are likely to be future participants in some form of adult education. This conclusion is almost certainly not valid; as Grotelueschen and Caulley (1977a) have shown, a number of personal and environmental factors must be brought into proper conjunction before a general desire to learn leads to specific action.

There is some evidence to show that adult Americans are less satisfied with the quality of their intellectual development than with any other aspect of their lives. For example, in March 1960, Project TALENT tested 400,000 secondary school students who made up a valid stratified sample of all students in grades 9 through 12 in the United States in that year. Fifteen years later, in a study reported by Flanagan and Russ-Eft (1976), a sample of 1,000 subjects representative of the earlier group were interviewed in depth about fifteen components of

Table 5. Percentage of professionals and of all respondents
who indicate various barriers to learning

	Professionals	All Respondents
Cost, including tuition and other expenses	31	53
Not enough time	65	46
Amount of time required to complete program	25	21
No way to get credit for a degree	3	5
Strict attendance requirements	8	15
Don't know what to learn or why	3	5
No place to study or practice	5	7
No child care	5	11
Courses aren't scheduled when desired	25	16
Don't want to go to school full time	29	35
No information about possible learning resources	18	16
No transportation	1	8
Too much red tape in getting enrolled	5	10
Hesitate to seem too ambitious	1	3
Friends or family don't like the idea	0	3
Home responsibilities	28	32
Job responsibilities	38	28
Not enough energy and stamina	10	9
Afraid that I'm too old to begin	6	17
Earlier low grades, not confident of ability	1	13
Don't meet requirements to begin program	1	21
Courses I want don't seem to be available	15	12
Don't enjoy studying	4	9
Tired of school, tired of classrooms	10	6
Other	6	5

the quality of their lives. They were asked not only how important each component was to them but also how satisfied they were with their present status in each respect. On "physical and mental health," for example, 98.2 percent thought it important or very important and 86.3 percent were satisfied or very satisfied with their status. One component was defined as "*Develop and use your mind* through learning, attending school, improving your understanding, or acquiring additional knowledge." Of the respondents, 83.9 percent thought this component to be important or very important, but only 54.2 percent were satisfied or very satisfied with their status. The disparity between value and present activity was far greater for this component than for any other. These data relate to the total thirty-year-old population, not merely to its members who work in professionalizing vocations; however, it is fair to assume that a substantial dissatisfaction does exist as far as the more specific group is concerned, and it may well be the most significant aspect of their discontent with the quality of their lives.

The Range of Total Participation

Some of the studies previously summarized in this chapter have been concerned with participation in a single activity or form of continuing education. This approach is adequate in helping to chart a target audience for a specific program at a given time, but it cannot provide the basis for an understanding of the extent of total participation. If a local society of veterinarians sponsors a series of lectures for its members, the analysis of who came and who did not is useful for deciding whether to have an additional series the following year and, if so, for mapping strategies to involve the nonattenders while encouraging the return of the people who came the first year. But members of the society have probably also been learning by other means, and all the analysis of attendance at the series determines is who found that specific activity to be both desirable and feasible. Nothing is known of the total participation in education of the veterinarians concerned.

Comprehensive involvement in learning of the members of professions is therefore becoming the focus of much current research. Chapter Four described some of the ways in which every professional develops a distinctive pattern of self-directed education influenced both by personal characteristics and by the special circumstances of the environment, including the stimuli provided by people and institutions who seek to advance continued learning. As character and circumstances change, so does this pattern. One dentist, for example, may read certain journals, consult specific reference works, go to the meetings both of the local dental society and of an informal special interest round table, and attend state and national conventions every year. This learning routine is so faithfully followed that it is truly continuous. In addition, he or she may, from time to time, attend a series of lectures, go to a workshop at a university, or take a study sabbatical. Such learning is intermittent but sufficiently regular to become part of an established way of life. Ten years later, some of these activities may have been dropped and others added. Another dentist may have a different pattern of reading, participation in group activities, and attendance at meetings, and the nature and extent of such activities will also change with passing time. A third dentist may engage only sporadically in learning; if any constellation of activities exists, it can be detected only in retrospect.

Since the early 1960s, interest in the measurement of participation in adult education has centered on the effort to discover the total learning patterns of individuals and to cluster them in meaningful ways. Researchers conducting these investigations usually identify, sometimes with the aid of qualified experts or actual participants, all the learning activities in which a person might engage during work time, leisure time, or both. The members of the sample studied may then be asked to indicate how extensively they take part in each activity. Alternatively the inquiry may be masked by asking people to indicate how they spend their time; in these cases, many activities are included as possibilities, but only items judged to be undertaken for educative reasons are scored. The sample population may include all kinds of people or be specific to a locality, a vocation, or a place of employment. The measurement of participation in an activity may be along a continuum, such as "frequently—seldom—never," or in terms of some scale. Instead of relying on judges to determine which activities are undertaken with educative intent, the investigator may ask the respondents to make that selection. These studies have been made of samples drawn from the general public, of participants in educational activities, and of the members of specific occupations, including professionalizing vocations.

All these studies show the same general distribution of participation. All respondents take part in some form of continuing education, even if only to a very limited extent. At one extreme, some people participate so variously and so extensively that it is hard to see how they get anything else done. The distribution curve of a sample shows some bunching near the lower end and an attenuation at the upper end, indicating that most people have a relatively low level of participation but that a few people are avid learners. Those investigators who have applied statistical tests, however, have found the distribution curve to be technically normal.

Most studies have dealt with samples of the general population, and the personal and social factors associated with extent of participation are too gross to be useful in explaining the differential participation of the members of professions. Among people in general, the extent of formal education is more closely associated with extent of formal learning activity than with any other factor, but this characteristic may have relatively less weight in a profession because all those who belong to it tend to have had about the same extent of formal study. Where differences in length of formal training do exist, they show a significant positive association with the extent of continuing education. As noted earlier, Berg (1973) found that past participation in continuing education is also a good indicator of present participation; the person most likely to be engaged in learning is one who has already taken part. People who are active in other aspects of professional advancement, such as committee membership or legislative persuasion, are also likely to have high learning participation. When the same instruments are given to the general public and to the members of a profession, the latter have a higher distribution of scores than the former, as might be expected from their superior education and financial resources. There is also a positive correlation between the extent of participation in leisure time and that in work time.

Orientations Toward and Away From Learning

The studies on motivation reported earlier in this chapter have been chiefly concerned with the reasons why individuals undertook specific activities; the ETS investigation is characteristic of this approach. But behind any relatively simple relationships may lie deeper configurations of value, as Bevis (1975) demonstrated when she showed that nurses with a dominant service component were more likely to engage in continuing education than those who held other role conceptions. Since the early 1960s, a number of investigators have tried to discover whether adults have basic orientations that generally lead to participation. These studies have been undertaken in a number of different places in several countries, but their results are basically similar.

Probably the most elaborate investigation yet published is that of Burgess (1971b), who collected data from 1,046 adults engaged in fifty-four different learning activities. Respondents were asked to indicate on a five-point scale how influential each of seventy reasons was in influencing their participation. (The list had been refined from an original collection of 5,773 reasons compiled by Burgess.) The responses were then examined by a complex process of factor analysis and were found to cluster into seven basic groups, known by Burgess as "orientations" (1971b, pp. 18–25):

1.   *The desire to know*: "a desire to gain knowledge for the sake of knowing: to grow in qualities and intellect and appreciation, to derive pleasure from learning, to enjoy mental exercises, and to remain in command of learning skills."

2. *The desire to reach a personal goal*: "the desire to gain knowledge in order to achieve a personal goal which the knowledge gained will make possible."

3. *The desire to reach a social goal*: "the desire . . . to learn certain knowledge or skills which will assist an individual to perform better the necessary functions as a contributing member of society."

4. *The desire to reach a religious goal*: "a desire to learn in order to meet felt obligations to a church, to some religious faith, or to some religious missionary effort."

5. *The desire to take part in social activity*: "the desire to take part in a social activity because the activity is enjoyed for its own sake regardless of what is intended to be taught at the activity."

6. *The desire to escape*: "the desire to escape from some other activity or situation which is unpleasant or tedious."

7. *The desire to comply with formal requirements*: "a desire which may be to earn credit required by an employer, to meet certain conditions required for membership by certain groups, and to meet requirements of a judge, of a social welfare worker, or of some other authority."

When these orientations had been identified, Burgess calculated the orientation of each of his 1,046 respondents. He found that 325 of them had a single dominant orientation (to know, 66; personal goal, 54; social goal, 54; religious goal, 42; social activity, 38; escape, 33; and formal requirements, 38), that another 592 had two or more dominant orientations, and that the orientations of only 129 could not be classified (Burgess, 1971a, p. 134).

The concept of adult learning orientations has not yet been widely used in the literature of continuing professional education, though some studies have moved into this line of thought. One such is that of Sovie (1972), who studied 237 staff nurses and identified eight orientations: learning; personal goal; occupational goal; professional goal; societal goal; need fulfillment; personal sociability, and professional sociability.

The studies of learning orientation have not been refined with adequate precision to build them into an overall theory of motivation or personality. At present, they must be accepted only as lists of observable and testable categories. It is safe to say, however, that some people have highly distinctive orientations toward learning, often so profoundly held that they cannot conceive of any other position. For example, in modern society, and certainly within the professions, many people believe so strongly that learning should be designed only to help accomplish personal or social goals that any other orientation seems unacceptable. Yet if Burgess's figures are to be accepted, the great majority of participants do have other orientations than the seeking of personal or social goals. The question of whether this latter observation is true as far as professionals are concerned remains unanswered. Some people suggest that because professionals are presumably among the most highly educated, resourceful, and broadly knowledgeable people in modern society, they should have a more diversified pattern of orientations than other people. The opposite conclusion is also argued, particularly by the enemies of professionalism: Highly specialized education of long duration makes those who undertake it far more narrow in their outlook than other people, and professionals are therefore more likely to have personal-goal or social-goal orientations than other people. I know of no study that demonstrates which of these hypotheses is correct.

Generalized reasons for not taking part in learning have also been studied in the United States and elsewhere, though none are restricted solely to professionals. One general investigation is that of Dao (1975). From a study of the literature and other sources, she compiled a list of 554 reasons for nonparticipation in continuing education activities. These were reduced by various analytical methods to 88. By the statistical technique of latent partition analysis applied to the scores given by twenty-four expert judges, she found that nine clusters of reasons emerged. The five most significant reasons in each cluster were then included in a longer list which was administered to 278 employees of 17 profit-making organizations. A projective technique was used, each respondent being asked, "How often do you believe each reason influences people not to participate in educational activities?" Answers were indicated on a seven-point scale. Dao assumed that the responses would indicate the reasons actually felt by the respondent, although he or she was ostensibly reporting on other people.

The nine clusters of reasons for nonparticipation in learning developed by Dao were:

1. Not enough time to participate in educational activities.
2. Individual and personal problems make it too difficult to participate. (This cluster includes all the obstacles caused by poor transportation, costs, ill health, problems of safety, and other factors.)
3. Too difficult to succeed in educational activities. (This cluster includes the fear that the instruction itself may be too demanding, that there will be insufficient time to devote to study, that ageing has caused abilities to decline, that a new group or new way of life will be too challenging, or that public failure will be harmful.)
4. Against the social norms to participate in educational activities. (This cluster includes general social disapproval as well as the fear of being ridiculed by peers, colleagues, or family members.)
5. Negative feelings toward the institution offering instruction.
6. Negative prior experiences in educational activities.
7. Results of educational activities not valued. (This cluster includes both the doubt that the learning will prove worthwhile and the conviction that experience, not education, is the best teacher.)
8. Indifference to educational activities.
9. Unawareness of educational activities available.

In Dao's sample of the general population, she found that clusters 1 and 9 were the most influential reasons given for nonparticipation. Cluster 7 was next in significance, followed by clusters 2, 3, 5, 6, and 8. These latter five were not differentiable in level and had only a moderate degree of influence. Clus-

ter 4 did not show any influential impact. The scores on all of
the clusters can be totaled to show a generalized measure of the
resistance to participation in learning experiences. The general
summary scores had a broad range and followed a normal distribution curve.

Dao's study, like those that preceded it, establishes the
fact that people do not necessarily reject specific learning activities only for simple or transitory reasons. Failure to participate
may be caused by a deeply ingrained attitude or group of attitudes that effectively prevents positive action. Even cluster 9,
unawareness of educational activities available, while perhaps
less frequently found among professionals than among people
generally, can be the consequence of a long and deeply held
"blindness" to the opportunities available. The task of securing
participation in a particular activity may involve not only widespread promotion but also the exploration of deep-seated resistance among the target audiences and the discovery of ways to
minimize it. To the extent that these negative orientations exist
in a profession, they will systematically impede its capacity to
provide a wholly satisfactory program of continuing education.

The Spread of Innovations

Studies of the zest for learning, or the lack of it, have
been essentially concerned with the mode of instruction; most
investigators have assumed that educational participation is associated with the effort to acquire mastery or competence. But,
as has already been pointed out, a different way to consider
education is in terms of the mode of performance, in which the
key evaluative question is; "What changes are brought about in
the practice of a professional that result, in part at least, from
education?" The phrase "in part at least" must always be used
in this connection, because substantial changes in professional
performance may result from many causes other than formal
educational participation. One way in which investigators have
measured change in performance is by charting the amount and
rate of adoption of innovations by practitioners. The study of
adoption has proceeded rapidly in many fields of practical in-

quiry and the analysis of this topic throws substantial light on the practice of continuing professional education.

In 1971, Rogers and Shoemaker synthesized the results of about 1,500 investigations that had been conducted with different groups throughout the world. An *innovation*, as the authors define it, "is an idea, practice, or object perceived as new by an individual. It matters little, so far as human behavior is concerned, whether or not an idea is 'objectively' new as measured by the lapse of time since its first use or discovery. It is the perceived or subjective newness of the idea for the individual that determines his reaction to it. If the idea seems new to the individual, it is an innovation" (Rogers and Shoemaker, 1971, p. 19). A study of the adoption of an innovation usually has several common elements. The investigator (1) defines the innovation in exact terms (a necessity that sometimes causes studies to be more concerned with concrete practices than with abstract conceptions), (2) identifies the population to be studied (such as foresters in state and national forests or optometrists practicing in New York State), (3) measures when the innovation was adopted by this population or by a valid sample of it; and (4) examines special factors associated with the rate of adoption.

It is common knowledge that some people put new practices into effect more rapidly than do other people. In their study of innovativeness in many cultures, Rogers and Shoemaker demonstrate that in terms of the speed of adoption of an innovation, people are distributed along a normal distribution curve. By laying off standard deviations from the average time of adoption, five categories have been identified. At the upper limit are the *innovators*, who make up about 2.5 percent of the distribution and whose chief characteristic is venturesomeness. Below them on the curve are: the *early adopters*, 13.5 percent (respectable); the *early majority*, 34 percent (deliberate); the *late majority*, 34 percent (skeptical); and the *laggards*, 16 percent (traditional). Investigators have used other divisions, have estimated them to be larger or smaller than just indicated, and have described them in different ways, but the formulation by Rogers and Shoemaker is the most broadly based summary of such studies. (The percentage estimates are for all the samples they analyzed. In the professions, the number of people in the various categories might well be substantially different from those just cited.)

Linkage between rate of adoption and participation in continuing education is also supported. Peterson and others (1956) found a positive correlation between a physician's skill in using new techniques and his interest in seeking new knowledge as evidenced by his subscription to professional journals. Averill (1964) studied 397 farm operators in three Kansas counties. Each had been identified as being generally an innovator, a leading adopter, a majority adopter, or a laggard based on the judgment of a panel of competent observers in each county. Educational participation was measured in nine activities: reading specialized farm magazines, reading general farm magazines, reading general magazines, amount of book reading, recency of book reading, currency of book reading, class and correspondence study experience, conference and institute attendance, and discussion group participation. Pronounced differences among the four adopter groups were found in the measures of participation in these activities. A general predisposition to adopt new practices was positively and highly significantly related to participation in the nine methods of learning, even when age, formal schooling, and socioeconomic status were controlled.

The direct linkage between continuing education and performance established by these two studies is reinforced by the positive correlations found by Rogers and Shoemaker between rate of adoption and each of the following factors: favorable attitude toward education; favorable attitude toward science; contact with people whose function is to bring about change; exposure to mass media; openness to interpersonal channels of communication; general social participation; cosmopolitanism as contrasted to localism; number of years of formal education; intelligence; and specialization of practice. All these factors are themselves learning activities, have been demonstrated by other studies to be positively associated with them, or logically would appear to have such an association.

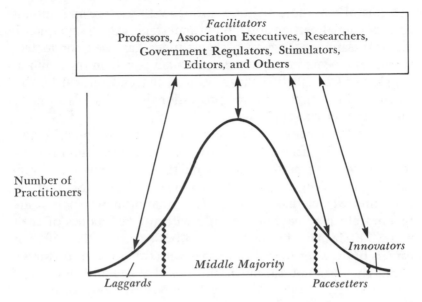

Figure 3. Classification of the members of a profession
according to extent of adoption of innovations

Five Groups of Professionals

The data presented throughout this chapter suggest that the members of a profession may be differentiated in the fashion indicated in Figure 3, regardless of whether the profession is considered as a whole or in some geographic area such as a state or a city. Active practitioners (regardless of their entrepreneurial, collective, hierarchical, or adjunct work settings) can be divided into four general groups that cannot be sharply distinguished from one another—as indicated by the jagged lines between them. A fifth group has withdrawn wholly or partially from active practice in order to fulfill various roles that advance and reinforce the profession; this group was designated in Chapter Four as "facilitators." The tendency of the individuals in this category to move in and out of practice is suggested by the double-pointed arrows.

The five groups will be described first in terms of their dominant attitudes toward their professional practice and then in terms of how those attitudes influence the nature and amount of educational participation they undertake. Almost no quantitative research bearing on such attitudes has been conducted, so the comments made here must remain largely in the realm of conjecture (though they have been tested and refined by discussion with many groups of professionals and by reactions to publication in several journals).

At the upper end of the continuum of active practitioners are the people, here called *innovators*, who continuously seek to improve their performance, sometimes in highly unconventional ways. They are attracted to ideas and practices that are still untested but that seem to offer great promise. Their desire to innovate may have to do only with the techniques of their work, but it may also lead them to push the frontiers of their careers outward or to make linkages with other realms of knowledge. They are not closely bound by the established ways of their profession and may actively oppose its institutions and their leaders, thereby often eliciting a counterrejection on the part of "the establishment." As Macchiavelli said, "There is nothing more difficult to undertake, more dangerous to conduct, or more uncertain in its success than the introduction of a new way of life. The innovator makes enemies of all those who did well under the old order, and he can expect only lukewarm support from those who may prosper under the new, partly because they fear the innovator's enemies, who have custom and law on their side, and partly because most men are incredulous, never really believing in new things unless they have tested them by long experience" (*The Prince*, chap. 6). It is not surprising that innovators seldom make up a large percentage of any population.

Innovators are likely to participate extensively in educational activities and to favor sophisticated learning pursuits. Innovators undertake investigations, have clear-cut plans of independent learning, seek and cherish part-time teaching positions, belong to groups which have restricted membership and which take pride in being more advanced in their practice than their colleagues, read highly specialized journals, attend invitational seminars, and leave their work occasionally to engage in full-time study. Innovators are so eager to seek the new that less arduous efforts to learn than their own may seem superficial or even meretricious to them. This special orientation often leads them to ignore or be contemptuous of formal programs of continuing learning. A significant number of innovators (particularly those who feel they are at or near their peak of occupational accomplishment) take delight in broadening their education beyond their basic professions in order to become expert in some other field of study.

The *pacesetters,* people who belong to the next group of active practitioners, feel the need to be progressive in their practice but are not eager to be the first to try a new idea. They wait until it has been fairly well tested before adopting it. This judgmental quality of their characters tends to win respect (which they value) and therefore to make them legitimizers of innovation for other people. Pacesetters look in two directions: toward the innovators and toward the majority adopters. They value opportunities to be exposed to new ideas and techniques, but they also maintain an attitude of conservatism toward avant-garde practices. Therefore, they seek to learn by the methods used by the innovators, though to a less whole-hearted degree. They are likely also to esteem membership in restricted societies, part-time faculty positions, and similar kinds of learning, though their aim may not be so much to gain knowledge as to prove to themselves and to others that they are part of the inner circle of the profession.

Yet the pacesetters are also concerned about the profession itself and feel a strong need to organize, conduct, or take part in its structures and functions. Thus pacesetters strongly support group learning endeavors and are leaders of such activities as meetings of professional societies, conventions, exhibits, short courses, lecture series, conferences, and efforts to learn within institutional settings such as schools, welfare agencies, hospitals, and libraries. The pacesetters are also the chief sponsors of the newer technologies of learning, such as films, closed-circuit color television, videotapes or videodisks, recordings or telephoned digests of research findings, self-scored examinations, computer-assisted instruction, or the use of simulated situations or case studies. Pacesetters often take part in these activities themselves, though they may do so with mixed motives; they want to learn, but they also want to lend to an activity the support of their presence as acknowledged leaders of the profession.

The *middle majority* make up the great body of those who practice the profession. Among them, in rapid or sluggish movement, innovations are gradually adopted. At the upper levels of this group, support for an innovation is often won because pacesetters have approved it. The people at the lower levels, who are often not in direct touch with the "leaders" of the profession, eventually adopt new practices because they have become so generally accepted that colleagues and clients would raise questions if older techniques were used.

The members of the middle majority, since their number is so large, have a broad spread of rates of adoption, ranging from those professionals who are just below the pacesetters to those who are just above the laggards, and include some people who will later move upward to one or slip downward to the other. The rate of educational participation varies in much the same fashion. As the level of participation by individuals declines, the number of reasons for resistance to learning increases as does the general distaste for or apathy toward learning. People below the mean may pay lip service to the idea of education but it is hard to win their attention to a specific learning activity and harder still to persuade them to participate in it.

The middle majority often set themselves apart from the innovators, who are—they are likely to think—too extreme in the advocacy of whatever is new and who are accused of living in a world removed from practical affairs. The feeling of rejection is reciprocated. Freymann (1964, p. 710) provided two examples of this separatism: "Among a vocal minority of practicing physicians can be found a thinly veiled antiintellectualism, preoccupation with medical economics, and resistance to change. In the academic community can be found islands of intellectual snobbery, startling ignorance of the quality of practice outside the university, and impatience with conservatism." Such a schism is not unique to medicine. This separation between the innovators on the one hand and a substantial number of middle majority adopters on the other hand highlights the importance of the pacesetters as intermediaries in any strategy of organized continuing education.

The final group of active professionals are the *laggards*, who learn only what they must know if they are to stay in practice. Their performance is so poor that they are a menace to their clients and a source of embarrassment to their colleagues. When young, they may have had their eyes fixed on the star of dedicated service to society; now they have fallen into the orbit of routine. They have arrived at this sad state along many roads: scarcity of competition, disillusionment with their profession, envy, apathy, unhappy personal life, alcoholism or other addictions, a fixation upon some single method, adequate private income, the tyranny of unbreakable habits of work, failure to perceive that the practice of their vocation has changed, low achievement motivation, failure to understand the need to keep on learning, belief that they can no longer learn, and many other reasons. Whatever the cause, they have built a house without windows, and now they live in the dark.

Laggards cause deep concern to their colleagues and to the policy makers of society. A profession has selected them, trained them, admitted them to practice, and must fight to protect their perquisites. If they are licensed, society has a formal stake in their ability. But laggards do not respond properly to their privileged position. Their ideas have hardened; their old skills deteriorate and they adopt few new ones, usually by a complex process of osmosis or by yielding to pressure. Their resistance to learning is high; they believe that it costs too much time and money, not realizing that ignorance is even more expensive. Their chief source of new information (and this is also true of the lower part of the middle majority) is salesmen of supplies, equipment, and services, who almost always surround their approach to a professional with some aura of education. In a comparison of pharmacists who did or did not participate in university-sponsored continuing education, Bernardi (1974) found that the two groups were strongly differentiated according to their sources of information. To a highly significant extent, the nonparticipants secured their information from sales and service representatives and from the descriptive brochures accompanying the materials purchased. Associates, supervisors, lecturers, authors, and others may try to help laggards solve their problems but the laggards can usually manage to find a difficulty for every solution.

Facilitators, the fifth group of professionals, may bear titles that reflect the profession they serve, but they share only part time or not at all in its central activity. A physician is judged by the progress of patients, an architect by the quality of buildings, and a social worker by the capacity to ameliorate personal and social ills. But the work of facilitators lies outside the mainstream of practice, though designed to uphold and strengthen it. They teach, do research, study, organize, administer, regulate, coordinate, and engage in other activities that advance the profession. They work in universities, associations, government offices, foundations, and other places. I will say more about facilitators here than about the other four groups, which are the foci of attention in most of the rest of the book.

The basically different functions of the practicing professional and the facilitator create an inherent and enduring tension. Kubie's significantly titled paper, "The Retreat from Patients" (1970), has developed one viewpoint of this difficulty in regard to psychiatry, but the issues explored may well be universal to all professions. It is argued by some people that facilitators who have not spent years in clinical practice simply cannot understand the profession or work effectively to assist and reinforce it. Even for a well-trained, experienced person, however, the dangers of being a facilitator are said to be great, because after a period of time, he or she is certain to lose the sense of uniqueness of the specific cases with which the professional must always deal. However, the facilitator must develop complicated special skills, such as research, teaching, editing, organizing, or administering. These tasks, which are necessary for the advancement of any profession, cannot be performed unless some people work at them full time, eschewing the laborious and time-consuming necessities required to deal with the cases confronted in practice. In fact these tasks may call for special kinds of competence for which the profession offers neither training nor experience.

The disparity between active professional practice and its facilitation is present in all the settings in which facilitators work and seems never to be resolved satisfactorily. Should the faculty of a professional school be full time, part time, or a combination of both? In an association, how should authority be divided between elected officers and employed staff? In a government office, can politically appointed senior officers control the tenured bureaucracy? Should a librarian who works within another profession be trained in that profession or in librarianship? The literature, discussion, and debate on these and allied matters are complex, voluminous, and long standing, being virtually as old as modern professionalism itself. No simple resolution of the problems has been found; rather, in every situation some accommodation to the realities of the moment must be reached.

Collectively, facilitators make up a group that is often high in prestige (however bureaucratic or pedestrian some of its members may be) because of its power to lead the profession and influence the individual advancement of its members. The group is also esteemed because many of its members are eminent and senior leaders of the profession. Some are stalwarts of conservatism, holding fast to the verities of the past. Some have been too long away from what Warner and Johnstone (1974, p. 18) have called "the real rough-and-tumble" of practice. Even those facilitators who serve as consultants do not get a sense of the current state of the field: "Consultants tend to be shown selected problems, and they do not have the responsibility of implementing their recommendations" (1974, p. 18). Other facilitators stand at the forefront of knowledge, deciding what research shall be fostered, conducting investigations, and disseminating their results by teaching, publication, and so forth. Because of their collective prestige, most facilitators conceive of themselves as innovators or pacesetters but, as Figure 3 suggests, they are actually drawn from all levels of practice, including the laggards. People no longer competent to practice a profession sometimes occupy safe berths in associations, government bureaus, foundations, and universities. If a facilitator wants to see a laggard, he often needs only to look in the mirror or glance into an adjoining office.

When a practicing professional becomes a facilitator, he or she enters the career sequence of educational needs suggested in Figure 2, learning how to prepare for change and then how to carry out new responsibilities. In their further maintenance education, facilitators tend to follow the habits of the basic group to which they belonged while in practice. If they had been innovators they are likely to remain innovators, though their attention may now be devoted less to the content of the profession itself than to the new frontiers of collective advancement in which they find themselves. The pacesetters and the members of the middle majority behave in their accustomed ways, and laggards can resist knowledge just as successfully on the staff of a journal, in the secretariat of an association or a government bureau, or as members of a university faculty as they could if they were in active practice.

Many facilitators are so wholly immersed in the mode of inquiry that they do not differentiate learning from the other activities of their lives. Paradoxically they may even deny that they are taking part in continuing education, a term they tend to restrict to the instruction mode. For example, many facilitators are on the faculty of professional schools. These men and women spend most of their time in research, reading, discussion, teaching, holding clinics, analyzing cases, and collectively trying to find out how to improve instruction. Periodically they take sabbatical leaves and sometimes they go on collective retreats. They perceive themselves as having a special way of life and sometimes do not realize that each of its elements would be regarded by other people as a way of learning. Other facilitators may be less devoted to inquiry than are faculty members, but each subgroup (such as editors, researchers, association or foundation executives, or government regulators) tends to have a pattern of life in which learning is more central or essential to its work than is usually the case with practicing professionals. To some degree, facilitators resemble Sir William Blackstone, author of the *Commentaries on the Laws of England*, of whom it was said, "It was not so much his learning that made the book as it was the book that made him learned" (Warden, 1938, p. 255).

Whether they perceive it or not, facilitators must bear the chief administrative burden of organized continuing education for the professions; in fact, their livelihood depends on it to a greater or lesser degree. Often they work directly with learners —teaching, giving lectures, writing papers, or editing. More frequently, they make the arrangements whereby other people, chiefly innovators and pacesetters, carry out major instructional responsibilities.

The collective mix of the facilitators in any specific situation has a great deal to do with the amount and kind of continuing education that a profession sponsors. If most of the facilitators, for example, are toward the right-hand side of the curve depicted in Figure 3, the program they produce will be characterized by vitality, novelty, and diversity. In this case, the members in the lower half of the distribution of the practitioners may criticize the program because it is too impractical or visionary or costs too much. If the mix of facilitators centers around the middle of the distribution—as it often does—the continuing educational activities provided will stay within a safe-and-sure pattern, following the routines dictated by custom. Meanwhile, the pacesetters will grace speakers' tables, and the innovators will go off on their own or form special groups that satisfy their hunger for learning. They withdraw from the main body of the career group and sometimes view it with disdain or scorn.

To suggest that these five categories exist is not to imply that individuals are locked forever into a single pattern of innovativeness or of study. Some people may welcome a new idea in one part of their lives and reject it in others; and the growth of responsibility turns many a young innovator into a middle-aged pacesetter, perhaps because all the innovations for which he or she fought have now been accomplished. However, the movement of individuals to different segments of the curve does not imply that the curve itself does not exist.

As mentioned in Chapter One, the dominant policy concerning continuing education in a number of professionalizing vocations is that more is better—more meetings, more courses, more lectures, more journals, more books, more everything. To implement this idea, one need only churn out a number of generalized programs for everyone who will come or use a variety of approaches, each one based on a special area of content or the need of a distinctive occupational group. But those who want to think about advancing a profession as a whole may first need to consider the distinctive educational requirements of each of the hypothesized categories.

Innovators need to find ways to explore the frontiers of the occupation, creating the new ideas and the tested knowledge that will eventually be diffused to other professionals through various channels. Pacesetters need to learn how to select the ideas that most need fostering and then how to exercise their special responsibilities for leadership to establish patterns of education that will bring about desired changes in performance. Whoever is responsible for a group of facilitators—the dean of a school, for example, or the administrator of a government bureau or a professional association—needs to recruit pacesetters and innovators and give them freedom to work and learn effectively.

The two chief concerns of organized continuing education today in all occupations are the same: how to speed up the learning of the majority adopters and how to reach the laggards. Debate ordinarily concerns whether it is better to use the stick or the carrot. The stick implies the threat of lawsuits or governmental regulation, compulsory continuing education, the fear of adverse publicity, the loss of the right to practice or of some valued perquisite, and the introduction of periodic relicensure. The general theory is that if minds are not cultivated, they should be plowed under. The carrot calls for the growth and enrichment of opportunities to learn until they are so pervasive and attractive that they become irresistible. Some greater use than at present of both approaches seems inevitable, though the mixture will vary from occupation to occupation and from time to time. The remainder of this book deals with the topic of how and by whom the carrot and the stick can be applied.

Chapter 6

Providers of
Continuing
Professional Education

*It is the business of the adult educator to bring system,
interest, plan, into the curriculum of life.*

Alvin Johnson

In this chapter and the two that follow, the focus is on organized programs designed to provide education for members of professions. These programs do not necessarily result in more learning than do the natural processes of practice or efforts to make such processes more educative. But most people who speak of continuing education have formal programs in mind, perhaps because they offer the greatest available opportunity for purposeful and ordered change within a profession or some segment of it. This chapter describes the frameworks in which they are developed and the institutions that sponsor them; Chapter Seven outlines the strategies that govern their design; and Chapter Eight suggests the methods by which their excellence can be estimated.

Institutions sponsor continuing education both directly and indirectly. In the former case, the institution has an immediate relationship with a learner or learners by providing lectures, workshops, journals, opportunities for discussion, or other of the myriad forms of educational assistance. In the latter case, the institution provides resources of some sort to enable a direct

165

provider to undertake or enhance its work. A single institution may carry out both functions. For example, a government bureau may furnish direct instruction to its own employees or to external groups of professionals, and it may also finance the work of other institutions that offer direct instructional services to special clienteles. The focus of attention in this book is upon direct provision, whether or not it is the sole function of the institutions described. This limitation is necessary because continuing professional education is now so widespread that, while central clusters of direct providers can be clearly discerned, the number of indirect providers appears almost limitless.

In most professions, basic education is usually offered by several different kinds of institutions. Even in a highly regulated occupation such as medicine, university-based, associational, independent, government-operated, and community-centered training programs exist. In law, the situation is even more complex than in medicine. In some of the newer professionalizing occupations—such as teaching, social work, and nursing—the variety of institutions that provide basic education and the programs they sponsor is so great as to defy enumerations or description.

The number of providers of continuing education is vastly greater than the providers of initial preparation for a profession. To seek to list for any profession the kinds of suppliers of instruction, much less the number of programs furnished by each kind, would be a virtually endless task. In this chapter, seven dominant forms of providers will be described: autonomous groups, professional associations, professional schools, the non-professional-school sectors of universities, places of employment, independent providers of learning opportunities, and purveyors of professional supplies and equipment. But these are merely rubrics, each of which contains a variety of specialized forms. In addition to the dominant seven, a number of other kinds of institutions—mentioned briefly in this chapter and elsewhere—provide continuing professional learning opportunities. In describing the seven kinds of basic providers, the distinctive strengths of each one will be identified. At the end of the chapter, the method by which professions mesh and evolve their designs of continuing education will be considered, as will the policies for financing them.

Autonomous Groups

The autonomous group is the most widely diffused major provider of continuing professional education and, for that reason, is the hardest to bring into focus. In this form of provision of training, a few members of a profession assemble periodically for fellowship, instruction, and discussion, the latter often serious and usually based on the common problems with which the group deals, each member slanting the focus wherever possible to his or her specific concerns. Autonomous groups have thousands of specific names. Some define a purpose, a process, or a profession—such as journal clubs, discussion circles, symposia, colloquia, seminars, teacher centers, physicians' round tables, or librarians' clubs. Others adopt completely irrelevant titles such as the Wednesday Society, the Jackson conference, or the No-Name Club; the purpose of the group is known only to the members, their intimates, and the other people who belong to the immediate subculture. Occasionally an autonomous group may own or maintain a clubhouse or suite of rooms, but usually such clubs meet in quarters that are borrowed or rented only for the times of their meetings.

Learning societies of this intimate sort have long been characteristic of many sectors of American life. The generalized pattern of development of a group seems to be for an individual leader or several like-minded persons, usually after some initial sounding of opinion, to propose a periodic schedule of meetings, invite other congenial and competent members to join, establish a working procedure, and then carry out the activity thus designed. The group may sustain its intellectual life by leadership from its own members or it may rely, at least occasionally, on speakers from outside. A successful group may be widely imitated or adapted in other locations, giving rise to what appears to be a spontaneous national movement. While many groups have only a short life, some last for generations or even centuries. Others die out for a while and are then revived. A few start as local autonomous groups but subsequently develop into multicelled organizations; the YMCA is an example of such growth.

The autonomous group based on a profession has not been deeply studied, but observation and frequency of reference indicates its pervasiveness. Guides and manuals describing how to create such groups are now appearing. At least five different but overlapping bases for organization can be readily observed. They are: employing institution, geographic area, subject specialty, distinctive personal attributes, and elitism.

The institutional base is found in collective and hierarchical work settings. For example, groups of lawyers in a large firm, doctors in a hospital, faculty members in a professional school, or principals in a city school system may maintain a club concerned with their immediate interests or, alternatively, one that helps them to enlarge their understanding of unfamiliar aspects of their profession. In either case, the group's activities are likely to be rooted in institutional policies and shared practices, as the members have all gone through the same selection process and work under similar conditions of employment.

A geographically based autonomous group is usually local, drawn from the practitioners in a community or a defined sector of a city. Occasionally, however, these clubs include members who work in a larger area, such as a state or a region. Geographically based groups are as likely to attract practitioners employed in entrepreneurial settings as in any other, particularly because many entrepreneurs use autonomous groups as opportunities to overcome the isolation of their lives.

The subject-specialty basis for an autonomous group occurs when some topic interests a number of professionals to such an extent that they want to collaborate on its investigation. This topic may be centered on a field of basic theory or technological advancement (such as nuclear physics or computers), on a field of application (such as space medicine or information retrieval systems), or on a special need (such as service to the economically deprived or therapy for the dying). Specialty-based autonomous groups are often short lived. They either disappear as soon as initial curiosities have been satisfied or they mature into full-scale professional associations, complete with their own structures and procedures.

As professions have broadened out in the twentieth century to include more heterogeneous kinds of people than before, clusterings based on the personal attributes of practitioners have multiplied. It is generally characteristic of professions today that they have subgroups of blacks and of women; in many cases, these are supplemented by other ethnic or special interest groups. While many entities are chiefly concerned with lobbying, pressure, militancy, and fraternalism, they often include such educative activities as the study of how best to achieve their collective goals, how to raise public and professional awareness of their existence and their contributions, and how to equip their members with competence that will help them equal or excel other practitioners.

Elitist autonomous groups are composed of self-chosen members of a profession who find a sense of congeniality in being in the forefront of practice. Many elitist groups start out in casual and informal ways, often being eclectic and inconstant in their rosters of membership. Several people discover a common interest in an innovation, develop a list of like-minded professionals, and circulate information to one another, perhaps never meeting formally as a group. These networks may appear to some people, both inside and outside their membership, to be primarily concerned with the use of influence and power, but the application of sanctions is usually thought by the members themselves to be wholly meritocratic, carried out in the name of advancement of knowledge, the establishment of standards, or the placement of people with enlightened understanding into positions of authority. Usually the formal collective endeavors of the group center on the education of its members. Influence is exercised, if at all, as an informal consequence of the relationships built up among the participating members.

Despite their casual beginnings, elitist autonomous groups sometimes become highly formalized into academies or societies with rigorous selection standards, frequent meetings, and subcommittees on special topics. The development and operation of elitist autonomous groups in theoretical fields, and particularly in the natural and behavioral sciences, has been extensively studied. In such cases they are often generically called "invisible colleges," a term used by Robert Boyle in England during the time of Cromwell, when scholars thought it dangerous to communicate with one another. Although little study of these entities in the professions has yet been produced, observation suggests that much of the professionalizing process may be guided by elitist groups, either directly or as a by-product, and that new groups constantly appear as that process continues.

Many autonomous groups seek to achieve new dimensions of knowledge, skill, and sensitiveness by the arduous study of topics not necessarily related to the occupation of the members. In some groups (often made up of people from several professions as well as of scholars, managers, and other highly educated individuals) each individual is challenged to demonstrate competence in some field of endeavor that may be far removed from occupational service. Throughout the country, for example, there exist independent literary and philosophical clubs, some of them more than a century old, whose members, chiefly professionals, read papers on abstruse topics to one another. These societies are supplemented by a vast number of other special interest groups with an almost infinite variety of interests but with learning, either narrowly or broadly conceived, as their central purpose. The self-enhancement characteristic of the professionalizing process, as described in Chapter Three, is often developed in such groups, particularly because the members of each profession who belong to them are often drawn together into a subcluster by special bonds of interest.

Autonomous groups can be powerful influences on the education of professionals in all work settings and at all levels of performance. Innovators may, in particular, be powerfully drawn to the idea of elitist activities, and pacesetters often like to be associated with them as well. A highly skilled practitioner of an advanced medical specialty once remarked to me that the twice-a-year meetings of a national selective association (limited to 300 members) to which he belonged were well worth attending despite their cost. "We keep about two years ahead of the other members of the profession," he said with pride. It was clear from observing him in action that even though many of his local colleagues thought him unorthodox, they covertly examined and appraised his techniques and subsequently adopted some of them.

Non-elitist groups also provide distinctive reinforcements to the learning process, strengthening institutional or geographic ties, building or extending awareness of subject specialties, and giving a sense of community and purpose to collections of individuals with common personal attributes. In the complex life of every profession, autonomous groups provide an important infrastructure, occasionally highly visible in individual instances but, on the whole, so closely related to everyday practice and often so transitory in nature that their collective importance is not recognized.

Associations

Associations are distinguished from autonomous groups in terms of size and complexity of structure. In a group, every member can have a sense of direct contact with every other member; the bonds of affiliation are frequently informal and often maintained by feelings of mutual commitment. An association usually has a complex structure, is so large that direct personal ties cannot bind the entire membership together, and has a well-defined and established position in the eyes of those who belong to it as well as to outsiders influenced by it. In the professions, associations vary greatly in number of members, in scope of purpose, in size and structure of staffs, and in the legal or quasi-legal rights bestowed on them by the government or assumed by their members. In the United States, each major profession is likely to have one or more comprehensive national associations, a complex array of general state, county, and local associations, and numerous specialized associations, each centered on a subspecialty or defined interest. Membership in an association may be restricted to those who have met rigorously defined requirements or may be open to anybody who wishes to participate and can pay for the privilege of doing so.

People belong to professional associations for many reasons. In some cases, membership is essential for the practice of a profession or establishes a basis for a fee schedule, but other reinforcing motives also exist. Among them are a need for status, a sense of commitment or calling, a desire to share in policy formation and implementation both within the profession and in the society in which it exists, a feeling of duty, a wish for fellowship and community, and a zest for education. An association meets these needs in many ways, including maintenance of a varied and graduated structure of responsibility through which members can develop their potential for leadership; sponsorship of conventions, conferences, workshops, and other gatherings; issuance of journals, books, newsletters, and other publications; support of legislative programs and other methods of influencing public policy; policing of its membership; and collaboration with external individuals, groups, and associations who have functions related to those of the profession.

In the charters and other basic documents of associations, "education" is often referred to in grand terms as being so pervasive a function that it permeates the entire range of purposes and processes just identified. In practice, however, the scope of what is called "the educational program" is often limited and may be hard to determine. In many cases it would probably be defined generically, though not always operationally, as having to do with the accreditation of professional schools or other training programs, the issuance of publications, the sponsorship of conventions and conferences, and the operation of special training programs, such as courses, conferences, workshops, and other activities clearly defined as instructional.

The organizational placement of these activities among the policy-making bodies of the association and within its administration usually reflects the conceptions of the function held by those in positions of power—conceptions that are often uncertain and variable. If an educational committee or division of the association exists, it may not include among its functions the sponsorship of publications or of conventions. These two programs are regarded as being so highly specialized as to require separate systems of control, particularly because they may produce a substantial percentage of the association's revenue, some of which may be required to cover nonlearning activities. If accreditation or licensure are professional association functions, they are also usually guided by special committees and staffs. The net effect is that, in many associations, the educational committee or division has responsibility for only a few specific activities, often characterized in terms of methods or processes, such as short courses, telelectures, or programs carried out by the mass media. The resulting divided authority often leads to ambiguity and imprecision.

If those who guide the affairs of an association wish to use it as a broad and comprehensive instrument of education for society and for increased professionalization of the vocation, several emphases and approaches seem to be particularly appropriate. One of these is to consider education as a major element in shaping the central policies and practices of the profession rather than merely giving lip service to that ideal in the charter or constitution of the association. In choosing the members of the decision-making groups and in the meetings and other activities those groups undertake, efforts must be made to broaden the knowledge and talents of actual or potential leaders so that they are less likely than before to act solely in terms of predetermined beliefs or as advocates of already-established points of view. To the extent that divergence of opinion requires discussion, the interaction of viewpoints can lead to an illumination that will be enhanced by the introduction of informed knowledge, concrete data, and opinions from outside sources. It often happens that the continuing enlightenment of established boards and committees is reinforced from time to time by the creation of special committees and commissions that examine the fundamentals of a problem or even of a whole profession or specialty group. Here the mode of inquiry is usually systematically undertaken and can eventually have profound consequences in the professionalization of the vocation.

Another appropriate initiative for a professional association is to implement its policy decisions by making them clear to all its members, to the outside publics with which it deals (such as the persons served, members of related professions, and legislative groups), and to other associations within the same profession. These policies may have to do with the work of the profession itself or with matters on which its members believe that the association's viewpoint should contribute to the shaping of public policy. To the extent that any such viewpoint is reasonable and based on data, it will appeal to thoughtful and objective people and, while it may not be labeled "educative," it will have the effect of adding to knowledge and enlarging understanding.

A professional association also has a special obligation to use the mode of instruction to enlighten and influence its members. It is for this reason that publications and conventions play so large a part in the provision of member services. Sometimes it is necessary to use widespread methods designed to reach everyone who belongs. In other cases, such as the American Library Association, the membership may be composed of a number of different specialty groups or of people with distinctive interests who congregate in specific sections or divisions. When this latter arrangement prevails, each subunit usually has some responsibility for guiding its own affairs, though the entire association must strike an appropriate balance in the attention given to the special interests of its membership.

Because of an association's breadth of service and continuity of coverage, its educational program has a special capacity to deliver discrete and not necessarily sequential messages. Journals and conventions are collections of separate and sometimes conflicting statements. In either of the two forms of dissemination, a common theme may serve as an integrating principle, but comprehensive unity is usually neither binding on authors and speakers nor completely worked out. Even when face-to-face educational methods—such as workshops or conferences —are held, they are often focused on special topics and of relatively brief duration.

Finally, professional associations often have a greater capacity to secure the assistance of a wide array of talent than do other major providers of education. In an association, all members meet together as formal equals. Positions of special authority, such as officers, committee chairmen, or other powerful posts, are temporarily held and subsequently relinquished, leaving a company of experienced senior members who have no more formal power than any of their colleagues. The recognition conferred by office or by medals and other testaments to outstanding accomplishment is highly prized and gives rise to efforts at excellence by many of the members. In its educational activities, therefore, an association is often able to secure the help of a more varied and experienced leadership than is available to other providers, who may be restricted to members of their own staffs and to people who hold specialized points of view or methods of approach.

Professional Schools

Professional schools collectively provide a massive offering of opportunities for continuing education, particularly in the instructional mode. There are many kinds and levels of such schools; some are free standing and others are parts of larger entities, most often universities. In a single profession, the patterns of training may be varied. Basic medical education may be offered by a curriculum in a university's biological sciences division, by a school that is part of a university's health professions complex, by a medical school with little relationship to training programs for the other health professions, or by an independent institution. Likewise, nurses are trained in hospital-based programs as well as in universities, colleges, community colleges, and special institutes or other organizations. In all this variety, however, two dominant frameworks of operations may be identified: the professional school that provides continuing education virtually autonomously and the school that operates such programs as parts of a larger network of service of a collaborative sort. These two frameworks (which actually are at the poles of a continuum of policy and practice) are not necessarily determined by the formal control of the program. A professional school situated in a university may operate as though it were independent of the rest of the institution, and a school that is formally separate, such as a theological seminary, may actually have strong affiliations with a university or with other organizations.

Autonomous operation. The great majority of professional schools that provide continuing education do so autonomously. The desire for a separatist approach appears to be in accordance with their natural habits of thought. During the years when leaders and supporters sought to establish these schools, the need for resources and recognition required single-minded intensity of purpose. By the time the schools had become accepted, so had the ways of thought that had been dominant in their early years. Faculty members have become so accustomed to a separatist approach to education, both on campus and off, that they have paid relatively little attention to the possibility of multiprogram or institution-wide collaboration even as far as baŝic professional training is concerned.

This viewpoint is maintained when continuing education is contemplated or undertaken. Professional school faculty members have in the past been generally apathetic or opposed to the provision of lifelong learning. The need to deal with full-time pre-service students, who are abundantly and often vociferously present and who have always been the center of concern of formal professional training, means that the desires and problems of adult student bodies (often unfamiliar, external, and dispersed) are not viewed as significant. The failure to provide continuing education can be more or less benign neglect, or it can be the result of a policy articulately championed on the ground that provision of continuing education would lead to frivolous dissipation of energy and create a diffusion of purposes that would detract from the school's other objectives. In a paper dealing with theological education, Rossman (1965, p. 229) summed up his thoughts by saying that the seminary should not only provide "a kind of monastery to which the parish clergy may come for periods of retreat and withdrawal from the world" but should also be the base "from which the theologians go forth for continuing study and involvement, with and for the clergy and the churches." In response, Clyde (1965, p. 232) argued that continuing education must be avoided in order that "the essential unity of the education of the ministry (that pearl without price!) might be preserved."

As a consequence of such differences of thought or of neglect, professional schools have been uneven in the extent and nature of their offering of continuing education. An abundance of self-congratulatory articles describing programs at individual schools exists, but provision of service is highly variable. A study by Chambers and Hamilton (1975b) of dental schools gloomily drew the conclusion that "these facts do not tend to strengthen the hope that dental schools will be able to meet the challenge to improve continuing education" (p. 237). Ripple (1974, p. 19), in contrast, reported that "almost all graduate schools of social work have continuing education programs, and in 1972, a total of sixty-three of them had fully planned programs with at least one full-time continuing education director or faculty member responsible on a year-round basis for development and administration of the program." And in 1974, the deans of medical schools agreed that one of the future changes most likely to occur in their institutions would be for continuing education to become a mission of equal importance to other medical center missions; 96 percent of the deans were in favor of this change (Keyes, Wilson, and Becker, 1975, p. 323).

The variability of the quality and quantity of continuing education services among schools in the same profession has often been caused by personality differences or the availability of special resources. A dean, a dominant faculty member, or a crucial committee can become convinced of the importance of educational service to active professionals and insist on the establishment of a strong program. An active, inventive, and influential director of continuing education can build a wide range of offerings, sometimes with only scanty resources; but many such programs flourish only as long as a dominant person or group retains influence. Some activities are financed by a governmental or philanthropic grant or other "soft" money; some of them last only as long as these special resources are available, while others manage to find continuing bases of support. But many social pressures are now beginning to reinforce continuing education. One is particularly significant as far as professional schools are concerned: When professional education was growing rapidly and institutions could exert a strong measure of selectivity, each could remain within its own bastion and concentrate upon a youth-centered program. These circumstances still exist for many professions, but others now find that they have difficulty attracting the number or the quality of students they would like to have. Underused faculty and facilities provide resources for continuing education, and the increased strength and visibility of a school that works actively with practitioners help it to recruit preservice students.

As time goes on, a new kind of competition will become evident as several institutions seek to serve the same relatively constant number of active practitioners. In most professions this competition is not yet evident because the need for education is great and the provision of learning opportunities is so relatively meager that wasteful duplications of service are not pronounced. As provision increases, however, problems of competition are likely to become progressively more severe. The conflict will be particularly acute when several schools of the same profession exist within the same city or state or, for other reasons, regard themselves as having the same service area. Limited coordination will occur either voluntarily or by the imposition of controls by some comprehensive authority, such as a state-wide chancellor of public higher education or a legislative committee. In the long run, however, the compelling determinant of success is likely to be excellence of programs and particularly the ingenuity with which needs of practitioners are defined and served. To some extent, also, the distinctive qualities of each professional school can be utilized in its continuing educational program, perhaps even enabling it to attract a national or regional audience.

One clear-cut mandate for a professional school is to assist the graduates of its own pre-service programs to continue their education. If a school has chosen students on the basis of probable learning potential, has carefully fostered the habit of independent study, and has devised a curriculum that assumes continued study, it would be strange to ignore the results of these efforts when graduates become active practitioners. If lifelong education is to be considered continuous, not sporadic, each school must remain in touch with its own alumni, offer services that take account of the special talents and needs of each person, help him or her to adjust effectively to a changing career line, transmit new knowledge and skills as they replace former beliefs and practices, and assist alumni to deal effectively with the problems encountered at each stage of the worklife. When the youth services of American higher education were rapidly expanding, efforts at continuing connection with alumni were seldom feasible; but as professional schools achieve a steady state or even experience a decline, they will find it easier to develop the concept of a lifelong student body that maintains a constantly changing interaction with a faculty. Computerized systems that compile cumulative records of services rendered to each student can greatly facilitate efforts to make this relationship more powerfully and continuously educative than it has been up to now.

Most of a professional school's continuing education should probably lie within the mode of instruction. Faculty members usually conduct, supervise, or are in other ways related to the studies that lead to the growth of the occupation's knowledge base. The pre-service curriculum in a well-qualified school is continually revised to eliminate obsolete ideas and introduce innovative ones. The attention of the faculty is therefore constantly called to information, methods, and conceptions that were not conveyed to earlier graduates but should now be learned by them. As new general concepts come to dominate the pre-service curriculum, they need to be interpreted to people already at work in the field. And, as may increasingly be the case, if a content area is eliminated from the pre-service program on the ground that it can be better learned after practical experience has made it meaningful, the faculty has a responsibility to make the subject matter available at the time it is needed. The autonomous school usually offers the content that is distinctive to the profession. Of the characteristics suggested in Chapter Three, conceptualizing, problem solving, and practical knowledge will probably be focused on by autonomous schools, although they also provide reinforcement for the collective identity goals.

In fulfilling these functions, professional schools have a greater opportunity than other major providers to offer lengthy, complex, or substantial kinds of learning experiences and to award certification of their successful completion. Colleges and universities have a long tradition of maintaining course sequences and of establishing accredited credentials. These institutions also ordinarily have more abundant and readily available physical facilities—housing and food, libraries, meeting rooms, laboratories, and other resources—than do other providers. Limitations on the use of both faculty and material resources are likely to be less stringent in the future than in the past because of the decline in the number of young pre-service students, and such changes should encourage substantial and intensive programs of continuing education.

Collaborative operation. At every university that has several professional schools, questions constantly arise as to the extent to which they should collaborate with one another and with nonprofessional departments of instruction in planning and conducting continuing education. On every campus, the specific issues depend upon the purpose and structure of the institution as it changes over time. On separate health sciences campuses, where the need for lifelong learning is particularly acute and generally well recognized, the essential commonality of the content and of the concern for patient care would seem to argue for collaboration of a fairly close sort. However, this inherent logic does not necessarily hold true in practice, and each professional school may remain as autonomous in providing continuing education as it would be in a comprehensive university.

The case for collaboration does not lie essentially in the fact that it would enable people from various professions to take the same courses, though in many respects interdisciplinary consideration of problems or content areas would add greatly to understanding of solutions or issues. The major gain to be achieved by collaboration lies rather in the fact, illustrated throughout this book, that most of the characteristics of professionalization are common to all occupations engaged in that process. To the extent that it is advanced by continuing education, a mutual interest and concern exists. If a committee on admissions in a school of nursing can find out how to discriminate between potential continuing learners and those who probably do not possess this trait, the general principles discovered may be relevant to all of the other professional schools on campus. The same is true of most of the other facets and activities of continuing professional education, though, as has already been noted, autonomous operation of programs is still the general rule among professional schools, particularly when each has a large measure of fiscal and administrative independence.

Universities

The separation of professional schools from one another is diminished by the determination of some universities to retain coherence and coordination among their common functions, including continuing education. This determination does not always exist; in 1977, for example, one major university had thirty-eight separate programs of continuing education, most of them situated in professional schools and each one shaping its own policies and devising its own practices. This case may be extreme. Most universities have general extension divisions with authority to operate institution-wide programs of educational services to adult learners and with control over the facilities and staffs required to provide these services. In some universities a substantial degree of centralization of authority has been achieved over all forms of continuing education, including those provided as part of the professionalization process. Despite all the difficulties that stand in the way of university-wide coordination, at least two strong arguments support its importance.

The first and more profound of these is that several of the major goals of the professionalization process cannot be achieved by a wholly autonomous approach. The practice of a profession is often inherently narrowing and, unless corrected by other influences, is likely to enclose the individual practitioner completely within the boundaries of the worklife, denying other aspects of his or her nature and constricting the focus of life to the immediately practical. The theoretical knowledge that underlies professional practice is ordinarily most advanced in the scholarly disciplines, and the practitioner will be denied direct access to essential understandings if study is restricted to what the professional school can convey. Nurses, for example, may need to study sociology, psychology, or pharmacology. Self-enhancement that helps a professional gain breadth and perspective must almost always lead to learning that is far afield from the work of the professional school. Several collective identity characteristics can be greatly aided by the use of disciplines outside the profession: instructional programs can profit from what has been learned from the formal study of education, the creation of a nurturing subculture can be enhanced by sociology, the legal reinforcement of a profession's standards can be aided by both law and political science, and the winning of public acceptance can be assisted by an awareness of the principles of communication and public relations. Professions can "cross-fertilize" one another by a common study of systematic continuing education, of credentialing, of the establishment of codes of ethical practice, and the development of rewards and penalties for practitioners. Even more directly, the members of some professions must constantly interact with one another in their practice, particularly in the fields of health, welfare, and education. One way to foster a harmonious relationship is by the use of collaborative forms of continuing education set within a university-wide framework.

The second reason an all-university approach is gradually seeming to be more and more sensible is that more efficient programs of service can thereby be provided. General extension divisions—serving either the whole institution or some significant segment, such as the health sciences—are building up staffs of competent programmers, often with advanced degrees in adult and continuing education. These divisions may have substantial physical resources, such as off-campus instructional units, residential centers for adults, television and radio stations or networks, telelecture systems, and programs of independent study using correspondence courses, modular lessons, audiovisual materials, and computer-assisted instruction. It is usually inefficient for a professional school to establish duplicative staffs and facilities chiefly on the ground that it alone should have entrée to its distinctive clientele. Increasingly, therefore, universities are appointing vice-presidents or other officials with responsibility for all continuing education. Coordination of programming is also sought through such devices as all-campus committees of assistant deans or other representatives of various professional curricula. The members of these groups can both learn from one another and help shape institutional policy.

An awareness of the values to be achieved by collaboration has led to a continuing conflict on many campuses between those faculty members and administrators who believe in autonomy and those who favor a coordinated institutional approach. In the 1970s, this conflict grew sharper, chiefly because of the growing relative significance of continuing education in the university's total program of service. By 1975, it had become clear to college and university administrators and faculty members that the declining attractiveness of higher education and the growing unemployment among highly trained persons was causing fewer and fewer young high school graduates to go to college and was influencing more and more of those who did enter to leave before completion of their courses of study. A substantial decline in traditional kinds of enrollment seemed inevitable in the 1980s, when the young people born in the high fertility years of 1946–1960 would have moved through the period of formal schooling and the rapid falling off of the fertility rate, which began in 1960, would create a much smaller pool than before of young people of traditional college age. During the steady growth in higher education of previous years, "formula budgeting," which related the amount of funds provided by legislatures or governing boards directly to the number of students served, had become commonplace in colleges and universities, particularly those under public control. While this policy is advantageous to growing institutions, it poses serious problems of financial adjustment to those that are declining. Continuing education of all sorts is one of the major ways in which the loss of students can be diminished and the surplus time of faculty members can be used. Therefore the desire of each separate part of a university to maintain or enhance its fiscal support came into ever sharper conflict with the desire to retain some sense of balance and unity in the entire institution.

The issues that arise from changing social trends must be debated and resolved specifically in terms of the constantly shifting structure and balance of power at individual institutions, no two of which are exactly alike. Continuing professional education is only one of the functions involved; most modern universities sponsor numerous nonprofessional extension services, many of which are now expanding. What universities confront, therefore, is a changing way of life in which a desire for institutionwide harmony must constantly be reconciled with the needs of special clienteles and with the relative degrees of initiative of various departments of instruction.

Future policy making may well follow a cyclical pattern. Let us consider a university with twenty-five continuing education programs, each one shaping its own policies and devising its own practices. The diversity and variety of service that flexibility allows may well be purchased at a cost of millions of dollars of duplicated services and a startlingly uneven level of competence of performance. In this case, it is likely that a budgetary or instructional leader will become aware of this cost or of the low level of some of the services provided and will move to bring the function under more centralized control. If this change does not occur from within, it may be imposed from without by the board of regents, the state board of higher education, or the legislature.

To assume that the resulting change in organization and procedure, however profound, will solve the problem is to ignore all past experience. Some units within the university will successfully resist change; they are too powerful to be forced to alter their practices. Other units within the reorganized framework will find ways to resist general policy and administrative control. New ventures will start up in unexpected places and find ways to remain independent. Often such new activities are created because innovative deans and faculty members believe that revenues produced by services rendered should go to the university unit that produced them. Meanwhile the consolidated unit may not have adequately strong leadership, sufficiently able staff members, or enough funds to offer services that meet university standards of excellence. If such conditions prevail, a drift toward decentralization begins, and it continues until a new demand for coordination becomes overpowering.

Employment Settings

The informal contacts and relationships that help to increase the knowledge and ability of professionals are usually found in the places where they work and in the social life in and around these places. The nature of this association and the ways in which it is deliberately made more educative have been described in Chapter Four. In addition, particularly when work is done in collaborative or hierarchical settings, formal provision is often made for education. Hospitals, schools, social agencies, and government departments (particularly the armed services) offer a vast array of opportunities of their own and also provide the stimulus and sometimes the resources for their staff members to take advantage of programs sponsored by other institutions.

The central educational task of employing institutions is to improve the quality of the services or products they provide to the people they serve. This goal may be interpreted broadly or narrowly. One employer may pay for almost any educational experience an employee desires on the grounds that each person knows best what he or she requires for personal growth and development. Another employer may support participation only in training activities that have a direct bearing on the immediate task the professional employee performs. At either extreme, the justification is the same. Education is secondary to service, a fact that is sometimes dramatically demonstrated when a new administration initiates policy changes or when lessened resources require financial stringency.

In the employment setting, the mode of performance can be most effectively used in designing programs of continuing education. An essential idea of professionalization is that a category of problems should be solved by the application of advanced bodies of knowledge; thus the adequacy with which that process is carried out must be the central concern of those employed in a workplace, and the need for education is made manifest and its goals shaped by the definition of specific inadequacies of personal or collective service. The program designed to improve performance is then shaped by the effort to meet the specific needs. For example, the cause of the problem in a specific setting may be defined as lack of technological skills, use of antiquated theories or methods, failure to establish effective internal relationships among a staff, or inability to reach a desired clientele. A learning program can be designed to deal with the identified need or needs, and the ultimate measure of its success will be the extent to which the inadequate performance that gave rise to the need for education is beneficially affected.

The mode of performance is appropriate to each of the three major kinds of professional work settings. A person in entrepreneurial practice can design and provide for himself or herself a program to advance greater personal expertise. In collective and small-scale institutional settings, the assessment of needs and the planning of ways in which they can be met are often handled informally, with the activity being initiated by a supervisor, a committee, or an individual professional. In large-scale organizations, particularly those which are hierarchic in form, careful and systematic career planning may be undertaken, usually coupled with systems of supervision. The typical military officer, for example, spends about one fourth of his whole career in some kind of training situation, and the design of his learning experience is unique because the competence required at advanced levels of command may grow increasingly specialized.

While the mode of performance may be the dominant method by which employing institutions provide education, whoever carries out these programs must also use the modes of instruction and inquiry. The former is needed when new knowledge, skill, or sensitiveness are to be conveyed, and the latter is required if decision-making processes are to have their full effect. Without the infusion of new ideas and ways of work through some form of organized instructional experiences and the involvement in planning of those who must carry out the plans, improvement is likely to be limited. For that matter, the offering of learning opportunities, no matter how skillfully conducted, may be insufficient to produce the desired results. Every institution develops an absorbing (sometimes all-encompassing) way of life for those associated with it; therefore, the improvement of performance is never easy unless an ethos that encourages or tolerates change is present or can be created. To achieve this atmosphere, it is sometimes necessary to establish new patterns or places of work, to reconstruct physical environments, to acquire new resources of materials and manpower, to change the overall composition of the staff, and to discharge or reassign those people who stand in the way of progress.

The instructional program sponsored by an institution for its own employed professionals is ordinarily conducted at the workplace itself. Sometimes staff retreats arc scheduled, clusters of professionals go away for educational programs, or study leave for individuals is granted; but the most common practice is to organize learning experiences at the employing institution. A hospital, for example, may introduce educational elements into its environment, such as specialty training programs, short courses, visiting lecturers, clinics, closed-circuit television broadcasts, a library and specialized book collections, group discussions, rooms to demonstrate new equipment, and support for such customary professional learning mechanisms as training clerkships, residencies, and courses for nurses. By sponsoring these programs, the hospital becomes an important educational center. Similarly, commercial and industrial establishments, particularly those which maintain substantial research and development units, may become substantial centers of instruction.

Education has also grown to be so important in a number of other work settings, particularly in government and industry, that investments have been made in separate training centers, some of which are fully equipped with residential accommodations, libraries, laboratories, and all of the other necessities of a university (except perhaps a football stadium). The use of these centers is usually not restricted to professional workers but includes a wide range of other staff members as well. To supplement these wholly owned facilities, employing agencies also make extensive use of hotels, motels, resorts, and residential centers operated by other educational institutions.

Independent Providers of Learning Opportunities

Independent providers are organized on a free-standing basis to provide specialized forms of continuing professional education. Some are operated for profit, some are formally defined as non-profit-making but may richly compensate their charter holders and officers, some are cooperative self-help ventures, and some are philanthropic foundations. Depending upon their specific nature and financial resources, they may charge for their services, offer them free, or subsidize the people who make use of them.

The most familiar independent suppliers are publishers, who have greatly aided the professionalizing processes of occupations. Textbooks introduce beginners to the knowledge base of their future work, and specialized manuals and reference works are available for consultation by practicing professionals. The need for publishers to compete with one another requires them to revise editions periodically, modernizing the content and often adding special aids to learning. Publishers also issue professional journals and have recently increased the distribution of many other communications materials as well, including microfilm, microfiche, programmed instruction, simulation games, and computer software.

Independent providers of education often sponsor direct instruction. Some of them, for example, offer intensive cram sessions to help professionals prepare for certifying examinations. Others offer standardized short courses, either centrally located or held sequentially in a number of locations, (reminiscent of circuit-riding preachers of early American life). Still other providers offer instruction in resort hotels, cruise ships, or foreign cities, supplementing teaching with recreation for the professional and his or her family. New learning techniques are often developed by such providers, and some proprietors express an evangelistic faith in the methods or materials they promote. In other cases, the "star system" is used to attract participation;

famous professionals are either proprietors of independent establishments or appear under the auspices of those who are.

Many institutions offer learning opportunities to individuals by providing free materials or instruction or by financing study grants. These agencies usually control financial resources that either have been left as bequests or are periodically provided by one or more donors. Some foundations are able to support numerous, varied, and generous programs of service; others are far more limited because of their lesser resources or creativeness. For the older, better established, and more remunerative professions, the aggregate educational offering of foundations is substantial. The opposite is true of the vocations that have not moved very far in the professionalization process and have not had time for their members to build up capital resources.

Some independent establishments that directly provide education promise more than they can perform, distribute shoddy materials and merchandise, pander to questionable motives, confuse means and ends, corrupt worthy motives, and create doubts about the value of continuing professional education. Many of these acts are cynically committed, often for profit, by people exploiting the desire to learn or the fear of governmental restrictions. Others result from excessive zeal, which makes so great a claim for a single approach to education that the part becomes a substitute for the whole and all balance and perspective is lost. (This has been the case, it is widely believed, with proponents of extreme forms of encounter group techniques.) Other weak programs are the result of simple incompetence; underequipped and overconfident individuals and groups try to maintain programs that are too elaborate for the resources available.

On balance, however, independent providers have made substantial contributions to continuing professional education, particularly as far as publishing is concerned. A solid base of printed material and other communications devices, continuously revised and expanded, supports many professionalizing occupations and constantly encourages all of them. Independent providers have often, in an enterprising spirit, pioneered in the identification of new goals, formats, and methods of instruction, thereby either establishing the foundations of their own success or making contributions that are later adopted by larger and better established providers of education. In addition, the careful fostering of outstanding talents has been encouraged by individualized instruction financed or provided by foundations and other similar agencies.

Most important, perhaps, has been the fact that independent providers have encouraged many leaders of professions to become familiar with what continuing education can do to help practitioners solve the problems they encounter in their work. Innovators and pacesetters may become so engrossed in the practice of their professions, in research and study, in administration, or in the leadership of associations that they have little insight into the way of life of their occupational colleagues. When these leaders are drawn, for profit or some other reason, onto the boards or staffs of philanthropic foundations or into the provision of instruction by a proprietary company, they may be required, sometimes despite their own initial wishes, to attend to the needs of the less accomplished members of the profession to which they belong. If these leaders are to write successful books and deliver successful lectures, they must learn to understand, communicate with, and influence the actions of their fellow professionals. For many people, continuing education ceases to be a dreary, remedial, and unrewarding effort and becomes a vital endeavor. As a consequence, a cadre of supporters for lifelong learning is created which often uses its influence to foster the provision of this kind of activity by other sponsors.

Purveyors of Professional Supplies and Equipment

Many professionals—including dentists, architects, pharmacists, and school administrators—must continually or periodically buy the supplies and equipment needed in their work. These professionals comprise the markets for the purveyors of these products, who approach their customers by personal calls, mail, advertising, maintaining exhibits at conventions, and in other ways. The purveyors may be representatives of the manufacturers of goods to be sold or staff members of separate sales organizations representing one or more manufacturers in a territory. Whatever their supporting framework may be, these salespeople are often equipped with elaborate brochures and warm personalities.

Purveyors have an important role to play in continuing education, particularly because they may be one of the few sources of outside information and training available to the relatively isolated and sometimes laggard professional, particularly one who is working as an entrepreneur. This kind of professional does not need to take initiative; it is the business of the purveyor to do that. While there is never any doubt that the major purpose of the purveyor is to sell, he or she can develop a relationship with a client, particularly one who is hungry for shop talk. Manufacturers, sales organizations, and brokers are responsive to the need for companionship. Many of them train their salespeople to use a "soft sell" approach. The heads of sales and distribution departments are prone to use such expressions as "giving greater attention to the needs and concerns of the library administrator," "providing the kinds of professional services that the osteopath has the right to expect of a supplier," "helping the dentist to deal with day-to-day problems," and "giving each customer served as much time as necessary to discuss all aspects of practice on a truly professional basis." While this approach may not yet be dominant, substantial efforts are being made to change the old image of high-pressure sales and to view the salesperson as a guide and consultant.

The influence of purveyors would logically appear to be greatest in aiding the adoption of a specific innovation, because most salespeople deal with only one product or class of products. In a study of physicians in four cities, Coleman, Katz, and Menzel (1966) found that 57 percent of their respondents had first heard of a new drug from the manufacturer's representative and an additional 18 percent had heard of it first from mailed promotional material. In contrast, only 7 percent named a professional journal as a primary source and another 7 percent named another physician. But this study showed that a "first mention" did not usually lead to adoption. About 90 percent of those who later prescribed the drug did so only after hearing about it from another source, and 62 percent needed confirmation from three or more sources. The precipitating causes of adoption were: a colleague, 28 percent; a professional journal, 21 percent; and a manufacturer's house organ, 21 percent.

In some cases, the purchase of equipment involves training in its use, either in the professional's office or in a special program maintained for the purpose. If the teaching is left to the salesperson, a simple show-and-tell procedure is usually provided, sometimes supplemented by drill and occasionally by use with actual clients. (In this latter respect, ethical questions may arise. Nobody would object to a salesperson using a new charge-out system for books with actual library patrons, but everybody would object to the seller of surgical equipment performing an operation on a patient unless that seller were himself a qualified surgeon.) If the equipment sold is complicated, special trainers may be required, carrying out their responsibilities either at the customer's office or at a special school established for the purpose. In the schools maintained by the manufacturers of advanced technological equipment, the educational and evaluative systems are sometimes very highly developed.

Purveyors of supplies and equipment are often important indirect providers of continuing education. Pharmaceutical manufacturers frequently provide grants to support lectures and conferences in the health sciences, particularly medicine. The possibility of conflict of interest in these cases arises, and codes of behavior for the recipients of these grants have been proposed.

Comprehensive Adequacy of Service

The quantity, nature, and quality of continuing education available to practitioners varies greatly in terms of geographic considerations, individual and institutional enterprise, and the extent of development of the profession itself. Because of the existence of multiple providers, however, a perennial double question is, "Who should do what and who should pay for it?" The answers are always local to each situation, are often compromises, and are in a constant state of flux. However, some general guides to action can be suggested.

The three modes of learning. To a very general extent, distinctions among providers of continuing professional education can be made on the basis of the three modes of learning. This is particularly true of the four most powerful and pervasive providers: professional associations, professional schools, comprehensive university programs, and controllers of employment settings. Associations usually become the ultimate arenas for the discussion, elaboration, debate, and determination of broad policy and hence have a special obligation to the mode of inquiry either for an entire profession or for that segment of it with which the association deals. The professional schools and comprehensive university programs have long been accustomed to the mode of instruction; it is, in fact, often their only form of educational service. In employment settings, the ultimate goal of teaching, whatever processes or structures are used, is improved performance. Thus each of the three modes provides a vital center, though never an all-encompassing arena, for the work of each of the primary providers. But this arena is sometimes so large that it overlaps at many places with those of other providers, and this fact often gives rise to jurisdictional problems.

Collaboration and competition. The profusion of offerings described in this chapter suggests the existence of a rapidly expanding educational market. In the past, when publications and conventions were the chief means by which practitioners continued their education, the task of instruction was essentially left to associations and to independent providers. Professional schools offered a few activities for alumni or gave courses taught by faculty members. Employers offered only those learning experiences that would directly aid their staff members and were primarily concerned with the kinds of knowledge required in a specific work setting. But that easy accommodation of function, although it still prevails in some places, is increasingly viewed as outmoded as it becomes apparent that the need for continuing education is so broad and pervasive that all providers have an important role to play.

A new provider will almost always find a pattern of services already in existence. It is a question of judgment, the wisdom of which will be tested pragmatically, whether the new program should directly compete in substance and form with those that have already succeeded or whether it should use an alternative conceptual approach or strategy of continuing education. The newcomer may find that its success depends not upon direct confrontation with established ideas and procedures but upon a novel and practical approach to offering assistance. In most places, a relatively free and rapidly expanding market exists, and those providers who cannot establish or maintain programs may be thinking too narrowly or too inexpertly about their task. Each of them is likely therefore to extend its own program unilaterally, serving such clienteles as it can attract and using available arts of public relations and special advantage to strengthen its service. If competition ensues, voices will immediately be heard proclaiming its virtues as being conducive to a higher quality of offering. The argument is, "Let the various providers do what seems best and the test of the marketplace will prevail."

In at least a few cases, competition has in fact become acute as various providers vie for the attention of professionals and perhaps for the funds that they can spend on their learning activities. For example, as noted earlier, within comprehensive university settings, competition often exists between a professional school and a general extension division or other continuing education office. Similar difficulties can appear among the other providers. This competition can lead to greater excellence, but it can also generate bitter struggles sometimes culminating in the decline, merger, or death of programs and institutions.

Although problems can arise with any of the modes of learning, the four major providers usually find themselves in the greatest danger of conflict in the mode of instruction, for several reasons. The mode of instruction is the most visible, widely understood, and highly structured of the methods of learning; its processes can be undertaken by any of the four providers, although not necessarily equally well; the mode of instruction is the usual basis for recredentialing; and the revenue derived from courses, journals, conferences, and other formalized learning episodes can be substantial.

In some cases, the various kinds of providers have worked out a coordinated pattern of offerings. For example, the Committee on Continuing Medical Education of the California Medical Association has followed this formula: "We do *not* undertake to be the purveyors of medical education; this is the task of the medical schools. But as they fulfill this task, we support them" (Petit, 1969, p. 1835). Many collaborative efforts in the continuing professional development of teachers have been identified by Davies and Aquino (1975). It is not difficult to find other similar blueprints or descriptions of patterns of collaboration.

But the potential demand for service is still so far from being met that in many professions formal continuing education is typically offered by providers who go their separate ways or who find it easy to collaborate with one another, sometimes by joint sponsorship of activities and sometimes by agreeing not to duplicate similar endeavors. The tendency toward coordination is accentuated by the fact that most providers have sufficiently distinctive missions so that the service responsibilities of each can be distinguished from those of others. Also, an overriding authority can mandate cooperation; for example, a university president or provost can insist that the professional school deans and the extension dean must work together. In many cases, too, the providers have a substantial overlapping of personnel. Faculty members of professional schools or extension divisions serve as officers of associations or consultants to employers. A network of influence within the profession reaches into all segments of its constituent organizations. If competition were to grow too aggressive or if one providing agency became too dominant, restraints would eventually be applied to preserve the dignity of the profession and avoid undue conflict or heavy-handed authoritarianism.

When the full range of possible goals and methods of continuing learning are considered, the dominant impression is still one of scarcity. It was said of Sir William Osler that, in the early days of modern medicine, "It is interesting to see how consistently he began anew at Oxford with precisely the same projects as those which had engaged him in Montreal, Philadelphia, and Baltimore. A consuming interest in libraries and librarians; the reunifying of an old medical society or the organization of new ones; the establishment of a medical journal, the bringing together of discordant elements in the profession, and the raising of money when money was needed" (Cushing, 1925, vol. 2,

p. 69). A similar pioneering enterprise is still necessary for most professions in most places at most times. Problems of coordination of specific services are sometimes encountered but for a long time to come the chief need will be for innovative and vigorous initiatives. No profession known to me has at any time or place succeeded in serving all the needs that might be met by continuing education.

Funding. No consistent policy of funding has been developed for continuing professional education, and the principles that determine the sources of revenue tend to be unique to individual situations. Some kinds of providers depend on specific forms of revenue; for example, members of autonomous groups almost always contribute their time and pay for any incidental expenses. Also, purveyors of equipment and supplies incorporate their expenses into the cost of what they sell—a price paid initially by the professionals served and ultimately by their clients. Associations depend on dues, advertisements, payment for special services rendered, and private or public grants. The question of cost and funding is a perennial, nagging problem in many cases but it appears surprisingly seldom in the general literature of continuing professional education. However, a few detailed studies have analyzed the costs of various kinds of continuing education. For example, one investigation of two-week university-based review courses for physicians itemized both direct costs (such as tuition fees, room, board, and travel expenses) and indirect costs (such as office overhead, loss of revenue, and payment to replace physicians). The average cost per participant in 1976 dollars was $5,353.49, ten times the registration fee and five times the direct costs (Faithe and others, 1979). Viewed in such terms as these, it becomes apparent that continuing professional education is a much more expensive individual and social expenditure than is often realized.

In discussions of the direct costs of funding, several alternative policies are usually proposed.

1. Professionals profit directly from their added knowledge; therefore learners themselves should pay the full cost of its acquisition. This policy guides the finances of all kinds of providers. Associations, professional schools, and comprehen-

sive university programs often establish continuing education as a separate budget item and require it to pay for itself. Independent providers usually make charges for their services and sometimes seek not only to regain costs but to make a profit.

2. The work of professionals benefits society; therefore the creation and maintenance of high standards of performance should be paid for by the public or by private sources established for the public good. This policy is generically applied to all skilled workers by income tax deductions, which pay part of the cost for the maintenance of competence. It is applied more specifically in the case of some professions—notably those in health and education—where a legislative or executive body determines which identified social needs must be met and uses public funds to pay for them. Also, foundations and other donors often make grants in terms of this same general policy.

3. The work of professionals is of benefit to those who employ them; therefore, their employers should pay for the cost of their continuing education, either by providing it directly or by making tuition reimbursements. This policy is used in both public and private sectors. It applies most fully in cases where the profession is wholly or largely restricted to one employer (as in the armed forces, the Catholic church, or a monopolistic industry) but it is used in many other situations as well.

4. Professionals profit generally from the advancement of their profession; therefore, they should collectively subsidize its educational activities. This policy governs education in all three modes and is almost universally recognized by the payment of membership fees to associations and of licensure or registration fees to appropriate bodies. Professionals also make great contributions of time and effort to the policy-making work of associations, to the deliberations of committees and commissions, and to the provision of instruction to colleagues.

In any given case, one of these financial policies may be dominant, but often they are combined. Accountants wishing to attend a conference may get travel grants from their firms, pay the costs of tuition fees themselves, and receive a tax deduction from the federal government on expenses for which they have not been reimbursed. The tuition fees from the conference may be lower than actual costs because a foundation has provided a partial subsidy and some staff members are contributing their services.

As was noted in Chapter Five, the second major obstacle to learning is usually expressed most simply and directly as "cost." Professionals feel this constraint to a lesser degree than do other people but it is still an important barrier. In fact, Sneed (1972, p. 226), basing his comments on the relatively highly paid professions of law and medicine, asserts that "Professionals do not participate more extensively in formal continuing education because they do not feel the benefits therefrom exceed the costs. These costs include opportunity costs, such as foregone earnings or leisure, as well as the direct costs of attendance. The benefits frequently are conjectural and only when they are immediate and palpable can attendance be assured. The key to increasing the demand for continuing education, therefore, is to reduce the costs and to increase the benefits."

Many of the strategies that aid a professional to find time for learning are also influential so far as the cost factor is concerned. For example, both the total man-hours and the dollars spent are far less when the lecturer travels to the audience than when the audience travels to the lecturer; therefore, the tuition fee can be lower in the former case. A number of strategies unrelated to the effective use of time can also be used to help defray the cost of learning to the learner: the designing of an activity so that it allows income tax deductions; the willingness of employers to pay tuition fees, travel, and other expenses; the sponsorship and financing of education by government agencies (such as those concerned with the armed services, health, welfare, or correction) as part of their basic missions; the granting of funds from government or private organizations to sponsors of activities or to the learners in them; the linking of financial rewards or promotions in rank to participation in education; the awareness of sponsors that continuing education is valuable for public relations and therefore should be provided as cheaply as possible; and the realization by a profession and its members that a demonstrated desire to avoid obsolescence is an excellent protection against militant consumerism expressed in legislation, appointments to licensing boards, malpractice suits, or other actions. However, all such aids serve only as easements. Ultimately a major part of the real cost of continuing education falls upon the individual practitioner; the acceptance of this obligation is part of the price which he or she must pay to secure the status, privileges, and exemptions that the occupation provides.

Chapter 7

Designing Programs of Learning

Policy is enunciated in rhetoric; it is realized in action.

Herbert Kaufman

Every sustained program of continuing education follows a pattern that is either predetermined or discernible in retrospect. A learner or an educator may design an activity in advance, usually recognizing that changing circumstances may later suggest modifications of the original plan. In other cases, the pattern emerges only at some end point when various learning episodes, each initiated for a specific purpose, are ultimately seen to have been linked together in a larger design. Each framework of action is unique to the person, group, or institution that undertakes it and to the situation in which it occurs. The examination of many patterns, however, reveals several general clusters. The purpose of this chapter is to identify and briefly describe the major methods and theories of learning strategy now being used by practitioners of the professions.

The present discussion of educational design cannot fully reflect either its wide scope or the depth of feeling with which it is usually treated. The presentation of methods and theories of learning makes up the bulk of the literature of continuing professional education, with many treatises on topics such as group process, simulation techniques, or systems theories. Most accounts are reportorial, some are pejorative, many are euphoric or evangelistic, and only a few are objectively evaluative. Moreover, because each profession tends in practice, though not

200

necessarily in theory, to hold itself apart from all others, each develops terms, abbreviations, or acronyms that become part of an esoteric code and often obscure similarities or differences. Insofar as is feasible, these special usages will be avoided here.

A general distinction is made between methods and theories of design. A method is taken to be a fairly simple and straightforward technique of learning or teaching such as reading, using a filmstrip, or participating in a class. (In the following pages, the terms *technique, process, procedure,* and *practice* will occasionally be used as synonyms for *method.*) Methods may be used alone or in combination; in the latter case, the pattern may become very complex. A theory of learning design, however, is ordinarily based on some conceptualization of the educative process itself or of the series of stages that should be followed in conducting it. For example, many theorists have based their practice on the transmission of subject matter; others have centered their attention on the needs established by the developing nature of the learner; and still others have focused on the learning demands imposed by adaptation to or advancement of the social milieu.

Traditional Methods

By the end of the 1940s, certain ways of conducting continuing professional education had been fairly well established. It was widely assumed at that time that they would meet any possible need that might arise. As it turned out, many new procedures have come into being, but traditional processes are still highly important. The dominant method of purposeful learning was, and still is, reading—of journals, monographs, books, manuals, and digests. A second method is the lecture or lecture discussion, which is offered at many different times and places by countless sponsors. A third method is the discussion group, usually locally sponsored and arising out of the need to keep up with the latest literature or to study difficult or unusual cases. A journal club, a meeting of a local society, or a "grand rounds" presentation and discussion are all examples of this way of learning. A fourth method is associated with the sales efforts of suppliers of goods and services, who use many means to instruct while they are seeking to persuade. This process involves first-hand contact with a salesperson and with the "literature" bountifully provided by the manufacturer.

These specific techniques are combined, often in complex and intricate ways, at conventions, which, because of the interaction of many stimuli, often have an impact greater than the separate effects of papers, business meetings, lectures, discussions, ceremonials, and exhibits. Conventions and other general assemblies also provide the major arenas in which the mode of inquiry is conducted. Committees meet, special interest groups press their distinctive points of view, policies are debated and decided, and leaders are chosen. The conceptual and the collective identity characteristics of professionalization (as identified in Chapter Two) are defined, debated, decided, and interpreted to the membership of the profession. Both instruction and inquiry modes are fostered, not only by all the processes mentioned above but also by the informal association that is a natural component of an intensive experience, which provides a continuing basis for the shop talk that shapes and reinforces opinions.

The traditional methods of continuing education are not necessarily static. For example, some professional journals have been transformed into strong educational instruments whose editors are concerned with readability, format, color, sequence of presentation of content, and the use of self-evaluative tests by their readers. Similarly many lectures, discussion groups, and sales presentations have taken on new forms and have become more appealing to modern tastes. Sometimes, however, the maintenance of tradition becomes, in effect, an objective. For example, the format of a journal may remain unchanged, except perhaps for its advertising pages. The formal program of a convention may be restricted to the reading aloud of papers in arbitrary order.

Whether the traditional methods have been adapted or remain in their original form, they have a power that in some circumstances still keeps them dominant. Haakenson (1972) has shown in a study of North Dakota pharmacists that personal lectures are less expensive and more effective (on a pretest-posttest cognitive-learning basis) than either correspondence study or audiovisual presentations. This finding serves as a warning that new methods should not be uncritically adopted merely because of their novelty or the enthusiasm of their proponents.

Technological Development

One of the chief ways in which traditional methods have been adapted or replaced has been through the application of new technological developments. The lecture delivered in person has been enhanced successively by the chalkboard, the slide, the flannel-board, the flip-chart, and the overhead projector as well as countless other devices. New systems of delivering lectures have been developed by the use of telephones, films, radio, television, audiotapes, and videotapes. At the same time, improved transportation has made it easy to take the lecturer to an audience or vice versa. Similarly reading has been greatly facilitated by xerography and other new and flexible ways of producing and using print.

While each technological development was first used to carry out a traditional mode, it tended eventually to give rise to new uses. In the field of entertainment, the cinema broke free from the conventions of the stage play; later on, television established its independence from cinema. So it has been in education. Television can offer an audience of millions to a lecturer, but inherently the medium has a variety and scope of presentation and application that allows it to be used in wholly novel ways. Much of the growth of continuing education has been brought about by the discovery of these new ways to use technological innovations.

Telephone. The telephone (and similar systems of long-range and usually interactive communication, such as citizen-band radio and "talk-back" television circuits) has been of much interest to educators engaged in continuing professional education. Among its uses are consultation with specialists, conference calls to discuss professional matters, and monitoring systems in which the practitioner is given step-by-step guidance in a complex technical procedure. In this use of telecommunications, learning is often a by-product of the diagnosis and treatment of clients, particularly those needing health care. As a straightforward educational device, however, the telephone has had at least two substantial applications.

The first is the telelecture, in which a speaker situated anywhere in the world can talk to an audience or audiences situated anywhere else, the chief limitations being the availability of suitable apparatus and the willingness of political systems to allow such communications. At the speaking end, the lecturer uses any convenient telephone. At the receiving end, special equipment is necessary so that the lecture can be sufficiently amplified to be heard by the audience and so that, at the end of the talk, questions can be addressed to the speaker by those who have listened to his or her presentation. A refinement of this method, pioneered by the dental profession, has been its extension to multiple audiences. In this case, a number of listening centers (at each of which an audience is assembled) can hear the same lecture and then (sometimes after a pause for discussion at the centers) can address questions to the speaker, the interchanges being heard throughout the system. The network can be established for a single event, but in several states a permanent system has been established, usually by a state university. The telelecture can have many useful adaptations. The talk itself can be put on audiotape or videotape, listening groups can be furnished with materials to supplement the lecture, and inquiry panels can help initiate and focus the discussion.

A second major informational use of the telephone is the preparation of a taped digest of current literature or opinion in a single profession. The tape may then be played continuously for a period of time on a designated telephone. A member of that profession, at his or her convenience, can dial the access number and acquire a modicum of knowledge along with references to other sources of data. Alternatively, a file of tapes on various topics may be stored at a center, available to any professional who requests that one of them be played.

Audiotape. Audiotapes have been widely used in at least four ways. First, periodical digests of new research and commentary are recorded onto tape cassettes and sent out to professionals who subscribe to the service and who play the tapes at their convenience. Second, addresses at conventions or specially prepared interviews with professional leaders are recorded. These may be purchased, borrowed from a materials center (such as a curriculum laboratory or a hospital library), or used by listening groups. Third, individual practitioners may make their own tapes. Now that recorders have been miniaturized and reduced in price and the time of tape cassettes lengthened, it is customary at professional gatherings to find members of an audience recording proceedings, which can be studied at leisure later on or shared with people who did not attend the meeting. Finally, audiotapes have been used in direct instruction, one example being the case in which the learner is able to compare his or her own pronunciation of a foreign language with that of an expert speaker. Special laboratory equipment and techniques based on this latter use of audiotapes have been devised for both individualized and collective study.

One advantage of purely auditory learning by telephone, audiotape, radio or any other mechanism is that it enables visually handicapped people to continue to learn. In addition, time that might otherwise be unproductive can be used—for example, when a professional plays a cassette while driving a car. The chief disadvantage of these learning processes, particularly when used by groups, is that listeners may find that despite their effort to concentrate, visual stimuli distract them from the educational message. To avoid this problem, designers of auditory learning programs often provide reinforcing visual materials to help focus attention.

Videotape. Videotape has all of the values of audiotape with the added stimulus of the integrated use of vision. This advantage has given rise to innovations that will gain in significance and usage as miniaturization and reduced cost cause television recorders and play-back mechanisms to be more flexibly used than is now the case. For example, the performance of a counselor can be recorded and subsequently made the subject of self-analysis as well as criticism by an instructor or by colleagues. Videotape makes it possible for people to see themselves as others see them, at least as far as external appearance is concerned, and thereby learn how to perfect their competence. For example, a brief course for teachers might take a learner through these steps: presentation by an instructor of the theory underlying the specific skills to be learned; viewing a film of a master teacher using them; videotaped recording of a classroom situation in which the learner tries to use them; study of the recording by the learner; joint analysis of the recording by the instructor and the learner; reteaching of the same material by the learner with a different group of students; and further self- and instructor-analysis (Borg and others, 1970).

Videotaped learning is not restricted to the acquisition of skills. For example, one elaborate study was designed to help physicians understand and perfect their analytical diagnostic skills. "The methods used involve the videotaping of physicians' work-ups using simulated patients, followed by a review of the videotape by the physician. The physician is encouraged to think aloud during the work-up about his reasoning processes. While reviewing the tape, he is again encouraged to comment on his reasoning during the workup" (Elstein, 1972, p. 91). The effect upon the physician may be profound. The investigators, who were primarily interested in research, discovered that the processes of diagnosis, as actually practiced, are far different from those generally taught in medical schools.

Videodisk. The videodisk is still in a primitive stage of development, prohibiting any informed estimation of its eventual effect. If it can be perfected and made inexpensive, its chief influence may well be similar to that of the prerecorded audiodisk. Individuals and institutions may make a collection of videodisks, each dealing with a discrete topic, which can be viewed and re-viewed in any chosen sequence as often as is desired. It will thus become a noninteractive instructional device for conveying knowledge, skills, and insights.

Limited outreach radio systems. These systems usually have only enough power to reach the boundaries of an institution such as a medical center or a university. The transmission of live talks or of audiotaped presentations can be carried throughout the place of employment, sometimes twenty-four hours a day, thus enabling those who must remain at their work stations to hear all or a part of the presentation and permitting the rebroadcasting of programs for those who could not listen the first time or would like to hear them again.

Closed-circuit television. This television mode, in which one-way transmission can be received only by specially adapted sets, can have the same kind of utility as limited outreach radio. The latter is still far more flexible than the former because of the miniaturization of the radio set. Television, however, particularly color television, has an impact that arises from the simultaneous capacity to listen and to view the stimuli presented. It is particularly useful in demonstrations of technique or in elaborate visual presentations. For example, a surgeon can show the steps of an operation, describing each one as it occurs, and the camera's eye can be far closer to the action than those of observers present in the room. The viewers can also be multiplied to almost any number, particularly if a videotape is made for subsequent use. Similarly an engineer or an architect can present a topic using models that can be closely observed by the viewers.

Cable television. With cable television, transmissions are carried to receiving sets by wire rather than through the atmosphere. This offers many advantages, chief of which is that, by the use of adaptors, a large number of channels becomes technologically accessible. Cable television enthusiasts see unlimited possibilities for its use and believe that the wiring of homes and other buildings for this purpose may eventually prove to be as significant as their earlier wiring for electricity and telephone service. A channel can be used by professions as a way of sending programs to the homes or workplaces of all their practitioners. Each program can be scheduled for a number of showings so that it can be seen at the convenience of more viewers. Videotape recorders can be used to tape broadcast programs and thereby build up a library for further study and review. Paullin (1971) has demonstrated in one investigation that participation was high among the general practitioners and internists who took part in a rather exacting course that included watching home-based television and taking both weekly and overall tests.

Courses lasted for either fourteen or twenty-eight weeks, and there was a significant positive correlation (at the .01 level) between extent of participation and cognitive learning gain.

Information-retrieval systems. Card catalogues and bibliographies are information-retrieval systems of long standing, but the computer has made possible the establishment of new networks of knowledge with access to a far larger body of source material than was ever the case previously. Local, regional, and national systems of information retrieval that permit the practitioner to find precisely the information needed have been successful in a few cases, such as the teaching and the health professions. Resources for a program of study can be readily found, as can the data needed to deal with specific problems. The use of these systems is likely to grow as their technology is perfected, as they grow less cumbersome, as their cost stabilizes, and as the capacity to use them effectively is more and more widely understood.

Many other forms of technological development have been created, some of which will be mentioned in subsequent pages. Computer-assisted instruction, for example, might have been mentioned here, but its deepest significance lies in the fact that it is a modularized approach to education, a method that can also use other technologies and that will be discussed later.

Basic Principles of Design

In addition to technological advances, another impetus to new endeavors in continuing professional education has been the interest of designers of learning experiences in working out new theories of design, each of which is founded on a single fundamental principle. The root idea of the design is often simple and familiar. Usually, however, the full achievement of the design requires not only sophisticated analysis but also intricate processes of change, sometimes made unusually difficult by the need to overcome dedicated opposition.

Constant self-monitoring of practice. Perhaps the most fruitful source of improvement in a profession occurs when its practitioners constantly monitor their own work, making judgments about success or failure and subsequently altering behavior as a consequence. While many outside influences can be brought to bear to stimulate changed skill, knowledge, and sensitiveness, it is ultimately true, as Osler said, that light comes "not from without us, only from within" (Osler, 1906, p. 109). This principle requires that the professional habitually think on two levels simultaneously. The primary requirement is to be absorbed in the task at hand, caring for successive particular cases and making any necessary arrangements for the care of others. For example, the social worker must concentrate upon a specific client, taking into account all distinctive needs while accommodating the service provided to the work of other professionals and to the use of relevant principles of social welfare. Yet it is necessary simultaneously to maintain a detached, cool, and appraising point of view, enabling the professional to observe the scene in which he or she is an actor. Experience is a hard teacher because it gives the test first, the lesson afterwards. Something can be learned, however, from every experience, and greater rewards will be gained if the learning is sought and does not come only as a by-product.

A good deal of the practical or clinical work of the preservice curriculum is devoted to the achievement of a self-monitoring capacity. Students are required to follow routines of practice until they are so thoroughly ingrained that they have become ineradicably habitual—or so their teachers hope. Case studies, field examples, and observed experiences are analyzed in depth, first by the professor and later by the student. The professor's running commentary shows that he or she is thinking at a different and deeper level than that apparent in the immediacies of the moment. In the conferences and informal conversations of the laboratory, office, school, or other field site, a discussion of cases, problems, successes, and failures keeps the budding professional constantly aware of the art with which advanced bodies of knowledge must constantly be applied in working with specific cases.

The practicing professional usually goes through stages in the practice of introspection. In the beginning, help may be supplied in the form of close supervision; the discussion of the details of each case by mentors and learners provides a model for the later processes of self-monitoring, when supervision is no longer provided. For example, a senior lawyer in a firm works with a junior lawyer, aiding in the process of refined analysis. The beginner who has no such help is usually so conscious of having to perform simultaneously (and often under stress) actions that have had to be learned over a long period of time that no time is left for the use of judgment or the refinement of technique. As time passes, constant repetition of the same activities leads to greater facility with immediate tasks and allows the possibility of constant self-monitoring. If this opportunity is seized, the self-analysis of error, the refinement of technique, and the solution of problems encountered in practice takes the individual as close to mastery of the profession as it is possible for him or her to get.

But the opportunity for introspection is sometimes not taken or is not followed through to fullest achievement. The succession of events can then lead to monotony and stereotyping. It is easy for the practitioner to fall into established routines, failing to note the subtle uniqueness of each case. To the extent that the capacity constantly to scrutinize practice is lost, so is the ability to learn; and it is not easily regained. It is widely believed that all that is required to correct this situation is to point out its dire consequences either to specific and presumably erring practitioners or to the profession at large. A number of professional leaders or lay observers have been content merely to criticize and to warn. Their criticisms have been rising steadily in volume and frequency, particularly since the middle 1960s. Their exhortations may have helped create a climate for change by preparing the way for the increased use of the instructional mode, for recertification and relicensure, and for structural changes in conditions of work that have increased the amount of supervision, the collegial review of performance, and the alteration of record-keeping systems so that they provide a clearer measure than before of the quality of performance. It is generally assumed by the sponsors of these actions that they will lead to self-monitoring by increasing the pressure upon the professional. But if this assumption were valid, one would expect the "scolding" (for that is what it has often become) to end. Instead it is increasing.

More positive ways of fostering the practice of effective self-monitoring lie somewhere near the heart of the methods to be described later in this chapter as well as the systems of evaluation and quality assessment that are analyzed in Chapters Eight and Nine. Better self-monitoring may be the ultimate result of admonition, but usually intervening steps must be taken to bring that result about. All forms of continuing professional education of whatever mode must ultimately be judged, at least in part, upon whether or not they encourage practitioners to have a steady concern for their own self-improvement.

Self-directed study. When an individual or a group identifies a learning goal and sets out to achieve it by independent study, using any resources available; self-directed study occurs. These endeavors may be brief or lengthy in duration, either by design or because the achievement of a goal takes longer than contemplated or leads on to the establishment of another, until, in some cases, a chain of related episodes has resulted. Probably every professional relies, at least occasionally and briefly, on self-directed study; some individuals virtually make it a way of life.

The general phenomenon of self-instruction has been most deeply studied by a group of Canadian scholars led by Tough (1971). Their investigations have been summarized, but further research is under way both by them and by other researchers. Most studies tend to stress the fact that introspective education is not only an alternate way of achieving learning goals when no other methods are available but also has unique values of its own—values that arise out of the intimacy with which the acquisition of knowledge must be interwoven with experience as well as with the necessary exercise of will. Dill, Crowston, and Elton (1965, p. 130) concluded, after studying the self-educational activities of seventy young managers, that their efforts produced some knowledge and skills "that cannot easily be taught"; further, self-directed study is "a source of self-confidence in facing a changing world."

The techniques of systematic self-education have not been taught to most professionals, probably because most professors believe that their students do not need such instruction.

Later on, busy professionals caught up in the pressures of practice may not know how to devise a workable plan for themselves and carry it through to completion. If their learning needs are not encompassed in some packaged plan, they must move into an area wholly unknown to themselves, and discover how to mark out a feasible pattern of work, identify and refine their goals, locate the proper learning materials, put them in the appropriate order, carry through or improve their original plan, and make some assessment of how much they have accomplished by such efforts. These tasks are not easy even in collective or institutional settings and become hard indeed for anyone engaged in entrepreneurial practice. In the arts of self-evaluation, most professionals are amateurs.

Mentorship. The student-mentor relationship has become the subject of deep theoretical analysis and, as a result, has given rise to many innovative programs in continuing professional education. The human constituents in this highly varied pattern are everywhere the same, however, and play out their parts in pre-service as well as continuing education. In this basic framework, a teacher, or occasionally a group of teachers, provides on an interactive basis instruction that is directly related to the specific needs of a person who seeks assistance. In a sense, all professional learning began with this form: a would-be lawyer "read law" in the office of a practitioner and a potential architect assisted one already established in practice. In the later years of the lifespan, the same pattern was used, though far less frequently and usually on an *ad hoc* basis: the established practitioner took time off to study in the office or clinic of an innovative specialist. In the early days of professional education, such teaching at either level was essentially a didactic and demonstrative exercise.

With the development of modern psychology, social psychology, and psychiatry, the dyadic relationship at the heart of mentorship was subjected to close analysis, with the result that learning patterns became greatly diversified. When a practicing professional is placed in the position of learning from another, the inner dynamics may take any one of a number of forms. The mentor may treat the learner as a colleague, teaching by nuance and serving as a sophisticated role model. The learner may be led by the mentor straightforwardly through a logical progression of tasks. The pattern may be one of total immersion, with the learner's full time and attention devoted to the task of learning, or alternatively it may be a part-time activity. The mentor may go through a psychoanalytic progression, moving from dependence to independence. The entire relationship may be one of challenge, the mentor putting the learner constantly on his or her mettle. The mentor may be willing to serve only as a resource person or as a guide to other resources, requiring the learner to take the full initiative for inquiry.

These patterns and countless variations can be found in continuing professional education. They most frequently exist in collective and hierarchical settings, in which instruction is related in some way to a collegial or supervisory relationship which, because it is intended to influence the pattern of later behavior, falls within the mode of performance. But the competitiveness of modern practice as well as the financial rewards (both directly and through tax incentives) of increased competence and additional credentials stimulate even entrepreneurs to take time from their practice to seek out mentors who can help them master needed skills.

Modularization. The modularization of instruction is an old principle that is finding countless new applications. The essential idea is to structure knowledge into meaningful and separable units and then to arrange them for instructional purposes according to some sequence of learning: from easy to hard; from early to late; from central to tangential; or from rudimentary to advanced. The division of the university curriculum into separate courses was an early example of this process, bringing about the same kind of profound changes as occurred in industry with the development of interchangeable parts. Later the development of the unit method of instruction in the schools carried modularization even further.

These early developments merely prepared the way, however, for the breaking up of knowledge into separate "bits" to be used in correspondence instruction, in programmed learning, and in computerized instruction. All three systems are adaptations of monitoring, but with stylized forms of interaction rather than direct contact. In correspondence instruction, every student must answer every question and therefore must be carried along through the entire compass of the subject matter. In programmed learning (presented by teaching machines, programmed books, or other devices), the learning is either straightforwardly sequential, with success on one step being required before advancement is possible, or "branched," in which the learner can follow more than one pathway. Computerized instruction has greatly amplified the range of possible approaches in ways that can scarcely be appreciated until they have been directly experienced. Various systems of teaching by computer have been developed, of which perhaps the best known program is PLATO, pioneered at the University of Illinois and now being applied to the continuing education of professionals as well as to many other instructional needs.

The idea of modularization has been carried forward in countless other ways as well, many of them using the printed word. The typical professional has many opportunities to buy "self-teaching books," packets of integrated learning materials, guided instruction, magazines with learning units or quiz sections, and manuals organized according to so-called "psychological" rather than logical principles. The torrent of new material makes it hard for the individual professional to find, despite many promises, precisely what he or she may require. Thus the volume of the new modularized materials is a blessing in disguise; sometimes the disguise seems almost perfect.

Broadening of content. The broadening of content to respond to a full range of motives has become a widely used principle in designing continuing professional education. Table 2 in Chapter Five shows that both the professionals who study and those who would like to study have many reasons for wanting to learn. Any complete program of continuing professional education, particularly one that accepts the self-enhancement goal of a professionalizing occupation, must therefore include a wide range of activities that give people the kinds of learning experience they really want.

Many programs are organized to include a recreational component for the participants and their families; in fact, pleasure is sometimes the chief component of the resulting program. Refreshment and repose are often deeply needed by hardworking professionals, and the combination of recreation and work can be beneficial. This broadening can occur within the design of a single activity. Some professional schools, for example, have introduced humanistic study or artistic experience into a course or workshop otherwise narrowly focused on professional expertise. A long week-end conference can be scheduled for professionals and their spouses to bring them out of the confines of a small community and offer them some of the cultural advantages of a large city or a cosmopolitan university. The broadening of content can also occur when a cultural institution makes special provisions for professionals; for example, an art museum might sponsor a series of courses or exhibits for teachers or librarians. Sometimes cosponsorship is involved, as when two associations, one based on a profession (perhaps social work) and the other on a field of study (perhaps world affairs) collaborate. The possibilities for such enlargement are infinite and often rewarding.

Purists sometimes argue that continuing professional education should always be based solely on established supporting disciplines or systems of practice related to the occupations. But if a course that does not conform to this dictate attracts a group of professionals who would not otherwise participate in education and helps them to practice their learning skills and build the informal bonds of association and affiliation that hold a profession together, it is hard to argue that diversity of curriculum should be frowned upon.

As discussed in Chapter Five, adult learners have complex patterns of motivation and orientation. An instructional activity may have meaning for the education of practitioners that was never intended by its sponsor. This fact suggests at least three strategies for increased participation. First, the language used in invitations, announcements, and promotional materials should adequately express all the benefits the sponsors of activities hope to provide in them so that they will attract potential participants for whom such values are important or even paramount. Second, supervisors or colleagues who seek to persuade a professional to engage in continuing education should use the specialized orientation of the person concerned; if that orientation is not known to the persuader it can usually be discovered fairly readily by discussion. Third, any teacher of an individual or group should learn as much as possible about the orientations of the person or persons taught in order to respond to them as fully and flexibly as possible. An enhanced sense of accomplishment by a participant in one activity increases the likelihood that he or she will engage in another. If the activity is a group learning situation, the teacher must assume that the students will have diverse motivations and orientations and must deal with that diversity either by adjusting his or her instruction to individuals or by using varied approaches in the general instruction of the group.

Intensive study for a lengthy period. This is an old and familiar design, widely exemplified in academic life, which has both the sabbatical and the nine-month contract. In the United States, intensive study arrangements for other professionals tend to be sporadic, individually initiated, and hard to achieve, but the number of study leaves is probably growing. In Europe, some governments have accepted the need to finance them, but investigation of these plans show that they have not yet become firmly established.

The value of intensive study depends on the period of time available, on the nature of the learning experiences undertaken, and on whether the service or study rendered occurs on the home site. For example, a professional in an institutional setting who is relieved of the customary work load but continues to go daily to the office and maintain the same informal social relationships as before may acquire a mass of new knowledge or bring to culmination some long-pursued investigations but is unlikely to achieve the freshness of outlook acquired by entering a new social or geographic setting. In the latter case, all the customary supports and reinforcements are removed, habitual routines are broken, the dangers of interruption are lessened, and new vantage points are established.

It has been hard in the past (and among many professions it is still hard) for senior professionals to engage in intensive study because they cannot neglect their responsibilities, because they are afraid of what might happen while they are away from their routines, and because they feel that such a course of action would be demeaning. In the hierarchical professions, the problem of how to establish extended study has often been solved by the creation of progressively advanced courses, the most advanced of which can be taken only by those who have achieved high-level status. In the military service, for example, there are lengthy programs of study whose students are generals and admirals. Somewhat similar patterns are to be found in large industries, particularly those which use advanced technologies.

Whether extended study leaves are individually arranged or offered in a systematic fashion, they are likely to increase in number. It may well become true, as Armer (1970, p. 80) predicts, that the advanced professional needs to engage in two forms of continuing education. The first and "lower" would be made up of all those individual and collective activities undertaken while still at work. "At the higher level, one would not attempt to hold down a job but would devote full time to education for a significant period of time (say six months to two years)." The ideal pattern at this higher level would be demanding, requiring extended study periodically (perhaps every five to seven years) throughout a worklife. Such a program would be costly but it would also be priceless.

Concentrated impact. The idea of concentrated impact suggests an exposure to knowledge in some depth during a relatively short period of time. Teachers may go individually or collectively to a community and provide brief but full-time instruction there. An example of this method of continuing professional education was the teachers' institute, which flourished at the time when the expansion of the public schools called for the in-service training of a large number of teachers. In a town or rural area, school would be dismissed for one or two days so that teachers could hear lectures from professors, who sometimes went on a circuit, delivering the same address five or six times a week in as many different locales. "Institute days" became a teacher's right, protected by state laws and regulations and with regularly appropriated funds to cover their costs. In some places, the habit continues but with less reliance on lectures and more on workshops and planning sessions. In recent years, the idea has been extended to other professions, though often on an episodic and sporadic basis.

An alternative pattern of concentrated impact calls for the learners to attend a course or conference, usually residential in character, in which full attention can be devoted to the study of a single topic. Such gatherings are hard to distinguish theoretically from conventions, though the latter usually are far more heterogeneous in character and do not require closeness and continuity of study. It is a common practice now for a convention to be surrounded with a cluster of satellite conferences, each one devoted to a single theme.

Since about 1950, the residential conference (as a method based on concentrated impact) has proliferated rapidly and may well be the most widely used form of continuing professional education. Many universities, associations, and employers have built continuing education centers to house conferences. Hotels, motels, and resorts secure much of their business by catering to this form of learning. In fact, the growth has been so great that, to many people, the term *continuing education* is virtually synonymous with residential conferences. This expansion in size and variety of offerings is facilitated by the rapid increase of transportation and the growth in the number and amenities of the centers, but the deeper causes of popularity lie elsewhere. The rise in the level of education has enlarged the potential audience, as has the increase in the number of professionalizing occupations. A conference solves difficulties caused by geographic separation. People with unusual and special responsibilities and interests who might otherwise be isolated can find or create communities that span the distances. Learners can escape the pressures of day-to-day life and concentrate fully on what they want to learn. Leaders and scarce resources can be shared, as can instructional aids and reinforcements. The art of conference design and management is quite advanced and can be used to achieve many purposes. Interaction with other individuals can be intense and challenging. New and rewarding personal contacts are often created. An absorbing though short-lived community is created, which provides a strong sense of reinforcement to learning and never completely disappears from the life and minds of its participants.

The residential conference can fit into the mode of instruction and may, in fact, be a short course. It can also fit into the mode of inquiry and has become one of the chief methods used in that mode. People come together from many places and backgrounds to work toward an outcome that cannot be fully discerned until the pooled knowledge and judgment of the persons concerned has brought about a consensus or has moved the group of people present closer to agreement than before. Many professions, for example, date crucial developmental stages in their growth from the time of a major conference, often giving it the name of the city or the institution where it was held or the chairman who presided.

Life-pattern analysis. This design aspect requires the examination of the typical life-styles of the members of a profession in order to discover the interstices into which education may best be fitted. Practicing teachers have been provided with summer or Saturday courses, while physicians and dentists often have their in-service education on Wednesday afternoons, the traditional off-duty time for those professionals. Suburban residents who work in the city may have programs scheduled at lunch time, in the late afternoon or, in at least one case, aboard a commuter train. This principle of design is complementary to the concentrated impact theory; the first fits study into the pattern of work, and the second interrupts work so that perspective on it can be gained. The two are not necessarily competitive, but in practical cases—particularly when scarce resources must be allocated—the principles may appear to be opposed to one another.

Just as the concentrated instruction available in the conference has certain advantages, so does that which is close to the practitioner, particularly if it is located in or near the workplace. The immediacy and vividness of the instruction, growing as it does from the problems faced every day at the very place where they are faced, has a striking impact. Costs are minimized, loss of time in travel is avoided, and study can take place without requiring the learner to leave the comforts of home. These advantages have turned factories and hospitals into learning places and have stimulated the growth of teacher centers and other local sites for learning.

Simulation techniques. This design—also called "games"— puts a learner into a situation that closely approximates what might be experienced in the practice of a profession and re- quires him or her to react in an appropriate fashion. In the "in- basket" approach, for example, a teacher learning to be a school principal may be given a packet of letters, reports, memos, and other documents reflecting the problems that typically come to a principal's attention. The learner is directed to respond appro- priately to each item. This method may be turned into a collec- tive technique by having a group of people react to the same stimuli and then discuss the results. The learners gain a sense of reality and of grappling with issues that have no easy or exact solutions but rely ultimately on the simultaneous application of principles.

A more sophisticated type of simulation requires the con- struction of a sequence of stimuli, each of which depends in some way on those preceding it. For example, a patient may be generally described to a physician, who is then asked to select from a list the conditions to be checked and the further infor- mation that is required. The requested information is supplied. In one or more steps, the doctor discovers what was extraneous and what was essential to his initial and his ultimate diagnoses. He then indicates the priority of steps to be taken, the advice to be given to the patient, and the subsequent treatment to be undertaken. Finally, the decisions made are checked against those which a panel of eminent physicians has chosen to be most preferable. This process can be carried out simply with pencil and paper or can be dealt with by a computer—the latter offering more rapid response and a wider latitude of choice.

In advanced training situations (particularly where so- phisticated computer technology is available), individuals or groups can follow the consequences of their individual or com- petitive reactions to problems set for them. For example, a mil- itary commander can try out the probable results of alternative moves on a hypothetical field of battle. In another type of "game," two commanders might play against each other, the computer working out the consequences of the moves of each one and presenting a new situation to which the other must respond.

All of these simulations test the appropriateness and the speed of the professional's response. The dolls, mock-ups, models, field exercises, aircraft trainers, and other devices that have proved useful in pre-service training are constantly amplified and made more complex, and, to some extent, are being used in continuing education. However, continuing education has not yet been as fertile a field for their development as have earlier stages of schooling.

Experiential learning. This term is now widely used to describe the education that occurs as a result of direct participation in the events of life. Its ultimate scope was stated in the middle of the nineteenth century by John Stuart Mill, who observed that education includes not only "whatever we do for ourselves, and whatever is done for us by others, for the express purpose of bringing us somewhat nearer to the perfection of our nature; it does more: in its largest acceptation, it comprehends even the indirect effects produced on character and on the human faculties, by things of which the direct purposes are quite different; by laws, by forms of government, by the industrial arts, by modes of social life; nay, even by physical facts not dependent on human will; by climate, soil, and local position. Whatever helps to shape the human being—to make the individual what he is, or hinder him from being what he is not—is part of his education" (Mill, 1874, p. 333).

As the American system of schooling was established, it was developed in essentially formal terms, gradually acquiring such rigidity that it seemed almost nothing could be learned except in a classroom or from a tutor. This system was reinforced by becoming the basis of evaluative and credentialing mechanisms, such as diplomas, degrees, certificates, and licenses. Rewards are often denied to those who cannot move through schools and universities, even if they are able to demonstrate their knowledge and competence. This extreme rigidity began to be corrected in the 1940s, partly as a result of the educational provisions made for members of the armed services in World War II, but the major changes did not occur until the 1970s.

In most continuing professional education, the learning that results from experience is its own reward, both in the pleasure inherent in inquiry and in the subsequent satisfaction and material benefits that flow from enhanced knowledge. But the elaborate credentialing systems that safeguard both the individual professional and the society he or she serves require the demonstration that continuing learning has occurred or, at any rate, has been attempted. Thus it becomes important to relate experiential learning to formal learning in such a way that they equate to or are compatible with one another. Modern thought on this subject tends to divide this problem into two parts: the validation of prior experience in terms of the extent to which it meets established criteria, and the designing of experiential bases for future learning episodes.

The validation of prior experience has heretofore been largely carried out by formal tests, some of them developed on an elaborately analytical basis. The accomplishment of college-level instruction, for example, is appraised by the College Level Examination Program administered by the College Board as well as by other course- or field-based tests. Within the specialties of the health sciences, proficiency examinations have been constructed not only to establish the basic competence required for entry into associations but also to enable the professional to continue to assess his knowledge from whatever source it might be derived.

A strong beginning has also been made on establishing equivalents between instruction offered in the armed forces, government, or industry and that provided by formal educational institutions. Thus either a career military person or someone with short-term service in the armed forces may be able to use the training afforded by the experience toward the awarding of a degree or a specialized credential. It seems likely that highly complex equivalency systems will eventually be devised, some based on specific professions—such as nursing, social work, and engineering—and some more broadly applicable in scope.

In the designing of future experiential learning episodes, much creative work was done in the 1970s, though most of it occurred at the pre-service level rather than in continuing education. At the latter level, however, the idea holds much promise. The basic idea that people need to have first-hand exposure to experience is as old as the laboratory period, the field trip, and the internship, but the newer systems provide for enhanced forms of experiential opportunity, learner initiative, evaluative mechanisms, and supervisory authority.

An educational episode (which may be developed in a myriad of contexts) usually begins when a learner and a counselor work out a contract in which the former agrees to undertake experiences that collectively seem likely to achieve a significant goal. For example, a social worker seeking to gain credit for a credential in psychiatric social work might devise a plan calling for visitation to several mental clinics, a period of intern service in a hospital, a series of interviews with administrators and staff members of other such institutions, and the reading of an agreed-upon list of books. As these experiences occur, the learner accumulates a series of documents: letters of certification that the visits have occurred, a diary recording the events of the internship, a rating scale of the quality of performance in the hospital, reports of the interviews, and reviews of the books read. These are combined into what is called a "portfolio," which is then submitted as evidence that the contract has been fulfilled. In highly formal systems, such as degree-structures, the contract and the portfolio may be reviewed by both mentors and monitoring committees.

It seems likely that devices such as contracts, portfolios, and other mechanisms will help make raw experience more focused, purposeful, and educative than it now is. These developments will assist in the task of credentialing either basic or advanced skills. In the long run, however, the major influence of the experiential learning movement may well be upon the stimulation of individuals to be more self-educative as they observe the ways in which guided practical experience leads to change in the competence of themselves and their colleagues.

Varied and complementary learning patterns. This is not itself a major guiding principle for the design of education but a useful corrective to a too-heavy reliance on any specific principle. As noted earlier, those who have sought to enlarge the roster of traditional methods of continuing professional education—and of other forms of adult education—have sometimes pressed so hard for a technological innovation or a simple principle of design that they have seemed to argue for its absolute and universal supremacy. For example, a group of professionals may be confronted with a three-day meeting conducted entirely by tele-lecture or computer-assisted instruction, or they may be asked to embark upon a training program that is solely experiential, with no introduction of basic theoretical analysis or interpretation of the meaning of what the learners are undertaking. These newer processes, if carried to excess, can become as monotonously tedious as can reading, lecturing, or discussing.

The group dynamics movement of the late 1940s and early 1950s was at first too doctrinaire, but it eventually led to the widespread realization that the involvement of learners in the processes of education could be greatly heightened by providing varied patterns of instruction. Buzz groups, reactor panels, nondirective discussion leadership, group consensus achievement techniques, and other devices were introduced in an effort to break up the rigidity of formal meetings. The effect of this movement, leading as it has to far more profound forms of encounter than before, has been permanent as far as additions to the creative processes of educational methodology are concerned. However, perhaps the broadest outcome has been the widespread realization that the maintenance of learner attention and involvement requires the use of varied educational techniques. The same effect has also been reinforced by the growing realization that the achievement of an objective calls for the use of the methods suited to its accomplishment. Also students have varied learning styles; a person who responds well to one method will not necessarily respond well to another.

This realization of the need for diversity in patterns of learning and teaching has led to increasing sophistication in the design of continuing professional education programs. It also acts as a deterrent to the proposing of simple methods as solutions to universal problems and aids the realization that the working out of learning programs will require far more intricate processes and ways of thought than have been characteristic in the past.

Complex Theories of Design

Most sponsors of continuing professional education have devoted their attention to patterns of learning already described in this chapter. Traditional methods have been refined through technological innovation and new basic principles of design have been worked out. The evaluation of these endeavors has almost always been based on such aspects as size of enrollment or attendance, maintenance of interest throughout a lengthy program, enthusiasm of learners, or performance on examinations. Other sponsors, however, have wanted to go beyond the immediacies of specific operation to see whether it was possible to define desirable end-products in terms of the improved performance of practitioners as a result of educational programs conducted. These desires have led to the growth of complex theories or systems of design.

Content and Process. Professions are based upon practical or theoretical bodies of knowledge and the skills and sensitiveness required to use them; therefore it has long seemed appropriate for continuing professional education to be focused solely upon helping practitioners to understand new content and to master new techniques. This theory of instruction has deep foundations in traditional processes of formal schooling. Its practice rests upon an analysis of what knowledge or skills should be conveyed in a given situation and how they may best be transmitted to the appropriate audience. If this essentially intellectual task is to be effective, it must be carried out only after due throught and careful analysis, with such subsequent revisions of processes as are needed but with the nature of the necessary designs always controlled by the content to be conveyed.

Widespread dissatisfaction with a purely content-centered approach to continuing professional education arose in the 1960s because of the all-too-apparent fact that it was not working satisfactorily. Bodies of knowledge were, for the most part, being adequately transmitted to practitioners by the medium of printed and oral presentations, but the transmission did not seem to be having the effect desired. Either working professionals were not absorbing the information available to them or they were not putting what they knew into practice. Also the non-content-based goals of the professionalizing process did not appear to be readily achievable by traditional methods. Something else was needed. The case was strongly put (in relation to physicians) by Miller (1967, p. 324): "There must be movement away from the content model, which encourages dependence upon teachers, to a process model, which demands a significant measure of self-reliance—a shift away from preoccupation with courses and methods toward an augmented concern for educational diagnosis and individualized therapy. It does not mean an immediate abandonment of present program forms, but it is likely to be accompanied by a slow erosion of the faith which presently supports them."

The movement toward replacing the content model with process models, or linking the two together so that content is part of the total constellation of process, has moved even more rapidly and in more diverse directions than Miller's prediction suggested it would. Educators in various professions who began to examine current thought in pedagogy and the social sciences found awaiting them sets of ideas and concepts that proved useful in offering freedom from traditional learning patterns. For example, Fleisher (1974, p. 210), advocating a system of influencing professionals which does not necessarily require formal instruction, notes that some readers will find it strange for him to call it "educational." He goes on: "To define education we must first define learning. Learning may be defined as a change of behavior. Education may then be defined as 'planned changes in behavior.' Using this definition may offend some, but it has an all-embracing quality that is supported by much educational literature." It is indeed supported, for this concept is part of the theory of curriculum and instruction developed by Ralph W. Tyler and his followers, which has dominated the practice of American schooling since the late 1940s.

In the effort to liberate themselves from the content model, continuing educators have found useful a number of other concepts of education. Most of the education provided for practicing professionals is still improvisational, with the design of each program or episode reflecting immediate needs and opportunities and taking advantage of immediately available resources. But in an effort to operate systematically and thereby gain the rewards of coherent program development, a number of models of overall design have been advanced, some of them arising from analyses of continuing professional education itself but many of them borrowed from the literature of adult education, psychology, or managerial control systems.

So strong is the belief that formal teaching is the only valid method of education that most of these models have been cast in the mode of instruction. This fact is particularly true of programs sponsored by professional schools; they are so strongly oriented to the classroom and laboratory that, intentionally or not, their planners begin with the idea that the other components of any model used will lead up to or flow from a process of instruction. In continuing professional education, however, the fact that learning often occurs in a workplace or under the sponsorship of some nonacademic authority has meant that theories of design must often be constructed so as to focus on the modes of performance or inquiry or must be so broadly framed that, as appropriate, they may be used for any of the three basic modes of learning. Several theories will be illustrated to show how they work out in practice.

An inductive model. A good way to put deductively derived systems into perspective is to begin by reporting on an inductive analysis. Pennington and Green (1976) created a general mode of program development by examining thirty-seven continuing educational activities in six professions—business administration, educational administration, law, teaching, social work, and medicine—which were conducted at five large midwestern universities. A flow-chart of the steps taken to develop each of the thirty-seven activities was studied. When the total group of charts was synthesized, the following sequential clusters of overlapping activities emerged:

1. *Originating the idea* from formal needs assessment, availability of funds, requests from potential clients, suggestions from faculty, legislative mandates, or other sources.
2. *Developing the idea* by exploring the extent of field interest, discovering the judgments of campus peers and administrative authorities, locating fellow planners, discov-

ering possible parallel programs, and engaging in other explorations.

3. *Making a commitment* by arranging for the instruction, outlining the logistics of recruitment and physical facilities, and laying other organizational and administrative groundwork.

4. *Developing the program*, a cluster of activities that overlaps the preceding one but deals essentially with such aspects of instructional design as determining and stating objectives, developing specific subject matter, and choosing the methods to be used.

5. *Teaching the course*, during which the plans are carried out but modified as required to accommodate the needs and desires of the learners as well as to other changing aspects of the situation.

6. *Evaluating the impact* by measuring the results, making judgments about their meaning, and using them to provide better planning in the future.

This list of inductively derived steps is similar to that found in many models of instructional planning expounded in the literature of education, though the rich context of the discussion by Pennington and Green presents interesting variations and interpretations. The reader cannot help but wonder whether the fifty-two people who reported on the thirty-seven programs were, in their various fashions, imposing upon the accounts of their own activities some memories of general patterns that had been described to them. But while a familiar general model emerged, it was not applied by the programmers with any rigor. Pennington and Green were particularly impressed, as a matter of fact, by the desultory, haphazard, and restricted fashion with which their informants used the pattern which they themselves put forward as a guide to action. The authors report: "Planners use the language of the classical model to label their planning actions. However, as they describe their planning actions it becomes clear that personal values, environmental constraints, available resource alternatives, and other factors impinge on the program development process" (Pennington and Green, 1976, p. 22). The reader may well regard this observation as commendation, not criticism, if it suggests that the planners concerned were sensitively responsive to the immediacies of the situations in which they found themselves.

It is probably wise to consider all theories of design as general guides to be used in an improvisational way—even in elaborate systems that have been worked out carefully in an effort to consider every contingency and possible decision point. In becoming familiar with an intricate pattern of behavior, it is necessary to follow it literally for a while until its routines become almost second nature, but mastery is not achieved until the user dominates the system and can employ it in a creative way.

A mode-of-performance model. A simple design that is essentially in the mode of performance was developed by Stearns and others (1974). Their purpose was to improve the availability of continuing professional educational facilities and programs in hospitals. For this purpose they used forty-two hospitals in New England that had volunteered to be in an experimental group and compared them with a matched control group. In the former group, clinically oriented medical school faculty members were used as consultants and were trained for the performance of that role as well as for the ability to use program-building processes. The educational staff members of the experimental hospitals were also given training on educational methods and technology. In each of two years, the consultants made one or more visits to their assigned hospitals and, on the basis of their consultations with staff members, provided written lists of suggestions for improvement.

Among the recommendations were: rotation of staff responsibility for planning and implementing programs; use of guest educators; development of an interhospital continuing education program; strengthening of the library; establishment of case presentations; and use of external resources for program development. Of the 353 recommendations made during the first year of the program, 60 percent were fully implemented at the end of eighteen months, 3 percent had been partially put into practice, and 37 percent had been rejected. The acceptance rate was significantly higher ($p < .05$) at the experimental than at the control hospitals. The authors concluded that "limited inputs by physicians acting as education program consultants and minimal training of community hospital [directors of medical education] can significantly facilitate development of hospital-based" continuing medical education programs. They also state that "large numbers of medical-school-based physician educators, with only a minimum of additional training and guidance, can bridge the so-called impediments of the town/gown schism and can function effectively as education program consultants to community hospitals" (Stearns and others, 1974, p. 1164).

Well-designed though this study was, its basic purpose was focused not on performance but on the provision of resources that could strengthen performance. For example, it is a potential asset for a hospital to have a stronger library than before, but its existence does not ensure that it will be used. The study might also have been stronger if the values to be derived from involvement in inquiry had been taken into account. While effective outside consultants will base their judgments in part on the interaction with local authorities, the recommendations in this study were ultimately based upon the judgments of physicians extraneous to the situation itself.

A triple-mode model. In the effort to take account of these limitations, a number of continuing educators in the health professions have evolved somewhat similar patterns, which operate simultaneously in all three modes of learning, sometimes stressing one and sometimes another. The intellectual roots of such models are more likely to be found in social psychology than in pedagogy and most of them owe a particular debt to Kurt Lewin and other change theorists. This debt may not always be a conscious one, for there are indications that, in many cases, theories and principles have been freshly conceived by their authors. The following synthesis of these approaches is based on the assumption that the program is being planned for some institutional entity, but, as noted later, the model can be used in other situations as well.*

*The model suggested here has been generalized to apply to many professional work settings, but it owes a great deal to formulations presented by Fleisher (1974), Charters and Blakely (1974), Brown and Fleisher (1971), and Brown and Uhl (1970).

1. A list of criteria is developed indicating the essential elements required for the performance of the functions of the entity. This entity might be an entire institution or a unit of service, such as a department of surgery in a hospital or the social studies program in a high school. This first step is wholly analytical and seeks to discover what is essential to the most effective operation of the entity. The resulting criteria should be stated in such a form that they are comprehensive, lend themselves to measurement, and are in conformity with enlightened practices. If such standards already exist generally, they can be adopted or adapted. Even so, the professionals employed in the entity should be sure that they understand the standards and agree that they are valid for local application.

2. On the basis of these criteria, the professionals involved —or some group of them—determine the standards of ideal accomplishment in the local setting. Thus, if the entity concerned is the language arts program of an elementary school, the curriculum committee, knowing both national norms and the school's own performance on the standardized tests, would set the maximum goals that might possibly be accomplished.

3. This same group also sets the minimal standards that can be accepted. While the second step establishes a ceiling, which in most cases is difficult to reach, the third establishes a floor—a standard or group of standards below which it is inexcusable to go, even in terms of the limitations that influence performance in a far-from-perfect world.

4. All staff members whose work is to be part of the collective process of staff improvement are informed of what steps have already been taken and approve of what has been done. In many cases, this result will already have been achieved, but where it has not, every effort should be made to gain total staff approval and assent to the collective effort.

5. Data are collected on the current performance of the entity as far as the identified criteria are concerned, the information being presented in terms of the standards already identified. These data are drawn from any source available, but most often from cumulative records on either a total or a sampling basis. Sometimes a lack of congruence exists between the data-

collection system and the statement of standards so that each must be adjusted and supplemented to conform to the other. The data on current performance may be collected by the professionals concerned, by special staff members (such as the medical record librarians in a hospital), by an outside evaluator, or by some combination.

6. Current performance is compared with the ideal and the minimally acceptable standards in order to highlight what are sometimes called "deficits of performance," and an effort is made to determine the causes for the differences between what is and what ought to be. The desired goals must be realistically set somewhere between the floor and the ceiling and must be based upon a candid estimate of the amount of change that can be accomplished in the time available and with the human and material resources at hand. The first inquiry into the causes of the deficits should be as free and open as possible, with group judgment finally narrowing the list to the basic reasons for the gaps between acceptable and unacceptable performance.

7. Programs of change are generally designed to correct identified deficits. The previous steps, if creatively conducted, will already have laid a basis for this seventh step and may, in fact, have suggested or even initiated revisions in processes. For example, a member of an engineering firm, upon identifying standards governing his work, may already have begun to revise it. In addition to these spontaneous changes, however, concerted efforts will ordinarily be necessary to raise the level of performance.

Some changes will be administrative, dealing with procedures or the provision of material resources. Fleisher (1974, pp. 209–210) illustrates this point with two examples from a cardiology clinic. It was agreed by the physicians involved that patients suffering from acute myocardial infarctions should be placed on heart monitors as soon as possible. In the clinic concerned, anecdotal evidence indicated that serious delays had often occurred and, in many cases cited, the data did not reveal the period of time between admission and the use of the monitor. The cause of the delay was determined to be the shortage of monitors and the absence of data arose from laxness in the use of time clocks. The appropriate changes could then be made by locating financial resources to buy more monitors and by rigorous supervision of the entry procedures.

It often happens, however, that a process of learning is required. In this case, a new sequence of steps is followed. It usually goes through a procedure similar to that by Pennington and Green (1976) cited earlier, although the term *instruction* must always be interpreted broadly to include a wide variety of stimuli aiming at cognitive or attitudinal accomplishments or the achievement of skills. Thus a design of continuing professional education in the mode of instruction is inserted into the larger design of a model, which also conforms to the modes of inquiry and performance. Some people have called a double design of this sort a "bi-cycle" model because it is composed of two series of steps that supplement one another but each of which makes up a completed but also prognostic plan of action.

8. The programs designed to remedy the identified deficits are carried out. In doing so, preordained activities should not be mechanically followed. Initial judgments as to how deficits may be remedied may prove to be incorrect, inadequate, or more stringent than necessary. Occasionally, also, further experience may cause the perception of the relative importance of the deficits to change so that programs are altered in their nature as well as in their style and form.

9. When the programs are completed, current performance on the standards is measured and then compared with earlier performance in order to determine what changes have occurred. The processes of analysis should lead on directly to the next step.

10. The best programs for further action are determined. The new standards should be at least maintained and, if possible, advanced so that they are closer than before to the ideal criteria. But this tenth step may take the staff or the committee all the way back to the reanalysis of basic criteria concerning the performance of the functions under consideration. The very process of continuing deliberation and education may have had profound consequences in the staff's understanding of the essential aspects of its work. Thus the tenth step completes

a cycle but resembles the first step, immediately starting a new sequence of actions, one which may once again involve the bi-cycle approach.

The triple-mode design, with appropriate adaptations to conform to circumstances, can be used in many settings rang-ing from the practice of a single entrepreneurial professional to the work of many individuals of different professions in a large organization. While clear advantages arise from the cumulative impact of a continuing program, briefer usage is also possible if necessary. In fact, it may even be useful for a staff to go through a very simple program with limited goals in order to gain expertise and enthusiasm before taking on a larger venture. In a few professional settings, most notably major health care institutions, efforts have been made to develop new record-keeping systems to aid in recording data and also allow for com-parisons to be made among institutions or between local and national norms. Johnson and Jackson (1979) have described an integrated medical-financial hospital information system that would provide an excellent basis for identifying needs on which educational programs could be based.

A flow-chart model. The most complex designs used in continuing professional education have arisen from the applica-tion of systems-analysis or managerial-control plans, in which each step in the process of designing or conducting a program is carefully analyzed and charted. These flow-charts can become extraordinarily involved. For example, Scriven (as described in Humble, 1973) has designed an algorithm to indicate how to take the first major step—the identification of training needs—in a straightforward two-person supervisory relationship. Thirty-two different actions are required to deal adequately with this process, and they are fitted together in complex ways. The first step is to determine whether Mr. X (the learner) understands his role in the department. If the answer is "no," then that role must be clarified. If the answer is "yes" or after the clarification has been made, it must be determined whether Mr. X's personal objectives, targets, and yardsticks of performance are defined to his satisfaction and that of the supervisor. If not, a process of refinement must be undertaken. If so, or after the refinement has occurred, a system of checking performance to measure such goals must be constructed. And so the algorithm proceeds. Sometimes a "no" answer leads to a series of steps before a "yes" answer can be given. Ultimately, by following one of several branched pathways, a determination is made of the learning needs of Mr. X, and a general strategy of training is defined. Specific forms of education can then be planned for him, and new algorithms can be designed for each of the subsequent steps in the learning process.

A carefully designed flow-chart model is ordinarily presented on a large sheet of paper with each step in a rectangular box linked by lines to one or more other boxes. Substantial time and effort are usually required even to comprehend the points being made. The mastery of the sequential processes so they can be used readily and flexibly is a major undertaking. However, the maker of an algorithm can appropriately argue that it is essential to have a clear delineation of basic steps in the correct sequence before an effective decision-making process can occur. It is also sometimes argued that the task of constructing such a flow-chart is a useful part of the mode of inquiry because it helps the individual or group who constructs it to focus attention upon the essentials that must be confronted in a given situation. Even if the chart is not subsequently followed (except in general terms) its construction has clarified the minds of those who made it.

A Note on All Programmatic Processes, Principles and Patterns

Throughout this chapter a point of view has been either implicit or suggested that should be stated here with emphasis. Every planner of a continuing education program—whether a learner or a designer of activities for other people—must remain in control of whatever process, principle, or pattern he or she finds useful. Learning can sometimes be greatly facilitated by a process but only if it is used skillfully and suitably and, equally important, is never employed in any circumstances for which it is not appropriate. A principle may provide dimensions of quality or quantity not previously attainable but only if it is applied correctly and is not carried beyond its limits of effectiveness. A pattern is a framework of decision points that reminds the planner of aspects to be considered and perhaps suggests a sequence to be followed. But the eventual results of the programs will be only as good as the decisions that have been made in using the model.

If this general point of view is accepted, the designers of programs will be freed from the absolutist and dogmatic stance which the proponents of either traditional or innovative methods so often adopt, either consciously or unconsciously. That freedom may be hard won, for it presupposes not only the awareness of a wide variety of ways of doing things but also a mastery of the knowledge and skills required for the proper use of each. The illustrations given in this chapter are but a few of the processes, principles, and designs now being used by one or more of the professions in their sponsorship of continuing education. The number of possibilities and ideas is not only growing but accelerating in its growth. Therefore, anyone who becomes dominated by some preexisting notion of how education should be planned is locked away not only from all present alternatives but also from those which are certain to arise in the future.

Chapter 8

Evaluation

This is the beginning of philosophy: the recognition of the conflicts among men, the search for their cause, the distrust and condemnation of opinion ... and the discovery of a standard of judgment.

Epictetus

Any consideration of continuing professional education must ultimately be concerned with the appraisal of its quality. Evaluation is usually undertaken within three possible frames of reference. The first has to do with the measurement of the results of formal educational activity of the sort described in Chapters Six and Seven. The second has to do with an assessment of the extent and quality of the developed ability of individual practitioners as a result of both formal study and the educational consequences of the worklife. The third is more general, having to do with an estimation of the level of performance of an entire profession or some significant sector of it; that judgment may be made by its members, by the people it serves, or by the general public.

The three frames of reference have become so closely intertwined in practice and discussion that it is hard to distinguish them. Arguments arise about whether it is better to take a formal course or to learn on the job—as though both were not complementary and necessary. It is also widely assumed that a record of participation in formal learning activities is the only substantive prerequisite for quality-control recredentialing, whereas actually many other methods are used. This blurring of important differences is one of the chief impediments to the appraisal of continuing professional education. In this book, therefore, the major efforts at evaluation will be described in terms of the three frameworks. The first two, those which are centrally educative in character, will be discussed in this chapter. The third, which has to do with the role of education in quality control, will be dealt with in Chapter Nine.

Measuring the Results of Formal Education

According to the traditional theory of professionalism, the ultimate rewards of education are intrinsic. The practitioner who learns is benefitted by increased skill, knowledge, or sensitiveness. He or she feels a growth in the power needed to cope with the problems that active practice presents; this greater competence is also apparent to both colleagues and clients. Increased accomplishment then stimulates the professional's appetite for further education, which may be carried out by persistent and long-term effort or by recurrent but separate episodes. The continuing desire to learn provides additional evidence of the value of education in the life and work of the practitioner.

For countless reasons, extrinsic evidence of accomplishment is also desired by those who undertake continuing professional education. People want to achieve specialty credentials, to be relicensed, to win increased compensation or more elevated position, to achieve formal status among their peers, to secure special awards, to win accreditation for their employing agencies, and in other ways to show tangible evidence that they are continuing learners. Even those people who chiefly value intrinsic awards sometimes also want extrinsic evidence of the amount and quality of their accomplishment. These and other motivations, many of which have appeared or been intensified in recent years as a result of the expansion of the professionalizing process, has led to a deep concern with extrinsic methods of assessing the results of formal education. Four major bases for such evaluation have emerged, and each will here be discussed in turn.

Extent of participation. The most widespread measure of continuing professional education is simply the number of hours spent in learning activities, usually in programs offered or approved by some such authority as a university or a professional

society. This measure is not related to how well the learner performs during participation or subsequently but only to how
much time has been spent. If examination questions are included in a program using this measure, their purpose is not to
evaluate accomplishment but to stimulate response, to foster
self-appraisal, to encourage completion of a sequential activity,
or to lead the learner to related aspects of content. Many systems of counting hours of participation have been developed,
but two generalized patterns have had widespread impact.

The first of these is the Physician's Recognition Award
(PRA), which was adopted by the American Medical Association in 1968. By July 1, 1979, a total of 178,232 such awards
had been granted. On the same date, 76,960 physicians held
valid awards (an award expires after a three-year period).* This
system is significant not only as a major form of credentialing in
its own right but also because it has become a model for other
professionalizing groups and has been widely accepted (either in
its original form or as adapted) as a basis for relicensure or renewal of membership in professional associations.

To receive this award, the physician is required to spend
at least 150 hours during a three-year period in one or more of
six categories of effort. Category 1 is made up of instructional
activities sponsored by institutions accredited for this purpose.
At least 60 hours must be spent in Category 1 activities, but
there is no upper limit to the number that may be used for the
PRA. As many as 45 hours may be spent in Category 2 activities,
which are those sponsored by nonaccredited institutions. An
equal number of hours may be spent in Category 3 activities,
which include the teaching by the applicant of present or potential physicians or other health professionals. Up to 40 hours
may be spent in Category 4 activities, which have to do with the
applicant's publications or other major demonstrations of medical knowledge, 10 hours being assigned for each paper or each
chapter of a book. As many as 45 hours may be spent in Category 5 activities, which are collectively designated as nonsuper-

*These data were provided by Jean Ayers of the American Medical
Association.

vised learning. This term includes carefully worked-out definitions of four subcategories: self-instruction; learning from a consultant; patient care review; and participation in self-assessment
procedures. (The consultant can also use the hours spent in
this way as Category 3 hours.) Category 6 includes meritorious
learning experiences that do not fit in other categories but are
undertaken, so far as possible, with the help of an accredited
organization. As many as 45 hours may be spent in activities in
this category. The total system has been continuously adapted
to meet changed circumstances, and many interpretations have
evolved to guide special cases.

    Category 4 activities are different from the others in that
hour equivalents are given for publishing activities. It is perhaps
for this reason that the term *credit hours* is used throughout the
system, although in all categories but 4 (and possibly 6) actual
contact hours are counted. The ascription of an automatic number of "hours" to activities not actually related to direct instruction is becoming commonplace. For example, in the American
Nurses' Association Mechanism for Accreditation of Continuing
Education in Nursing, a complete short course may be printed
in an issue of the *American Journal of Nursing*. The nurse studies
the material, sends $10 for a computer-scored examination, gets
a score of pass or fail, and, if the former is achieved, earns ten
"contact hours" of credit in any voluntary or mandatory state
program of relicensure or state association renewal that honors
such self-directed instruction. But variations such as the Category 4 activities of the AMA or the magazine-conveyed "contact
hours" of the ANA are still atypical. Most systems of accounting for continuing professional education are based solely on
clock hours.

    The second widely used system of measuring continuing
education in terms of extent of participation is the continuing
education unit (CEU) which was first developed by a national
task force made up of representatives of higher educational
associations and government bureaus. The plans for such a unit
were developed during 1968 to 1970, and the concepts used
were widely tested in 1970 and 1971; since then this method of
measurement has become widespread. One CEU is defined as

ten contact hours of participation in an organized continuing education experience under responsible sponsorship, capable direction, and qualified instruction. Elaborate and comprehensive criteria have been enunciated by various sponsors to assure responsible providers and high standards, and an extensive campaign has been mounted to launch the new unit of measurement.

The desire of the sponsors of the CEU has been to establish a method of recording participation that will parallel the credit course. The intention was to design a unit that would be easily measured, flexible as to method, transferrable from one record-keeping system to another, combinable in various ways to meet concentration-and-dispersion content requirements of degrees and certificates, usable as a metering device for measuring the instructional loads of teaching staffs and the payment requirements of funding agencies, and capable of serving in other ways as the coin of the continuing education realm. It has been argued that the CEU is not capable of being standardized as to quality or integrity of sponsorship, but, its proponents quickly respond, neither is the credit course. Even more significantly, they observe, faculty members resist almost any effort at imposing external standards of uniformity and consistency upon their right to determine the content and methods they use in their courses. Why should reputable sponsors of the CEU not have equal freedom?

The success of the campaign to launch the CEU and the evidence that it met a real need was demonstrated by its immediate and broad-based acceptance. Many sponsors of educational activities began to award CEUs, and they were accepted by many credentialing and funding agencies. The Council on the Continuing Education Unit has been created both to advance the concept and to establish even firmer controls over quality.

As yet, however, the CEU has never had full acceptance and has encountered formal opposition from engineering groups as well as members of other professions. Many people believe that the chief problem with the CEU is that no strong legitimizing body accredits the institutions permitted to award it. The task force that created the CEU and the council that fosters it have set high standards for the maintenance of its quality, and in most settings those standards may well have been maintained. Unfortunately, however, the CEU has sometimes been mismanaged or incorrectly perceived. Institutions of dubious quality or questionable motives have awarded it. Sometimes it has been granted merely as an award for ten hours of essentially unintegrated instruction. Some educators have proposed that equivalency tables be established, equating CEUs with academic credits; it has been assumed by some people that such tables already exist. Most devastating of all, perhaps, is the fact that the CEU has sometimes become the object of ridicule, being seen as merely a pretentious synonym for "chair warming." As a result of these difficulties, the ultimate fate of the unit is uncertain.

The essential problem of all measures of extent of participation, including the Physician's Recognition Award and the CEU, is that they carry no assurance that desired changes in the competence or performance of participants have occurred. While both external evaluation and self-appraisal may be included, neither is required by definition. Moreover the meaning of attendance is unclear, and the actual presence of participants is hard to certify without turning the sponsors into doorkeepers, a deeply unprofessional and often ineffective role. For example: a three-hour meeting is scheduled. The full roster of participants is present at the beginning and attendance is recorded. Fairly soon, however, people begin to slip away, some of them physically, some mentally. At the end of the period, everyone is back and ready for the final check-out. They all receive three hours on their attendance records. These episodes are not rare, and every session in which such behavior does occur outrages the people who are honestly concerned with the maintenance or advancement of professionalization.

A person working for a credential in a single activity based on participation usually receives a diploma or certificate, which serves as an emblem of accomplishment. The institution offering the activity should keep records of its successful "graduates" but often does not do so or maintains them in inaccessible places. The problem of record keeping becomes far greater in complex systems, where evidences of completion of activities under multiple sponsorship are required. Here the burden falls simultaneously on the learner, on the multiple providers of educational activities, on the institution that awards the credential, and perhaps eventually on some independent record-keeping organization. Master systems of computerized "credit banks" have often been proposed as the most efficient way of centralizing this responsibility, but it is not yet clear who would control such systems and how their data would be programmed and stored.

Another problem with using participation as a measure of evaluation is that little or no interchange is possible among the myriad plans being developed. When each profession deals solely with matters distinctive to its work, the need for interchange among systems and cumulative records may not be very great and therefore fairly easy to handle. But in programs that provide fields of content common to several professions or that offer general or basic education, accommodation and compilation are difficult to arrange. Professionals who seek credentials may find themselves locked into one or another scheme for securing them with no acceptable way of using resources that are more available or even superior to those required.

Perhaps the greatest difficulty with using participation as the basis of evaluation is that it tends to restrict the goals of continuing education to the mode of instruction. Category 4 of the PRA is a clear exception to this limitation, but not many others exist. Thus the scope of continuing education is narrowed so that "keeping up to date" is virtually its only purpose, and effective professionalization (with all of its need for improved inquiry and performance) is hampered because learning tends to be restricted to only a few characteristics of its total process.

The limitations of extent of participation as an evaluation tool have caused much opposition to continuing professional education, particularly when it is the only form of appraisal used. While every new program starts out in a spirit of innovation and optimism, the net result is often one of general cynicism based upon and often reinforced by anecdotes showing how profitless "time serving" has proved to be or how casually participants have undertaken it.

Extent of learner satisfaction. A common method of assessing the quality of an educational activity is to determine how its students judge it. This method places emphasis on the evaluation of the program rather than of the learner. A substantial body of literature has developed on studies of learner satisfaction in schools and colleges, including the impact of the assessments upon later instruction. In continuing professional education, learners are often asked to fill out evaluation questionnaires at the close of instruction or subsequently. In situations where many activities are offered, a standard reporting form may be used so that comparisons can be made among them. Usually a good deal of weight is given to these assessments because it is believed that professionals are particularly well equipped by their sophistication to make decisions about the quality of their instruction.

Institutions can also receive this same form of scrutiny. For example, White and Buchman (1978) have reported a study of the continuing educational activities of 469 certified public accountants in Colorado. Their average age was thirty-four, they had practiced an average of eleven years in public accounting, and during the four years previous to the study they had participated fairly extensively and at a rapidly growing rate in various forms of continuing education. Among other questions, the respondents were asked to judge the relevance and the quality of activities sponsored by various kinds of institutions. Formal in-firm training was given the highest ranking for both relevance and quality. Second and third in both categories were courses sponsored by the American Institute of Certified Public Accountants (or the comparable state society) and presentations by an instructor, discussion leader, or speaker. In the ten categories of sponsorship, one of which was "other," there was a fairly substantial congruence between the two rankings, with one notable exception. University or college credit courses were judged to be fourth in quality and tenth in relevance. (The comparable figures for noncredit courses were eighth and seventh.)

Most people take learner satisfaction at face value as a highly significant measure. It is assumed that the learner is the best or ultimate judge of quality. A parallel belief holds that experienced and mature learners are even better judges than beginners and young people. In recent years, however, faith in these assumptions has been diminished by several studies showing that when the actual accomplishment of students in schools and colleges was compared with their estimate of the quality of instruction, a negative correlation resulted. Cognitive gain was higher in classes the students disliked than in those they liked. These studies have come under bitter attack as being deficient in design and comprehensiveness, but they did at least cause educators to examine more closely than before the assumption that student judgment is the criterion against which performance should be measured.

Meanwhile the belief that experienced and mature professionals can be relied upon for accurate judgments about the quality of teaching was seriously shaken by the so-called "Dr. Fox studies." In the original investigation (Naftulin, Ware, and Donnelly, 1973), a professional actor was given a fictitious name (Dr. Myron L. Fox), identity (an authority on the application of mathematics to human behavior), and *curriculum vita*. He gave a lecture entitled "Mathematical Game Theory as Applied to Physician Education," which was based on authentic material. In his one-hour presentation and the ensuing thirty-minute discussion, "Dr. Fox" made what the authors of the study called "an excessive use of double talk, neologisms, non sequiturs, and contradictory statements." He also used much "parenthetical humor and meaningless references to unrelated topics." His general manner was warm, enthusiastic, and friendly. The original presentation was made to a select audience of psychiatrists, psychologists, and social workers. The entire proceedings were videotaped and later shown to two other groups, one of which was similar to the first and the other of which was made up of advanced graduate students who had had field experience. The response of all three groups, as expressed on a questionnaire, was overwhelmingly positive, even to such questions as "Did he present his material in a well-organized form?"

The first study led to a series of others. In one of them the same actor as in the earlier study was engaged to present six videotaped lectures, all on the same topic. Three were delivered in the seductive fashion used in the first study; the other three were straightforward presentations. In each set of three, one was high, one was medium, and one was low in content, conveying twenty-six, fourteen, and four substantive points respectively. Six matched groups of undergraduate and graduate students were shown these videotapes and asked to take cognitive tests on the material and fill out evaluation instruments. The cognitive scores were positively correlated with the level of content presented, but the high-seduction films in all cases produced higher scores than did the low-seduction films. In fact the cognitive scores of those students who saw the high-seduction low-content film were higher than those who saw the low-seduction high-content film. Other related topics have been considered in other studies (Williams and Ware, 1976; Ware and Williams, 1977; Williams and Ware, 1977), one notable finding being that the "Dr. Fox effect" is not a single-lecture phenomenon but lasts during at least two sequential presentations.

Nobody would wish to discard learner assessment as a useful instrument for evaluating instruction merely on the basis of these and other studies, particularly because some of them are still controversial. These investigations do suggest, however, that an uncritical acceptance of student judgments is no longer warranted. This conclusion is further emphasized by the increasing trend in educational research toward studying the differential responses of learners to various methods of instruction. Students vary greatly in their learning styles and make judgments accordingly. Thus a generalized averaging out of responses to questionnaires may tend to obscure rather than to reveal information. But, accepting all such limitations, two conclusions still appear feasible: First, student judgments can provide one form of information on the relative success of an educational activity, particularly when included with other indications of success such as the measurement of increased competence or performance. Second, if a skillful use by an instructor of "seductive" presentation increases the amount learned by the students, it would seem profitable to learn how to be seductive.

Accomplishment of a learning plan. The demonstration by learners of their level of attained accomplishment follows patterns and principles that have become commonplace at all levels of formal education and are not unique to continuing professional education. Measurement is considered an integral part of a learning design, however brief or lengthy, simple or complex. Goals are stated so that their accomplishment can either be evaluated directly or give rise to evaluation criteria. A system of measurement of results is devised that permits such evaluation. A pretest is often given to determine the students' entry knowledge or ability and special needs. During the course of instruction, increased knowledge and ability are monitored, continuously or periodically, to determine what changes in either learning procedures or goals should be made; this is called "formative evaluation." At the conclusion, the final accomplishment by the learners is assessed; this is called "summative evaluation."

The systems of measurement used to assess accomplishment can be of many forms, though educators in the professions tend to think in terms of either pencil-and-paper or "practical" tests, the latter showing the extent of the students' learning in various ways, most of which simulate real-life situations. In the 1970s, an increased interest has been shown in measuring competence. This emphasis calls for the statement of goals in operational terms, including the full range of cognitive, affective, and skill capacities required to perform specific actions, such as arriving at the correct diagnosis of a complex problem or demonstrating the capacity to create a work of art. Often competence-based education calls for the organization of content into modular units, each of which can be separately mastered. In other circumstances, the term describes efforts to place emphasis on behaviorally described objectives and complex evaluative systems which assess skill and sensitiveness as well as cognition.

The theoretical framework of evaluating the accomplishment of a learning plan, as summarized in the two preceding paragraphs, has dominated the thought of continuing professional educators partly because it has been highly developed in conventional forms of schooling and partly because much of the work done in the mode of instruction occurs in settings in which learning is operationally divorced from actual practice. A college or university, an association, or an independent establishment often sponsors a course that is a separate, self-contained unit not directly related to practice. Ultimate achievement in such

an activity is the attainment of mastery by the learner or
learners. It is of no concern to the leaders of the course whether
or not this mastery is used after it is achieved. Surprisingly
enough, even the continuing professional educators who sponsor activities in workplaces sometimes do not take advantage
of their closeness to practice to go beyond mastery or competence to performance. This strange outcome is the result of the
belief or assumption that education should be separated formally from other activities in order to give it adequate clarification and stature.

Those who teach or learn by the mode of inquiry cannot
follow a predetermined plan such as that usually adopted for
the mode of instruction. Thus a professional association that
needs to frame new policies or solve a problem can only outline
initial positions and establish principles and preliminary schedules to guide its efforts. As the plan of inquiry unfolds, its form
may be altered or supplemented by evaluative decisions made
by its participants or sponsors. When the process has ended and
the ultimate outcomes have been decided, the immediate evaluation will rest upon subjective judgment by the people concerned. The ultimate appraisal will be pragmatic. Do the results
of the inquiry work?

Measurement of performance. In many employment situations, the measurement of the extent of improved performance
as a result of formal learning is often built into the career line of
the professionals involved. The example of officers in the armed
forces has already been given, but the same practice is followed
in many other settings as well, particularly those which are collective or hierarchical. An individual who undertakes a program
of self-improvement is expected, on its completion, to be able
to understand and do things that were not possible before. This
change is most evident when the learning program is part of induction into a new specialty or level of service or when an individual who has not been in practice decides to resume work. If
a member of a law firm is asked by her partners to prepare herself to handle a new category of cases, if an engineer is chosen
to head a new unit in her firm, or if a trained nurse who has
been absent from his profession decides to take up his duties

again, he or she must ordinarily make systematic preparation to undertake the new responsibilities. The test of how well that preparation was carried out is determined by the ability with which the new duties are handled. Even when the basic aim is not induction into a new responsibility but maintenance or modernization on a continuing job, it is usually expected by the learners and their associates that the newly learned competence will be displayed in the normal course of work.

The closest association between learning and performance occurs in educational activities sponsored by those who control the workplace. If a course is offered by a hospital for a category of its employees or a curriculum-planning workshop is held under the auspices of a local school system for its teachers, the possibility exists of a close relationship between learning and practice, each enriching the other so that immediate, though often subtle, changes in practice occur. In these cases, the mode of inquiry may be used as well as the mode of instruction, because the professionals involved may be led to question established dogma and bring their experience to bear on the shaping of new principles and policies for either the hospital or the school.

In other forms of sponsorship, a linkage between learning and performance can be established, though it is often carried out on a sporadic, generalized, and subjective basis. Tuition reimbursement plans are usually established by their sponsors to serve as both an employee benefit system and as a means of upgrading the work of the people who take part in the programs for which reimbursement is provided. Discussions with personnel managers indicated that tuition reimbursement programs are valuable but that they are often among the first items cut from budgets in times of financial stringency. I am not aware of any carefully controlled studies that measure the extent to which learning acquired under a tuition reimbursement plan influenced performance, particularly as far as professionals are concerned. However, one study of the employees of the city of Milwaukee who had taken advantage of a tuition reimbursement plan must have included a large number of professionals (Milwaukee Personnel Department Training Unit, 1977). Of the sample queried,

90 percent felt that the courses taken improved their performance, and 60 percent felt that it aided their chance for promotion. Of those who had actually been promoted, 87 percent felt
that they had been aided by their learning experiences. When
supervisors in the system were questioned as to the value of tuition reimbursement, 80 percent felt that it was a useful way to
overcome job deficiencies, 93 percent felt that it was a good
way to prepare for promotion, and 79 percent felt that it helped
employees to keep up to date on new developments in their
fields. When these supervisors were asked about what had actually occurred in their departments as a result of participation in
learning, 79 percent said that quality of job performance generally improved, 69 percent said that employees did more work
than before, and 89 percent said that employees had improved
their chances of advancement. Only a few supervisors felt that
participation in the plan had been used as a way to help employees find jobs with other employers.

The follow-up of participants by sponsors of educational
activities tends to be sporadic. The provider of a course or workshop may decide to send out a questionnaire to its participants
some time after they have settled back into their work habits,
asking them how participation in the activity has changed their
performance. The results of such inquiries usually vary greatly
from one situation to another, are based on uncertain recollec-
tions, and are not validated by external reports of either the extent of change or its quality.

Research investigations that probe deeper than questionnaires reveal subtleties not always apparent to those who assess
the improvement of practice as a result of learning. One such
study was reported by Chambers and others (1976a), who wished
to measure the impact of a continuing education course on the
actual behavior of entrepreneurial dentists. The subjects were
the members of an autonomous study club, which meant that
they had a sustained interest in continuing learning. The results,
therefore, cannot be generalized to all dentists or all professionals but are sufficiently provocative to be worth reporting.

Precourse and postcourse visits were made by two investigators to the offices of the fifteen dentists in the sample in order

to measure performance in ten dimensions of behavior that are logically related to the content of the course. A rating scale was used independently by the two observers, and any differences were reconciled by discussion. The average dentist studied made changes in almost half the categories after taking the course. The details of the changes are significant and interesting but too complex to be summarized here. However, the investigators reached several broad conclusions.

First, the dentists did not follow exactly the advice given by the instructor but modified "the information and procedures suggested in the course to fit their own needs and the constraints of their practices" (p. 548). These adaptations were not caused by any lack of understanding of what had been suggested or any desire to cut costs. "Typically the dentist can give a well thought out rationale in support of his failure to incorporate course material in its original form" (p. 548). An important methodological implication here is that the measurement of changed performance should not rely heavily on detailed checklists or predetermined criteria but must be capable of assessing variations in recommended procedures made necessary by diverse practice.

Second, the judgment of the dentists about what changes were important to them and therefore deserved to be reported varied markedly from comparable judgments of the evaluators. Thus the self-report technique of measuring changes in performance, particularly when based on categories established by the investigator, may have limited value when assessments are made of the influence of continuing education.

Third, the motives of the dentists for taking the course were complex, and varied substantially from one person to another. This finding bears out the general research summarized in Chapter Five, but this study (1976a, p. 550) comes to an additional and important conclusion: "The motives of practitioners could have been used to predict behavioral change resulting from course attendance." This conclusion reinforces the contention that in continuing professional education, it is important for a self-directed learner to understand his or her own goals and for the instructors of any group effort to be aware of the variety of reasons for participation that motivate the people concerned.

Measuring the Results of Total Educative Processes

The evaluation of a professional's learning must be broader and more significant than the measurement of competence and performance achieved in any single educational program or sequence of programs. This is the growing belief of professionalizing groups as they move toward a greater sense of individual and collective responsibility for their actions. Learning occurs chiefly as a by-product of alert and self-monitored experience and is strongly reinforced both by efforts to make that experience more educative and by participation in formal instructional activities. The net result is reflected in the quality of practice demonstrated by an individual practitioner, by groups of professionals in various settings, and by a professionalizing occupation as a whole.

Appraisal is always ultimately subjective, but it can be greatly aided by the development of refined measurement instruments. Methods by which judgments are made concerning the competence or performance of working professionals are still relatively primitive. However, many people are working in experimental, pilot, and demonstration settings to perfect techniques, and it is hoped that eventually this effort will lead to systems of appraisal that can be widely applied.

Peer appraisal. The more common term *peer review* is not used here for two reasons. First, *review* does not suggest assessment of quality as strongly as does *appraisal*, and quality assessment is essential to the process described here. Second, *peer review* has a second and probably more widely used meaning that is not intended here; it includes the many procedures in which scholars and professionals allocate financial and other resources to the projects of fellow specialists. Controversies surround the use of such procedures, particularly by the government (Gustafson, 1975), and the lack of clarity caused by two meanings of the same term is often compounded by the conflict to which each usage tends to give rise.

Peer appraisal is based on the belief, as Freidson and Rhea (1965, p. 107) put it, that "professionals have the special privilege of freedom from the control of outsiders" and must accept the accompanying obligation to make qualitative judgments about one another. In various situations, therefore, a group of professionals, usually working in a collective or hierarchical setting, systematically scrutinize the work of their colleagues and make these analyses available to the persons concerned. This information is sometimes made a part of the permanent (usually confidential) records of the institution and is often used as the basis for promotion, retention, or elimination. Peer appraisal systems of this sort have been in existence for many years with the faculty members of universities. For example, the faculty of a professional school may maintain a complex system of judgment of all its members until they have secured tenure—and sometimes even beyond that point. Judgments are customarily made by colleagues from the same institution, but external referees are sometimes involved. Usually the pattern followed at each institution is unique, though imitation or adaptation of particular features is often found.

Many relatively simple ways have been devised to provide professional peer appraisal in nonacademic settings. The staff of a school or a social work agency can establish a committee, usually with a rotating membership, to monitor competence. The pathologists at a hospital can report on actual causes of death as revealed by autopsies, contrasting them with the diagnoses of attending physicians. In a city school system, the standardized test scores received by children in elementary school can be reported on a class-by-class or school-by-school basis, thereby highlighting problem situations that need to be examined to determine whether teacher incompetence is one of the causes. A simple peer appraisal system may require the members of some well-defined and interactive group of professionals to fill out rating scales on their colleagues, thereby developing a mutual system of judgment. Freidson and Rhea (1965) describe such a system developed among the members of a medical clinic staff, and Gage (1972) suggests a similar plan as it might work in a school setting. Such rating scales may have value, particularly if they are refined and based on thorough observations; but (as with any other form of peer appraisal) they represent person-to-person judgment in which an individual with one set of standards evaluates another individual who may or may not have identical values.

Because the practice of formal peer appraisal has been widely practiced in the past few years, the awareness of what constitutes a comprehensive system has grown more and more substantial, and several apparently indispensable elements have been defined. They are summarized in the following paragraphs.

1. An organizing framework or system of professional colleagueship should serve as an encompassing network of professionals. Examples are a law firm, a hospital nursing staff, or a school. As Sanazaro and Worth (1978, p. 1171) have pointed out, "Systematic assessment and assurance of the quality of medical care are now major elements of national health policy." This conclusion, amply buttressed by congressional activity, has meant that health care units seeking federal funds must develop systems of peer appraisal.

2. A formal structure of appraisal should be created. It is most often guided by or actually carried out by a committee chosen by the professionals involved, with a sufficient rotation of membership so that everyone within the encompassing network has an eventual obligation and opportunity to serve. To most professionals, self-control is essential. Schless, a physician, has argued this in relation to medicine, and his words could be echoed by leaders in every other profession: "The alternative to successful self-determined peer review programs is painfully obvious, and might well result in politically imposed standards aimed solely at reducing dollar costs but oblivious to possibly greatly increased expense in terms of the quality of medical care. It is this *quality* which we are responsible for bringing to the public" (Schless, 1972, p. 1061).

3. A statement of the standards of good practice should be developed. These standards can be adapted from national codes of ethics or from examples used in other peer appraisal networks but must be applied to local practice and refined frequently enough to remain consistent with the best modern prac-

tice. These criteria should be clearly stated so that they can be used to measure actual performance. For example, Laventurier (1972) provides a detailed description of a flexible system of seven broad criteria used by the pharmacists providing drugs authorized by Medicaid in the San Joaquin area of California. The House of Delegates of the American Association of Dental Schools has adopted five general principles to govern peer appraisal in dentistry and has spelled out in detail what experiences students in dental schools should have to prepare them for careers in which such appraisal will be an established part of a practitioner's life.

4. Some objective body of data or systematic observation (or both) should be available to serve as the basis for judgment. It is at this point that many peer appraisal systems fail. Satisfactory systems for measuring performance are hard to devise. In a number of professions, particularly those associated with health, record-keeping systems are being developed to provide a basis for judgment, but none have yet been universally accepted. Indeed, one of the problems of those who design peer appraisal systems is that they are constantly drawn away from their primary tasks by lengthy and sometimes exhausting arguments on the merits of various systems of recording and retrieving data. Sanazaro and Worth (1978, p. 1171) have amply documented their assertion that "the relations between 'process measures' (i.e., what physicians do to and for patients in providing medical care) and 'outcomes' (i.e., the results of that care) have been defined conceptually, empirically, operationally and experimentally." Similar problems have been found in the rating of teachers in terms of their use of certain processes compared with the grades received by their students on standardized tests.

5. Some practitioners should be chosen for close scrutiny. Ideally peer appraisal systems should be so established and maintained as to deal with the full range of quality of practice, not merely with the people who cause problems. Some networks are small enough so that every member's performance can be periodically reviewed. For example, one pediatric unit in a prepaid health care system randomly chooses an appointment hour each

week; the survey committee then studies the cases being cared for by each physician and nurse at that time. In the normal course of work, allowing for the rotation of time assignments, each professional's work is sampled frequently. In larger networks, individuals may be selected for scrutiny on a sampling basis. Sometimes special attention is given to those individuals whose quality of performance is called into question. The need for detailed examination in these cases may arise from any of a number of sources, such as client complaints, negative comments by fellow workers, or indications that some established criterion of good practice is not being followed. Laventurier (1972) cites an example of this third indicator: the drugs issued to each Medicaid client by each pharmacist in a peer appraisal network are recorded and cumulative records are kept for each physician, pharmacist, and patient. Normal ranges of prescriptions of each kind of drug and of total patient patterns of drug use are defined. Cases that fall well outside the range of normal practice are brought to the committee's attention.

6. Each professional should be made aware of his or her performance rating. The methods of communication include many different written forms and oral interviews, but a central idea of all reporting mechanisms must be that the evaluation has been made by peers whom the person concerned has had a part in choosing and according to criteria to which he or she assents. If negative comments must be made, counseling by colleagues is always a difficult interpersonal activity, but this difficulty will be diminished if the peer appraisal system is known to be objective.

7. In the event of consistently poor performance, penalties should be applied, their nature varying with the gravity and frequency of the offenses as well as with the options for action available. Among the penalties most commonly invoked are formal warnings, written reprimands, denial of promotion or of salary increase, withdrawal of access to needed resources, discharge from employment, and loss of the right to practice.

A successful peer appraisal program provides important incentives for continuing education. To an innate zest for learning is added the collective pressures of the colleagues with whom each person is most immediately and directly associated. The desire of the professionals in the network to do well on subsequent reviews leads to a general responsiveness to both formal and informal opportunities to learn. Also the results of peer appraisal may lead to awareness of deficiencies that can be remedied by education either for an individual or for many or all of the members of the network.

Despite the obvious values of peer appraisal systems, however, they still have serious flaws. The difference between process and outcome (as mentioned by Sanazaro and Worth, 1978) is present in all professions. Moreover, every profession has schisms and factions, the most prominent being that between practitioners who hold fast to customary values and patterns of behavior and those who espouse emergent values in what they may even choose to call a "new professionalism." The latter tend to have a more egalitarian viewpoint, expressed in a community-wide commitment to service, than the former. This difference in turn sets up a dichotomy in peer ranking that can be destructive, particularly in collective and hierarchical settings. Other differences—for example between subject-centered and child-centered teachers or between clergy interested in social reform and personal salvation—can also make it difficult or impossible to set the criteria for peer appraisal. Factors that have nothing to do with competence can also blur the lines of assessment—sex, age, ethnic origin, religion, wealth, and length of residence in the community.

Years of work and field testing lie ahead before systems of peer appraisal can be sufficiently perfected to allow their widespread adoption even within a single profession. Until that time, informal peer appraisal of the types suggested in Chapter Four will continue to operate. Within any community and, to a lesser degree, within larger population groups, those who belong to any profession make constant judgments about the competence of their colleagues which, however imperfectly and subjectively based, are nonetheless far reaching in their impact. Informal peer appraisal influences all practitioners but probably has its most important impact on two groups of professionals. One cluster is made up of the innovators, the pacesetters, and the top portion of the middle majority; the second cluster, at the other end of the innovativeness scale, consists of the worst laggards. The former seek status, greater compensation, and the personal satisfaction of being at or near the forefront of practice. The latter desperately seek to retain their right to practice, usually in the face of clear-cut threats to their livelihood or licenses.

Complex self-assessment programs. These forms of self-testing have spread very rapidly since the late 1960s. They are used chiefly by the health professions and particularly by medical specialty groups. On July 1, 1979, in the medical field alone, thirty-one self-assessment programs were in existence, most of them sponsored by national organizations.* While specific systems vary widely in detail, most of them consist of lengthy examinations that purport to test all of the essential aspects of a profession or one of its specialties. These examinations are taken voluntarily by practitioners, and the results are reported confidentially to them.

The purpose of these examinations is to give a professional practitioner, particularly one who is highly specialized, an accurate assessment of his or her current state of the knowledge of the profession. John Hubbard of the National Board of Medical Examiners defined the self-assessment examination's principle by quoting St. Paul's epistle to the Galatians: "For if a man thinketh himself to be something when he is nothing, he deceiveth himself. But let each man prove his own worth and then shall he have his glorying in regard to himself alone, and not of his neighbor" (Hubbard, 1971b, p. 424). The method by which each professional proves his own worth can be generally sketched as follows: Sponsorship of a program is initiated by a general or specialized professional association. The essential knowledge base of the profession is analyzed by a group of its leaders into its component practical and theoretical subfields. A committee of content specialists is formed for each one and, in collaboration with specialists in test construction, this committee writes and refines a cluster of questions (usually multiple choice)

*This information was supplied by Jean Ayers of the American Medical Association.

which, taken as a group, fairly represents the body of content involved. Out of these separate efforts, a total test of perhaps 750 items is constructed and reviewed in its totality, both by an overall committee and by pilot groups to whom the test is administered. When the process of validation has been completed, all practitioners of the profession or specialty group are given the opportunity to take the test, usually paying a fee to do so. The questions are answered at the convenience of the respondent, who may or may not be allowed to use available sources of information. The completed examination is then returned, sometimes with fairly elaborate safeguards of secrecy. For example, it may be sent by the professional to a bonded delivery service, which is the only agency to know the coded number of that copy of the examination. When it has been scored, results are sent back to the intermediary, which then transmits them to the individual in a plain envelope with a preaddressed label.

The information provided to the practitioner is sometimes quite complex. He or she will probably receive a group of scores, one for the entire examination and others for each of the subtopics. These may be raw scores (number right and number wrong), but they are often put in perspective by being compared with those of others taking the test. The practitioner may be told, for example, that he or she is in the top 10 percent of the respondents overall but is in the third decile for one subtopic and the seventh for another. For each question that has been missed, the practitioner may receive an aid to knowledge, such as a citation to the literature, a reprint of a published paper, or a specially prepared abstract of the data supporting the right answer. The examinee may also be provided with more general counsel by receiving an individualized message; perhaps one which has been prepared by a computer. A surgeon may, for example, be given this assessment: "Congratulations on your performance in category 1. Your knowledge of gastrointestinal surgery is outstanding in comparison with your specialty peers. The evaluation of your knowledge in the field of metabolism, shock, and surgical endocrinology suggests the need for remedial postgraduate education" (Hubbard, 1971b, p. 424). Meanwhile the leaders of the profession may receive an analysis of each item on the examination based on the scores of all the people who have taken it. This summation shows which areas of content are least well understood by those now practicing in the field, thus defining the goals of intensive direct efforts at education to be carried out through journal articles, conventions, conferences, and other means. Presumably the next round of tests would show whether these efforts have been successful.

The self-assessment examination is forward looking and is an instrument that combines evaluation with education at every point: at the time the examination is taken (if the use of outside resources is permitted); in the detailed follow-up of error by the study of why the correct answers are correct; in the advice given as to general areas of weakness; and in the educative activities that follow the analysis of the total pattern of responses to the examination. Thus the proponents of this form of self-assessment have tended to refer to it as a "learning examination," encouraging the professional toward the achievement of excellence, in contrast to tests for licensure, which establish basic competence to practice the profession.

The self-assessment examination, however, has three interrelated limitations. The first of these is that even in subspecialties, some practitioners work in fields so concentrated that the cost of developing special examinations for them would be very high. In some alterations of the basic techniques, therefore, one set of questions is given to all practitioners, the assumption being that however rarefied their practice may be a common body of knowledge is essential. The respondent also identifies one or more specialized areas applicable to his or her practice. The analysis of responses can then be made for both the section of the examination that tests the common body of knowledge and for each of the subsets, enabling the practitioner to know his or her ranking in each one and providing program suggestions for continuing educators as to areas of need for knowledge. Alternatively the examinee answers only those questions which seem relevant. The possibility of establishing comparability is thereby destroyed, but the reports on the responses to individual test items provide valid though limited learning experiences.

A second problem is that these examinations tend to test particularized knowledge and understanding but not skill or the complex interaction of factors that must be used in dealing with specific cases. Efforts have been made to remedy this difficulty by introducing "client management" problems, which ask the respondent to deal with complex situations similar to those which occur in practice. For example, in tests constructed for pediatricians and psychiatrists, the Educational Testing Service has items in which "a clinical problem is presented and followed by possible diagnostic or management options. When an option is selected, the physician marks it with a special crayon, and the answer, printed in invisible ink, becomes visible. The information provided directs the physician to the next decision point, where other options are made available. This pattern is repeated until the case is resolved" ("Trend Toward Self-Assessment . . . ," 1976, p. 3). It is also possible, though expensive, to require professionals to take examinations at places where advanced forms of testing are available. Complex computerized client management cases can be developed and simulation techniques can require the professional to demonstrate physical skills.

A third problem is that because examinations are voluntary, they may be taken only by innovators, pacesetters, and the upper part of the middle majority, leaving those professionals who are in the lower half of the profession relatively untouched. Nobody seems to know of any good way to increase the percentage drawn from this last group, though many conscientious efforts have been made to do so. Self-assessment, if it remains wholly voluntary, may prove useful chiefly for refining and extending the capacities of the more competent members of professions. This outcome would be desirable, particularly because the tendency toward complacency of people in these groups may lead them to be less knowledgeable than they think they are. While no distributions of scores are made publicly available, it has been reported to me confidentially that in at least the early forms of such examinations the distribution of scores followed a customary distribution curve with an item failure rate of from 2 to 99 percent. If this is still true, ample evidence of the need to learn exists among the leaders of the professions concerned.

Self-appraisal examinations are not all at the same level of sophistication. In the early days, some specialty groups did no more than use tests no longer used by boards for original certification. Extreme caution about confidentiality has led some professions to fail to take full educational advantage of more innovative systems. For example, some examinations are self-scored; as a result, the practitioner knows only a raw score—not one that compares his or her performance to that of fellow professionals. Such a practice also allows no follow-up of educational assistance. In other cases that do use central scoring, item analyses are forbidden, thus depriving the profession of a knowledge of areas that need remediation.

While failures to take full advantage of modern forms of self-examination still exist, the rapid advance in their use has been extraordinary. The advance has been so great, in fact, that an obvious next step has occurred to many people: Why not make this examination the basis for certification in a specialty group or even relicensure in the profession itself? As might well be imagined, strenuous objections to this idea have been expressed. Many of them arise from opposition to the very idea of recredentialing, an opposition that will be considered fully in the next chapter. It can also be argued that licensure examinations and self-appraisal examinations exist for different reasons. The self-appraisal examination is essentially constructed as a learning instrument that makes broad suggestions of what may be known, understood, or done in a profession. Its designers contemplate an almost limitless ceiling, not a floor, as is the case with a licensure examination, which must establish a "cutting level" below which one fails. If there were to be an examination for the revalidation of a certificate or license, the current test taken for basic credentialing might be better suited for the purpose than a self-appraisal form. For example, the reexamination for a drivers' license is identical to the original examination, though the "cutting level" may be different.

Those who argue that recredentialing should be based on self-appraisal examinations are not daunted by these criticisms. They try to allay worries by noting that the failure to be recredentialed does not necessarily mean that the credential is withdrawn. The original credential is merely dated (perhaps with a large red date overprinted on the document). Clients who see these credentials (often prominently displayed on the wall) can then be aware of the "vintage" of the professional's knowledge. The educative aspects of the examination can be retained, but the need for revalidation would increase the number of people who expose themselves to the opportunity provided. A "cutting level" would be needed but might initially be set fairly low and subsequently raised as a broader basis of familiarity with the new instrument is established.

Some people are not prepared to accept so gradual an approach. When Senator Edward Kennedy discussed self-appraisal examinations at a meeting in 1974 of the Senate Subcommittee on Health, he argued strongly that all of the medical specialty groups should have such a plan in operation on a mandatory basis in less than five years (U.S. Senate, 1974, p. 821). While his hope has not been realized, the groundwork for its eventual accomplishment has been progressively laid by the building up of the number of tests and techniques for constructing them. Leaders of professions outside the health field are looking closely at this progress and, with the passage of time, the scope of self-appraisal examinations may broaden until they become both more familiar and more acceptable as bases for recredentialing.

In 1971, when self-appraisal examinations were in their infancy, a group of specialists convened a special workshop sponsored by the American Medical Association. The summary of the proceedings ends with the comment: "On the basis of the information gathered here, it is possible to conclude that self-assessment programs will have wide support, will continue to develop, will probably be offered by most of the professional organizations eventually, and will probably be among the major continuing education efforts of most of the professional societies" (American Medical Association, 1971, p. 9). Events since 1971 have borne out this prophecy.

Formal staff appraisal. Formal systems of staff appraisal are common in organizations. In fully worked out programs, reviews of work performance are made, usually annually, by supervisors. Each review is based on the job description of the employee concerned and is usually both written and oral. This system may call for an initial appraisal by the supervisor with ratings of past performance and recommendations for future improvement, and the latter may include participation in formal or informal learning activities. This preliminary rating is then discussed with the employee, who has the right to question judgments, ask for changes, point out inhibiting limitations in his work environment or in the policies of the organization, and suggest alternate courses of action for the future. The actual freedom of the employee to be open and direct in this discussion depends greatly on the relationship he or she has with the supervisor.

After the interview, a final rating is made and placed in the employee's personnel record. Ordinarily he or she has the right to inspect it and sometimes to make a formal rejoinder, which is also filed. In some cases, the rating is reviewed by an individual or committee with greater authority and may, along with ratings of other employees, become a part of the evaluation of the supervisor by the next level of authority. Ratings influence compensation and other benefits, including promotion. They also form a continuing record of an employee's progress, because one item that influences subsequent ratings is the extent to which the plan for improvement of the previous year has been carried out.

The extent to which the formal staff appraisal of professionals corresponds to this general system is influenced by the nature of the situations in which professionals work hierarchically. When the entire structure of an organization is professional, as in an engineering or pharmaceutical firm, or when a special professional corps exists within a general administrative structure, as in a specialized government bureau or in a research and development department of an industrial corporation, the system of staff appraisal is usually not very different from that used under other circumstances, although the nature of the profession will influence the criteria of the rating system. When the professional is an adjunct employee, however, his or her rating must often be made by a generalist administrator or by a member of another profession, which means that important differences of interpretation and understanding may occur. A school principal's rating of a nurse or a librarian, for example, must take into account the fact that their work proceeds according to different standards than do those of the teachers who are their colleagues. The same is true of the corporation vice-president who must oversee the rating systems of the engineering and research department heads. An important learning experience of most senior executives is determined by their need to appraise the work of diversified specialist individuals or groups.

The importance of continuing education in the processes of formal staff appraisal should be crucial, though it is sometimes ignored or treated lightly. In the context of an intimate and direct appraisal of work, the professional is made aware of another person's perception of the quality of his or her performance. On the basis of this evidence of need, a program for the future is designed to include both formal instruction and informal reconstruction of the physical or social work setting to make it more educative. Deficiencies in performance are perceived as challenges to be met and not as personal inadequacies. Abrahamson (1967, p. 84) has reported that "generally social workers seem much less hostile to the idea of supervision than many other professional groups"; he ascribes this fact to their interpretation of supervision "as educational rather than administrative in purpose."

As far as professionals are concerned, staff appraisal programs are likely to become more learning-oriented as continuing education grows in importance and availability. Individuals who are eager to learn will find more opportunities than before to do so and may gain financial and other support from their employers for their educational endeavors. Individuals whose capacity to perform effectively is diminishing will have their deficiencies brought to their attention by supervisors who are aware that new standards must be met and that the means for doing so are readily available. No organization wishes to employ a professional whose credentials are antiquated, and the increasing concern for recredentialing provides a useful means by which supervisors can insist on maintaining adequate performance.

A Concluding Note

The deep concern with professional improvement that led
to the development of the evaluative systems described in this
chapter has stimulated the growth of many excellent educational programs but has also encouraged some activities that are
hard to defend. Much of the ballooning effort labeled "continuing education" is still characterized either by eager directness
and naive faith or by an apparent belief that only marginal efforts and uninspired instruction are needed to bring practitioners to ever higher levels of performance. One faculty member in
a professional school referred to continuing education as "shout-
ing out of the window," and an analysis of the programs at his
institution shows the aptness of his metaphor: Faculty members
who can be persuaded to do so give lectures on subjects of their
own choosing to audiences they do not know, who have assembled only because they want to put in enough hours of classroom attendance so that they can meet a relicensure requirement. Unfortunately such programs are distressingly common
throughout the country. As a result, every profession now has
members who vigorously oppose what they regard as the excessive promotion of continuing education. As the balloon continues to expand, they believe, it is increasingly likely to become
difficult to manage and may eventually burst. An account of
the annual Congress on Medical Education in 1977 began with
the question, "Is medicine rushing headlong into a billion-dollar
enterprise—continuing medical education—whose problems we
underestimate and whose value we overestimate?" ("Continuing
Medical Education," 1977, p. 11). A summary of the addresses
at the congress made it clear that many of the speakers would
answer "yes" on both points.

Current disenchantment, however, may imply that the
leaders of professions have not yet developed a subtlety and
constancy of approach to continuing professional education to
match the complex processes they use at earlier levels of teaching. At the beginning of the twentieth century, basic preparation for the then-established professions was provided in ways
that seem incredibly simple by today's standards. Eighty years

later, these systems of pre-service education have become complex and costly. Furthermore, new clusters of professions have not only come into being but also have developed elaborate patterns of basic education. It seems likely that, in the years just ahead, continuing education will mature in concept and grow in size until it becomes at least as important as initial training has come to be. This increase in significance will be enhanced by an ever-greater concern for quality assurance, the topic of the next chapter.

Chapter 9

Assuring Professional Quality Through Continuing Education

> *The attainment of proficiency, the pushing of your skill with attention to the most delicate shades of excellence, is a matter of vital concern. Efficiency of a practically flawless kind may be reached naturally in the struggle for bread. But there is something beyond—a higher point, a subtle and unmistakable touch of love and pride beyond mere skill; almost an inspiration which gives to all work that finish which is almost art—which is art.*
>
> Joseph Conrad

As was noted in Chapter One, continuing education moved into a new era in the 1960s, when professions first became subject to widespread attack. Until then, the need for a professional to keep up to date had been accepted as an individual obligation enforced by self-discipline and by sanctions applied by colleagues and persons served. The link between level of performance and extent of continued learning was clear but not widely stressed. However, the sudden decline of many professions in public esteem and an accompanying growth of criticism from within their own memberships gave rise to serious concerns about what might be done to improve both the substance and the image of practice. The most immediate positive reaction was to emphasize the old but neglected idea of continuing education. It was thought that earnest and, if possible, innovative efforts to help practitioners learn might greatly improve performance, disarm criticism, and build defenses against malpractice suits, loss of certification, and the requirement of compulsory periodic relicensure or other forms of recredentialing. As a result, every characteristic of the professionalizing process eventually became linked with learning.

But nothing is a panacea for the problems of modern professions, not even education. Other ways to assure high quality have been added to self-policing and the enforcement of codes of practice. Among these essentials are the use of operational routines that prevent or minimize error, the development of patterns of service that take account of changing times, the enactment of laws and the establishment of regulations to safeguard the public interest, and the vigilant determination of the people served that high standards will be maintained. These policies and practices are not additions to education; they are interwoven with it. The purpose of this chapter is to identify the major quality controls now being used or advocated and to indicate how continuing education reinforces them. Many previously considered topics will again be reviewed; this time the focus is directly upon quality control, not upon education.

As always, the effort to achieve excellence must be based on the realization that it is ultimately subjective. Procedures can be refined, outcomes can be measured, authorities can be cited, precedents can be followed, and data can be brought to bear upon decision-making processes, but qualitative conclusions must always be judgmental. To hope that if some specific procedure is followed the right answer will always be produced is to rely upon dogma. In any situation, past experience may have shown that one way of doing things is generally best, but in particular cases unknown factors may exist. This is one of the most important lessons a professional, who must always be practical and pragmatic, should learn.

The Case Against the Professions

The modern effort to assure quality of performance is based upon the attacks now launched against the professions, which have always been subject to condemnation. There are numerous collections of witty or damaging charges made in previous eras against specific occupations. Many of them sound startlingly up to date, but actually a profound difference exists between old and modern attacks. The difference lies chiefly in the fact that the people who belong to professionalizing occupations have increased so greatly in number and in their proportion to the rest of the population that they are brought in some fashion into the life of virtually everyone. Problems that were once small are now writ large. With size has come complexity. A neighborhood shop may have inherently the same problems as a mammoth department store, but in the latter case they are magnified, specialized, and intricately interrelated. So it is with modern professions when compared with their predecessors. With the growth of the knowledge bases on which practice must rely, the development of a more egalitarian society, the rise to visibility and power of new categories of occupations, and the development of rapid and pervasive communication, the professions have become universally recognized phenomena of modern life. Their great contributions to society have won them favor and renown but a combination of many other reverberant actions and forces have also brought them into a disfavor that is both particularized to their individual members and generalized to the idea of professionalism itself.

The causes of this disfavor are as immediate as the faulty behavior of a single practitioner and as pervasive as the widespread feeling of disquiet that has diminished respect for all forms of authority in modern society. The heart of the difficulty—at least as it relates to systems of quality control—lies in the changed relationship of the professional to his or her profession. Now that the number of people in every occupation has grown substantially, the capacity of the collective groups to police their members has greatly diminished. Also, as the number of practitioners increases, so does the probability that some of them will be ineffective or unethical. It cannot be argued that the growth itself has been bad, for it has been mandated by the urgent needs of society, but one of the unintended consequences has been a dramatic increase in the belief that better methods of quality control are necessary to remedy errors and deficiencies.

One cluster of accusations focuses on the alleged failure of the professions to develop comprehensive service systems to care for all of the people who need help, particularly the poor and the socially least franchised. Specific allegations take many forms: traditional methods of service do not meet new needs; the number of practitioners is held down to keep fees high; elitism excludes from the profession people who might be better equipped to aid the unserved than can present practitioners; competition and jealousy set up jurisdictions of service that work against comprehensive coverage; the spatial distribution of practitioners is uneven; impoverished or remote geographic areas can attract only the least competent practitioners; and professionals lobby against and otherwise impede legislative and administrative regulations that would remedy present deficiencies.

A second cluster of accusations asserts that professionals always put their own self-interest ahead of the public welfare, even though they have presumably been called to their work by a special sense of mission, are trained directly or indirectly at public expense, owe their livelihood to the people they serve, and are often granted special privileges and immunities. Among specific charges are: conspiring to inhibit or prevent competition; protecting erring colleagues; charging excessive fees; and trying to have all the economic advantages of trade unionism while retaining professional status.

The third cluster of accusations insists that the practices of a profession demonstrate incompetence, inattention, dogmatism, lack of feeling, or malevolence. Some specific charges are: conservatism; faddism; coldness and impersonality; recommendation of unneeded procedures; experimentation at the expense of the public or the persons who should be served; adherence to unnecessary and time-wasting rigidities of procedure; mindless and continued enforcement of regulations that are intended to work in one way but actually work in another; ignorance of new ideas and practices; and failure to develop adequate systems of monitoring quality. On this last point, Brook and Avery

(1976, p. 227), commenting on the American medical care system, noted that "new conceptual frameworks for assessing quality have not been developed in the last two decades."

These charges do not reflect the current overall state of practice in any professionalizing occupation, much less the self-image of its practitioners, but they do suggest the range of problems that require attention if public and personal confidence is to be restored. Every unfortunate incident involving an individual or a group is generalized to a whole profession or even to the idea of professionalism. To the extent that collective reputation declines, so does the social status and self-esteem of practitioners. This interactive effect is accentuated by the fact that when an individual's accomplishment is outstanding, the credit goes to the person; when he or she commits a venal act, even one not associated with work, the profession itself is likely to share in the blame. People tend to be identified by the occupations in which they engage; for example, headlines read "architect accused of killing wife," "engineer gets manslaughter verdict," or "librarian fined for hit-and-run driving." This characteristic is true of all occupations but there are more professionals now than there used to be; so they are noticed more. Also the prestige of the professions and the awareness that their members have special privileges draws particular attention to the errant ways of individual members. Quality controls are not designed to prevent nonoccupational transgressions, but the task of quality control is made more difficult by the public relations problems these transgressions cause.

Professionals ordinarily feel keenly the attacks levied against their own occupation and may even believe that they alone have been singled out for condemnation. In practice, however, they themselves often raise the same charges against other professions and, in fact, some professions work fairly consistently to criticize or police others. Every malpractice suit, for example, can be viewed as an attack by a member of the legal profession on a practitioner of some other profession. Physicians usually feel themselves to be the senior partners in all health care teams; thus, to some extent they act individually and collectively as the monitors of other health professions.

While professionalism itself has come under attack, the inter-relationship among professions both adds to the criticism and provides some assurances of quality.

Present Controls

As American professions began to move beyond the frag-mentation and individualistic approaches of earlier days toward more disciplined and systematic ways of serving society, their efforts to control quality were chiefly oriented to original entry into service. The growth of these efforts has been, as Shimberg, Esser, and Kruger said of licensure, "a haphazard, uncoordin-ated, and chaotic process" (1972, p. 1), varying from occupa-tion to occupation, from time to time, and from place to place. The ultimate results, however, have been impressive. Some form of accreditation of training programs is virtually universal and many work settings must also achieve standards of good prac-tice. The certification of the competence of individuals by as-sociations and their licensure by the state is widespread. Admis-sion to specialty groups is rigorously controlled, as is the right to practice in specific work settings. Thus success has been sub-stantially achieved in the establishment of a basic level of com-petence that an individual must reach before being allowed to work as a fully qualified practitioner in an institution that meets accepted standards.

The controls now being developed to monitor a lifetime of practice are in part adaptations of the regulatory devices that govern entry into a profession and in part systems that grow out of its ongoing practice. Reaccreditation, relicensure, and recerti-fication (usually known collectively as recredentialing) seem logically to follow the initial use of such procedures, though they are more readily accepted by institutions than by individ-uals. Few people doubt the need for periodic appraisal of train-ing programs or workplaces (such as schools or hospitals), but many object to the requirement that practitioners themselves should be subject to any regular reexamination of their compe-tence or performance. In both cases, however, adaptations of initial entry systems have been insufficient to assure quality, and many other methods of regulation or influence have been introduced during the course of the worklife of professionals.

Taken as a whole, the old and new control systems vary widely in every respect. Some are applied to an entire profession or some segment of it; others are aimed at individuals. Some are disciplinary in intent; others are intended to provide incentives for competence. Some are simple; others are complex. Some are based almost entirely on education; others involve it to only a slight degree. For the most part they are related to one another only tangentially if at all—and this fact influences their treatment in this chapter. They will be grouped into three analytical clusters, but each form of quality control is actually undertaken separately, a fact that will be manifested in the discussion of each of them.

Altering Established Control Systems

Most of the recent attempts to assure professional quality have centered on the adaption or supplementation of the systems used to regulate entry into a profession or its specialized practice as well as of the traditional methods of self-policing. However, even those people who have been most progressive in rethinking such systems as accreditation and licensure to make them conform to new ways of thought have often failed to be equally progressive in considering how customary patterns of education should be changed. A leader of a profession may be strongly in favor of relicensure and yet assume that traditional forms of instruction will suffice to achieve the ends desired. The need for lifelong quality assurance must influence traditional control systems, but it must also determine how their requirements are to be met, at least in part, by continuing education.

Reshaping accreditation. In general, it may be said that accreditation is a process by which an organization, either established independently or as part of a larger structure, approves an institution or a program as meeting certain predetermined criteria that are accepted as adequate tests of the level of quality of service provided. Accreditation is thus usually applied in two different situations: First, concerning the professions,

the most widespread application has been to the process of preparing individuals for entry into the occupation. The second
application has been the accreditation of the places where the
work of the profession is actually carried out; widely known examples of this latter application are health-care centers, welfare
services, and secondary schools. These two applications overlap
to some extent, because an educational institution, such as
a school of forestry or of social work, is itself a workplace in
which professionals are employed. In the following discussion,
an arbitrary distinction will be drawn between educational and
workplace accreditation, because the implications of life-long
continuing education are somewhat different for each application. In all such cases, periodic reaccreditation is required to
ensure that standards are maintained and that the attention of
the staff members of the institution or program is frequently
drawn to a direct consideration of the ends and means of the
work they do.

In educational accreditation, attention is here focused on
the examination of professional programs, not upon that broader
process which scrutinizes the total nature and scope of services
of a college or university within which such programs exist.
Each professionalizing occupation establishes its own method
of judging the quality of pre-service training programs and sets
up a formal apparatus and procedure to accredit them. In the
past, continuing education has not been an important aspect of
this process, but that omission must now be remedied if lifelong
learning is to be taken seriously. Among the criteria by which
training programs must be judged, several relate to continuing
education. How well has pre-service instruction been designed
to include only those aspects of content which lay a sound
foundation and prepare people for initial practice, leaving for
later learning those topics which can better be studied if and
when they are needed? How effectively has the faculty of the
pre-service training program designed its formal processes and
presentation so as to prepare and encourage graduates to be
continuing learners? How successfully does the institution seeking accreditation provide, either alone or collaboratively, meaningful and extensive continuing educational opportunities for

professionals already at work in the field? These questions are no more difficult to answer than any of the others which accrediting teams must ask.

In workplace accreditation, the central aim is to be certain that quality assurance is adequately maintained. This goal calls for the audit of both practices and accomplishment. How well are the processes used being carried out? What is the outcome of the work that professionals do for the people served? A school, a hospital, or a psychiatric center must have evidence of the excellence of its performance so that it can be held accountable for what it does or what happens as a result of what it does. Thus quality assurance must be built into the pattern of its work from the very beginning on the basis of process, outcome, or both. The pursuit of excellence should be the constant goal of every staff, but success in achieving it must be periodically reassessed.

The chief task of education under these circumstances is to help deal with the needs revealed by the process of accreditation. The patterns of learning sketched in Chapter Seven as well as the less formal processes mentioned in Chapter Four are both relevant here. In addition, those who engage in workplace accreditation must make it their business to examine the provision of continuing education to the professional staff so that they can maintain and advance the competence required for their present service and also prepare for and function effectively in positions of greater or different responsibility than those they presently hold.

In any accreditation process, inquiries are usually made concerning the level of educational attainment reached by the staff, because it is usually assumed that qualified people must have appropriate basic credentials. It is only a small additional step to make reaccreditation of the institution dependent in part on a demonstration that the professionals employed have increased their level of formal training, have been appropriately recredentialed, or have otherwise demonstrated that they have maintained or increased their ability to perform their duties. When this step is taken, powerful reinforcement is given to all other formal systems of quality assurance.

Reshaping general licensure or certification. As was noted in Chapter Four, a license is issued by a governmental body whereas a certificate is issued by a private organization or association. Either one is based on the examination of whether individuals meet predetermined criteria established by the granting agency. Competence is measured in a number of ways, among which are: achievement of at least a passing score on an examination; completion of an approved program of study; demonstration of satisfactory performance; and testimony from a recognized authority that the individual should have the right to practice. Sometimes two or three basic methods are used; for example, completion of an approved program of study may be required before an applicant is admitted to an examination that measures knowledge or competence. Some professions (such as most forms of librarianship) have no system of licensure or certification. In these cases, the professional degree itself becomes the establishing credential.

Many thoughtful and experienced people have examined professional credentialing and come to very different conclusions about it. Some hold the *laissez faire* view that the whole system is top heavy, overelaborate, inherently meaningless, and an unwarranted intrusion on civil liberties; they believe that all or part of the apparatus should be abandoned. At the opposite extreme are those who think that credentialing is an essential safeguard to society and that its processes should be even more tightly controlled and centrally administered than they now are. The latter opinion has been strengthened by punitive actions by legislative bodies and public administrators. It should be understood, therefore, that all discussions about the nature of credentialing occur within the context of a continuing conflict as to whether it should exist.

Whatever process leads to the initial awarding of a license or certificate, relatively little attention is paid by examiners to the interest of potential professionals in continuing education or to their ability to devise a plan for carrying it out. It would not be difficult to inquire about either matter. Attitudes toward lifelong learning could be measured, as could awareness of resources and the ability to design a personal learning program.

Some systems of credentialing require reports on field experience; this is the case, for example, in the awarding of the CPA. In all systems, evidence could be provided of the extent and quality of noncompulsory learning that the applicant has undertaken. Methods of collecting evidence of this sort will need to be tried, evaluated, and perfected, but good starts have already been made in some professions and in the general field of adult education. The leaders of any profession who wish to do so can take steps to introduce or advance this new criterion of credentialing into established systems of issuing certificates and licenses or into new systems that may be devised.

Reshaping specialty certification and diplomas. With the growing complexity of all the professions, the provision of specialized service is gradually becoming the normal way to practice. In medicine, specialty organizations have been particularly highly developed and provide elaborate systems of certification and continuing reinforcement of their members. In such fields as dentistry, comparable institutions have been developed but not as extensively as in medicine. In many professions, diplomas signifying at least a minimum mastery of specialized competence are issued by universities, associations, government authorities, or special boards. In other professions, special interest groups exist and even develop voluntary societies, but their structure may be rather loose so that they resemble "invisible colleges," more than formal associations.

Where organized structures of specialty certification exist, the same kinds of evidence of concern and capacity for continuing education can be required as is the case in general licensure and certification. The possibility of securing evidence of performance measures is even greater for the specialties than for general practice, because preparation for credentialing is usually heavily practical. A person who is admitted to a specialty board examination must have undergone a fairly lengthy period of direct tutelage while serving clients. One of the measures used in certification is the report of the applicant's mentor concerning his or her knowledge and capacity. Estimates of future growth potential are also earnestly sought. As Holden (1970, p. 1017) has observed, "Greater efforts are being made continually by many boards to devise either written or oral questions that will evaluate the candidate's ability to function independently." This independence assumes a personal capacity to conduct a practice, an ability that presupposes a strong need to continue to learn. Sometimes the applicant's need is taken for granted, but increasingly it must become the subject of special inquiry.

The countless diploma and certificate programs that abound in the professions cannot do as much in fostering continuing education as a means of quality assurance as can specialty board certification. Ordinarily the programs that prepare for such credentials last for relatively brief periods (though some may extend for two or more years) and combine both instruction and supervised practical service. However it is possible in the learning activities themselves to foster a sense of personal commitment to continuing education and an ability to undertake it. In the award of the credential, measures of these traits may be sketchy, but they can at least serve as signals of the importance attached by awarding authorities to lifelong learning.

Recredentialing practitioners. The idea of periodically recredentialing practitioners struck most professions with explosive force in the last half of the 1960s. Until then it was almost universally taken for granted that the acquisition of initial general or special competence coupled with the expectation that every professional would voluntarily maintain, apply, and advance his or her knowledge and skills throughout a lifetime would be sufficient guarantees of continued excellence of performance. But for reasons that have been described throughout this book and as a result of heated debates at all levels of every professionalizing occupation, it is now widely accepted that there should be periodic reassessments of competence to ensure the individual professional, the people he or she serves, and society in general that a high level of performance is being maintained. A few examples will indicate the strength of this conviction. The Task Force on Continuing Competence in Pharmacy, created by the American Association of Colleges of Pharmacy and the American Pharmaceutical Association, accepted as its first assumption that "in the interests of the public welfare, pharmactists should be subject to evaluation and relicensure at periodic intervals" ("The Continuing Competence of Pharmacists," 1975, p. 432). The American Board of Medical Specialties has adopted a set of guidelines on recertification for specialty groups, the first of which is "recertification should assure, through periodic evaluations, the physician's continuing competence in the chosen area of specialty practice" (*Continuing Medical Education Newsletter*, 1978, p. 4). The editor of the *New England Journal of Medicine*, worried lest the specialty groups might retreat from this position, has commented, "We can't have it both ways. We cannot defend the use of objective tests to determine which physicians are qualified as specialists while criticizing the use of tests to measure continuing competence. Even if we grant that the examination appropriate for young physicians just completing their specialty training may not be suitable for specialists who have been in practice for many years, it does not follow that we should reject any kind of recertification examination" (Relman, 1979, p. 779).

One reason for resistance to recredentialing, and particularly to general relicensure, is the belief that it might sooner or later become a life-or-death matter for every practitioner concerned. Whatever tests or procedures are established, the failure to perform adequately might lead immediately or eventually to the denial of the right to practice. Although the whole conception of recredentialing would become meaningless if this ultimate penalty were not present, it is usually suggested by advocates of relicensure or recertification that lesser sanctions should customarily be applied. Recency of successful assessment might grow to be an important index of success and might be displayed prominently on credentials, be posted in places of business, appear on lists of practitioners in directories and advertisements, and become a criterion for employment and promotion. Loss of membership in general or specialized associations might be a penalty for failure to be recredentialed. A third consequence might be denial of access to facilitating services, such as hospitals, clinics, or university resources. In recredentialing, probationary status might be given on the first failure of reassessment, thus allowing time for intensive effort on the part of the practitioner concerned to bring his or her work up to an acceptable level of performance. (This practice is common in the accreditation of workplaces.) Other penalties and sanctions will almost certainly be developed to fit various circumstances as the relative merits of various systems of recredentialing are identified.

While these systems may deal with any aspects of the professionalizing process (as is also true of original credentialing), the tendency so far has been to restrict the content to the performance characteristics identified in Chapter Three and, most specifically, to the mastery of theoretical and practical knowledge and the capacity to solve the problems that arise during the course of practice. Occasionally attention is paid to the governing conceptual framework, the standards of ethical practice, or the relationships between the profession and other occupational groups with which it may work. However, the other characteristics of professionalization are not often considered, nor is the extent of mastery of the continuing education process.

The full range of evidence on which recredentialing could be based has scarcely been considered. Most of those who discuss the matter have taken it for granted that some evidence of participation in formal education is the only feasible test. As a result, *mandatory continuing education* has incorrectly become a synonym for *relicensure, recertification*, and, more generally, the whole concept of recredentialing. The two are separated here because they are essentially distinct from one another. The belief that they are identical prevents the constructive thought that will lead eventually to satisfactory systems whereby all professionals can maintain or improve high levels of performance.

Any specific program for recredentialing should be developed in terms of identified criteria that are particular to the situation. In a given situation, some criteria are already evident and others will appear as a result of further experience. Some seem to be mutually contradictory and require that balances be struck between opposites. But all of the criteria listed here have been brought forward in the literature on this topic; each has its strong proponents, though in some cases a criterion has been advanced as a way of demonstrating that recredentialing is not feasible according to any presently known methods of measurement. These are the most frequently named criteria:

1.   Whatever immediate tests may be used, any ultimately satisfactory system of recredentialing should be based on excellence in the performance of duties in the work settings of the profession.

2.   A system of recredentialing should be reliable; that is, if it were repeated, no significant variance in the result should occur.

3.   A system of recredentialing should be based on a valid sample of the full range of behaviors actually required of the professional—not just on part of them.

4.   A system of recredentialing should take account of the increasing diversification of professions so that the present performance of individuals is assessed in terms of their defined areas of competence. Parker (1974, p. 476) makes this point vividly: "There may be some reason for requiring the novice lawyer to know a little bit about everything, but the criminal law practitioner, for example, who confines his practice to the criminal branch of litigation, is certainly entitled to forget what he knew and to forego keeping up in wills and trusts law. In fact, it would be counter-productive to the maintenance of his competence in criminal law practice to have to learn all of the intricacies of the Uniform Probate Code."

5.   A system of recredentialing should take account of the fundamental body of knowledge and practice that gives unity and coherence to the entire profession. For example, high school teachers should be specialists in their content fields, but they should also be able to demonstrate their awareness and use of the basic principles common to all aspects of teaching as a profession.

6.   A system of recredentialing should take account of changes in work assignments that occur during the course of a practitioner's career. In this respect recredentialing differs from initial licensure or certification that tests the general knowledge and competence required to enter

a profession. The nature of some of these career movements was described in Chapter Four.

7. A system of recredentialing must use the time of the
    practicing professional economically.

8. A system of recredentialing should be readily adminis-
    trable so that it can be used efficiently to deal with large
    numbers of people.

9. A system of recredentialing should be monitored by ob-
    jective and impartial authorities in both the content dealt
    with and the measurement techniques used.

Mandatory continuing education. Either mandatory or
voluntary recredentialing can take place by any of the methods
of evaluation suggested in Chapter Eight, such as peer review,
examinations of various sorts, or evidences of satisfactory completion of a plan of study. Practically speaking, however, relicensure and recertification have almost always occurred as
a result of the presentation of evidence that a practitioner has
participated to some extent in formally organized educational
activity. Perhaps this is true because, as Maslow (1966) once
observed, if the only tool a man has is a hammer, he tends to
treat everything as if it were a nail. It is possible to assess various other forms of measurement and come finally to the conclusion that, for the present at least, extent of participation is
best, but it is premature to accept it as being virtually synonymous now and forever with recredentialing.

Mandatory continuing education is, however, now widely
accepted in terms of recredentialing. Charts are frequently published showing how many professions in how many states have
established a compulsory participation requirement as official
policy. Careful tallies are also kept for each profession. As of
July 1, 1979, twenty states had some legal requirement for
physicians to use continuing medical education as a basis for
relicensure and in four other states such a requirement had been
authorized by the legislature but not yet implemented. In eighteen states such education had been made a condition of continuing membership in state medical societies. In all, thirty-seven
states, the District of Columbia, and Puerto Rico had taken
some action toward making continuing medical education com-

pulsory for either licensure or membership renewal. Thirteen medical specialty societies had established continuing medical education programs; in seven, participation in such programs was required for continuing membership. All twenty-two medical specialty boards had provided for recertification, though in only two cases was it mandatory. Seventeen of the boards had started their programs or set the date on which recertification is to begin; in some cases initiation of the practice will not start before 1986.*

Half or more of the members of several professions that have been recently studied are in favor of mandatory continuing education as a basis for relicensure or recertification. In an inquiry made of 1,705 physicians in Georgia in January 1978, 1,044 (61.2 percent) favored some form of it, while 394 (23.1 percent) were opposed, the remainder expressing no opinion (*Continuing Medical Education Newsletter*, 1978). Of 115 nurses working in small hospitals in the Boston area, 53 percent felt that continuing education should be required for relicensure (Larocco and Polit, 1978). A study of 423 Colorado accountants who had been living for four years under a system of mandatory continuing education showed that 83 percent favored it (White and Buchman, 1978). A somewhat older investigation (Leete and Loeb, 1975) of the opinions of 209 attorneys showed that only 43.5 percent favored required continuing education; a more recent study might show greater favorable response.

In some surveys, efforts have been made to discover what personal traits or employment circumstances are most likely to be associated with support for compulsory continuing education. These investigations are too scanty and too varied to allow for much comparison. In all studies that treat the age of respondents as a variable, however, it seems clear that the older the professional, the less likely he or she is to favor mandatory recredentialing or compulsory education. There is less decisive evidence that both level of formal education and extent of participation in professional associations are positively linked with support.

However, all is not well as far as mandatory continuing education as a basis for recredentialing is concerned. Opposition

*These data were provided by Jean Ayers of the American Medical Association.

to its present form is not restricted to the old, the relatively ignorant, and the professionally isolated. Chambers and Hamilton (1975a) have made strong assertions that continuing dental education is not sufficiently varied and flexible to allow its results to be accurately measured. Pennington and Moore (1976), after looking broadly at the whole field of continuing professional education, adopt the Socratic approach and raise twenty-seven clusters of questions addressed to the public, the professions, educators, and individual practitioners. And Storey (1978, p. 1416), in a slashing assault on a too-hasty acceptance of mandatory continuing medical education, says that "there is a tide in the affairs of men that—taken at the flood—can sweep them out to sea."

This last attack is particularly direct and vigorous. It focuses on the Physician's Recognition Award of the American Medical Association which, Storey asserts, has created a multi-million-dollar market in entrepreneurial educational activity of an uncoordinated and largely uncontrolled sort that is maintained largely for public relations reasons. The heart of the difficulty, Storey suggests, is that medical authorities have accepted unevaluated participation as the chief form of education and have therefore gone astray by adopting a system that is ultimately unrelated to performance and therefore can carry no assurance of its improvement. The questions and difficulties raised by Storey and other authors all go back to the point that the means now being used for recredentialing are not sufficient to achieve the goals sought.

Disciplinary procedures. Within every profession, the most effective form of discipline is probably informal. The weaknesses of a practitioner come to be known to his associates who, sooner or later, apply sanctions (see Chapter Four). In entrepreneurial practice, the number of clients dwindles and access to resources declines. In collective or hierarchical practice, jobs are lost, promotions are denied, or individual practitioners are personally rejected by their colleagues. These informal sanctions work in all professions, including those which do not have formal systems of certification and licensure, but as methods of quality assurances they can not be relied upon; otherwise the powerful attacks upon professions would not carry the weight they do. It is well to remember, however, that direct and formal approaches are always undergirded by the informal routines of the worklife of professionals.

In most professions formal disciplinary procedures are established by associations, public regulatory agencies, and workplaces. Where no system exists, the need to improvise a procedure sometimes occurs, as when part of a church congregation wishes to remove its pastor. Any such process—whether pre-established or independently initiated—usually calls for the bringing of charges, the presentation of evidence, the holding of hearings, and the conduct of a quasi-judicial process, sometimes of great magnitude if the case is contested. The ultimate non-criminal penalty is removal of the right to practice the profession, though other lesser sanctions can be applied, including the compulsion to undertake continuing education.

The holding of a formal hearing of this sort is always a weighty and expensive process and is never undertaken lightly, particularly because a miasma of doubt, distrust, allegation of bad motives, hard feelings, and counterclaims almost always arises. Usually a professional must be very obviously incompetent or commit some overt and patently wrong act before his or her colleagues will initiate charges and hold fast in their prosecution. Figures on just how widespread such procedures may be are hard to uncover. On January 26, 1976, however, the *New York Times* reported on the revocation of medical licenses for the years 1971 through 1974. During that period, there were approximately 320,000 licensed physicians in the country, of whom 16,000 were estimated by two competent observers to be incompetent or unfit. However, an average of only 72 licenses were revoked each year (Rensberger, 1976). One never knows, in any profession, how many people voluntarily surrender their licenses under threat or fear of detection or because they know they are incompetent, but the disparity between judged incompetence and actual convictions in the case of medicine would seem to be more than any profession could bear.

The chief influence of formal trial processes upon continuing education probably arises from the stimulus they give to participation in learning activities. People who suspect that they are incapable or uninformed may be made uneasy by the feeling that they might be detected and brought to trial themselves. More specifically, any case usually receives a great deal of attention, and its details attract the notice of other practitioners who may not have realized until then that they themselves are engaging in questionable or outmoded practices. Needs for learning are thus made evident and are sometimes acted upon.

Direct citizen participation. Most professionals are accustomed to working in circumstances in which major policies are established by citizen authority. Usually, however, the impact of this control is relatively general, being exercised by Congress, state legislatures, or governing boards. The individual practitioner has been insulated from direct lay authority either by being in independent entrepreneurial practice or by the fact that protection is afforded in collective or hierarchical settings by one or more layers of administrators. As far as the inner workings of a profession are concerned, fairly complete control has usually been left in the hands of practitioners. Even government regulators are usually chosen from among the membership of the profession being regulated. A very sound reason for self-control is the fact that only those who understand the arcane knowledge of a highly advanced craft and have shared in the experiences its practice affords can comprehend the central issues that govern its existence. How could a nonprofessional person possibly deal with intricate matters such as accreditation, licensure, certification, or disciplinary action?

Several interacting factors now operate to modify this point of view. Professions come under continuing attack as being strongly concerned with monopolistic self-interest at the expense of the public. Government funds are required to take care of the needs of professions or the people they serve, and the acceptance of these funds is accompanied by social control. Populist governors are affronted by any limitations of their power to appoint members of regulating boards. Professional association leaders recognize that they need to broaden their bases of citizen involvement and understanding in order to increase public support. Slowly, therefore, a previously insurmountable barrier has been overcome, and lay citizens have begun to be appointed to positions of regulation and control in governments and associations. Usually this direct influence is through appointment to boards or other collective entities where a majority of members are professionals; but the presence of even one candid, independent, and influential lay person can make a substantial difference in the process of shaping decisions and in their acceptance by the public.

A full report of this shift in policy has not yet been written. Indeed, scarcely enough history exists to provide a substantial account or to make any judgment of the effect of the change. From various shreds of evidence, however, it appears that the first "citizen" appointees are usually members of other professions and therefore are well able to make transitions between the problems of their own occupations and the difficulties of the one they are asked to help govern or police. As time goes on, however, appointees come from broader and broader spheres of influence. All general and anecdotal evidence suggests that these people seem to have done well. They inform themselves on issues, ask sensible questions, help protect the profession from attack, represent it in centers of influence which it had not previously penetrated, and, most important, they bring broad-based judgment to bear on issues that previously have been seen only narrowly. As testimony has been provided about these advantages, resistance to citizen representation on professional boards has gradually declined. When the governor of a western state appointed lay members to all state boards of this sort in 1977, his action came as recognition of an established trend, not as a striking innovation.

It remains to be determined whether close citizen involvement will improve the quality of service provided by the professions. The first appointees appear, on the whole, to have been sensitive and experienced people, well able to judge how to play their roles effectively. As time goes on, less capable and less sophisticated people may well be appointed, with unhappy results. It will not require many unfortunate incidents to bring this episode of citizen involvement to an end or to cause a sense of disillusionment about it. Both the professions themselves and the appointing authorities will need to take care that this promising innovation matures into a desirable established practice.

As far as the continuing education implications of citizen involvement are concerned, the major influence discernible thus far has to do with the mode of inquiry. Different kinds of people expressing new ideas are beginning to be heard within the professions and, as a result, some of the characteristics of professionalizing occupations may be influenced. As for the modes of instruction and performance, changes will doubtless occur, but it is too early to assess their ultimate nature and influence.

Altering Practice to Achieve Higher Quality

Quality assurance systems throughout a lifetime of practice—not just at its beginning or when major disciplinary actions are required—are beginning to receive the full, deep, and sustained attention of the leaders of most professions. New emphases upon the maintenance of quality of performance throughout a career calls for a reshaping of much of the worklife of many professionals. The assumption that a threshold of competence can be established early in a practitioner's life, which he or she then accepts as a basis for striving to reach ever higher levels of performance, has been sufficiently discredited so that at least some of the pacesetters of every profession have realized that they must take assertive positive action during the course of practice to assure the maintenance and improvement of quality. Much of this action concerns a reshaping of former habits and policies, but new ideas are also being adopted. The three approaches considered here have special relevance to continuing professional education.

Career advancement. Beyond the initial threshold of competence lie all the specific requirements that must be met in a lifetime of practice as professsionals advance through their careers. It is here that the distinctions among entrepreneurial, collective, and hierarchical practice are most significant. In the first of these three types of work settings, the individual makes his or her way alone, somehow acquiring needed capital, setting up a practice, attracting a clientele, establishing necessary contacts, gaining admission to appropriate associations and organizations, and moving through the successive stages of a career that are specific to the person or place concerned. In collective and hierarchical practice, the individual enters a system and moves forward in terms of its rules and customs, feeling strongly the need to guide his or her actions so as to take advantage of opportunities and avoid pitfalls. In collective settings, advancement often comes in subtle and poorly understood ways. For example, it is hard to identify, at least from the outside, the patterns of influence in a large legal or accounting firm. In hierarchical settings, and particularly in the professions based on them, the line of advancement is more clearly apparent, as the examples of school and hospital administration suggest.

At points where decisions are made about the admission or advancement of individuals, some form of quality control is always presumed to exist. When a physician is allowed to practice in a hospital, an attorney is admitted to plead before a court, a member of an architectural firm is made its managing partner, or a military officer is promoted to a higher rank, the decision is always stated in terms of merit. Experienced people know that other factors (such as wealth, chance, favoritism, or compromise) are always present, cynics believe them to be dominant, and apologists include them in the definition of merit. But quality in its best sense, can never be assured unless excellence of performance is truly the basis of selection at all the points in a career line in which decisions about advancement must be made.

Continuing professional education is crucially important in reinforcing all advancement decisions. People must prepare themselves for special perquisites or for advancement or, if they do not do so, must learn their new duties after they have assumed them. Chapter Four dwelt at some length on the kinds of educational activity required by changes in position, specialization, or rank as well as by a move from one work setting to another. Generalized instruction aimed at a whole profession or large sectors of it is being greatly supplemented by specialized courses designed to consider the needs of special categories of people. Engineers and pharmacists learn how to be managers, teachers learn how to be principals, and lawyers learn how to be appellate court judges. The greatest growth in professional education is likely to occur by the provision of a constantly growing number of closely defined and intricately detailed forms of career advancement learning experiences.

Payment and promotion systems. Compensation is but one aspect of career advancement, but it is so much the basis of distinctive forms of thought and action as to suggest separate treatment here. In the normal course of events, the ability of a professional to provide service is generally thought to be roughly proportional to the amount of compensation received and the extent to which psychic and other rewards are provided. Abundant anecdotal evidence suggests that this conventional wisdom does not always accord with reality, but the assumption is more likely to be correct than its converse. The assumption probably holds true for all three of the major settings in which professionals work, though each has its distinctive opportunities and constraints.

To the extent that a free choice exists among entrepreneurial professionals, the more competent are likely to have more clients and to be able to charger higher fees than their competitors. As in any other application of classic economic theory, the marketplace is presumed to provide the best assurance of quality. In reality, few completely free marketplaces exist as far as such professionals are concerned and, in fact, one of the major charges against professionalization is that it works systematically to restrict competition and even to achieve monopoly. However, insofar as competition does exist, continuing education has a practical advantage, because one of the bases of choice by clients is the extent to which various practitioners have mastered new knowledge and technique and show clear evidence of having done so.

Hierarchical and collective settings often provide organized reward schedules based to some extent on continuing education. In a public school, for example, a multitrack system may be used in which each teacher is located on a level defined in terms of the highest academic degree he or she has received. Increases in compensation then occur on the basis of length of tenure, estimates of merit, and participation in learning activities. If a significant increment of education, such as the winning of an advanced degree, is achieved, the individual moves to a higher track and, as time goes on, receives more substantial increments than those on the lower track. Many people doubt that mechanical systems of this sort have any direct relationship to quality assurance, but the systems are convenient ways of linking financial reward to educational effort and therefore have an appeal to many people.

The social importance of continuing professional learning has led many governmental and private agencies to provide subsidies to individuals for further study. This financing has its chief value in helping to lower cost barriers but also often has status-raising benefits, particularly when grants are given as a result of competitions or achieve importance in the occupation, such as the Prix de Rome for architects or the Nieman Fellowships for journalists. In the United States, governmental payments have usually been restricted to specific categories of people, often determined by occupation. Large sums have been spent by the federal government to enable teachers to attend short courses on how to teach the "new mathematics" and other curricula devised by experts, and other grants provide continuing education for health professionals. In some European countries, in contrast, generalized grants are available; they permit extended periods of full-time study with allocations for both living and tuition costs. These funds are not available solely for professional studies, but they do provide substantial assistance for at least some people interested in these forms of learning.

Changing work patterns. Every profession is in the throes of profound change not merely in the ways it provides service but also in its internal control mechanisms. Most changes are brought about by growth of the knowledge base of the profession, by the adoption of innovations in practice, by competition, or by demands for service, but some have been devised as quality controls or have developed in such a fashion that they have become important in assuring excellence of service.

The most pervasive changes in work patterns are those having to do with the elaboration and refinement of procedures of practice. Several examples will demonstrate this point.

1. Computerization has speeded up customary processes, provided vast data storage and retrieval possibilities, made

possible the simultaneous examination of a broad array
of data, and developed the capacity for sequential systems of analysis that respond immediately to changing
situations.

2. The collaboration of various kinds of specialists in the
handling of specific problems has in many cases brought
about a new definition of roles and relationships that
conforms to a basic pattern even as it deals with the immediacies of specific actions.

3. The practice management of entrepreneurs is facilitated
by elaborately worked out procedures that are often reinforced by specialized machines, printed forms, and
manuals of operation.

4. In hierarchies, systems analysis has become a way of
thought that has generated countless methods of analyzing data and opinions and arriving logically at decisions.

Professions have always depended upon procedural ways
of work, and so the vast changes of recent years use familiar
basic concepts, even though the impact of an instrument (such
as the computer) or of an idea (such as systems analysis) may
seem to bring about qualitative rather than quantitative alterations in practice. All these approaches, simple or elaborate, are
ultimately used and controlled by the mind of the professional,
but they help the person involved both to take account of all
relevant factors and to reduce to routine the processes that can
be dealt with in that fashion. In work arrangements that require
collaboration, each person involved serves as a monitor for all
of the others. A system is a great help in assuring that things
will be done in the right way and therefore contributes greatly
to process evaluation. To the extent that it leads to successful
results, it also aids in outcome evaluation.

Each new system that is seriously considered for introduction into practice by a professional requires a period of
inquiry during which the feasibility of adopting it is considered.
If the decision is affirmative, there ensues a period of instruction. Sometimes only a brief introduction is needed, and mastery
is achieved by habituation. Sometimes the new way of work is
so complex that it requires an intensive period of training. Sub-

sequently the professional is likely to discover that he or she is once again going through the familiar process of first carrying out the steps required in a monotonous and routine fashion and then, as familiarity with the elements of the total process is gained, of gradually being able to move with greater swiftness as a higher level of performance is achieved. Quality is fully controlled, however, only when, despite the rapidity of thought and action, the separate elements are given their proper weight in the handling of each case.

Sometimes change is so great that it calls for a completely new organization of the service provided. For example, in caring for orphans, social workers turned long ago from asylums to foster homes. Hospitals are being supplemented with various forms of health maintenance and support organizations, thereby influencing the methods of work of all the health professions. When new basic patterns such as these are proposed, they influence not only the people who are engaged in them but also the employees of other allied services. For everyone concerned, the movement through the three modes of learning takes place much as it does with less profound changes of practice. At least in the early days of major innovations, however, the mode of inquiry is often both deepened and lengthened by the fact that the new institution or service is moving foward on an uncharted course of action with few reference points to guide it. This sense of pioneering, often made more intense by a strong emotional commitment, adds greatly to the motivation to learn and to examine the results of learning, thereby facilitating the achievement of high quality.

Direct Pressures

Attacks on professions and professionalism come from many quarters, some of which are ventilations of anger and frustration and some of which are sermons or admonitions to take certain unspecified actions. Other attacks, however, lead more or less directly to corrective action or apply pressures that are so immediate or intense that they require a response intended to eliminate impediments to excellence. Four of these latter forms of pressure will be considered here because of their implications for continuing professional education.

Attacks on a profession by its members. One of the major charges against professions is that their members protect one another, even in clear-cut cases of wrongdoing. As is true of any other human group, the members of a profession feel that they must present a united front to the general public; indeed the preservation of the mystique of arcane knowledge requires that those who share it must defend the common guild and usually its individual members. The essence of mutual guardianship was expressed when in the second century B.C., one Egyptian accountant wrote the following note to another: "You should know that an inspector of temple finances has arrived in these parts and intends to review your accounts also. Do not be unduly disturbed, however, for I will get you off. As quickly as you can, write up your books and bring them here to me, for he is a very strict fellow. If you cannot bring the books yourself, at any rate send them to me and I will see you through, for I have become friendly with him" (Newgarden, 1970, p. 38).

But within a profession, when those who belong to it are talking to one another, plain speaking is the norm and sharp criticism frequent. And because acrimonious discussions are often reported in the media as news items or feature stories, public awareness of the great differences between a united exterior and an inner dissension is itself a cause of general cynicism which, in various ways, may lead the profession to feel more beleaguered than before, thereby increasing its internal dissension.

The responsible innovators, pacesetters, and facilitators of a profession are usually those who see most clearly the need to cleanse it of its imperfections. Warren Burger, Chief Justice of the United States, seems never to lose an opportunity to state his views on the low status of law and the problems of the judiciary. Among other comments, he has observed that up to 50 percent of the attorneys who handle litigation are unfit to do so. The article in the *Wall Street Journal* (February 24, 1975) that reported that estimate also quoted other authorities who had come to the same general conclusion. One judge said, "You almost cringe up there on the bench," as he recounted the evi-

dences of carelessness and incompetence that he was daily required to witness (Green, 1975, p. 1). Many attorneys have
similar observations to make about the judges before whom
they must appear. In the *New York Times,* Philip Kurland
(1975, p. 35) has asserted, for example, that judges are usually
appointed as a reward for political services and that "there is
a greater proportion of incompetent judges than of incompetent counsel." When such comments become sufficiently
widespread within any profession, they can create a climate of
opinion that leads to corrective action. Law schools and bar
associations stimulated by such criticisms have been led to provide many seminars and workshops to train attorneys in lawyering skills and to assist judges in carrying out their work responsibly. More fundamentally, the initial preparation of lawyers
has come under sharp scrutiny. Law school faculty members
and other leaders of the bar are thinking about new ways to
help students move from instruction in jurisprudence toward
the capacity to engage competently in practice. The degree of
success of this transition will be of crucial importance in laying
the future foundations of continuing legal education.

Strong expressions of disagreement with the status quo
on the part of the members of a profession have an immediacy
of impact that external attacks seldom achieve. It is hard to
impugn the motives of one's own colleagues or to argue that
they have not been initiated into the mysteries or the practice
of the craft and are therefore speaking from ignorance. Dissi-
dent members tend to become the nuclei of reform groups, each
of which has a platform of changes it hopes to accomplish. As
these groups press their cases, often winning influence as they do
so, they initiate a process of education by the mode of inquiry
that may eventually profoundly influence the policies and practices of the profession and do a great deal to instruct its practitioners and eventually lead them to change their performance.

Consumer concern. Somewhat the same effect is produced
when any of the people served by a profession become active in
protesting its incompetence, narrow practices, invasion of personal rights, self-aggrandizement, or secretiveness. The professions have not been the sole or even the chief targets of consum-

erism, but they have been directly influenced as it has become a general phenomenon in modern society. People have increasingly shown a collective determination to help guide and direct important aspects of their own lives. Out of a few initial and scattered efforts, a general movement has grown, with advocates of specific causes creating a mutuality of effort in which each assists the others. The practices of professions are sometimes sufficiently similar so that one campaign reinforces or leads to another. For example, the belief that pharmacists should prominently post the prices of drugs is not very different from the belief that attorneys should inform clients in advance of the base rates of various legal services.

In the 1960s, the initial waves of consumer demands were often expressed in an intemperate or even vitriolic fashion and resulted in violence or in passive resistance aimed at work stoppage. The first response of the professionals concerned—including social workers, hospital administrators, and professional school faculty members—was one of outraged indignation. This response was explained as a natural reaction against the attacks upon their hard-won knowledge, experience, and ethical standards, but dispassionate outside observers often could not distinguish it from the pomposity sometimes shown by businessmen, politicians, and others also under this kind of attack. It was not long, however, before cooler—or wilier—heads prevailed on both sides and, as a result, many methods of compliance with demands were somehow absorbed into practice in various ways.

As the 1960s drew to a close, however, it seemed at least remotely possible that the professions might have to make such concessions to demand that they would either disappear or be forced to accept a markedly inferior place in society. Haug and Sussman (1969, p. 160) dispassionately analyzed the phenomenon of "the revolt of the client" and came to the conclusion that one of two eventualities was likely. There might be a "process of deprofessionalization, involving both narrower bounds for autonomy and lowered status" or the result might be "a blessing in disguise," one which would "enable the professional to give up the 'whole man' approach to service and treatment, and enable him to revert to a more specialized expert role."

In the case of some individuals or groups, one of these results may already have been brought about. It is the opinion of many people that the heyday of the professions has long since passed. But in most cases, professionals—learning by the mode of inquiry—have discovered how to adjust to the demands made upon them by acceding to them, by building reasoned defenses against them, or by achieving compromises acceptable to all points of view. The world did not come to an end when various clients' "bills of rights" were adopted or when professionals were brought more and more into the world of competition and told that they could no longer object to advertising their services. In fact, the "whole man" approach to which Haug and Sussman referred has often been fostered, not negated, by changed relationships between professionals and clients, and wise and effective decisions have been made by the involvement in policy-making processes of representatives of the publics served.

In this latter connection, a distinction should be made between *citizen* representation, in which people are chosen because of their breadth of viewpoint, and *special interest* representation, in which nonprofessionals are deliberately chosen as counter-forces to a vested interest. People selected because of race, religion, sex, neighborhood of residence, or any similar attribute are likely to be expected to make decisions solely in terms of this one characteristic and to be made to feel, if they do not do so already, that they should not express a balanced perspective. They become the special watch-dogs of a profession, accenting its negative attributes and stressing conflict. While it is too soon to make any ultimate judgments about the social effectiveness of the special interest monitoring of professions, anecdotal evidence suggests that it often presents new problems at least as great as those it was designed to correct. Any system constructed along such adversary lines may ultimately fall of its own ponderousness and because few people have a continuing appetite for conflict.

But consumerism is far from having run its course, and professions are constantly encountering fresh demands and new surprises. To meet such attacks, all three modes of learning have been required in the past and will presumably be needed in the future. Learning occurs in response to the answering of a series of questions. How can a new proposal—often stated as a challenge—best be dealt with? How can all practitioners be taught the changes necessary in a response to demands made? How can such changes then be put into effect and reinforced? Some people will always argue that "bowing to outside demands" lessens rather than enhances quality assurance, but the validity of their contention depends on somebody's judgment as to whether the "bowing" is a craven abandonment of principle or a reasoned response to a forceful argument.

Mass media interest and concern. A significant phenomenon of professionalization in recent years has been the extent to which the media of communication have taken an interest in it. Investigative journalism has always been part of the American scene (though the Watergate incident has given it recent prominence) and accounts of specific professions or of professions in general have been staple items of reporting. But professions have become more newsworthy as they have grown in importance and controversy. Newspapers, broadcasting networks, and other mass media now have specialized reporters in religion, education, health, welfare, and other areas of service in which professionals work.

While the media have been eager to report positive breakthroughs in the work of various professions or in their supporting disciplines, the general tone of much reporting has grown increasingly negative. The account of the inadequacies of lawyers in the *Wall Street Journal* has already been mentioned. An even more powerful and sustained attack on the medical profession was mounted by the *New York Times* on January 26 to 30, 1976, when five lengthy accounts were given on successive days focusing on: the number and variety of incompetent doctors; the large amount of unnecessary surgery; the unwarranted and dangerous prescription of drugs; the reluctance of physicians to criticize their colleagues; and the ways in which a patient can choose a doctor and evaluate the care given. This series had been extensively researched by the reporter, Boyce Rensberger. It was widely read by leading physicians as well as by the gen-

eral public and has had a continuing influence far greater than
most newspaper stories. More general treatments sometimes
supplement those dealing with specific professions. A cover
story of *Business Week* dealt with "The Troubled Professions"
(1976, p. 127) and had as its subtitle "Society is pummeling
lawyers, accountants, architects, engineers, and doctors—and
changing their role."

There are numerous accounts of this sort, and all are intended for the general public or some defined segment of it and
provide information and opinion to many people. Included in
their audience are many professionals for whom the widespread
exposure of issues and problems has special implications. This
exposure can help build a sense of unity among the members
of one or more professions as they face the need to build a common defense against attack. It can highlight general ills and specific practices to which practitioners should be alerted though,
depending on circumstances and temperaments, responses may
vary greatly. Most profoundly, it indicates that topics which
were hitherto private are now public. As a result, the older professions may feel less sacrosanct and the new ones may feel
a pride of recognition. In any of these cases, action by the professionals concerned is stimulated and often leads to the use of
the three modes of education, thus ultimately influencing the
quality of service rendered to the publics served.

Government decisions and judgments. Most professions,
even those which do not themselves have specially defined legal
rights and obligations, have established networks of contact
with legislative bodies, regulatory agencies, public commissions,
and administrative policy makers. Facilitators and pacesetters
are often heavily involved in influencing legislative decisions,
being assisted in this process by people who are not members
of the profession but are expert in public relations or the wield-
ing of influence. Advocacy of this sort is particularly necessary,
because many policy makers are hostile to the practices of specific professions, basing their opposition on all the charges
summarized earlier. Public decisions about governing policies
or their applications within a profession can sometimes still be
quietly and intimately dealt with, "all in the family," but intimacy of this sort is less and less frequently found.

In the United States, the courts have also become powerful policy makers for the professions. The best-known example of this influence lies in malpractice suits, which, beginning in a few professions and with moderately sized awards, have spread to other professions and given rise to very large payments. The judicial system itself cannot be blamed for the growth of this form of litigiousness, but it is the arena in which its expression is realized. But courts have gone far beyond the rendering of decisions. In the courts of appeal—and particularly in the Supreme Court—where decisions are made by judges rather than by juries, rules have been handed down that have had profound consequences. The 1954 school desegregation decision of the Supreme Court suggests how deeply a decision can influence professional thoughts and activities, particularly when it is subsequently buttressed by legislative enactments and administrative guidelines. In the making of court decisions, organized professional groups (with the possible exception of those related to law) have a great deal less power than they do with more broadly representative bodies.

All these decisions and rulings have profound influence not only on quality assurance but on the very definition of quality; thus, the consequences for continuing education of various forms of government action are profound. While any issue is being debated and decided, the attention of the profession, and particularly of its most influential members, is drawn to it. Often there is a need to discuss and debate the issues until alternative positions become clear and, if possible, an agreement can be reached by compromise, consensus, or vote. When a profession's wishes are established, the task is to mobilize an informed opinion so that it can be brought to bear in an appropriate way upon the centers of decision. On other occasions, particularly when controversial matters are before a court or administrative tribunal, at least some people must study the alternative courses of action that should be followed if various decisions are reached. Once a new program has been enacted or a ruling has been made, all professionals influenced by the new policies and practices must learn how to live according to them. The processes mentioned in this paragraph are often called "public relations," "politicking," or "strategy mapping," but both in themselves and in their consequences they are to some extent educational, using all three modes of learning.

Future Expansion

The expansion of continuing education is certain to be sustained. There are slight evidences that the present antagonism against the professions may already have passed its peak and be subsiding, partly as a result of the steps taken to counter it. But any relaxation of dedicated efforts to maintain quality will start new waves of criticism. Learning must occur throughout the lifespan and must assume new and more complex forms. The plans to establish basic educational programs for those entering the professions were thought in the first quarter of this century to be visionary, but they have now been realized at levels far beyond those of the original dreams. Continuing education will follow the same pattern of growth; what we hardly dare prophesy today will be seen by later generations as efforts to achieve a manifest necessity.

Chapter 10

A Program for Action

Although a man's work may indeed be a good clue to his personal and social fate, it is a clue that leads us—and the individual himself—not by a clear and single track to a known goal, but into a maze full of dead-ends and of unexpected adventures.

Everett Cherrington Hughes

Too few professionals continue to learn throughout their lives, and the opportunities provided to aid and encourage them to do so are far less abundant than they should be. These twin assumptions underlie this whole book, even though they have only occasionally been made as explicit as they were at the end of Chapter Nine. I am not alone in holding these views. As the citations used earlier suggest, many authors share the same beliefs and argue or preach their truth. Continuing professional learners are not everywhere present and docile. They must be identified and eagerly sought, and this fact permeates and will long continue to permeate the practice of continuing professional education. In this final summing-up, therefore, the central themes that have guided the analysis in the foregoing chapters will be restated as working policies to be used in enlarging the scope of present programs and in encouraging a greater response to them.

Before undertaking this task, I should stress again the fact that learning deficiency is far from universal among present professionals. Many practitioners have worked out patterns of continuous or recurrent learning for themselves that precisely suit their needs and desires and fully meet their obligations to soci-

303

ety. Despite limited resources, particularly of time, these professionals are constantly observing, reflecting, reading, discussing, and taking part in organized programs of instruction, incorporating into their performance what they learn by all such means. They do the best they can and as much as any realistic observer could expect of them. These optimal learners can serve as role models for colleagues less assiduous in learning than themselves. Some people go even further; they spend so much time learning that they neglect the people they are supposed to serve or reduce themselves to immobility because they cannot harmonize the depth of their knowledge with the swift flow of their practice. But such extreme cases are not yet numerous enough to constitute a serious problem.

It might seem easy to project an ideal pattern of continuing learning for all professions by using the optimal learners as examples or, alternatively, by combining and extrapolating into an indefinite future the best theory and practice from all the seventeen professions compared in this book, along with insights from other occupations where excellent ideas have been excellently achieved. But while vocations can be compared, they cannot be blended. Their inherent natures differ. The adversary system of law builds into its practice a systematized struggle that challenges lawyers to learn how to defeat one another. Health professionals also do battle but against chiefly impersonal forces and in a spirit of collaborative support. Other opportunities or constraints exist at the core of every other profession, making each one unique. In addition to these disparities in practice, occupations have progressed to different levels of accomplishment in their achievement of professionalizing characteristics. Each has a distinctive profile of successes and failures. Because of these dissimilarities in both nature and achievement, the leaders of each profession and their social sponsors must design a tailor-made system of lifespan education, creating their own innovations, but also adopting or adapting whatever they can learn from the successes achieved by those who face comparable situations in other professions.

Such a task is never easy. The lack of sophistication in many continuing education programs is all the more suprising because the work of an architect, engineer, dentist, social worker, or any other professional demands the skilled use of intricate and complex techniques, the comprehension of abstruse knowledge, and the application of sensitive understanding. Every profession requires diagnoses, therapies, strategies, designs, controls, and prescriptions to be subtly designed and painstakingly adjusted to the circumstances presented by specific problem cases. In their own continuing learning endeavors, however, many professionals seem willing to accept simple programs of direct action. For them, continuing education often means only listening to a lecture or using a new communication technique. The purpose of such endeavors is usually to convey information or provide training in a new skill; such simple goals cannot be disdained but neither can they be deeply admired. Sponsors of activities frequently act as though participation is enough. The learner may not be required to demonstrate increased competence or performance; indeed it is sometimes thought that it would be undignified to suggest that he or she should have to do so. It seems to be assumed that if simple aims are sought by simple methods, improvements in complex performance will inevitably occur.

Throughout this book, it has been suggested that the needs of individuals, professions, or society can be adequately served by programs of continuing education only if they are developed in terms of certain basic ideas that may be easy to understand but that are often difficult to work out in practice, particularly as their applications interact with one another. Up to this point, these conceptions have been used to describe past, present, and proposed activity. Now, if they are to be considered prescriptively, they must be stated more directly than before. It would be going too far to call them rules or principles since they have not been adequately validated by experiment. To the extent, however, that they achieve assent either by their statement here or by their exposition on earlier pages, they may be considered to be working policies for the future.

1. *The primary responsibility for learning should rest on the individual.* It is the ideal of every profession, stated or implied in its code of ethics, that each professional should feel

a deep and continuing concern that his or her own education be carried out at a high level throughout a lifetime of practice. To be sure, all people have a similar need if they are to fulfill their potentialities, but professionals must feel it with special urgency, for once they achieve their formal status, they are usually protected in it for life. They must try to learn from each new situation, no matter how familiar, by viewing it creatively. They must collaborate actively with other professionals who are also trying to maintain the life and vitality of their thought and practice. They must participate in groups and associations that provide new ways to scrutinize and improve practice. They must remove themselves from that practice from time to time for intensive periods of study, thereby not merely acquiring new knowledge but also gaining a broader perspective so that, upon returning to service, they view matters in a new light. They must, in short, use every means of continuing education available so that their work retains the dedication, lucidity, and freshness of its early years. Only in this way can lifelong education achieve its essential continuity, one phase blending into another as new ideas and techniques are constantly absorbed in a gradual fashion.

In the self-monitoring of education as of other human activities, both desire and ability are crucial. As Churchill, quoted earlier on the importance of desire in learning, also observed, "Where my reason, imagination, or interest were not engaged I would not or could not learn" (1930, p. 13). A profession has the collective responsibility to honor and foster this zest for learning in all its members from the time of initial selection through the formal period of preparation and subsequently during all the years of practice. It has a similar obligation to help its members develop the ability to learn how to learn, through formal training, the setting of personal examples, and the provision of many alternative systems of education designed to be available and congenial to individuals who differ widely in their preferred learning styles.

2. *The goals of professional education, including those of continuing learning, should be concerned with the entire process of professionalization.* The fourteen characteristics identi-

fied in Chapter Three and any others that may define an occupation's growth toward professionalization need to be considered in the total educational program. In present practice, the goals are often far too restricted, sometimes being limited only to efforts to keep up to date on new developments in the profession or in the basic disciplines that underlie its practice. Meanwhile, much of the active life and thought of the profession occurs outside the purview of its educational program and without the benefits of its disciplined processes.

Every person who practices a profession needs to understand the evolving nature of its central mission, to be aware of relevant new developments in its basic disciplines, to improve competence, to use the theories and techniques of innovative practice, to apply the ethical principles required in a constantly changing work and social environment, to strengthen and sustain a responsibly coherent profession in all the ways suggested in Chapter Three, to preserve an appropriate perspective on worklife and not be engulfed by it, to collaborate with members of other professions whose self-conceptions and ways of work are also continuously evolving, and to represent the profession responsibly in all relationships with the persons he or she serves.

These general goals establish an ideal that may never be achieved but that needs constantly to be sought in intricate and varied ways. As yet, the contribution of continuing education to the advancement of all of the characteristics of professionalization has not been fully thought through. Nor is it clear that all professions must consider all these characteristics in the same order. Wilensky's view that the pathway toward progress and acclaim is always and inflexibly the same, as discussed in Chapter Two, may prove in the long run to be correct, but his idea of an inexorable destiny does not accord with the sense of free will felt by the leaders of most professions. They want to exercise control over their own actions, following the routes they choose themselves, working systematically or sporadically on the achievement of those characteristics that permit them to make immediate and significant advances, and using education as one of the major ways of doing so. I think they are right.

3. *Continuing education should be considered as part of an entire process of learning that continues throughout the life-span.* This idea wins universal acceptance as an abstraction but is seldom thought about except in negative terms. Professional schools are often critical about the quality of the earlier education of their entrants and may impose demands intended to make it better. Those who hire credentialed practitioners often deplore the caliber of education provided in professional schools. And those who observe the performance of elder workers marvel that they have been able to stay in practice with so little evidence of having learned anything as the result of experience. Many formal programs of continuing education have been established to remedy the deficiencies of basic professional education. In 1910, Flexner (p. 174) observed that "The postgraduate school as developed in the United States may be characterized as a 'compensatory adjustment.' It is an effort to mend a machine that was predestined to break down. Inevitably, the more conscientious and intelligent men trained in most of the medical schools herein described must become aware of their unfitness for the responsibilities of medical practice; the postgraduate school was established to do what the medical school had failed to accomplish." Today programs organized substantially for the same purpose are found in some employing institutions, such as hospitals or law firms, where the intent is not to develop some specialty or acquaint the learner with new usages but to provide remedial education that will correct or reinforce the basic pre-service program.

But little or no action has yet been taken on the positive and creative idea that each profession should design a program of education that will occur during the whole lifespan. As modern professional schools have achieved the great strength they now possess, they have become the central institutions in all considerations of formal learning. "Teacher education" or "dental education" are shorthand terms for what colleges of education or dental schools do. The views on continuing education of the faculties of such institutions tend to be characterized as either traditional or progressive. The traditional view holds that a professional school should focus entirely on the initial preparation of professionals, teaching them for only a short span of years but so intensively that what they learn will be structural for their thoughts and actions ever after. The liberal view enlarges to some extent the work of the school; while instruction still centers on the pre-service years, continuing education is provided to reinforce or revise what has been learned in those years.

But a new and emerging view goes well beyond either of these positions and must therefore be termed "radical." It holds that professional education must be reconceptualized as an activity that normally occurs throughout all of life. The preparatory school is no longer seen as the centerpiece of education but merely as one of its providers. It performs essential tasks and is therefore indispensable, but it must be regarded as taking its appropriate place among other equally needed providers of learning experience as it is extended throughout an entire career. In setting a full program of lifespan learning in place, policy makers and administrators both in and out of the profession may need to plan for a progression of developmental stages. The moon-landing program of the 1960s called for several sequences of action: an unmanned satellite circling the earth, a manned flight in space, a manned orbital flight around the earth, a manned orbital flight around the moon, a landing on the moon, and a vehicular exploration of the moon's surface. Even before the first phase was accomplished, people were at work designing the later stages. Perhaps such a phasing effort will be required in many professions for continuing education and the programs of recredentialing that it will need.

4. *The patterns and methods of continuing education should be planned and conducted in terms of one or more of three modes of education: inquiry, instruction, and performance.* These modes are familiar in day-to-day life, but they have not been adequately conceptualized as distinctive methods of approach to learning. As has been noted earlier, instruction—in all its myriad forms—is usually taken as being virtually synonymous with education. Professionals also find it easy to accept the idea that a policy-forming committee or a staff retreat can be considered educative, though they usually do not think

very much about the fact that such forms of learning by inquiry operate on entirely different theoretical premises and follow different practices than do those based on instruction. The same fact is true of education designed specifically to improve performance; the learning activities involved may follow the purpose or form of either instruction or inquiry, but they are importantly changed by being interwoven with other methods of seeking improvement, such as the use of financial incentives, the revision of regulations, or the reorganization of personnel.

Because of the confusion of terms and frameworks, a certain amount of chaos and conflict now exists as far as the fundamental conceptualization of continuing education is concerned. It can be roundly condemned as a professional activity by somebody who thinks it means only formal instruction and who believes that experience is the best teacher. Such a person might warmly approve the auditing of performance in an employment institution as a basis for an improvement program and yet never think that one aspect of that program could be considered to be education. Another person could scorn a meeting based on inquiry as being merely the exploration of prejudices, not realizing that the identification of differing viewpoints is necessary for the ultimate creation of a shared concensus, which is itself a learning gain.

As the nature of these three modes and the distinctions among them become more evident in the next quarter century, a better and broader conceptualization of the full dimensions of continuing professional education may well emerge. Many of the quarrels, reservations, and complaints of the present will disappear when it is understood that the choice is not whether continuing education (as some single form of it may be defined) should or should not exist but rather what methods drawn from the three basic modes may best be selected or mixed to achieve that purpose.

5. *The provision of continuing education should expand so that it pervades all aspects of professional life.* As the realization grows that continuing education can take many forms and be used for many purposes, it seems likely that the number and kind of providers and the designs for learning that they offer

will continue to grow in size, proliferate in form, and ceaselessly combine and recombine. Much of the fascination of education (at least for Americans) lies in the invention and adaptation of new devices, processes, and systems, as well as in the fostering of competitive or collaborative programs of sponsorship. Nothing now in prospect suggests that what has already occurred is any more than a prologue to a much more complex future. Some of these processes and sponsors will become established as they meet the tests imposed by educationally and economically sound usefulness, while others—including some that are now flourishing—will decline and even disappear. In the long run, however, the range of opportunities will become vastly enlarged as more and more people recognize how intimately learning is related not only to the maintenance of present accomplishments but also to the hopes for further professionalization.

Why—it may be asked—is such an expansion likely? There are many answers. The social forces that have already led to the elaborate monitoring of the professions are likely to gain strength. Occupations will continue to want to professionalize. As the needs of the country for highly skilled manpower are met, the concentration on early education will be replaced by a more balanced viewpoint involving the entire lifespan. This shift will enable a larger share of human and material resources to be devoted to continuing education. Moreover, success will lead to success. As theoreticians and practitioners gain an ever firmer grasp of how to use the three learning modes, how to redesign the stages of professional education to achieve greater articulation, and how to establish and maintain defensible systems of recredentialing, the effective innovations of each occupation will serve as stimuli and encouragement to others.

But continuing education will not only grow; it will diversify. The programs of the past have tended to be monolithic, standardized, and undifferentiated, often giving rise to manifest absurdities. As McKenna (1978, p. 18) observed, "It seems ludicrous to suggest that, simply because continuing education is mandatory, the maternal and child clinical specialist [in nursing] attend a seminar on Environmental Health in India from the standpoint of a sanitary engineer in order to have continuing education units on a record somewhere which says 'See I have done it.'" This kind of heavy-handed compliance to arbitrary regulations is being replaced by more sensitive and thoughtful programs that respond to the general and specific needs of practitioners, are presented in interesting and informative ways, and achieve collective as well as individual goals. The special needs of people in each of the five basic employment settings are being addressed; entrepreneurial, collective, hierarchical, adjunct, and facilitative practitioners are less likely than before to be lumped together. Innovators, pacesetters, middle-majority adopters, and laggards are being approached in terms of their distinctive natures, and strategies based on the innovation-adoption curve are being used to transmit new ideas and practices. Specialized activities are developing to suit the needs of people moving from one kind of occupational position or setting to another.

As this diversification grows, so do the ways of coping with it. Many professionals seeking education still have great difficulty in finding exactly what they want. The problem is gradually being solved, however, not only by a growth in learning opportunities that makes them more readily available but also because intermediary devices and processes are being initiated. Registries of continuing educational opportunities appear in professional journals or special publications, activities are advertised widely, and clearinghouses and other "brokering" services are becoming available. As yet, such services are being provided almost wholly within the confines of single professions, but in at least a few cases the members of several professions are being simultaneously helped to locate useful offerings.

Anybody who looks out over the present terrain of continuing professional education finds it filled with jurisdictional conflicts and tensions, a few of which have been mentioned in Chapter Six. It is hard not to be caught up in such battles, which are often more vivid and colorful than are substantive questions of purpose, learning procedures, and changes in performance. If saturation in service had been achieved or if the field had matured, it would be important at this point to try to think through the allocations of function. Anybody who keeps up with the swift flow of events, however, will note frequent changes in the sponsorship of activities and in the creation and realignment of alliances. Offerings are expanding so rapidly that their future sponsorship is hard to predict on either a short-term basis or in the long run. While master plans and memoranda of agreement will always be needed to establish and stabilize operations at various times and places, rapid expansion soon requires the revision of all such formal arrangements.

6. *Professions should collaborate on the planning and provision of continuing education.* While recognizing the ultimate uniqueness of each profession, this book has stressed the similarity of their problems. The occupations have not been considered one by one, as is customarily the case with comparative studies in this field, but on the basis of cross-cutting analyses of structures and functions, as well as of problems and solutions. It seems unnecessary at this point, therefore, to stress the significance of a commonality that would not abandon present patterns and systems but enrich them by a wider realization of their interdependence. Greater collaboration in continuing education might achieve substantial financial economies and would almost certainly ensure higher quality and comprehensiveness of service. Professionals could be encouraged to work together in the service of the public, cooperation could diminish competition and factionalism, resources could be shared, and, most important, the principles and methods used by one profession to solve its continuing education problems could be used by other professions.

This collaboration can occur at any of the places of collective assembly of the professions with appropriate matters being considered at each one. Those that come prominently to mind are universities, health center campuses, places such as hospitals with practitioners from a number of disciplines, state government offices that license professionals, state boards of higher education, regional accrediting associations, university consortiums, national associations of universities, national testing services, and regional compacts. Such a listing barely begins the roster of places where professionals might work together fruitfully and where a passion for universal principles may keep them from being dominated by the practices of any one profession.

7. *The processes of recredentialing should be thoroughly rethought and redeveloped to determine the appropriate role of continuing education.* While the organized professions and the general public establish policy controls at many different points and in many different ways, credentialing and recredentialing of both individuals and institutions are the most general and conspicuous ways by which quality and public accountability are assured. So far as continuing education is concerned, the requirement of relicensure of practitioners has been a major means of assuring enrollments and attendance at organized instructional activities. It has been noted in Chapter Nine that "mandatory continuing education" is often a virtual synonym for "relicensure," though the two have no necessary connection.

The issues involved in the complex relationships between continuing education and credentialing have been so fully explored in earlier chapters, particularly Eight and Nine, that they require no restatement here. The conclusion to which they lead, however, must be that a primary need in the advancement of professionalization is for a systematic, flexible, and sophisticated approach to credentialing and recredentialing. The counting of hours of exposure to instruction, the achievement of passing scores on theoretical and practical tests, the accumulation of reports of successful experience, the favorable results of peer and supervisory reviews, and other existing or to-be-discovered evidences of positive accomplishment must all be considered and appraised to see how they can best be fitted into comprehensive systems that can assure the profession and the general public that continuing education is being used creatively to help practitioners perform their responsibilities in a satisfactory fashion. Similar efforts must also be made to improve the processes by which both educational and service institutions are accredited.

The distinction between process and outcome systems of credentialing is clear, but the latter has been so hard to apply that reliance has been almost entirely placed on the former. In licensure a good many ways have been found to measure the extent of an individual's exposure to instruction or to assess the resulting knowledge or competence, but as yet those who practice the craft of evaluation have not found very many ways to measure the effect of that teaching on the quality of actual performance. The professional must apply sensitiveness, knowledge, and ability to the successful handling of a succession of particular cases in actual field conditions, often under stress. Only if continuing education can improve the practitioner's accomplishments in these respects can it be said to be wholly successful. Similarly a training program or a service institution may have excellent resources, all of which it can count, but the ultimate test of its success lies in the contribution it makes to the quality of performance of the people it instructs or to the successful results of the services it performs. A great deal of work remains to be done to devise new measures of accomplishment that will probably first be developed and used under research conditions but that can eventually be adapted for use on widespread and readily administrable bases. Only on this kind of quality assessment can any broadly acceptable systems of relicensure and reaccreditation be based.

Who should do all of the many things suggested in this chapter? The facilitators, the innovators, and the pacesetters will need to take the initiative, but the ultimate answer to the question is: all people who are concerned with the maintenance and improvement of professions and professionalization, whatever the setting in which they work. In the capacity of professionals to create and adopt new ideas of continuing education, the customary range from innovators to laggards almost certainly applies. Therefore, some people will do a great deal to advance such learning, and others will do little or nothing. But everybody has an opportunity to help, even if it is only to set a personal example.

The preface to this book says that its purpose is to advance the process by which greater conceptual coherence may be brought to the educational endeavors of those who practice professions in the United States. To the extent that this advancement is achieved, it must go forward on the basis of ideas that are still being formulated and tested. Great designs may someday emerge—as they already have in the pre-service educational programs of some professions. As yet it is too early to say what they may be because our vision of what might be accomplished is too narrow. The task for this generation is to move ahead as creatively as possible, amid all the distractions and complexities of practice, to aid professionals—whether in natural employment settings or in specially designed educational situations—constantly to refine their sensitiveness, enlarge their conceptions, add to their knowledge, and perfect their skills so that they can discharge their responsibilities within the context of their own personalities and the needs of the society of which they are collectively a part.

References

Abbott, E. *Social Welfare and Professional Education.* Chicago: University of Chicago Press, 1931.

Abrahamson, M. (Ed.). *The Professional in the Organization.* Chicago: Rand McNally, 1967.

Abrahamson, S. "Evaluation in Continuing Medical Education." *Journal of the American Medical Association,* 1968, *206,* 625–628.

Acheson, H. W. K. "The Clinical Records as an Aid to Continuing Education in General Practice: A Medical Self-Audit." *British Journal of Medical Education,* 1972, *6,* 26–28.

Adams, F. H. "Continuing Education, Education Needs and Standards." *American Journal of Cardiology,* 1974, *34,* 439–443.

Adams, S. "A Self-Study Tool for Independent Learning in Nursing." *Journal of Continuing Nursing Education,* 1971, *2,* 27–31.

Adler, N. "Survey of Continuing Education." *Journal of the California Dental Association,* 1969, *45,* 132–136.

Akenson, D. H., and Beecher, R. S. "Speculations on Change of College Major." *College and University,* 1967, *42,* 175–180.

Allen, H. R. *Open Door to Learning.* Urbana: University of Illinois Press, 1963.

Allen, L. A. "The Growth of Professionalism in the Adult Educational Movement, 1928–1958." Unpublished doctoral dissertation, University of Chicago, 1961.

Allen, L. A. *Continuing Education Needs of Special Librarians.* New York: Special Libraries Association, 1974.

Allouard, P. "The Present Situation of Continuing Education in France Among Engineers and in Schools of Engineering." In

The School and Continuing Education. Paris: UNESCO Press, 1972.

Alspaugh, D. Y. *A Bibliography of Materials on Legal Education.* New York: New York University School of Law, 1965.

American Association of Colleges for Teacher Education. *Time for Decision in Teacher Education.* Washington, D.C.: American Association of Colleges for Teacher Education, 1973.

American Association of Dental Schools. "Statement on Peer Review." *Journal of Dental Education,* 1978, *42,* 410.

American Board of Medical Specialties. *Proceedings of the Conference on Extending Validity of Certification, March 24, 1976.* Chicago: American Board of Medical Specialties, 1976.

American Council on Education. *Survey of Dentistry.* Washington, D.C.: American Council on Education, 1961.

American Dental Association. *Guidelines for Continuing Dental Education.* Chicago: American Dental Association, 1974.

American Institute of Certified Public Accountants. *Professional Accounting in 30 Countries.* New York: American Institute of Certified Public Accountants, 1975.

American Law Institute. *Continuing Legal Education for Professional Competence and Responsibility.* Report of the Arden House Conference, December 16–19, 1958. Philadelphia: American Law Institute, 1959.

American Law Institute. *Goals for CLE and Means for Attaining Them.* Report on the 1968 National Conference on Continuing Legal Education, University of Chicago Center for Continuing Education, October 11–13, 1968. Philadelphia: American Law Institute, 1969.

American Medical Association. *Proceedings of the Self-Assessment Workshop, June 2, 1971.* Chicago: American Medical Association, 1971.

American Medical Association. *Peer Review Manual.* Vols. 1 and 2. Chicago: American Medical Association, 1972.

American Nurses' Association. *A Position Paper: Educational Preparation for Nurse Practitioners and Assistants to Nurses.* New York: American Nurses' Association, 1965.

American Nurses' Association. *Avenues for Continued Learning.* New York: American Nurses' Association, 1967.

American Society for Engineering Education. *Goals of Engineering Education.* Washington, D.C.: American Society for Engineering Education, 1968.

Anderson, R. K. "The Continued Education and Training of Regulatory Veterinarians." *Journal of the American Veterinary Medical Association,* 1970, *157,* 1888–1893.

Andrews, J. D. W. "Growth of a Teacher." *Journal of Higher Education,* 1978, *49,* 136–150.

Anglo American Conference on Continuing Medical Education. *Proceedings.* London: Royal Society of Medicine, 1974.

Anlyan, W. G. "Recommendations for the Future of the Continuum of Medical Education." *New England Journal of Medicine,* 1977, *297,* 110–112.

Arden House II: Toward Excellence in Continuing Legal Education. Philadelphia: Joint Committee on Continuing Legal Education of the American Law Institute and the American Bar Association, 1964.

Argyris, C. "Conditions for Competence Acquisition and Therapy." *Journal of Applied Behavioral Science,* 1968, *4,* 147–177.

Argyris, C., and Schön, D. A. *Theory in Practice: Increasing Professional Effectiveness.* San Francisco: Jossey-Bass, 1974.

Armer, P. "The Individual: His Privacy, Self-Image, and Obsolescence." In *The Management of Information and Knowledge.* Washington, D.C.: McGrath, 1970.

Ashby, E. *Adapting Universities to a Technological Society.* San Francisco: Jossey-Bass, 1974.

Asheim, L. E. "Education and Manpower for Librarianship." *ALA Bulletin,* 1968, *62,* 1096–1106.

Association of American Law Schools. *Anatomy of Modern Legal Education.* St. Paul, Minn.: West, 1961.

Association of Hospital Directors of Medical Education. "The Director of Medical Education in the Teaching Hospital." *Journal of the American Medical Association,* 1965, *192,* 1055–1060.

Association for Hospital Medical Education. *Role of Community Hospitals in Continuing Education of Health Professionals: Final Report to the National Library of Medicine.* Springfield,

Va.: National Technical Information Service, 1975.

Astin, A. W. *Four Critical Years: Effects of College on Beliefs, Attitudes, and Knowledge.* San Francisco: Jossey-Bass, 1977.

Astin, A. W., and Panos, R. J. *The Educational and Vocational Development of College Students.* Washington, D.C.: American Council on Education, 1969.

Auerbach, J. S. *Unequal Justice.* New York: Oxford University Press, 1975.

Averill, T. H. "Educational Participation and Openness to New Ideas." Unpublished doctoral dissertation, University of Chicago, 1964.

Ayers, J. *Continuing Medical Education Fact Sheet, January 1, 1979.* Chicago: American Medical Association, 1979.

Back, K. W. *Beyond Words.* New York: Russell Sage Foundation, 1972.

Bailit, H., and others. "Quality of Dental Care: Development of Standards." *Journal of the American Dental Association,* 1974, *89,* 842–853.

Baird, L. L. "Medical Schools Differ in Important Ways." *Findings, 3* (4), 5–8.

Bannister, T. C. (Ed.). *The Architect at Mid-Century: Evolution and Achievement.* New York: Reinhold, 1954.

Barker, B. D. "Administration and Evaluation of Continuing Educational Programs." *Journal of the American College of Dentists,* 1969, *36,* 171–178.

Barnett, C. "The Education of Military Elites." *Journal of Contemporary History,* 1967, *2,* 15–35.

Barton, J. C. "A Commonsense Approach to CME Organization." *The Hospital Medical Staff,* 1979, *8,* 10–13.

Barzun, J. "The Professions Under Siege: Private Practice Versus Public Need." *Journal of the American Dental Association,* 1979, *98,* 672–677.

Bauer, J. C., and Bush, R. G. "Dentists' Attitudes Toward Continuing Dental Education: Nontopic Factors of Demand for Courses." *Journal of Dental Education,* 1978, *42,* 623–626.

Beamer, E. G. "Continuing Education: A Professional Requirement." *Journal of Accountancy,* 1972, *133* (1), 33–39.

Becker, H. S. "Some Problems of Professionalism." *Adult Edu-*

cation, 1956, *6,* 101–105.

Becker, H. S. "The Nature of a Profession." In N. B. Henry (Ed.), *Education for the Professions.* Chicago: University of Chicago Press, 1962.

Becker, H. S., and Carper, J. W. "The Development of Identification with an Occupation." *American Journal of Sociology,* 1956a, *61,* 289–298.

Becker, H. S., and Carper, J. W. "The Elements of Identification with an Occupation." *American Sociological Review,* 1956b, *21,* 341–348.

Becker, H. S., and Greer, B. "The Fate of Idealism in Medical School." *American Sociological Review,* 1958, *23,* 50–58.

Becker, H. S., and others. *Boys in White: Student Culture in Medical School.* Chicago: University of Chicago Press, 1961.

Becker, H. S., and others (Eds.). *Institutions and the Person.* Chicago: Aldine, 1968.

Becker, M. H. "Factors Affecting Diffusion of Innovations Among Health Professionals." *American Journal of Public Health and the Nation's Health,* 1970, *60,* 294–304.

Bell, D. "The Dispossessed—1962," *Columbia University Forum,* 1962, *5* (Fall), 4–12.

Belth, M. *Education as a Discipline.* Boston: Allyn & Bacon, 1965.

Ben-David, J. "The Professional Role of the Physician in Bureaucratized Medicine: A Study in Role Conflict." *Human Relations,* 1958, *11,* 255–274.

Ben-David, J. "Role and Innovation in Medicine." *American Journal of Sociology,* 1960, *65,* 557–568.

Ben-David, J. "Professions in the Class System of Present-Day Societies." *Current Sociology,* 1964, *12,* 247–330.

Bennett, H. H. "Continuing Education: A Survey of Staff Development Programs." *School Libraries,* 1970, *19,* 11–20.

Bennis, W. G., Benne, K. D., and Chin, R. (Eds.). *The Planning of Change: Readings in the Applied Behavioral Sciences.* (2nd ed.) New York: Holt, Rinehart and Winston, 1971.

Benthall-Nietzel, D. "An Empirical Investigation of the Relationship Between Lawyering Skills and Legal Education." *Kentucky Law Journal,* 1974–75, *63,* 373–397.

Bentley, H. "The Medical Center and the Continuing Education of the Practicing Physician." *Pediatric Clinics of North America,* 1969, *16,* 809–813.

Berg, H. M. "Factors Differentiating Participant and Nonparticipant Nurses in Continuing Education." Unpublished doctoral dissertation, Columbia University, 1973.

Berg, I. "Education and Performance: Some Problems." *Journal of Higher Education,* 1972a, *43,* 192–202.

Berg, I. (Ed.). *Human Resources and Economic Welfare.* New York: Columbia University Press, 1972b.

Bergsten, U. *Adult Education in Relation to Work and Leisure.* Stockholm, Sweden: Almqvist and Wiksell, 1977.

Bernardi, V. W. "A Comparison of Selected Variables Associated with Participation in Pharmacy Continuing Education Programs." Unpublished doctoral dissertation, University of Connecticut, 1974.

Bertram, D., and others. "Evaluation of Continuing Medical Education: A Literature Review." *Health Education Monographs,* 1977, *5* (4, entire issue).

Berube, M. R., and Gittell, M. "In Whose Interest is 'The Public Interest'?" *Social Policy,* 1970, *1,* 5–9.

Beuter, J. H. "Teaching, Learning, Doing: Integrated Forest Resource Management." *Journal of Forestry,* 1975, *73,* 94–98.

Bevis, M. E. "The Continuing Learning Activities of Neophyte Nurses." *Adult Education,* 1975, *25,* 169–191.

Bidwell, C. E. "The Young Professional in the Army." *American Sociological Review,* 1961, *26,* 360–372.

Bidwell, C. E. "Students and Schools: Some Observations on Client Trust in Client-Serving Occupations." In *Organizations and Clients.* Columbus, Ohio: Merrill, 1970.

Bierer, B. W. *A Short History of Veterinary Medicine in America.* East Lansing: Michigan State University Press, 1955.

Bigelow, D. (Ed.). *The Liberal Arts and Teacher Education: A Confrontation.* Lincoln: University of Nebraska Press, 1971.

Bishop, M. *The Middle Ages.* New York: American Heritage Press, 1970.

Bjorn, J. C., and Cross, H. D. *The Problem-Oriented Private*

Practice of Medicine. Chicago: Modern Hospital Press, 1970.

Blaney, K. D. "A National Study of Directors of Medical Education." *Journal of Medical Education,* 1967, *42,* 660–665.

Blauch, L. E. (Ed.). *Education for the Professions.* Washington, D.C.: U.S. Office of Education, 1955.

Bledstein, B. J. *The Culture of Professionalism: The Middle Class and the Development of Higher Education in America.* New York: Norton, 1977.

Blizzard, S. W. "The Minister's Dilemma." *Christian Century,* 1956, *73,* 508–510.

Block, J. R. *Ventures in Judicial Education.* Chicago: National Council of Juvenile Court Judges, n.d.

Blockstein, W. L. "Aiding Professional Growth Through Continuing Education." *Journal of the American Pharmaceutical Association,* 1965, *n.s.5,* 422–424.

Blockstein, W. L. "Myths and Realities: Continuing Pharmaceutical Education." *Journal of the American Pharmaceutical Association,* 1967, *n.s.7,* 10–12.

Blockstein, W. L. "Developing a Program for Continuing Education for a College of Pharmacy." *American Journal of Pharmaceutical Education,* 1969, *33,* 767–773.

Bloomfield, D. K. "A Role for Practicing Physicians in Basic Medical Science Education." *Journal of the American Medical Association,* 1972, *221,* 187–188.

Bloomquist, H., and Kinney, M. M. "Continuing Education of Medical Librarians: Continuing Education in the Professions." *Medical Library Association Bulletin,* 1967, *51,* 357–367.

Boffey, P. M. "Nader and the Scientists: A Call for Responsibility." *Science,* 1971, *171,* 549–551.

Bohne, C. J., Jr. "Objectives of Professional Education and Training." In J. D. Edwards and others (Eds.), *Accounting Education: Problems and Prospects.* New York: American Accounting Association, 1974.

Boley, B. A. (Ed.). *Crossfire in Professional Education: Students, the Professions, and Society.* New York: Pergamon, 1977.

Borg, W. R., and others. *The Mini Course: A Microteaching Approach to Teacher Education.* Beverly Hills, Calif.: Macmillan Educational Services, 1970.

Bowers, T. A. "Student Attitudes Toward Journalism as a Major and a Career." *Journalism Quarterly,* 1974, *51,* 265–269.

Boyer, B. B., and Cramton, R. C. "American Legal Education: An Agenda for Research and Reform." *Research Contributions of the American Bar Foundation,* 1974, *1,* 221–297.

Boyette, R., Blount, W., and Petaway, K. "The Plight of the New Careerist." *American Journal of Orthopsychiatry,* 1971, *41,* 237–238.

Bradfield, R. M. *A Natural History of Associations.* (2 vols.) New York: International Universities Press, 1973.

Bramley, G. *World Trends in Library Education.* London: Clive Bingley, 1975.

Braucher, C. "A Comparative Analysis of Three Years of Continuing Education Activity." *American Journal of Pharmaceutical Education,* 1970, *34,* 234–240.

Braude, L. *Work and Workers.* New York: Praeger, 1975.

Brauner, C. J. *American Educational Theory.* Englewood Cliffs, N.J.: Prentice-Hall, 1964.

Brenner, M. N., and Koch, W. H., Jr. *Continuing Education Among Social Workers: Highlight Report of a Study.* Madison, Wis.: University of Wisconsin Extension, 1973.

Brenner, M. N., and Koch, W. H., Jr. "Continuing Education Among Social Workers: Patterns and Profiles." In *Approaches to Innovation in Social Work Education.* New York: Council on Social Work Education, 1974.

Bretz, R. *A Taxonomy of Communication Media.* Englewood Cliffs, N.J.: Educational Technology Publications, 1971.

Bright, W. E. "How One Company Manages Its Human Resources." *Harvard Business Review,* 1976, *54,* 81–93.

Brodie, D. C., and Heaney, R. P. "Need for Reform in Health Professions Accrediting." *Science,* 1978, *201,* 589–593.

Brodman, E. "A Philosophy of Continuing Education." *Bulletin of the Medical Library Association,* 1968, *56,* 145–149.

Brodsky, N. "The Professional Education of Officers." *Phi Delta Kappan,* 1967, *48,* 429–432.

Brody, B. L., and Stokes, J. "Use of Professional Time by Internists and General Practitioners in Group and Solo Practice." *Annals of Internal Medicine,* 1970, *73,* 741–749.

Brook, R. H. "Quality of Care Assessment: Choosing a Method for Peer Review." *New England Journal of Medicine,* 1973, *288,* 1323–1329.

Brook, R. H., and Avery, A. D. "Quality Assurance Mechanisms in the United States: From There to Where?" In G. McLachlan (Ed.), *A Question of Quality?* London: Oxford University Press, 1976.

Brook, R. H., and Williams, K. N. "Evaluation of the New Mexico Peer-Review System 1971–1973." *Medical Care, Supplement,* December 1976.

Brown, B. J. (Ed.). "Continuing Education: Who Cares?" *Nursing Administration Quarterly,* 1978, *2* (entire issue).

Brown, C. R., Jr., and Fleisher, D. S. "The Bicycle Concept: Relating Continuing Education Directly to Patient Care." *New England Journal of Medicine,* 1971, *284,* 88–97.

Brown, C. R., Jr., and Uhl, H. S. M. "Mandatory Continuing Education: Sense or Nonsense? *Journal of the American Medical Association,* 1970, *213,* 1660–1668.

Brown, M., and others. "A Retraining Program for Inactive Physicians." *California Medicine,* 1969, *111,* 396–400.

Brown, T. E. "Vocational Crises and Occupational Satisfaction Among Ministers." *Princeton Seminary Bulletin,* 1970, *63,* 52–62.

Brustein, R. "The Case for Professionalism." *New Republic,* 1969, *160* (17), 16–18.

Bucher, R. "Pathology: A Study of Social Movements Within a Profession." *Social Problems,* 1962, *10,* 40–51.

Bucher, R., and Stelling, J. "Characteristics of Professional Organizations." *Journal of Health and Social Behavior,* 1969, *10,* 3–15.

Bucher, R., Stelling, J., and Dommermuth, P. "Differential Prior Socialization: A Comparison of Four Professional Training Programs." *Social Forces,* 1969, *48,* 213–223.

Bucher, R., and Strauss, A. "Professions in Process." *American Journal of Sociology,* 1961, *66,* 325–334.

Buck, C. R., Jr., and White, K. L. "Peer Review: Impact of a System Based on Billing Claims." *New England Journal of*

Medicine, 1974, *291,* 877–883.

Buckley, J. W. *In Search of Identity.* Los Angeles: Study Center in Accounting and Information Systems, Graduate School of Management, University of California, Los Angeles, 1972.

Buckley, J. W., and Buckley, M. H. *The Accounting Profession.* Los Angeles: Melville, 1974.

Buerki, R. A. "Historical Development of Continuing Pharmaceutical Education in American Universities." Unpublished doctoral dissertation, Ohio State University, 1972.

Bullough, V. L. *The Development of Medicine as a Profession.* New York: Hafner, 1966.

Bundy, M. "A Report from an Academic Utopia." *Harper's Magazine,* 1962, *224,* 10–15.

Bundy, M. L., and Wasserman, P. "Professionalism Reconsidered." *College & Research Libraries,* 1968, *29,* 2–26.

Bureau of Library and Information Science Research, Graduate School of Library Service, Rutgers University. "New Jersey Library Manpower: Patterns and Projections." In *Library Education in New Jersey.* Trenton: New Jersey Department of Education, 1972.

Bureau of Research and Planning, California Medical Association. "Physician Opinions About Continuing Education Programs." *California Medicine,* 1969, *111,* 132–139.

Burg, F. D., Grosse, M. E., and Kay, C. F. "A National Self-Assessment Program in Internal Medicine." *Annals of Internal Medicine,* 1979, *90,* 100–107.

Burgess, P. "The Educational Orientations of Adult Participants in Group Educational Activities." Unpublished doctoral dissertation, University of Chicago, 1971a.

Burgess, P. "Reasons for Adult Participation in Group Educational Activities." *Adult Education,* 1971b, *22,* 3–29.

Burgwardt, F. C., and Biedenbach, J. M. *CES Directors Handbook.* Washington, D.C.: American Society for Engineering Education, 1975.

Burke, E. M. "Citizen Participation Strategies." *Journal of the American Institute of Planners,* 1968, *34,* 287–294.

Burkett, G., and Knafl, K. "Judgement and Decision Making in a Medical Specialty." *Sociology of Work and Occupations,* 1974, *1,* 82–109.

Butler, P. "Librarianship as a Profession." *Library Quarterly*, 1951, *21*, 235–247.

Byrne, D. R., Hines, S. A., and McCleary, L. E. *The Senior High School Principalship*. Vol. 1. Reston, Va.: National Association of Secondary School Principals, 1978.

Cafferetta, G. L., and others. "Continuing Education: Attitudes, Interests and Experiences of Practicing Dentists." *Journal of Dental Education*, 1975, *39*, 793–800.

Calhoun, D. H. *Professional Lives in America*. Cambridge, Mass.: Harvard University Press, 1965.

California Medical Association. *A Survey of Continuing Medical Education for Physicians: Part I and Part II*. San Francisco: California Medical Association, 1969.

Callan, L. B., Parlette, N., and Leonard, A. R. "Twelve-State Survey of Needs and Interests in Continuing Education in Public Health." *Public Health Reports*, 1969, *84*, 741–755.

Campbell, A. B. "The Adult Educator in the Hospital Setting." *Adult Leadership*, 1971, *19*, 331–332, 355.

Campeau, P. L. "Selective Review of the Results of Research on the Use of Audiovisual Media to Teach Adults." *AV Communication Review*, 1974, *22*, 5–40.

Caplan, R. M. "Relating Undergraduate Medical Education." *Journal of Medical Education*, 1975, *52*, 674–676.

Carey, J. L. *The Rise of the Accounting Profession*. (2 vols.) New York: American Institute of Certified Public Accountants, 1969–1970.

Carey, R. G. "Correlates of Satisfaction in the Priesthood." *Administrative Science Quarterly*, 1972, *17*, 185–195.

Carlin, J. E. *Lawyer's Ethics*. New York: Russell Sage Foundation, 1966.

Carlson, A. B. "Research Will Lead to Performance Tests for Lawyers." *Findings*, 1976, *3* (2), 1–4.

Carlson, A. B., and Werts, C. E. *Relationships Among Law School Predictors, Law School Performance, and Bar Examination Results*. Princeton, N.J.: Educational Testing Service, 1976.

Carmichael, H. T. "Continuing Education for Psychiatrists." *American Journal of Psychiatry*, 1968, *125*, 135–136.

Carnegie Commission on Higher Education. *Higher Education*

and the Nation's Health Policies for Medical and Dental Education. New York: McGraw-Hill, 1970.

Carnegie Commission on Higher Education. *Toward a Learning Society: Alternative Channels to Life, Work, and Service.* New York: McGraw-Hill, 1973.

Carmichael, H., Small, S. M., and Regan, P. F. *Prospects and Proposals: Lifetime Learning for Psychiatrists.* Washington, D.C.: American Psychiatric Association, 1972.

Carp, A., Peterson, R., and Roelfs, P. *Learning Interests and Experiences of Adult Americans.* Berkeley: Educational Testing Service, 1973.

Carp, A., Peterson, R., and Roelfs, P. "Adult Learning Interests and Experiences." In K. P. Cross, J. R. Valley, and Associates (Eds.), *Planning Non-Traditional Programs: An Analysis of the Issues for Postsecondary Education.* San Francisco: Jossey-Bass, 1974.

Carroll, C. E. *The Professionalization of Education for Librarianship.* Metuchen, N.J.: Scarecrow Press, 1970.

Carr-Saunders, A. M., and Wilson, P. A. *The Professions.* London: Oxford University Press, 1933.

Carr-Saunders, A. M., and Wilson, P. A. "Professions." In E. R. A. Seligman (Ed.), *Encyclopaedia of the Social Sciences.* Vol. 12. New York: Macmillan, 1934.

Castle, C. H., and Storey, P. B. "Physicians' Needs and Interests in Continuing Medical Education." *Journal of the American Medical Association,* 1968, *206,* 611–614.

Centra, J. A. "The Student as Godfather? The Impact of Student Ratings on Academia." In J. D. Edwards (Ed.), *Accounting Education: Problems and Prospects.* New York: American Accounting Association, 1974.

Chambers, D. W., and Hamilton, D. L. "Continuing Dental Education: Reasonable Answers to Unreasonable Questions." *Journal of the American Dental Association,* 1975a, *90,* 116–120.

Chambers, D. W., and Hamilton, D. L. "A Survey of Resources of Continuing Education Programs in American Dental Schools." *Journal of Dental Education,* 1975b, *39,* 234–238.

Chambers, D. W., and others. "An Investigation of Behavior

Change in Continuing Dental Education." *Journal of Dental Education,* 1976a, *40,* 546–550.

Chambers, D. W., and others. "Means of Improving Continuing Dental Education." *Journal of Dental Education,* 1976b, *40,* 222–226.

Chapman, C. B. "Doctors and Their Autonomy: Past Events and Future Prospects." *Science,* 1978, *200,* 851–856.

Charnley, A. *Paid Educational Leave: A Report of Practice in France, Germany and Sweden.* London: Hart-Davis, 1976.

Charters, A. N., and Blakely, R. J. "The Management of Continuing Learning: A Model of Continuing Education as a Problem-Solving Strategy for Health Manpower." In U.S. Department of Health, Education, and Welfare, *Fostering the Growing Need to Learn.* DHEW Publication no. (HRA) 74–3112. Washington, D.C.: U.S. Government Printing Office, 1974.

Cheit, E. F. *The Useful Arts and the Liberal Tradition.* New York: McGraw-Hill, 1975.

Chenault, J., and Burnford, F. *Human Services Professional Education.* New York: McGraw-Hill, 1978.

Chiang, K. S. "The Invisible College in Nuclear Physics." Unpublished master's thesis, University of Chicago, 1974.

Christie, R. W. "Letter to the Editor." *New England Journal of Medicine,* 1970, *282,* 877.

Church, C. A. "A Nonacademic View of Continuing Engineering Education." *Journal of Continuing Education and Training,* 1971, *1,* 65–71.

Churchill, W. S. *A Roving Commission.* New York: Scribner's, 1930.

Churchill, W. S. *Thoughts and Adventures.* London: Thornton Butterworth, 1932.

Churchwell, C. D. *The Shaping of American Library Education.* Chicago: American Library Association, 1975.

Citizens Commission on Graduate Medical Education. *Graduate Education of Physicians.* Chicago: American Medical Association, 1966.

Clare, R. L., Jr. "Incompetency and the Responsibility of Courts and Law Schools." *St. John's Law Review,* 1976, *50,* 463–473.

Cless, E. L. "Social Change and Professional Continuing Educators." *Adult Leadership,* 1972, *20,* 273–274, 299.

Clyde, J. D. "Should Primary Responsibility Rest on the Seminary? No!" *Theological Education,* 1965, *1,* 229–232.

"CME Data on Physicians Disciplined by the California Board of Medical Quality Assurance." *Continuing Medical Education Newsletter,* 1979, *8* (4), 4–5.

Cogan, M. L. "Toward a Definition of Profession." *Harvard Educational Review,* 1953, *23,* 33–50.

Cogan, M. L. "The Problem of Defining a Profession." *Annals of the American Academy of Political and Social Science,* 1955, *297,* 105–111.

Coggeshall, L. T. *Planning for Medical Progress Through Education.* Evanston, Ill.: Association of American Medical Colleges, 1965.

Cohen, H. S., and Miike, L. H. *Developments in Health Manpower Licensure.* Washington, D.C.: U.S. Department of Health, Education, and Welfare, 1973.

Cohen, H. S., and Miike, L. H. "Toward a More Responsive System of Professional Licensure." *International Journal of Health Services,* 1974, *4,* 268.

Coleman, J. S., Katz, E., and Menzel, H. *Medical Innovation, A Diffusion Study.* Indianapolis: Bobbs-Merrill, 1966.

Combs, A. W., and others. *The Professional Education of Teachers.* (2nd ed.) Boston: Allyn & Bacon, 1974.

Commission on Education for Health Administration. *A Future Agenda.* Vol. 3. Ann Arbor, Mich.: Health Administration Press, 1977.

Commission on Medical Education. *Medical Education: Final Report.* New York: Office of the Director of the Study, 1932.

Compendium on Continuing Education Accreditation in the Health Professions. Washington, D.C.: Association for Academic Health Centers, 1978.

Competence in the Medical Professions: A Strategy. Washington, D.C.: U.S. Department of Health, Education, and Welfare, 1977.

Conant, J. B. *The Education of American Teachers.* New York: McGraw-Hill, 1963.

Condliffe, P. G., and Furnia, A. H. (Eds.). *Reform of Medical Education.* Washington, D.C.: U.S. Department of Health, Education, and Welfare, 1970.

"Consumer Involvement in the Delivery of Social Service." *Human Needs,* 1973, *1* (9), 3–35.

"The Continuing Competence of Pharmacists." *Journal of the American Pharmaceutical Association,* 1975, *n.s.15,* 432.

"Continuing Education: Joint Body Needed." *Royal Institute of British Architects Journal,* 1970, *77,* 430.

"Continuing Education of Chemistry's Manpower." In *Chemistry in the Economy.* Washington, D.C.: American Chemical Society, 1973.

The Continuing Education of Engineers. Proceedings of the FEANI–UNESCO Seminar, Helsinki, August 21–24, 1972. Paris: UNESCO Press, 1974.

"Continuing Education of the Practicing Physician: A Statement by the Committee on Medical Education of the New York Academy of Medicine." *Bulletin of the New York Academy of Medicine,* 1970, *46,* 892–905.

"Continuing Liberal Education for the Physician." *New England Journal of Medicine,* 1964, *270,* 561–562.

"Continuing Medical Education: Is Its Value Overestimated?" *American Medical News,* February 7, 1977.

Continuing Medical Education Newsletter, 1978, *7,* 4.

Coombs, R. H., and Vincent, C. E. (Eds.). *Psychosocial Aspects of Medical Training.* Springfield, Ill.: Thomas, 1971.

Cooper, S. S., and Hornback, M. S. *Continuing Nursing Education.* New York: McGraw-Hill, 1973.

Cooper, S. S., and Lutze, R. S. "Dial N for Nursing." *Adult Leadership,* 1970, *19,* 178–180, 202–203.

Copeland, H. "Organizational Personality and the Continuing Learning Activity of Adults." Unpublished doctoral dissertation, University of Chicago, 1969.

Corby, C. S. "Continuing Education: Are You Being Taken for a Ride?" *Dental Economics,* 1979, *6,* 42–47.

Cordtz, D. "Change Begins in the Doctor's Office." *Fortune,* 1970, *81,* 84–89, 130–134.

Corrigan, R. E., and Kaufman, R. *Why System Engineering.*

Belmont, Calif.: Fearon, 1965.

Corwin, R. G. "The Professional Employee: A Study of Conflict in Nursing Roles." *American Journal of Sociology*, 1961, *66*, 604–615.

Corwin, R. G. *Militant Professionalism.* New York: Appleton-Century-Crofts, 1970.

Council of Medical Specialty Societies. *Proceedings of the Conference for Accreditation of Continuing Medical Education, January 20–21, 1979.* Lake Forest, Ill.: Council of Medical Specialty Societies, 1979.

Council on Social Work Education. *Guide to Continuing Education for Schools of Social Work.* New York: Council on Social Work Education, 1974.

Cowan, A. "General Comments on Continuing Education." *International Dental Journal*, 1975, *25*, 1–7.

Crane, D. *Invisible Colleges.* Chicago: University of Chicago Press, 1972.

Craven, O., Todd, A. L., and Ziegler, J. H. (Eds.). *Theological Education as Professional Education.* Dayton, Ohio: American Association of Theological Schools, 1969.

Credentialing Health Manpower. Washington, D.C.: U.S. Department of Health, Education, and Welfare, 1977.

Curtiss, F., and others. *Continuing Education in Nursing.* Boulder, Colo.: Western Interstate Commission for Higher Education, 1969.

Cushing, H. *The Life of Sir William Osler.* (2 vols.) Oxford, England: Clarendon Press, 1925.

Daeschner, C. "Continuing Medical Education Through Self-Evaluation." *Pediatrics*, 1970, *45*, 729–731.

Daniels, A. "The Captive Professional: Bureaucratic Limitations in the Practice of Military Psychiatry." *Journal of Health and Social Behavior*, 1969, *10*, 255–265.

Daniels, W. "Variations in Needs of Pharmacists for Continuing Education." *American Journal of Pharmaceutical Education*, 1969, *33*, 729–734.

Dao, M. N.-S. C. "The Orientations Toward Nonparticipation in Adult Education." Unpublished doctoral dissertation, University of Chicago, 1975.

Darby, D., and Weiss, R. "Continuing Education Outside the

Dental School Setting." *Journal of the American Dental Association,* 1965, *70,* 1488–1496.

Darling, J. R., and Bussom, R. S. "A Comparative Analysis of the Attitudes of Dentists Toward the Advertising of Their Fees and Services." *Journal of Dental Education,* 1977, *41,* 59–67.

Darwin, C. *The Autobiography of Charles Darwin: 1809–1882.* London: Collins, 1958. (Originally published 1887.)

Davidson, L., and others. *Guides for the Establishment of Refresher Courses for Registered Nurses.* New York: American Nurses' Association, 1968.

Davies, H. M., and Aquino, J. T. "Collaboration in Continuing Professional Development." *Journal of Teacher Education,* 1975, *26,* 274–277.

Davis, D. A. "Continuing Education in the Community Hospital: An Interprofessional Approach." *Journal of Medical Education,* 1977, *52,* 745–751.

Davis, F. (Ed.). *The Nursing Profession: Five Sociological Essays.* New York: Wiley, 1966.

Davis, F. "Professional Socialization as Subjective Experience: The Process of Doctrinal Conversion among Student Nurses." In. H. S. Becker and others (Eds.), *Institutions and the Person.* Chicago: Aldine, 1968.

Davis, J. A. *Undergraduate Career Decisions.* Chicago: Aldine, 1965.

Davis, S. "Entrepreneurial Succession." *Administrative Science Quarterly,* 1968, *13,* 402–416.

Decker, B., and Bonner, P. (Eds.). *PSRO: Organization for Regional Peer Review.* Cambridge, Mass.: Ballinger, 1973.

DeLancy, P. *The Licensing of Professions in West Virginia.* Chicago: Foundation Press, 1938.

de Lodzia, G. "Procedural Training: The Next Step in Medical Education." *Journal of Medical Education,* 1970, *45,* 421–433.

DeMuth, J. E., Kirk, K. W., and Weinswig, M. H. "Continuing Education for Nonpracticing Professionals: A Case Study of a Program for Pharmacists." *Adult Education,* 1976, *26,* 157–166.

Denemark, G. W., and Yff, J. (Eds.). *Obligation for Reform:*

The Final Report of the Higher Education Task Force on Improvement and Reform in American Education. Washington, D.C.: American Association of Colleges for Teacher Education, 1974.

Denzin, N. K., and Mettlin, C. J. "Incomplete Professionalization: The Case of Pharmacy." *Social Forces,* 1968, *43,* 375–381.

DeProspo, E. R., and Huang, T. "Continuing Education for the Library Administrator: His Needs." In *Administration and Change: Continuing Education in Library Administration.* New Brunswick, N.J.: Rutgers University Press, 1969.

Derbyshire, R. C. "What Should the Profession Do About the Incompetent Physician?" *Journal of the American Medical Association,* 1965, *194,* 119–122.

Derbyshire, R. C. *Medical Licensure and Discipline in the United States.* Baltimore: Johns Hopkins University Press, 1969.

Derbyshire, R. C. "One State's Farewell to Lifelong Licensure." *Medical Opinion,* 1971, *7* (7), 56–67.

Devaney, K. (Ed.). *Essays on Teachers' Centers.* San Francisco: Far West Laboratory for Educational Research and Development, 1975.

Devaney, K., and Thorn, L. *Exploring Teachers' Centers.* San Francisco: Far West Laboratory for Educational Research and Development, 1975.

Dill, W. R., Crowston, W. B. S., and Elton, E. J. "Strategies for Self-Education." *Harvard Business Review,* 1965, *43,* 119–130.

Dimond, E. G. "The Open Medical School." *Journal of the American Medical Association,* 1965, *194,* 162–166.

Dimond, E. G. "National Resources for Continuing Medical Education." *Journal of the American Medical Association,* 1968, *206,* 617–620.

Djonovich, D. J. *Legal Education: A Selective Bibliography.* Dobbs Ferry, N.Y.: Oceana Publications, 1970.

Dobson, J. "Doctors in Literature." *Library Association Record,* 1969, *71,* 269–274.

"Doing Better and Feeling Worse." *Daedalus,* 1977, Winter (entire issue).

Dollinger, M. R., and others. "A Novel Program of Continuing Medical Education." *Journal of the American Medical Association,* 1972, *220,* 714–716.

Donabedian, A. "The Quality of Medical Care." *Science,* 1978, *200,* 856–864.

Dorros, S. *Teaching as a Profession.* Columbus, Ohio: Merrill, 1968.

Drake, D. *Medical School.* New York: Rawson, Wade 1978.

Dreeben, R. *The Failure of Teaching: Schools and the Work of Teachers.* Glenview, Ill.: Scott, Foresman, 1970.

Dryer, B. V. "Lifetime Learning for Physicians: Principles, Practices, Proposals." *Journal of Medical Education,* 1962, *37* (6, Part 2, entire issue).

Dryer, B. V. "A Nationwide Plan for Continuing Medical Education." *Journal of the American Medical Association,* 1964, *189,* 123–127.

Dubin, S. S. *Professional Obsolescence.* Lexington, Mass.: Lexington Books, 1971a.

Dubin, S. S. "Motivational Factors in Professional Updating." In S. S. Dubin (Ed.), *Professional Obsolescence.* Lexington, Mass.: Lexington Books, 1971b.

Dubin, S. S. "Obsolescence or Lifelong Education: A Choice for the Professional." *American Psychologist.* 1972a, *27,* 468–498.

Dubin, S. S. "The Psychology of Keeping Up-to-date." *Chemtech,* 1972b, *2,* 393–397.

Dubin, S. S., Alderman, E., and Marlow, L. "Keeping Managers and Supervisors in Local Government Up-to-date." *Public Administration Review,* 1969, *29,* 294–298.

Dubin, S. S. and Cohen, D. M. "Motivation to Update from a Systems Approach." *Engineering Education,* 1970, *60,* 366–368.

Dubin, S. S., Shelton, H., and McConnell, J. (Eds.). *Maintaining Professional and Technical Competence of the Older Engineer.* Washington, D.C.: American Society for Engineering Education, 1974.

Ducker, D. "The Myth of Professional Isolation Among Physicians in Nonurban Areas." *Journal of Medical Education,*

1977, *52*, 991–998.

Duffy, J. *The Healers.* New York: McGraw-Hill, 1976.

Dumont, M. P. "The Changing Face of Professionalism." *Social Policy,* 1970, *1,* 26–31.

Dunkin, M. J., and Biddle, B. J. *The Study of Teaching.* New York: Holt, Rinehart and Winston, 1974.

Dunn, R. E. "Legal Education and the Attitudes of Practicing Attorneys." *Journal of Legal Education,* 1969, *22,* 220–226.

Durkheim, E. *Professional Ethics and Civic Morals.* London: Routledge & Kegan Paul, 1957.

Ebert, R. H. "Medical Education in the United States." *Daedalus,* 1977, Winter, 171–184.

Education for Professional Responsibility. Proceedings of the Inter-Professions Conference on Education for Professional Responsibility. Buck Hill Falls, Pennsylvania, April 12–14, 1948. Pittsburgh: Carnegie Press, 1948.

Education Technology: Definition and Glossary of Terms. Washington, D.C.: Association for Educational Communications and Technology, 1977.

"Education in the 1970's: Teaching for an Altered Reality." *Architectural Record,* 1970, *148,* 128–133.

Edwards, J. D. (Ed.). *Accounting Education: Problems and Prospects.* New York: American Accounting Association, 1974.

Egdahl, R. H., and Gertman, P. M. *Quality Health Care: The Role of Continuing Medical Education.* Germantown, Md.: Apen Systems Corp., 1977.

Egelston, E. M. "The Effects of Allied Health Licensure Laws and Program Accreditation Standards upon the Selection, Preparation, Job Definition, and Continuing Education of Allied Health Personnel." Unpublished doctoral dissertation, University of Chicago, 1973.

Eidell, T. L., and Kitchel, J. M. (Eds.). *Knowledge Production and Utilization in Educational Administration.* Eugene, Ore.: Center for the Advanced Study of Educational Administration, University of Oregon, 1968.

Eisley, J. (Eds.). *Engineering Education and a Lifetime of Learning.* Washington, D.C.: American Society for Engineering Education, 1975.

Elkinton, J. R. "Self-Assessment of Medical Knowledge." *Annals of Internal Medicine,* 1968, *68,* 247–249.

Ellis, P. G. "A Case for Professional Registration." *Engineering Education,* 1969, *60,* 329–330.

Elmina, M. P. *Learning Needs of Registered Nurses.* New York: Teachers College Press, Columbia University, 1967.

Elstein, A. S., and others. "Methods and Theory in the Study of Medical Inquiry." *Journal of Medical Education,* 1972, *47,* 85–92.

Enarson, H. L. "New Strategies for Universities in the Education of the Professional." In *A Future Agenda.* Ann Arbor, Mich.: Health Administration Press, 1977.

Engel, G. L. "Professional Autonomy and Bureaucratic Organization." *Administrative Science Quarterly,* 1970, *15,* 12–21.

Engel, G. L. "The Need for a New Medical Model: A Challenge for Biomedicine." *Science,* 1977, *196,* 133–137.

Ennis, P. H., and Winger, H. W. (Eds.). *Seven Questions about the Profession of Librarianship.* Chicago: University of Chicago Press, 1962.

Etzioni, A. (Ed.). *The Semi-Professions and Their Organization.* New York: Free Press, 1969.

Faithe, M. E., and others. "The Cost of Continuing Medical Education for Family Physicians." *Journal of the American Medical Association,* 1979, *242,* 449–450.

Farber, S. M. "Greatest Challenge in Medicine Today: Continuing Education." *Journal of the American Medical Association,* 1965, *193,* 432–435.

Farmer, J. A., Jr., and Williams, R. G. "An Educational Strategy for Professional Career Change." *Adult Leadership,* 1971, *19,* 318–330, 353.

Faruqee, S., and Lauffer, A. (Eds.). *Social Work Continuing Education Yearbook: 1973.* Ann Arbor: Continuing Education Program, School of Social Work, University of Michigan, 1973.

Feather, N. T. *Values in Education and Society.* New York: Free Press, 1975.

Federman, D. "Continuing Education in Medicine." *American Journal of the Medical Sciences,* 1970, *259,* 237–241.

Feiman, S. (Ed.). *Teacher Centers: What Place in Education?* Chicago: Center for Policy Study, University of Chicago, 1978.

Ferdinand, T. N. "On the Obsolescence of Scientists and Engineers." *American Scientist,* 1966, *54,* 46–56.

Ference, T. P., Goldner, F. H., and Ritti, R. R. "Priest and Church: The Professionalization of an Organization." *American Behavioral Scientist,* 1971, *14,* 507–524.

Fessel, W. J., and Van Brunt, E. E. "Assessing Quality of Care from the Medical Record." *New England Journal of Medicine,* 1972, *286,* 134–138.

Fichter, J. H. *Religion as an Occupation: A Study in the Sociology of Professions.* South Bend, Ind.: University of Notre Dame Press, 1961.

Fields, C. M. "The Qualities Admissions Tests Don't Identify." *Chronicle of Higher Education,* August 7, 1978.

Fiester, K. "Upgrading Hospital Workers." *Manpower,* 1970, *2,* 24–27.

"Final Report of the Goals Committee." *Journal of Engineering Education,* 1968, *58,* 369–446.

Flanagan, J. C., and Russ-Eft, D. *An Empirical Study to Aid in Formulating Educational Goals.* Palo Alto, Calif.: American Institutes for Research, 1976.

Fleisher, D. S. "Priorities and Data Bases: Their Relationship to Continuing Education." In U.S. Department of Health, Education, and Welfare, *Fostering the Growing Need to Learn.* Washington, D.C.: U.S. Government Printing Office, 1974.

Flexner, A. *Medical Education in the United States and Canada.* New York: Carnegie Foundation for the Advancement of Teaching, 1910.

Flexner, A. "Is Social Work a Profession?" *School and Society,* 1915, *1,* 901–911.

Florio, D. H., and Koff, R. H. *Model State Legislation: Continuing Professional Education for School Personnel.* Washington, D.C.: National Institute of Education, 1977.

Ford, R. N. *Motivation Through the Work Itself.* Montreal: Canadian Management Centre, 1971.

Form, W. H. "Occupations and Careers." In D. L. Sills (Ed.),

International Encyclopedia of the Social Sciences. Vol. 11. New York: Macmillan, 1968.

Fortier, C. B. "A Study of Continuing Education Needs of Clergymen in Lafayette Parish, Louisiana, 1972." Unpublished doctoral dissertation, Louisiana State University, 1972.

Foshay, A. W. (Ed.). *The Professional as Educator.* New York: Teachers College, Columbia University, 1970.

Fox, R. C. "Training for Uncertainty." In R. K. Merton, G. C. Reader, and P. L. Kendall (Eds.), *The Student Physician.* Cambridge, Mass.: Harvard University Press, 1957.

Frager, S. R., and Rhodes, G. "Continuing Education Among Social Service Personnel." *NUEA Spectator,* 1975, *39* (21), 25–28.

Francis, P. R. "Competency of Health Professionals: An Approach for Continuing Education." *Journal of the American Dental Association,* 1976, *92,* 1119–1123.

Francis, V., and others. "Gaps in Doctor-Patient Communication." *New England Journal of Medicine,* 1969, *280,* 535.

Frandson, P. E. "Continuing Education of the Professions: Issues, Ethics, and Conflicts." *NUEA Spectator,* 1975a, *39* (21), 5–10.

Frandson, P. E. "In Setting Standards for the Professions, Greater Role Urged for Universities." *Los Angeles Times,* Sept. 28, 1975b.

Frazier, H. S., and Hiatt, H. H. "Evaluation of Medical Practices." *Science,* 1978, *200,* 875–878.

Freidson, E. "The Impurity of Professional Authority." In H. S. Becker and others (Eds.), *Institutions and the Person.* Chicago: Aldine, 1968a.

Freidson, E. "Medical Personnel." In D. L. Sills (Ed.), *International Encyclopedia of the Social Sciences.* Vol. 10. New York: Macmillan, 1968b.

Freidson, E. *Professional Dominance: The Social Structure of Medical Care.* New York: Atherton Press, 1970a.

Freidson, E. *Profession of Medicine.* New York: Dodd, Mead, 1970b.

Freidson, E. "Professionalism: The Doctor's Dilemma." *Social Policy,* 1971a, *1,* 35–40.

Freidson, E. (Ed.). *The Professions and Their Prospects.* Beverly Hills, Calif.: Sage Publications, 1971b.

Freidson, E., and Rhea, B. "Processes of Control in a Company of Equals." *Social Problems.* 1963, *11,* 119–131.

Freidson, E., and Rhea, B. "Knowledge and Judgement in Professional Evaluations." *Administrative Science Quarterly,* 1965, *10,* 107–124.

Frey, L. A., Shatz, E., and Katz, E. A. "Continuing Education: Teaching Staff to Teach." *Social Work,* 1974, *55,* 360–368.

Friday, H. H. "Continuing Legal Education: Historical Background, Recent Developments, and the Future." *St. John's Law Review,* 1976, *50,* 502–512.

Freund, P. A. "The Legal Profession." In K. S. Lynd (Ed.), *The Professions* in America. Boston: Beacon Press, 1967.

Freymann, J. G. "Leadership in American Medicine." *New England Journal of Medicine,* 1964, *270,* 710–720.

Freymann, J. G. "The Community Hospital as a Major Focus for Continuing Medical Education." *Journal of the American Medical Association,* 1968, *206,* 615–616.

Fry, J. *The New Approach to Medicine: Principles and Priorities.* Lancaster, England: MTP Press, 1978.

Fulchiero, A., and others. "Can the PSRO's be Cost Effective?" *New England Journal of Medicine,* 1978, *299,* 574–580.

Funkenstein, D. H. "Medical Students, Medical Schools, and Society During Three Eras." In R. H. Coombs and C. E. Vincent (Eds.), *Psychosocial Aspects of Medical Training.* Springfield, Ill.: Thomas, 1971.

Gage, N. L. *Teacher Effectiveness and Teacher Education.* Palo Alto, Calif.: Pacific Books, 1972.

Gamble, C. C., Jr. *The Continuing Theological Education of the American Minister.* Richmond, Va.: Union Theological Seminary, 1960.

Gardner, J. W. *Self-Renewal.* New York: Harper & Row, 1963.

Gartner, A. *Paraprofessionals and Their Performance.* New York: Praeger, 1971.

Gartner, A. *The Preparation of Human Service Professionals.* New York: Human Sciences Press, 1976.

Gartner, M. G. "Was the Mayflower Filled with Lawyers?" *Wall Street Journal,* March 1, 1978, p. 20.

Garvey, W. D., Lin, N., and Nelson, C. E. "Communication in the Physical and Social Sciences." *Science,* 1970, *170,* 1166–1173.

Gaver, M. V. "The Educational Third Dimension: I. Continuing Education to Meet the Personalized Criteria of Librarians." *Library Trends,* 1971, *20,* 118–143.

Geer, B. "Teaching." In D. L. Sills (Ed.), *International Encyclopedia of the Social Sciences.* Vol. 15. New York: Macmillan, 1968.

George, J. L., Dubin, S. S., and Nead, B. M. "What Foresters Need to Do to Keep Up to Date." *Journal of Forestry,* 1974, *72,* 288–289.

Gessner, P. K. "Evaluation of Instruction." *Science,* 1973, *180,* 566–570.

Gilb, C. L. *Hidden Hierarchies.* New York: Harper & Row, 1966.

Gilder, J. (Ed.). *Policies for Lifelong Education.* Washington, D.C.: American Association of Community and Junior Colleges, 1979.

Ginzberg, E. "The Professionalization of the U.S. Labor Force." *Scientific American,* 1979, *240* (3), 48–53.

Ginzberg, E., and Yohalem, A. M. (Eds.). *The University Medical Center and the Metropolis.* New York: Josiah Macy Jr. Foundation, 1974.

Glaser, B. (Ed.). *Organizational Careers.* Chicago: Aldine, 1968.

Glass, J. C., Jr. "The Professional Churchman and Continuing Education." *Adult Leadership,* 1972, *20,* 349–350.

Glazer, N. "The Schools of the Minor Professions." *Minerva,* 1974, *10,* 346–364.

Gold, N. "Continuing Legal Education: A New Direction." *Ottawa Law Review,* 1975, *7,* 62–84.

Goldner, F. H., and Ritti, R. R. "Professionalization as Career Immobility." *American Journal of Sociology,* 1967, *72,* 489–502.

Goldstein, R. L., and others. "Data for Peer Review: Acquisition and Use." *Annals of Internal Medicine,* 1975, *82,* 262–267.

Goode, W. J. "Community Within a Community: The Professions." *American Sociological Review,* 1957, *22,* 194–200.

Goode, W. J. "Encroachment, Charlatanism, and the Emerging

Profession: Psychology, Sociology, and Medicine." *American Sociological Review,* 1960, *25,* 903–914.

Goode, W. J. "The Librarian: From Occupation to Profession?" *Library Quarterly,* 1961, *31,* 306–318.

Goode, W. J. "The Theoretical Limits of Professionalization." In A. Etzioni (Ed.), *The Semi-Professions and Their Organization.* New York: Free Press, 1969.

Gordon, N. *The Rabbi.* New York: McGraw-Hill, 1965.

Gorman, C. A. "Board Examinations: Arbitrary Rites." *New England Journal of Medicine,* 1969, *280,* 960–961.

Gossett, W. T. "Future of Continuing Legal Education." *American Bar Association Journal,* 1969, *55,* 132–134.

Gough, H. G. "Some Predictive Implications of Premedical Scientific Competence and Preferences." *Journal of Medical Education,* 1978, *53,* 291–300.

Graber, J. B., and Brodie, D. C. *Challenge to Pharmacy in the 70's.* Washington, D.C.: U.S. Department of Health, Education, and Welfare, 1972.

Grabowski, S. M. "The Telephone as an Instructional Method in Adult Education." *Adult Leadership,* 1972, *21,* 105–107.

Graham, J. W., and DeMarais, D. R. "Continuing Dental Education Requirements for State Dental Relicensure and Constituent Society Membership." *Journal of the American Dental Association,* 1975, *90,* 966–970.

Graham, J. W., and others. "Continuing Education in U.S. Dental Schools." *Journal of the American Dental Association,* 1976, *92,* 1225–1229.

Grayson, L. P., and Biedenbach, J. M. (Eds.). *Proceedings, First World Conference on Continuing Engineering Education, Mexico, April 25–27, 1979.* Washington, D.C.: American Society for Engineering Education, 1979.

Green, W. E. "Inept Advocates?" *Wall Street Journal,* February 24, 1975, *55,* 1, 17.

Greenblatt, M., Sharaf, M. R., and Stone, E. M. *Dynamics of Institutional Change: The Hospital in Transition.* Pittsburgh: University of Pittsburgh Press, 1971.

Greenfield, H. I. *Allied Health Manpower: Trends and Prospects.* New York: Columbia University Press, 1969.

Greenwood, E. "Attributes of a Profession." In S. Nosow and W. Form (Eds.), *Man, Work and Society.* New York: Basic Books, 1962.

Griffith, B. C., and Mullins, N. C. "Coherent Social Groups in Scientific Change." *Science,* 1972, *177,* 959–964.

Griffith, W. S. "Perspectives on Professional Education." *Connecticut Medicine,* 1976, *40,* 779–786.

Grose, R. F. "How Long is a Credit? When is a Course?" *College and University,* 1970, *46,* 20–32.

Gross, R., and Osterman, P. (Eds.). *The New Professionals.* New York: Simon & Schuster, 1972.

Grosser, C., Henry, W. E., and Kelly, J. G. (Eds.). *Nonprofessionals in the Human Services.* San Francisco: Jossey-Bass, 1969.

Groteleuschen, A. D., and Caulley, D. N. "A Model for Studying Determinants of Intention to Participate in Continuing Professional Education." *Adult Education,* 1977a, *28,* 22–37.

Grotelueschen, A. D., and Caulley, D. N. "A Model for Studying Determinants of Intention to Participate in Continuing Professional Education.* Urbana-Champaign, Ill.: Office for the Study of Continuing Professional Education, University of Illinois, 1977b.

Guelzo, C. M. "The Long Hard Climb to Professionalism." *United States Naval Institution Journal,* 1961, *106,* 32–51.

Gustafson, J. M. "Theological Education as Professional Education." In O. Craven, A. L. Todd, and J. H. Ziegler (Eds.), *Theological Education as Professional Education.* Dayton, Ohio: American Association of Theological Schools, 1969.

Gustafson, J. M. "On the Threshold of a New Age." In J. B. Hofrenning (Ed.), *The Continuing Quest.* Minneapolis: Augsburg Publishing House, 1970.

Gustafson, T. "The Controversy over Peer Review." *Science,* 1975, *190,* 1060–1066.

Gutzman, S. D. "Career-Long Sabbatical." *Library Journal,* 1969, *94,* 3411–3415.

Haakenson, P. N. "A Cost-Benefit Analysis of Three Formal Methods of Presenting Continuing Education Material to Pharmacists in North Dakota." Unpublished doctoral dissertation, University of Wisconsin, 1972.

Haber, D., and Cohen, J. *The Law School of Tomorrow.* New Brunswick, N.J.: Rutgers University Press, 1968.

Haberman, M., and Stinnett, T. M. *Teacher Education and the New Profession of Teaching.* Berkeley, Calif.: McCutchan, 1974.

Hackett, J. W. *The Profession of Arms.* London: The Times Publishing Co., 1963.

Hakansson, N. H. "Where We Are in Accounting." *Accounting Review,* 1978, *53,* 717–725.

Hall, O. "The Informal Organization of the Medical Profession." *Canadian Journal of Economics and Political Science,* 1946, *12,* 30–44.

Hall, O. "The Stages of a Medical Career." *American Journal of Sociology,* 1948, *53,* 327–336.

Hall, O. "Types of Medical Careers." *American Journal of Sociology,* 1949, *55,* 243–253.

Hall, R. H. "Professionalization and Bureaucratization." *American Sociological Review,* 1968, *33,* 92–104.

Hall, R. H. *Occupations and the Social Structure.* Englewood Cliffs, N.J.: Prentice-Hall, 1969.

Halmos, P. *The Personal Service Society.* New York: Schocken Books, 1970.

Hamachek, D. E. (Ed.). *The Self in Growth, Teaching and Learning.* Englewood Cliffs, N.J.: Prentice-Hall, 1965.

Hamburg, J. (Ed.). *Review of Allied Health Education.* Vol. 1. Lexington: University Press of Kentucky, 1974.

Hapgood, M. (Ed.). *Supporting the Learning Teacher: A Source Book for Teacher Centers.* New York: Agathon Press, 1975.

Harel, G. I. "Earnings in Pharmacy and Investment in Pharmacy Education." *The Apothecary,* 1975, *87,* 9–11, 36–38.

Harlow, N., and others. *Administration and Change: Continuing Education in Library Administration.* New Brunswick, N.J.: Rutgers University Press, 1969.

Harrington, F. H. "Continuing Professional Education: An Outside View." *Continuum,* 1977a, *41* (4), 1–4.

Harrington, F. H. *The Future of Adult Education: New Responsibilities of Colleges and Universities.* San Francisco: Jossey-Bass, 1977b.

Harrison, J. C. "Advanced Study: A Mid-Atlantic Point of View." In L. E. Bone (Ed.), *Library Education: An International Survey.* Champaign, Ill.: Graduate School of Library Science, University of Illinois, 1968.

Harvey, J. F., and Lambert, B. "The Educational Third Dimension: II. Programs for Continuing Library Education." *Library Trends,* 1971, *20,* 144–153.

Hatfield, H. R. "An Historical Defense of Bookkeeping." In M. Moonitz and A. C. Littleton (Eds.), *Significant Accounting Essays.* Englewood Cliff, N.J.: Prentice-Hall, 1965.

Haug, M. R., and Sussman, M. B. "Professionalism and the Public." *Sociological Inquiry,* 1968, *39* (1), 57–68.

Haug, M. R., and Sussman, M. B. "Professional Autonomy and the Revolt of the Client." *Social Problems,* 1969, *17,* 153–161.

Havelock, R. G., and others. *Planning for Innovation Through Dissemination and Utilization of Knowledge.* Ann Arbor: Institute for Social Research, University of Michigan, 1969.

Heath, D. H. "Academic Predictors of Adult Maturity and Competence." *Journal of Higher Education,* 1977, *48,* 613–632.

Henry, N. B. (Ed.). *Education for the Professions.* 61st Yearbook, Pt. 2. Chicago: National Society for the Study of Education, 1962.

Henry, R. (Ed.). *Ends and Means: The National Conference on Continuing Education in Nursing.* Syracuse, N.Y.: Syracuse University Publications in Continuing Education, 1971.

Hiatt, P. "Continuing Education." *College & Research Libraries,* 1973a, *34,* 101–102.

Hiatt, P. "Continuing Education and PNLA [Pacific National Library Association]." *PNLA Quarterly,* 1973b, *37,* 10–16.

Hiatt, P. "WICHE Continuing Education Programs for Library Personnel." *Illinois Libraries,* 1973c, *55,* 332–336.

Hickson, D. J., and Thomas, M. W. "Professionalization in Britain: A Preliminary Measurement." *Sociology,* 1969, *3,* 37–53.

Hiltner, S. "The Essentials of Professional Education." *Journal of Higher Education,* 1954a, *25,* 245–255.

Hiltner, S. "From the Obvious to the Significant." *Journal of Higher Education,* 1954b, *25,* 245–255.

Hinton, L. *Engineer and Engineering.* London: Oxford University Press, 1970.

Hodge, R. W., Siegel, P. M., and Rossi, P. H. "Occupational Prestige in the United States, 1925–63." *American Journal of Sociology,* 1964, *70,* 286–302.

Hodgkinson, H. L. "Adult Development: Implications for Faculty and Administrators." *Educational Record,* 1974, *55,* 263–274.

Hofrenning, J. B. (Ed.). *The Continuing Quest: Opportunities, Resources, and Programs in Post-Seminary Education.* Minneapolis: Augsburg, 1970.

Holden, W. D. "Specialty Board Certification as a Measure of Professional Competence." *Journal of the American Medical Association,* 1970, *213,* 1016–1018.

Holder, A. R. *Medical Mapractice Law.* New York: Wiley, 1975.

Hollister, J. E. "The Minister's Time, Leisure and Continuing Education: A Study of Time Use, Participation in Leisure Activities and Continuing Education." Unpublished doctoral dissertation, University of California, Berkeley, 1968.

Hood, A. B. "Predicting Achievement in Dental Schools." *Journal of Dental Education,* 1963, *27,* 148–155.

Hospital Research and Educational Trust. *Training and Continuing Education: A Handbook for Health Care Institutions.* Chicago: Health Research and Educational Trust, 1970.

Hospital Research and Educational Trust. *Supervisory Training: The University, the Community College, and the Hospital.* Chicago: Health Research and Educational Trust, 1971.

Houle, C. O. *The Design of Education.* San Francisco: Jossey-Bass, 1972.

Houle, C. O. "The Changing Goals of Education in the Perspective of Lifelong Learning." *International Review of Education,* 1974, *20,* 430–445.

Howsom, R. B., and others. *Educating a Profession.* Washington, D.C.: American Association of Colleges for Teacher Education, 1976.

Hoyt, D. P. *The Relationship Between College Grades and Adult Achievement: A Review of the Literature.* Iowa City: American College Testing Program, 1965.

Hoyt, D. P. "College Grades and Adult Accomplishment: A Review of Research." *Educational Record,* 1966, *47,* 70–75.

Hubbard, H. B. (Ed.). *Symposium on Education in Veterinary Public Health and Veterinary Medicine.* Washington, D.C.: Pan American Health Organization, 1969.

Hubbard, J. P. *Measuring Medical Education.* Philadelphia: Lea and Febiger, 1971a.

Hubbard, J. P. "Self-Education and Self-Assessment as a New Method for Continuing Medical Education." *Archives of Surgery,* 1971b, *103,* 422–424.

Hudson, C. "The Responsibility of the University in the Continuing Education of Physicians." *Journal of Medical Education,* 1968, *413,* 526–531.

Hughes, E. C. *Men and Their Work.* London: Collier-Macmillan, 1958.

Hughes, E. C. "Education for a Profession." In P. H. Ennis and H. W. Winger (Eds.), *Seven Questions About the Profession of Librarianship.* Chicago: University of Chicago Press, 1962.

Hughes, E. C., and others. *Education for the Professions of Medicine, Law, Theology, and Social Welfare.* New York: McGraw-Hill, 1973.

Humble, J. (Ed.). *Improving the Performance of the Experienced Manager.* New York: McGraw-Hill, 1973.

Huntington, S. P. *The Soldier and the State: The Theory and Politics of Civil-Military Relations.* Cambridge, Mass.: Harvard University Press, 1957.

Hurst, J. W., and Walker, H. K. (Eds.). *The Problem-Oriented System.* New York: Medcom Press, 1972.

Illich, I. *Medical Nemesis: The Expropriation of Health.* New York: Pantheon, 1976.

"Inept Advocates?" *Wall Street Journal,* 1975, *55* (92), 1, 17.

Ingalls, J. P., and Arceri, J. *A Training Guide to Andragogy: Its Concepts, Experiences and Application.* Washington, D.C.: U.S. Department of Health, Education, and Welfare, 1972.

Ingelfinger, F. J. "Annual Discourse: Swinging Copy and Sober Science." *New England Journal of Medicine,* 1969, *281,* 526–532.

Ingelfinger, F. J. "Medical Literature: The Campus Without Tumult." *Science,* 1970, *169,* 831–837.

Ingelfinger, F. J. "The Graying of Grand Rounds." *New England Journal of Medicine,* 1978, *299,* 772.

Inkeles, A., and Rossi, P. H. "National Comparisons of Occupational Prestige." *American Journal of Sociology,* 1956, *61,* 329–339.

Insel, S. A., Hoggard, R., and Robinson, B. A. *Continuing Education for Licensed Professionals in California.* San Francisco: California State University, 1972.

Institute for the Study of Health and Society. *Young Doctors, Health Care, and the American Future.* Proceedings of the 2nd National House Staff Conference, Washington, D.C.: Institute for the Study of Health and Society, 1972.

International Labour Office, Geneva. "Paid Educational Leave." *Convergence,* 1973, *6,* 71–86.

Jackson, J. A. (Ed.). *Professions and Professionalization.* London: Cambridge University Press, 1970.

Jackson, M. A. "Continuing Education in Eight Allied Health Professional Organizations." *Adult Leadership,* 1977, *27,* 153–156.

Jackson of Burnley, Lord. "The Magnitude of Occupational Obsolescence in Engineering and Science." In S. S. Dubin (Ed.), *Professional Obsolescence.* Lexington, Mass.: Lexington Books, 1971.

James of Rusholme, Lord. *Teacher Education and Training.* London: Her Majesty's Stationery Office, 1972.

Jampol, M., Sager, R., and Daily, F. "Continuing Education in Group Practice." *American Journal of Public Health,* 1967, *57,* 1729–1753.

Janowitz, M. *The Professional Soldier: A Social and Political Portrait.* Glencoe, Ill.: Free Press, 1960.

Janowitz, M., and Little, R. W. (Eds.). *Sociology and the Military Establishment.* (3rd. ed.) Beverly Hills, Calif.: Sage Publications, 1974.

Jason, H. "A Study of Medical Teaching Practices." *Journal of Medical Education,* 1962, *37,* 1258–1284.

Jason, H. "The Relevance of Medical Education to Medical Practice." *Journal of the American Medical Association,* 1970, *212,* 2092–2095.

Jerge, C. "Looking at the Next 10 Years in Continuing Education." *Journal of the Academy of General Dentistry,* 1971, *19,* 27–29.

Jessup, G. "Updating the Royal Air Forces Training." In S. S. Dubin (Ed.), *Professional Obsolescence.* Lexington, Mass.: Lexington Books, 1971.

Jobe, B. "A Survey of Continuing Pharmaceutical Education." *American Journal of Pharmaceutical Education,* 1968, *32,* 611–615.

Johnson, M. E., and Jackson, R. M. "An Integrated Medical-Financial Hospital Information System: Utilization of the Ancillary Services as the Basic Modules." In R. H. Shannon (Ed.). *Hospital Information Systems.* Amsterdam: North-Holland Publishing, 1979.

Johnson, T. J. *Professions and Power.* London: Macmillan, 1972.

Johnstone, Q., and Hopson, D., Jr. *Lawyers and Their Work.* Indianapolis: Bobbs-Merrill, 1967.

Jones, R. W. "Forestry's Changing Ecology." *Environmental Education,* 1970, *2* (2), 29–31.

Jordan, A. A., Jr. "Officer Education." In R. W. Little (Ed.), *Handbook of Military Institutions.* Beverly Hills, Calif.: Sage Publications, 1971.

Kallen, D., and Bengtsson, J. *Recurrent Education: A Strategy for Lifelong Learning.* Paris: Organisation for Economic Co-operation and Development, 1973.

Kanter, R. M. *Men and Women of the Corporation.* New York: Basic Books, 1977.

Kaplan, A. C., and Veri, C. *The Continuing Education Unit.* DeKalb, Ill.: ERIC Clearinghouse in Career Education, 1974.

Kaplan, N. M. "The Support of Continuing Medical Education by Pharmaceutical Companies." *New England Journal of Medicine,* 1979, *300,* 194–196.

Kasaba, R., and Abato, B. *Scientific Design of a Hospital Training System.* Rockville, Md.: National Center for Health Services Research and Development, 1971.

Katz, D., and Kahn, R. L. *The Social Psychology of Organizations.* New York: Wiley, 1965.

Katzen, M. *Mass Communication: Teaching and Studies at Universities.* Paris: UNESCO Press, 1975.

Kaufman, H. *The Forest Ranger.* Baltimore: Johns Hopkins University Press, 1960.

Kay, J. H. "Architecture Education Needs a New Blueprint."
   Change, 1975, *7* (5), 34–38.

Keeton, M. T., and Associates. *Experiential Learning: Rationale,
   Characteristics, and Assessment.* San Francisco: Jossey-Bass,
   1976.

Kenny, L. A. "Continuing Education for Academic Librarianship." *California Librarian,* 1969, *30,* 199–202.

Kern, H., and others. "Continuing Education in Psychiatry:
   A Report of a Program Based Upon the Inductive Method."
   Johns Hopkins Medical Journal, 1968, *122,* 78–84.

Keyes, J. A., Wilson, M. P., and Becker, J. "The Future of Medical Education: Forecast of the Council of Deans." *Journal of
   Medical Education,* 1975, *50,* 319–327.

Kinsinger, R. E. (Ed.). *Health Technicians.* Chicago: Ferguson,
   1970.

Kirkpatrick, D. *A Practical Guide for Supervisory Training and
   Development.* Reading, Mass.: Addison-Wesley, 1971.

Kirkwood, R. "The Myths of Accreditation." *Educational Record,* 1973, *54,* 211–215.

Klever, G. "The Value Orientations and the Educational Participation of Clergymen." Unpublished doctoral dissertation,
   University of Chicago, 1966.

Knapp, D. E., and others. "The Pharmacist as Perceived by Physicians, Patrons, and Other Pharmacists." *Journal of the
   American Pharmaceutical Association,* 1969, *9,* 80.

Knowles, A. S. (Ed.). *The International Encyclopedia of Higher
   Education.* San Francisco: Jossey-Bass, 1977.

Knowles, M. S. *The Modern Practice of Adult Education.* New
   York: Association Press, 1970.

Knox, A. B. "Continuing Legal Education of Nebraska Lawyers."
   Nebraska Bar Journal, 1964, *13,* 121–136.

Koch, W. H. "Continuing Education and Professionalism Among
   Social Workers." Unpublished doctoral dissertation, University of Chicago, 1973.

Koch, W. H., and Brenner, M. N. "Continuing Education for
   Social Service: Implications from a Study of Learners."
   Journal of Education for Social Work, 1976, *12,* 71–77.

Kollaritsch, F. P. "Job Migration Pattern of Accounting." *Management Accounting,* 1968, *49,* 52–55.

Kortendick, J. J. "Continuing Education and Library Administration." *American Library Association Bulletin,* 1967, *61,* 268–272.

Kortendick, J. J. "Continuing Education for Librarians." In H. Borko (Ed.), *Targets for Research in Library Education.* Chicago: American Library Association, 1973.

Kortendick, J. J., and Stone, E. W. *Job Dimensions and Educational Needs in Librarianship.* Chicago: American Library Association, 1971.

Kotasek, J. "The Idea of Continuing Education in the Current Reform of Educational Systems and Teacher Training." In *The School and Continuing Education.* Paris: UNESCO Press, 1972.

Kotzan, J. A., and Jowdy, A. W. "Differential Attitudes Toward an Adult Education Program for Pharmacists." *Adult Education,* 1970, *21,* 20–28.

Krause, E. A. *The Sociology of Occupations.* Boston: Little, Brown, 1971.

Kress, G. C. "Continuing Education: Does It Affect the Practice of Dentistry?" *Journal of the American Dental Association,* 1979, *99,* 448–455.

Krowka, M. J., and Peck, O. C. "Continuing Medical Education as Viewed by Medical Students." *Journal of Medical Education,* 1979, *54,* 53–54.

Kubie, L. S. "The Retreat from Patients." *International Journal of Psychiatry,* 1970, *9,* 693–711.

Kulski, J. E. "Means of Survival." *AIA Journal,* 1968, *45,* 45–46.

Kurland, P. B. "Polishing the Bar." *New York Times,* April 24, 1975, *123,* 35.

Landis, B. Y. (Ed.). "Ethical Standards and Professional Conduct." *Annals of the American Academy of Political and Social Science,* 1955, *297* (January, entire issue).

Larocco, S. L., and Polit, D. F. "A Study of Nurses' Attitudes Toward Mandatory Continuing Education for Relicensure." *Journal of Continuing Education in Nursing,* 1978, *9,* 25–35.

Larson, M. S. *The Rise of Professionalism.* Berkeley: University of California Press, 1977.

Lauffer, A. "Continuing Education as Problem-Focused Extension." *Journal of Education for Social Work,* 1972, *8,* 40–49.

Lauffer, A. *The Practice of Continuing Education in the Human Services.* New York: McGraw-Hill, 1977.

Lauffer, A. *Doing Continuing Education and Staff Development.* New York: McGraw-Hill, 1978.

Laventurier, M. "Utilization and Peer Review by Pharmacists." *Journal of the American Pharmaceutical Association,* 1972, *n.s.12,* 166–170.

Lebeaux, C. N. "Learning to Live on the Curve." In *Education for Social Work: Proceedings of the Twelfth Annual Meeting, Toronto, Canada, January 29–February 1, 1964.* New York: Council on Social Work Education, 1964.

Lee, B. J. "Financial Support for Continuing Education." *Journal of Continuing Education in Nursing,* 1971, *5,* 7–12.

Leete, B. A., and Loeb, S. E. "Continuing Legal Education: Should It Be Compulsory?" *Journal of Legal Education,* 1975, *27,* 110–115.

Lefferts, G., Jr. "Demand and Supply." *AIA Journal,* 1968, *45,* 46–49.

Lemberger, M. A., and McCormick, W. C. "Continuing Education as a Lifelong Process." *American Journal of Pharmaceutical Education,* 1976, *40,* 170–173.

Lembke, V. C., Smith, J. H., and Tidwell, V. H. "Compulsory Continuing Education for CPAs." *Journal of Accountancy,* 1970, *129* (4), 61–65.

Leslie, L. L. *Innovative Programs in Education for the Professions.* University Park: Center for the Study of Higher Education, Pennsylvania State University, 1974.

Levine, A. I. "Shaping Our Future." *CPA Journal,* 1973, *43,* 91–93.

Levit, E. J., and Holden, W. D. "Specialty Board Certification Rates: A Longitudinal Tracking Study of US Medical School Graduates." *Journal of the American Medical Association,* 1978, *239,* 407–412.

Levitt, M., and Langsley, D. G. "The Education of Psychiatrists." *Change,* 1974, *6,* 30–35.

Levy, M. *Accounting Goes Public.* Philadelphia: University of Pennsylvania Press, 1977.

Lewis, C., and Hassanein, R. "Continuing Medical Education:

An Epidemiological Evaluation." *New England Journal of Medicine,* 1970, *282,* 254–259.

Lewis, R., and Maude, A. *Professional People.* London: Phoenix House, 1952.

Lieberman, M. *Education as a Profession.* Englewood Cliffs, N.J.: Prentice-Hall, 1956.

Light, I. "Development and Growth of New Allied Health Fields." *Journal of the American Medical Association,* 1969, *210,* 114–120.

Lindsay, C. A., Morrison, J. L., and Kelley, E. J. "Professional Obsolescence: Implications for Continuing Professional Education." *Adult Education,* 1974, *25* (1), 3–21.

Lockard, W. T., Jr. "Survey of Cost of Continuing Medical Education Programs." *Continuing Medical Education Newsletter,* 1978, *7* (10), 2–4.

Loewenberg, F. M. "Social Workers and Indigenous Nonprofessionals: Some Structural Dilemmas." *Social Work,* 1968, *13,* 65–71.

Long, H. B., and Lord, C. B. *The Continuing Education Unit: Concept, Issues, and Use.* Athens: University of Georgia Center for Continuing Education, 1978.

Long, L. D. "The Evaluation of Continuing Education Efforts." *American Journal of Public Health and the Nation's Health,* 1969, *59,* 967–973.

Lortie, D. C. "From Laymen to Lawmen: Law School, Careers, and Professional Socialization." *Harvard Educational Review,* 1959, *22,* 352–359.

Lortie, D. C. "The Balance of Control and Autonomy in Elementary School Teaching." In A. Etzioni (Ed.), *The Semi-Professions and Their Organization.* New York: Free Press, 1969.

Lortie, D. C. *School-Teacher, a Sociological Study.* Chicago: University of Chicago Press, 1975.

Lubove, R. *The Professional Altruist.* Cambridge: Harvard University Press, 1965.

Lusterman, S. "Education in Industry." In D. W. Vermilye (Ed.), *Relating Work and Education: Current Issues in Higher Education 1977.* San Francisco: Jossey-Bass, 1977.

Luvaas, J. *The Education of an Army: British Military Thought 1815–1940.* Chicago: University of Chicago Press, 1964.

Lynch, P. D., and Blackstone, P. L. *Institutional Roles for In-Service Education of School Administrators.* Albuquerque: Department of Educational Administration and Foundations, University of New Mexico, 1966.

Lynn, K. S. (Ed.). *The Professions in America.* Boston: Beacon Press, 1965.

Lysaught, J. P. "Enhanced Capacity for Self-Instruction." *Journal of Medical Education,* 1969, *44,* 580–584.

Lysaught, J. P. *An Abstract for Action.* New York: McGraw-Hill, 1970.

McCarty, D. J., and Associates. *New Perspectives on Teacher Education.* San Francisco: Jossey-Bass, 1973.

McCatty, C. "Patterns of Learning Projects Among Physical and Health Education Teachers." *Reporting Classroom Research,* 1976, *5* (2), 7–8.

Maccoby, M. *The Gamesman.* New York: Simon & Schuster, 1977.

McCord, J. H. "A View from the Halls of Ivy: A Law Professor Looks at Continuing Legal Action." *Illinois Bar Journal,* 1969, *57,* 824–829.

McCormack, T. H. "The Druggists' Dilemma: Problems of a Marginal Occupation." *American Journal of Sociology,* 1955, *61,* 308–315.

McGehee, E. H., and others. "The Philadelphia County Medical Society Self-Evaluation Examination." *Journal of Medical Education,* 1974, *49,* 993–995.

McGlothlin, W. J. *Patterns of Professional Education.* New York: Putnam's, 1960.

McGlothlin, W. J. *The Professional Schools.* New York: Center for Applied Research in Education, 1964.

McGlothlin, W. J. "Continuing Education in the Professions." *Journal of Education for Librarianship,* 1972, *13,* 3–15.

McGrath, E. J. *The Adult Student in Buffalo.* Buffalo: The Buffalo Foundation, 1938.

McGrath, E. J. *Liberal Education in the Professions.* New York: Columbia University Press, 1959.

McGuire, C. H., Solomon, L. M., and Bashook, P. G. *Construction and Use of Written Simulations.* New York: Psychological Corporation, 1976.

McKenna, M. E. "A Perspective on the Impact of Mandatory Continuing Education on Publicly Supported Colleges and Universities." *Journal of Continuing Education in Nursing,* 1978, *9,* 15–20.

McKillop, W. "Continuing Education for the Osteopathic Physician." *The D.O.,* 1970, *10,* unpaged.

McLachlan, G. (Ed.). *A Question of Quality.* London: Oxford University Press, 1976.

McLaughlin, C. P., and Penchansky, R. "Diffusion of Innovation in Medicine: A Problem of Continuing Medical Education." *Journal of Medical Education,* 1965, *40,* 437–447.

McNerny, W. J. "The Quandary of Quality Assessment." *New England Journal of Medicine,* 1976, *295,* 1505–1511.

McTernan, E. J. "Development of an Administrative Pattern for a Program of Continuing Professional Education for Six Selected Allied Health Fields." Unpublished doctoral dissertation, Boston University, 1974.

McWhinney, I. R. "Medical Knowledge and the Rise of Technology." *Journal of Medicine and Philosophy,* 1978, *3,* 293–304.

Mager, R. F. *Preparing Instructional Objectives.* Belmont, Calif.: Fearon, 1961.

Mager, R. F. *Developing Attitudes Toward Learning.* Belmont, Calif.: Fearon, 1968.

Mager, R. F. *Goal Analysis.* Blemont, Calif.: Fearon, 1972.

Mager, R. F., and Beach, K. M., Jr. *Developing Vocational Instruction.* Belmont, Calif.: Fearon, 1967.

Mager, R. F., and Pipe, P. *Analyzing Performance Problems.* Belmont, Calif.: Fearon, 1970.

Mahan, J. M., and others. "Patient Referrals: A Behavioral Outcome of Continuing Medical Education." *Journal of Medical Education,* 1978, *53,* 210–211.

Males, A. R. "The Education of the Architect." In J. D. Turner and J. Rushton (Eds.), *Education for the Professions.* Manchester, England: Manchester University Press, 1976.

Mali, P. "Measurement of Obsolescence in Engineering Practitioners." *Continuing Education,* 1970, *3* (2), 3, 57–63.

Manning, P. R., and others. "Continuing Medical Education: Linking the Community Hospital and the Medical School." *Journal of Medical Education,* 1979, *54,* 461–470.

Marcotte, D. B., and Held, J. P. "A Conceptual Model for Attitude Assessment in All Areas of Medical Education." *Journal of Medical Education,* 1978, *53,* 310–314.

Marcson, S. *The Scientist in American Industry.* Princeton, N.J.: Department of Economics, Princeton University, 1960.

Margulies, N., and Raia, A. P. "Scientists, Engineers, and Technological Obsolescence." *California Management Review,* 1967, *10,* 43–48.

Masland, J. W., and Radway, L. I. *Soldiers and Scholars.* Princeton, N.J.: Princeton University Press, 1957.

Maslow, A. *The Psychology of Science: A Reconnaissance.* New York: Harper & Row, 1966.

Mauksch, H. O. "The Organizational Context of Nursing Practice." In F. Davis (Ed.), *The Nursing Profession.* New York: Wiley, 1966.

Mawardi, B. H. "Satisfactions, Dissatisfactions, and Causes of Stress in Medical Practice." *Journal of the American Medical Association,* 1979, *241,* 1483–1486.

Mayhew, L. B. *Graduate and Professional Education, 1980.* New York: McGraw-Hill, 1970.

Mayhew, L. B. *Changing Practices in Education for the Professions.* Atlanta, Ga.: Southern Regional Education Board, 1971.

Mayhew, L. B. *Higher Education for Occupations.* Atlanta, Ga.: Southern Regional Education Board, 1974.

Mayhew, L. B., and Ford, P. J. *Reform in Graduate and Professional Education.* San Francisco: Jossey-Bass, 1974.

Mead, M. *Continuities in Cultural Evolution.* New Haven: Yale University Press, 1964.

Medical Malpractice. Washington, D.C.: U.S. Department of Health, Education, and Welfare, 1973.

Meeting the Educational Needs of the Newly Admitted Lawyer. Philadelphia: Joint Committee on Continuing Legal Education of the American Law Institute and the American Bar

Association, 1968.

Menges, R. J. "Assessing Readiness for Professional Practice." *Review of Educational Research,* 1975, *45,* 173–207.

Menzel, H. "Scientific Communication: Five Themes from Social Science Research." *American Psychologist,* 1966, *21,* 999–1004.

Merton, R. K. "The Functions of the Professional Association." *American Journal of Nursing,* 1958, *58,* 50–54.

Merton, R. K., and others. *The Student Physician.* Cambridge, Mass.: Harvard University Press, 1957.

Messersmith, E. J. "PDP's Development." *AIA Journal,* 1968, *45,* 49–51.

Meyer, C. H. *Staff Development in Social Welfare Agencies.* New York: Columbia University Press, 1966.

Meyer, H. J. "Professionalization and Social Work." In A. Kahn (Ed.), *Issues in American Social Work.* New York: Columbia University Press, 1959.

Meyer, H. J. "Social Work." In D. L. Sills (Ed.), *International Encyclopedia of the Social Sciences.* Vol. 14. New York: Macmillan, 1968.

Meyer, T. *CME and Professional Growth: The Physician's Protection.* Chicago: Illinois Council on Continuing Medical Education, 1973.

Milgrom, P. "Continuing Education and the Prospect for a National Standard of Dental Care." *Journal of Dental Education,* 1974, *38,* 482–486.

Mill, J. S. *Dissertations and Discussions.* Vol. 4. New York: Holt, 1874.

Miller, E. H. "The Identification of Continuing Education Needs for Practicing Dentists in Nebraska." Unpublished doctoral dissertation, University of Nebraska, 1972.

Miller, G. E. "Adventures in Pedagogy," *Journal of the American Medical Association,* 1956, *162,* 1448–1450.

Miller, G. E. (Ed.). *Teaching and Learning in Medical School.* Cambridge, Mass.: Harvard University Press, 1961.

Miller, G. E. "Medical Care: Its Social and Organizational Aspects." *New England Journal of Medicine,* 1963, *269,* 295–299.

Miller, G. E. "Medical Education Research and Development."

Journal of the American Medical Association, 1966, *197,* 992–995.

Miller, G. E. "Continuing Education for What?" *Journal of Medical Education,* 1967, *42,* 320–326.

Miller, G. E. "The Continuing Education of Physicians." *New England Journal of Medicine,* 1973, *269,* 295–299.

Miller, G. E., and Harless, W. G. *Instructional Technology and Continuing Medical Education.* Washington, D.C.: Academy for Educational Development, 1970.

Miller, H. M. "Career Development of Engineers in Industry." *Engineering Education,* 1969, *59,* 1113–1116.

Miller, J. W. *Organizational Structure of Nongovernmental Postsecondary Accreditation: Relationship to Uses of Accreditation.* Washington, D.C.: National Commission on Accrediting, 1973.

Miller, J. W., and Mills, O. (Eds.). *Credentialing Educational Accomplishment.* Washington, D.C.: American Council on Education, 1978.

Miller, N., and Botsman, P. B. "Continuing Education for Extension Agents." *Human Ecology Forum,* 1975, *6,* 14–17.

Miller, S. J. *Prescription for Leadership: Training for the Medical Elite.* Chicago: Aldine-Atherton, 1969.

Miller, W. E. "Application of Adult Learning Procedures to an Orthopedic Problem." *Southern Medical Journal,* 1974, *67,* 319–327.

Millerson, G. *The Qualifying Associations.* London: Routledge & Kegan Paul, 1964.

Millis, J. S. *The Graduate Education of Physicians.* Chicago: American Medical Association, 1966.

Millis, J. S. *A Rational Public Policy for Medical Education and Its Financing.* Cleveland: National Fund for Medical Education, 1971.

Mills, E. W., and Koval, J. P. *Stress in Ministry.* Washington, D.C.: Ministerial Studies Board, 1971.

Milwaukee Personnel Department Training Unit. "Tuition Reimbursement in Employee Productivity and OD: A Survey." *Public Personnel Management,* 1977, *6,* 166–172.

Monahan, J. "The Flexner Report: A Study in Polemics." Paper presented at the American Educational Research Association meeting, Washington, D.C., April 2, 1975.

Montagna, P. D. "Professionalization and Bureaucratization in Large Professional Organizations." *American Journal of Sociology*, 1968, *74*, 138–145.

Moore, D. C., Jr. (Ed.). *Mandatory Continuing Education: Prospects and Dilemmas for Professionals.* Urbana-Champaign: Office of Continuing Education and Public Service, University of Illinois, 1976.

Moore, W. E., and Rosenblum, G. W. *The Professions: Roles and Rules.* New York: Russell Sage Foundation, 1970.

Mooth, A. E. *Developing the Supervisory Skills of the Nurse: A Behavioral Science Approach.* New York: Macmillan, 1966.

Moran, V. "Study of Comparison of Independent Learning Activities vs. Attendance at Staff Development by Staff Nurses." *Journal of Continuing Education in Nursing*, 1977, *8*, 14–21.

Moreland, C. C. *Professional Education of the Bar: Growth and Perspectives.* Chicago: American Bar Foundation, 1972.

Mosher, F. C. "Professions in Public Service." *Public Administration Review*, 1978, *38*, 144–150.

Moxley, J. H. "Legislation and Social Pressures for Continuing Education." *Journal of the American College of Dentists*, 1969, *36*, 154–164.

Munk, R. J., and Lovett, M. *Hospitalwide Education and Training.* Chicago: Hospital Research and Educational Trust, 1977.

Murray, W., and Sobieszek, B. *Sources of Self-Evaluation: A Formal Theory of Significant Others and Social Influence.* New York: Wiley, 1974.

Mushkin, S. J. (Ed.). *Recurrent Education.* Washington, D.C.: U.S. National Institute of Education, 1974.

Myers, E. D. *Education in the Perspective of History.* New York: Harper & Row, 1960.

Nader, R. "The Engineer's Professional Role: Universities, Corporations, and Professional Societies." *Engineering Education*, 1967, *57*, 450–454.

Nader, R. "Law Schools and Law Firms." *New Republic*, 1969,

161 (15), 20–23.

Nadler, L., and Nadler, Z. *The Conference Book.* Houston: Gulf, 1977.

Naftulin, D. H., Ware, J. E., Jr., and Donnelly, F. A. "The Dr. Fox Lecture: A Paradigm of Educational Seduction." *Journal of Medical Education, 1973, 48,* 630–635.

Nakamoto, J., and Verner, C. *Continuing Education in the Health Professions: A Review of the Literature, 1960-1970.* Syracuse, N.Y.: ERIC Clearinghouse on Adult Education, 1973.

National Commission on Accrediting. *Optometry: Education for the Profession.* Report of the National Study of Optometric Education. Washington, D.C.: National Commission on Accrediting, 1973.

National Commission on Libraries and Information Science. *Continuing Library and Information Science Education.* Washington, D.C.: Department of Health, Education, and Welfare, 1974.

National Institute of Mental Health. *Continuing Education: Agent of Change.* Rockville, Md.: National Institute of Mental Health, 1971.

National Institute of Mental Health. *Continuing Education in Mental Health.* Rockville, Md.: National Institute of Mental Health, 1974.

National Research Council. *The Invisible University.* Washington, D.C.: National Academy of Sciences, 1969.

National Science Foundation. *Continuing Education for R&D Centers.* Washington, D.C.: National Science Foundation, 1969.

National Task Force on the Continuing Education Unit. *The Continuing Education Unit: Criteria and Guidelines.* Washington: National University Extension Association, 1974.

Nattress, L. W., Jr. (Ed.). *Continuing Education for the Professions.* Chicago: Natresources, 1970.

Nelson, C., and Pollock, D. (Eds.). *Communication Among Scientists and Engineers.* Lexington, Mass.: Heath, 1970.

Netherton, J. D. "The Relationship Between Educational Participation and the Innovativeness of County Extension Agents."

Unpublished doctoral dissertation, University of Chicago, 1967.

Neuhouser, D. *The Relationship Between Administrative Activities and Hospital Performance.* Chicago: Center for Health Administration Studies, University of Chicago, 1971.

Newell, J. A. "A Strategy for Seminary-Related Continuing Education for Pastors." Unpublished doctoral dissertation, Southern Baptist Theological Seminary, 1974.

Newgarden, A. "Historical Development: Chronology of Major Influences." In G. B. Mueller and C. H. Smith (Eds.), *Accounting: A Book of Readings.* New York: Holt, Rinehart and Winston, 1970.

Newman, C. *New Axis.* Boston: Houghton Mifflin, 1966.

Newman, I. M. (Ed.). *Consumer Behavior in the Health Marketplace.* Lincoln: Nebraska Center for Health Education, 1976.

Neylan, M. S., and others. "An Interprofessional Approach to Continuing Education in the Health Sciences." *Journal of Continuing Education in Nursing,* 1971, *2* (4), 21–28.

Nicely, R. F., and Wiens, B. J. "Student Suggestions for the Design of Off-Campus Professional Education Courses." *NUEA Spectator,* 1975, *38,* 21–25.

Niebuhr, H. R., and Williams, D. D. (Eds.). *The Ministry in Historical Perspectives.* New York: Harper & Row, 1956.

Niebuhr, H. R., Williams, D. D., and Gustafson, J. M. *The Advancement of Theological Education.* New York: Harper & Row, 1957.

Nonet, P., and Carlin, J. E. "Law: The Legal Profession." In D. L. Sills (Ed.), *International Encyclopedia of the Social Sciences.* Vol. 9. New York: Macmillan, 1968.

Norland, I. J., and McConnell, J. O. (Eds.). *Continuing Engineering Studies Series.* Washington, D.C.: American Society for Engineering Education, 1973.

Nosow, S., and Form, W. (Eds.). *Man, Work and Society.* New York: Basic Books, 1962.

Nowlen, P. M. "Continuing Education for the Professions." *Continuum, 41* (4), 9–11.

O'Keefe, M. *The Adult, Education and Public Policy.* Cambridge, Mass.: Apsen Institute Program in Education for a Changing Society, 1977.

Olesen, V. L., and Whittaker, E. W. *The Silent Dialogue: A Study in the Social Psychology of Professional Socialization.* San Francisco: Jossey-Bass, 1968.

Organization for Economic Cooperation and Development. *Strategies for Innovation in Education.* Paris: Organization for Economic Cooperation and Development, 1973.

Organization for Economic Cooperation and Development. *Selection and Certification in Education and Employment.* Paris: Organization for Economic Cooperation and Development, 1977.

Osman, M. E. "The Case Survey: Self-Portrait of a Profession." *American Institute of Architects Journal,* 1974, *62,* 38–39, 65.

Osler, W. *Aequanimitas.* London: Lewis, 1906.

Owens, J. C., and others. "Continuing Education for the Rural Physician." *Journal of the American Medical Association,* 1979, *211,* 1261–1263.

Oxford University Commission. *Report.* London: Her Majesty's Stationery Office, 1852.

"P.D.P." *AIA Journal,* 1968, *45,* 44–54.

Packer, H. L., and Ehrlich, T. *New Directions in Legal Education.* New York: McGraw-Hill, 1972.

Palmer, W. L. "Medical Education, Research, and Patient Care: A Commentary." *Pharos of Alpha Omega Alpha,* 1971, *34* (2), 58–62, 74.

Parker, D. H. "Periodic Recertification of Lawyers: A Comparative Study of Programs for Maintaining Professional Competence." *Utah Law Review,* 1974, *1974,* 470–480.

Parlette, N. "Evaluation of Continuing Education." *American Journal of Public Health,* 1970, *60,* 316–321.

Parry, N., and Parry, J. *The Rise of the Medical Profession.* London: Croom Helm, 1976.

Parsons, T. "Professions." In D. L. Sills, (Ed.), *International Encyclopedia of the Social Sciences.* Vol. 12. New York: Macmillan, 1968.

Paullin, A. K. "Participation, Learning Achievement, and Perceived Benefit in a Televised Continuing Medical Education

Program." Unpublished doctoral dissertation, Catholic University of America, 1971.

Pawlina, A. M. "From the Editors." *Apothecary,* 1976, *88,* 6, 39–42.

Payne, B. C. "Continued Evolution of a System of Medical Care Appraisal." *Journal of the American Medical Association,* 1967, *204,* 536–540.

Pennington, F. C., and Green, J. "Comparative Analysis of Program Development Processes in Six Professions." *Adult Education,* 1976, *27,* 13–23.

Pennington, F. C., and Moore, D. E., Jr. "Issues Related to Mandatory Continuing Education for Professionals." *NUEA Spectator,* 1976, *40,* 5–8.

Perlmutter, F. D. (Ed.). *A Design for Social Work Practice.* New York: Columbia University Press, 1974.

Perrucci, R., and Gerstle, J. E. *Profession Without Community: Engineers in American Society.* New York: Random House, 1969.

Perry, J. W. "Career Mobility in Allied Health Education." *Journal of the American Medical Association,* 1969, *210,* 107–110.

Peter, L. J., and Hull, R. *The Peter Principle.* New York: William Morris, 1969.

Peterson, O. L., Spain, L., and Greenburg, B. "The Physicians' Medical Intellectual Life." *Journal of Medical Education,* 1956, *31,* 74–93.

Peterson, O. L., and others. "Analytical Study of North Carolina General Practice." *Journal of Medical Education,* 1956, *31,* 1–165.

Petit, D. W. "State Medical Association's Role in the Continuing Education of the Practicing Physician." *Journal of the American Medical Association,* 1969, *208,* 1835–1838.

Petit, D. W. "The Physician Recognition Award." *Journal of the American Medical Association,* 1970, *213,* 1668–1670.

Phaneuf, M. C. *The Nursing Audit: Profile for Excellence.* New York: Appleton-Century-Crofts, 1972.

Pharmacists for the Future. Ann Arbor: Health Administration Press, 1975.

Phipps, W. J. "The Development of Attitudes Toward Continu-

ing Professional Learning in Collegiate Nursing Students."
Unpublished doctoral dissertation, University of Chicago,
1977.

"Physician Opinions About Continuing Education Programs."
California Medicine, 1969, *111,* 132–139.

Pigors, P., and others. *Professional Nursing Practice: Cases and
Issues.* New York: McGraw-Hill, 1967.

Pincus, W. "The Lawyer's Professional Responsibility." *Journal
of Legal Education,* 1969, *22,* 1–21.

Pool, I. deS., Schramm, W., and others (Eds.). *Handbook of
Communication.* Chicago: Rand McNally, 1973.

Posnak, R. L. "The Decline and Fall of Cratchit . . ." *Journal of
Accountancy,* 1970, *129,* 59–63.

Powell, D. R. *Continuing Teacher Education: The University's
Role.* Evanston, Ill.: Center for the Teaching Professions,
Northwestern University, 1974.

Practicing Law Institute. *Continuing Legal Education.* New
York: Practicing Law Institute, 1973.

Price, D. J. deS., and Beaver, D. deB. "Collaboration in an Invisible College." *American Psychologist,* 1966, *21,* 1011–1018.

Price, E. M. *Learning Needs of Registered Nurses.* New York:
Teachers College Press, Columbia University, 1967.

Professional and Nonprofessional Duties in Libraries. London:
Library Association, 1974.

Proffitt, J. R. "Professions and the Public: A Crossroads of Interest." *American Journal of Medical Technology,* 1971,
37, 3.

Proust, M. *The Guermantes Way.* London: Chatto & Windus,
1966.

Purcell, E. F. (Ed.). *Recent Trends in Medical Education.* New
York: Josiah Macy Jr. Foundation, 1976.

Pusey, N. M., and Taylor, C. L. *Ministry for Tomorrow.* New
York: Seabury Press, 1967.

Reader, W. J. *Professional Men.* London: Weidenfeld and Nicol-
son, 1966.

Reed, A. Z. *Present-Day Law Schools in the United States and
Canada.* New York: Carnegie Foundation for the Advancement of Teaching, 1928.

Reedy, B. L. *The New Health Practitioners in America.* London: King Edward's Hospital Fund for London, 1978.

Reiss, A. J., Jr., and others. *Occupations and Social Status.* New York: Free Press, 1961.

Relman, A. S. "Recertification: Will We Retreat?" *New England Journal of Medicine,* 1979, *301,* 778–779.

Rensberger, B. "Few Doctors Ever Report Colleagues' Incompetence." *New York Times,* January 29, 1976, *125,* 1, 24.

Resnick, N. "Continuing Education: Programs in Four Diverse Institutions." *Journal of the American Dental Association,* 1975, *90,* 1214–1218.

"Revolution in Architectural Education." *Progressive Architecture,* 1967, *48,* 136–147.

Rezler, A. G., Hudson, E. K., and Flanagan, G. C. "Medical Clerkship in Five Different Settings." *British Journal of Medical Education,* 1970, *4,* 130–137.

Richards, R. K., Pool, P., and Jason, H. "The Physician-Educator Project." *Audiovisual Instruction,* 1971, *16,* 30–33.

Richards, R. K. *Continuing Medical Education.* New Haven: Yale University Press, 1978.

Richards, R. K., and Stein, D. "Mandatory Continuing Education in Medicine: A Challenge to Adult Educators." *NUEA Spectator,* 1975, *39* (21), 20–24.

Riddle, J. W. "Trends in Certification as it Applies to Licensure." *Continuing Medical Education Newsletter,* 1978, *7* (12), 2–7.

Ripple, L. *Report to the Task Force on Structure and Quality in Social Work Education.* New York: Council on Social Work Education, 1974.

Ritti, R. R., Ference, T. P., and Goldner, F. H. "Professions and Their Plausibility." *Sociology of Work and Occupations,* 1974, *1,* 24–51.

Ritzer, G. *Man and His Work: Conflict and Change.* New York: Meredith, 1972.

Rivlin, A. M. *Systematic Thinking for Social Action.* Washington, D.C.: Brookings Institution, 1971.

Roark, A. C. "Veterinarians Seek a New Image." *Chronicle of Higher Education,* March 14, 1977.

Roberts, S. L. *Behavioral Concepts in Nursing Throughout the*

Life Span. Englewood Cliffs, N.J.: Prentice-Hall, 1978.

Robertson, J. "When the Name of the Game is Changing, How Do We Keep the Score." *Accounting, Organizations, and Society,* 1976, *1,* 91–95.

Rockart, J. F., and Scott, M. S. *Computers and the Learning Process in Higher Education.* New York: McGraw-Hill, 1975.

Rodin, M., and Rodin, B. "Student Evaluations of Teachers." *Science,* 1972, *177,* 1164–1166.

Rodowskas, C., and Evanson, R. "Continuing Education in Pharmacy: Motivation and Content." *American Journal of Pharmaceutical Education,* 1965, *24,* 393–403.

Roe, A. "Community Resources Centers." *American Psychologist,* 1970, *25,* 1033–1040.

Rogers, E. M., and Shoemaker, F. F. *Communicating Innovations.* New York: Free Press, 1971.

Rose, G. "Issues in Professionalism: British Social Work Triumphant." In F. D. Perlmutter (Ed.), *A Design for Social Work Practice.* New York: Columbia University Press, 1974.

Rose, S. W. "A New System for Professional Growth." *American Institute of Architects Journal,* 1972, *57,* 14.

Rosengren, W. R., and Lefton, M. (Eds.). *Organizations and Clients.* Columbus, Ohio: Merrill, 1970.

Rosenstein, A. B. *A Study of a Profession and Professional Education.* Los Angeles: School of Engineering and Applied Science, University of California, 1968.

Rossman, P. "Should Primary Responsibility Rest on the Seminary? Yes!" *Theological Education,* 1965, *1,* 226–229.

Roth, J. A. "Professionalism: The Sociologists Decoy." *Sociology of Work and Occupations,* 1974, *1,* 6–23.

Rothman, R. A. "Problems of Knowledge and Obsolescence Among Professionals: A Case Study in Dentistry." *Social Science Quarterly,* 1974, *55,* 743–752.

Rubin, L. (Ed.). *Improving Inservice Education: Proposals and Procedures for Change.* Boston: Allyn & Bacon, 1975.

Rudd, J. H. "The Goals of PDP." *AIA Journal,* 1968, *45,* 52–54.

Ruhe, C. "Problems in Accreditation of Continuing Education Programs." *Journal of Medical Education,* 1968, *43,* 815–822.

Ryan, K. *Teacher Education.* Chicago: National Society for the Study of Education, 1975.

Sanazaro, P. J. "Medical Audit, Continuing Medical Education, and Quality Assurance." *Western Journal of Medicine*, 1976, *125*, 241-252.

Sanazaro, P. J., and others. "Research and Development in Quality Assurance: The Experimental Medical Care Review Organization Program." *New England Journal of Medicine*, 1972, *287*, 1125-1131.

Sanazaro, P. J., and Worth, R. M. "Concurrent Quality Assurance in Hospital Care." *New England Journal of Medicine*, 1978, *298*, 1171-1177.

Schechter, D. S. *Agenda for Continuing Education: A Challenge to Health Care Institutions.* Chicago: Hospital Research and Educational Trust, 1974.

Schechter, D. S., and O'Farrell, T. M. *Universities, Colleges, and Hospitals: Partners in Continuing Education.* Battle Creek, Mich.: W. K. Kellogg Foundation, 1972.

Schein, E. H. "The Role Innovator and His Education." *Technology Review*, 1970, *72*, 33-37.

Schein, E. H. *Professional Education.* New York: McGraw-Hill, 1972.

Schiff, S. K. "Training the Professional." *University of Chicago Magazine*, 1970, *62* (4), 9-14.

Schless, J. M. "Peer Review as an Educational Challenge." *Journal of the American Medical Association*, 1972, *219*, 1060-1062.

Schlotfeldt, R. M. "The Nurse's View of the Changing Nurse-Physician Relationship." *Journal of Medical Education*, 1965, *40*, 772-777.

Schmertz, M. F. "Design for the 1970s: A New Professional Conscience." *Architectural Record*, 1970, *148*, 118-127.

Schoen, H. L., and Hunt, T. C. "The Effect of Technology on Instruction: The Literature of the Last Twenty Years." *Association for Educational Data Systems Journal*, 1977, *10*, 68-80.

Schott, R. L. "Public Administration as a Profession: Problems and Prospects." *Public Administration Review*, 1976, *36*, 253-259.

Schrader, A. W. "Motive For and Form of Participation in Continuing Professional Education." Unpublished doctoral dissertation, University of Michigan, 1973.

Schwartz, M. L. "Law Schools and Ethics." *Chronicle of Higher Education,* December 9, 1972.

Schwartz, W. B., and Komesar, N. K. "Doctors, Damages and Deterrence." *New England Journal of Medicine,* 1978, *298,* 1282–1289.

Selden, W. K. *Accreditation: A Struggle Over Standards in Higher Education.* New York: Harper & Row, 1960.

Selden, W. K. *Study of Accreditation of Selected Health Education Programs.* Washington, D.C.: National Commission on Accrediting, 1972.

Selden, W. K., and Porter, H. V. *Accreditation: Its Purposes and Uses.* Washington, D.C.: Council on Postsecondary Accreditation, 1977.

Senior, J. R. *Toward the Measurement of Competence in Medicine.* Philadelphia: University of Pennsylvania Press, 1976.

Shawyer, J. R. "The Need of Continuing Education from the Standpoint of the Hospital Administrator." *Ohio State Medical Journal,* 1970, *224,* 218–221.

Shelburne, J. C., and Groves, K. J. *Education in the Armed Forces.* New York: Center for Applied Research in Education, 1965.

Shelburne, J. C., Groves, K. J., and Brokaw, L. D. "Military Education." In R. L. Ebel (Ed.), *Encyclopedia of Educational Research.* (4th ed.) New York: Macmillan, 1969.

Sheldon, E. B., and Moore, W. E. *Indicators of Social Change.* New York: Russell Sage Foundation, 1968.

Shepard, C. R. "History of Continuing Medical Education in the United States since 1930." *Journal of Medical Education,* 1960, *35,* 740–758.

Shils, Edward. "Intellectuals." In D. L. Sills (Ed.), *International Encyclopedia of the Social Sciences.* Vol. 7. New York: Macmillan, 1968.

Shimberg, B. S. "Continuing Education and Licensing." In D. W. Vermilye (Ed.), *Relating Work and Education: Current Issues in Higher Education 1977.* San Francisco: Jossey-Bass, 1977.

Shimberg, B. S., Esser, B. F., and Kruger, D. H. *Occupational Licensing: Practices and Policies.* Washington, D. C.: Public Affairs Press, 1972.

Shulman, L. S., and Keislar, E. R. *Learning by Discovery: A Critical Appraisal.* Chicago: Rand McNally, 1966.

Siegler, M. "A Legacy of Osler." *Journal of the American Medical Association,* 1978, *239,* 951–956.

Sigerist, H. E. *Medicine and Human Welfare.* New Haven, Conn.: Yale University Press, 1941.

Simpson, I. H. "Patterns of Socialization into Professions: The Case of Student Nurses." *Sociological Inquiry,* 1967, *37,* 47–54.

Simpson, M. A. *Medical Education: A Critical Approach.* London: Butterworths, 1972.

Slater, C. H. (Ed.). *The Education and Roles of Nursing Service Administrators.* Battle Creek, Mich.: W. K. Kellogg Foundation, 1978.

Slavin, S., and Perlmutter, F. D. "Perspectives for Education and Training." In F. D. Perlmutter (Ed.), *A Design for Social Work Practice.* New York: Columbia University Press, 1974.

Slocum, W. L. *Occupational Careers: A Sociological Perspective.* Chicago: Aldine, 1966.

Smith, B. O., Cohen, S. B., and Pearl, A. *Teachers for the Real World.* Washington, D. C.: American Association of Colleges for Teacher Education, 1969.

Smith, C. M. *How to Become a Bishop Without Really Trying.* New York: Pocket Books, 1966.

Smith, H. A. "Professional Education: Taps or Reveille?" *School Science and Mathematics,* 1969, *69,* 43–52.

Smith, R. M., Aker, G. F., and Kidd, J. R. (Eds.). *Handbook of Adult Education.* New York: Macmillan, 1970.

Smithcors, J. F. *The American Veterinary Profession.* Ames: Iowa State University Press, 1963.

Sneed, J. T. "Continuing Education in the Professions." *Journal of Higher Education,* 1972, *43,* 223–238.

Sobey, F. *The Nonprofessional Revolution in Mental Health.* New York: Columbia University Press, 1970.

Soffen, J. *Faculty Development in Professional Education.* New York: Council on Social Work Education, 1967.

Solomon, D. N. "Ethnic and Class Differences Among Hospitals as Contingencies in Medical Careers." *American Journal of Sociology,* 1961, *65,* 463–471.

Sovie, M. D. "The Relationships of Learning Orientation, Nursing Activity and Continuing Education." Unpublished doctoral dissertation, Syracuse University, 1972.

Spacek, L. *A Search for Fairness in Financial Reporting to the Public.* Chicago: Arthur Anderson, 1969 and 1973.

Spaeth, J. L., and Greeley, A. M. *Recent Alumni and Higher Education.* New York: McGraw-Hill, 1970.

Spencer, H. *Principles of Sociology.* Vol. 3. New York: D. Appleton, 1900.

Spikes, F. "A Multidimensional Program Planning Model for Continuing Nursing Education." *Lifelong Learning, the Adult Years,* 1978, *1* (6), 4–8.

Stearns, N. S., Getchell, M. E., and Gold, R. R. *Continuing Medical Education in Community Hospitals: A Manual for Program Development.* Boston: Massachusetts Medical Society, 1971.

Stearns, N. S., and others. "Impact of Program Development Consultation on Continuing Medical Education in Hospitals." *Journal of Medical Education,* 1974, *49,* 1158–1165.

Stein, J. J. "Re-Examination and Re-Certification of Physicians." *California Medicine,* 1968, *109,* 175–177.

Stein, L. S. *Your Personal Learning Plan: A Handbook for Physicians.* Chicago: Illinois Council on Continuing Medical Education, 1973.

Stein, L. S. *How to Start a CME Program in Your Hospital or Medical Society.* Chicago: Illinois Council on Continuing Medical Education, 1976.

Stein, L. S. *Setting Directions in Continuing Medical Education: Purposes, Goals and Objectives.* Chicago: Illinois Council on Continuing Medical Education, 1978.

Stein, L. S., and Byyny, R. L. *Case Discussion and Problem Solving.* Chicago: Illinois Council on Continuing Medical Education, 1975.

Stern, M. R. "The Invisible University." *NUEA Spectator,* 1975, *39,* 11–14.

Stern, M. R. "The Politics of Continuing Professional Education." *Adult Leadership,* 1977, *25,* 226–228, 250–252.

Stevenson, R. L. *Records of a Family of Engineers.* The Works of Robert Louis Stevenson. Vailima Edition, Vol. 12. London: W. Heinemann, 1922. (Originally published 1893.)

Stinnett, T. M. (Ed.). *The Teacher Dropout*. Itasca, Ill.: F. E. Peacock, 1970.

Stinnett, T. M. "Certification of Teachers." In L. C. Deighton (Ed.), *The Encyclopedia of Education*. Vol. 8. New York: Macmillan, 1971a.

Stinnett, T. M. "Trends in Teacher Certification." *Science Teacher*, 1971b, *38* (2), 24–25.

Stone, E. W. "Continuing Education in Librarianship: Ideas for Action." *American Libraries*, 1970, *1*, 543–551.

Stone, E. W. (Ed.). *New Directions in Staff Development: Moving from Ideas to Action*. Chicago: American Library Association, 1971a.

Stone, E. W. (Ed.). "Personnel Development and Continuing Education in Libraries." *Library Trends*, 1971b, *20* (entire issue).

Storey, P. B. "Mandatory Continuing Medical Education: One Step Forward—Two Steps Back." *New England Journal of Medicine*, 1978, *298*, 1416–1418.

Storey, P. B., Williamson, J. W., and Castle, H. C. *Continuing Medical Education, A New Emphasis*. Chicago: American Medical Association, 1968.

Storey, R. K. *The Search for Accounting Principles*. New York: American Institute of Certified Public Accountants, 1964.

Strauss, A., and others. *The Professional Scientist: A Study of American Chemists*. Chicago: Aldine, 1962.

Strauss, G. "Professionalism and Occupational Associations." *Industrial Relations*, 1963, *2*, 7–31.

Striner, H. E. *Continuing Education as a National Capital Investment*. Kalamazoo, Mich.: W. E. Upjohn Institute for Employment Research, 1972.

Stross, J. K., and Harlan, W. R. "The Impact of Mandatory Continuing Medical Education." *Journal of the American Medical Association*, 1978, *239*, 2663–2666.

Stross, J. K., and Harlan, W. R. "The Dissemination of New Medical Information," *Journal of the American Medical Association*, 1979, *241*, 2622–2644.

Strother, G. B., and Swinford, D. N. "Recertification and Relicensure: Implications for the University." *NUEA Spectator,* 1975, *38,* 5–9.

"Survey Shows Slow but Strong Movement in States Toward Mandatory Continuing Education." *American Journal of Nursing,* 1978, *78,* 766ff.

Szczypkowski, R. B. "The Participation of Philanthropic Foundations in Continuing Professional Education." Unpublished doctoral dissertation, Columbia University, 1971.

Taubenhaus, L. "The Hospital Record as a Tool for Assessment of Physician Postgraduate Educational Needs in the Cardiovascular Field." *Journal of the American Geriatric Society,* 1969, *17,* 1025–1033.

Taylor, E. B. "Relationship Between the Career Changes of Lawyers and Their Participation in Continuing Legal Education." Unpublished doctoral dissertation, University of Nebraska, 1967.

Taylor, E. H., Jr. "Wealth, Poverty and Social Change: A Suggestion for a Balanced Curriculum." *Journal of Legal Education,* 1969, *22,* 227–239.

"Theological Schools and the Continuing Education of Ministers." *Theological Education,* 1965, *1,* 197–248.

Thomas, L. "How to Fix the Premedical Curriculum." *New England Journal of Medicine,* 1978, *298,* 1180–1181.

Thomas, W. I. "The Relation of the Medicine-Man to the Origin of the Professional Occupations." *The Decennial Publications, University of Chicago,* 1903, *4,* 241–256.

Thompson, E. K. "A New Look at Registration and Licensing." *Architectural Record,* 1971, *150,* 9–10.

Thompson, R. E. "Beyond Medical Audit: Relating Medical Care Evaluation to Patient Care." *Resident & Staff Physician,* 1978, *24,* 91–93.

Thornbury, R. E. (Ed.). *Teachers Centres.* New York: Agathon Press, 1974.

Titmuss, R. M. "The Relationship Between Schools of Social Work, Social Research, and Social Policy." *Journal of Education for Social Work,* 1965, *1,* 68–75.

Toren, N. *Social Work: The Case of a Semi-Profession.* Beverly

Hills, Calif.: Sage Publications, 1972.

Tough, A. *The Adult's Learning Projects.* Toronto: Ontario Institute for Studies in Education, 1971.

Tough, A. "Major Learning Efforts: Recent Research and Future Directions." *Adult Education,* 1978, *28,* 250–263.

Towle, C. *The Learner in Education for the Professions.* Chicago: University of Chicago Press, 1954.

Tracey, W. R. *Designing Training and Development Systems.* New York: American Management Association, 1971.

"Trend Toward Self-Assessment Tests Growing Among Several Professions." *ETS Developments,* 1976, *23,* 2–3.

Trivett, D. A. *Accreditation and Institutional Eligibility.* Washington, D.C.: American Association for Higher Education, 1976.

"The Troubled Professions." *Business Week,* August 16, 1976, pp. 126–38.

Truesdell, C. "The Scholar: A Species Threatened by Professions." *Critical Inquiry,* 1976, *2,* 631–648.

Turner, J. D., and Rushton, J. (Eds.). *Education for the Professions.* Manchester, England: Manchester University Press, 1976.

Tyer, T. E. (Ed.). "Continuing Education." *Illinois Libraries,* 1974, *56* (entire issue).

Tyler, R. W. "More Effective Education for the Professions." In I. Berg (Ed.), *Human Resources and Economic Welfare.* New York: Columbia University Press, 1972.

U.S. Department of Health, Education, and Welfare. *Fostering the Growing Need to Learn.* DHEW publication no. (HRA) 74–3112. Washington, D.C.: U.S. Government Printing Office, 1974.

U.S. Senate, Committee on Labor and Public Welfare, Subcommittee on Health. *Health Manpower, 1974.* Hearings on S. 3585, Pt.2, June 24, 1974, 93rd Congress, 2nd Session.

University of British Columbia, University Extension. *Continuing Education in the Professions: A Symposium.* Vancouver, B.C.: University of British Columbia, 1962.

University of Illinois, Center for the Study of Medical Education. *Continuing Education for the Health Professions.* Chicago: University of Illinois, 1966.

Unterberger, S. H. "The Lawyer's 1976 View of Continuing Legal Education." *The Practical Lawyer*, 1976, *22*, 71–108.

Utterback, J. M. "Innovation in Industry and the Diffusion of Technology." *Science*, 1974, *183*, 620–626.

Vander Meer, A. W. "Legislatures, the Courts, and Teacher Education." *School Review*, 1974, *82*, 281–292.

Vander Meer, A. W., and Lyons, M. D. "Professional Fields and the Liberal Arts." *Educational Record*, 1979, *60*, 197–201.

Vander Weele, R. "An Evaluation of the Need for Continuing Education and Professional Development for Certified Public Accountants." Unpublished doctoral dissertation, University of Wisconsin, 1972.

Van Doorn, J. "The Officer Corps: A Fusion of Profession and Organization." *European Journal of Sociology*, 1965, *6*, 262–282.

Vermilye, D. W. (Ed.). *Lifelong Learners—A New Clientele for Higher Education: Current Issues in Higher Education 1974*. San Francisco: Jossey-Bass, 1974.

Vermilye, D. W. (Ed.). *Relating Work and Education: Current Issues in Higher Education 1977*. San Francisco: Jossey-Bass, 1977.

Viner, J. "A Modest Proposal for Some Stress on Scholarship in Graduate Training." *Brown University Papers*, 1950, *24*, 2.

Vollan, D. *Postgraduate Medical Education in the United States*. Chicago: American Medical Association, 1955.

Vollmer, H. M., and Mills, D. L. (Eds.). *Professionalization*. Englewood Cliffs, N.J.: Prentice-Hall, 1966.

Walsh, J. "Stanford School of Medicine: III. Varieties of Medical Experience." *Science*, 1971, *171*, 785–787.

Walton, J., and Kuethe, J. L. (Eds.). *The Discipline of Education*. Madison: University of Wisconsin Press, 1963.

Warden, L. C. *The Life of Blackstone*. Charlottesville, Va.: Mishie, 1938.

Wardwell, W. I. "The Reduction of Strain in a Marginal Social Role." *American Journal of Sociology*, 1955, *61*, 16–25.

Ware, J. E., Jr., and Williams, R. G. "The Dr. Fox Effect: A Study of Lecturer Effectiveness and Ratings of Instruction." *Journal of Medical Education,* 1975, *50,* 149–156.

Ware, J. E., Jr., and Williams, R. G. "Discriminant Analysis of Student Ratings as a Means of Identifying Lecturers Who Differ in Enthusiasm or Information-Giving." *Educational and Psychological Measurement,* 1977, *37,* 627–639.

Warner, F., and Johnstone, R. E. "Continuing Education for Engineers." In *The Continuing Education of Engineers.* Paris: UNESCO Press, 1974.

Waters, J. H. "Audit System Upgrades Performance, Downplays Discipline." *The Hospital Medical Staff,* 1979, *8* (June), 2–6.

Webb, S., and Webb, B. "Special Supplement on Professional Associations." *New Statesman,* 1917, *9* (211), special supplement.

Webster, M., and Sobieszek, B. *Sources of Self-Evaluation: A Formal Theory of Significant Others and Social Influence.* New York: Wiley, 1974.

Weed, L. L. *Medical Records, Medical Education, and Patient Care.* Cleveland, Ohio: Case Western Reserve University, 1969.

Weigand, J. E. (Ed.). *Developing Teacher Competencies.* Englewood Cliffs, N.J.: Prentice-Hall, 1971.

Wenrich, W. J., and others. "Informal Educators for Practicing Physicians." *Journal of Medical Education,* 1971, *46,* 299–305.

Wesbury, S. A., Mosher, J. E., and Sachs, M. A. "Continuing Education: An Approach Toward Structure and a Call for Help." *Hospital & Health Services Administration,* 1978, *23,* 68–78.

White, G. E., and Buchman, T. "A Study of the Effectiveness of the Continuing Education Requirement for Certified Public Accountants." *Continuum,* 1978, *42* (3), 21–23.

White, W. D., and Robbins, A. "Role of On-the-job Training in a Clinical Laboratory." *Monthly Labor Review,* 1971, *94* (3), 65–69.

Whitehead, A. N. *Science and the Modern World.* New York: Macmillan, 1926.

Whiting, J. "The Medical Practitioners' View of Continuing Medical Education." *Archives of Dermatology,* 1967, *96,*

132–146.

Wiegand, R. "Factors Related to Participation in Continuing Education Among a Selected Group of Graduate Engineers." Unpublished doctoral dissertation, Florida State University, 1966.

Wilcox, J., Saltford, R. A., and Veres, H. C. *Continuing Education: Bridging the Information Gap.* Ithaca, N.Y.: Cornell Institute for Research and Development in Occupational Education, 1975.

Wildman, I. J. "Education: A Lifelong Process." *Law Library Journal,* 1972, *65,* 130–133.

Wilensky, H. L. "The Professionalization of Everyone?" *American Journal of Sociology,* 1964, *70,* 137–158.

Williams, R., Walker, J., and Fletcher, C. "International Review of Staff Appraisal Practices: Current Trends and Issues." *Public Personnel Management,* 1977, *6,* 5–12.

Williams, R. G., and Ware, J. E., Jr. "Validity of Student Ratings of Instruction Under Different Incentive Conditions: A Further Study of the Dr. Fox Effect." *Journal of Educational Psychology,* 1976, *68,* 48–56.

Williams, R. G., and Ware, J. E., Jr. "An Extended Visit with Dr. Fox: Validity of Student Satisfaction with Instruction Ratings after Repeated Exposures to a Lecturer." *American Educational Research Journal,* 1977, *14,* 449–457.

Williamson, J. W., Alexander, M., and Miller, G. E. "Priorities in Patient-Care Research and Continuing Medical Education." *Journal of the American Medical Association,* 1968, *204,* 303–308.

Wilson, P. T. "Continuing Education for Psychiatrists: Programs and Techniques." *American Journal of Psychiatry,* 1969, *125,* 1729–1732.

Wilson, R. N. *The Sociology of Health.* New York: Random House, 1970.

Wirtz, W. *The Boundless Resource: A Prospectus for an Education-Work Policy.* Washington, D.C.: New Republic Book Co., 1975.

Wittemann, J. K., and Currier, G. F. "Motives to Enter the Dental Profession: Students, Practitioners, Faculty." *Journal of*

Dental Education, 1976, *40,* 265–268.

Wittrock, J. W. "The General Practitioner and Continuing Education." *Journal of the American Dental Association,* 1977, *94,* 1065–1067.

Wolkin, P. A. "The Present Status of Continuing Legal Education in the United States." *Journal of Legal Education,* 1968, *20,* 614–619.

"Workshop on Continuing Education." *Journal of Dental Education,* 1964, *28,* 297–359.

Wretha, W. W., and Fine, S. A. *A Systems Approach to New Careers.* Kalamazoo, Mich.: Upjohn Institute for Employment Research, 1969.

Wright, R. R. "The Role of the Law School in Continuing Education." *University of Pittsburgh Law Review,* 1966, *28,* 19–36.

Young, R., and Cummings, P. "Speaking from Experience: Portrait of a Training Executive." *Training and Development Journal,* 1977, *31,* 21–22.

Zelby, L. W. "Student-Faculty Evaluation." *Science,* 1974, *183,* 1267–1270.

Zelikoff, S. B. "On the Obsolescence and Retraining of Engineering Personnel." *Training and Development Journal,* 1969, *23,* 3–15.

Zintel, H. A. "Education and the Assessment of Surgical Knowledge." *Surgery, Gynecology & Obstetrics,* 1971, *133,* 659–660.

Znaniecki, F. *The Social Role of the Man of Knowledge.* New York: Columbia University Press, 1940.

Name Index

Subject Index

A

Academic performance prediction, 81–82

Accounting, 50; career mobility in, 103; continuing education studies of, 244, 284; induction practices in, 93–94, 278

Accreditation, 52, 54; reshaping of, 274–276. *See also* Credentialing

Acculturation in professions, 57–59, 87. *See also* Life-style

Adjunct practice, 98–99, 101

Administrative professionals, 36, 49–50, 73, 100

Admissions tests, and academic performance, 81–82. *See also* Tests

Adult education: orientations in, 149–150; participation studies in, 146–147; specialists in, 16, 59. *See also* Continuing Education; Education; Learning

Advancement of Learning, The (Bacon), 40

Age, and learning, 120–121, 284

"Allied" professions, 68–70

Alumni, continuing education services to, 178–179

Amateur, 64

American Association of Colleges of Pharmacy, 279–280

American Association of Dental Schools, House of Delegates, 255–256

American Bar Association, 53

American Board of Medical Specialists, 280

American Council on Education, 38

American Institute of Certified Public Accountants, 244

American Journal of Nursing, 240

American Library Association, 55, 174

American Medical Association, 263, 284*n*, 285; Physicians Recognition Award, 239–240, 242, 243, 285

American Nurses' Association, Mechanism for Accreditation of Continuing Education in Nursing, 240

American Pharmaceutical Association, 279–280

Applied knowledge. *See* Practice

Apprenticeship programs, 93–94

Architectural Record, 37

Architecture, 28; concepts of, 37–38; life-styles in, 83

Association of American Law Schools, 53

Associations: and collective identity, 50–51; educational functions of, 169, 171–175, 193; elite type, 111–112; informal type, 111; and licensing, 55–56, 239–240; private type, 56; and professional policy, 59–60

Attorneys. *See* Courts; Law; Legal Profession

Audiotapes in education, 204–205

Autonomous educational groups, 167–171

Autonomous professions, 68

Avignon, University of, 3